DEVELOPING THE LONERGAN LEGACY

Historical, Theoretical, and Existential Themes

Edited by Frederick E. Crowe and Michael Vertin

Comprising twenty papers, including six never before published, this long-awaited work spans the fifty-year career of noted theologian Frederick E. Crowe, a scholar who has devoted himself to studying, expounding, and making available the writings of Bernard Lonergan, the well-known Canadian Jesuit philosopher and theologian who died in 1984. The publication of these papers, compiled by Michael Vertin, is a tribute to both their subject and their author.

Developing the Lonergan Legacy both recounts the history of Lonergan's work in philosophy and theology and offers significant theoretical and existential developments of that work. Divided into two sections – 'Studies,' which examines the historical context of Lonergan and his writings, and 'Essays,' which applies Lonergan's work in different directions – the essays in this volume are motivated by Crowe's deep concern for the concrete intellectual, moral, and religious welfare of his readers, of all those whom his readers might influence, and ultimately of the entire human community. Vertin's meticulous editing and thoughtful sequencing highlight the uniquely spiritual character of Crowe's works.

FREDERICK E. CROWE was a co-founder of the Lonergan Research Institute and a professor at the Toronto School of Theology, University of Toronto.

MICHAEL VERTIN is a professor in the Department of Philosophy at the University of Toronto.

Developing the Lonergan Legacy

Historical, Theoretical, and Existential Themes

Frederick E. Crowe

Edited by Michael Vertin

UNIVERSITY OF TORONTO PRESS
Toronto Buffalo London

Toronto Buffalo London
www.utpublishing.com

Reprinted in paperback 2016

ISBN 978-0-8020-8938-0 (cloth) ISBN 978-1-4875-2053-3 (paper)

Lonergan Studies

Library and Archives Canada Cataloguing in Publication

Crowe, Frederick E.
Developing the Lonergan legacy : historical, theoretical, and existential themes / Frederick E. Crowe ; edited by Michael Vertin.

Includes index and bibliographical references.
ISBN 978-0-8020-8938-0 (bound). – ISBN 978-1-4875-2053-3 (paperback)

1. Lonergan, Bernard J. F. (Bernard Joseph Francis), 1904–1984. 2. Theology. I. Vertin, Michael, 1939– . II. Title.

BX4705.L75C763 2004 230′.2092 C2004-901375-0

University of Toronto Press acknowledges the financial assistance to its publishing program of the Canada Council for the Arts and the Ontario Arts Council, an agency of the Goverment of Ontario.

Funded by the Government of Canada
Financé par le gouvernement du Canada

Contents

Part Two: Essays

Editor's Introduction

Frederick Crowe's engagement with the work of Bernard Lonergan began in the late 1940s when, as a Jesuit scholastic at Christ the King Seminary (later Regis College) in Toronto, he had Lonergan as one of his theology professors. Lonergan was writing his *Verbum*[1] articles during that period; and Crowe, eleven years his junior, was mightily impressed by his professor's scholarly erudition, intellectual creativity, and theological balance. He eventually sought out Lonergan to direct his licentiate thesis, 'The Unity of the Virtues in St Thomas Aquinas' (1950); and something of Lonergan's influence extended into the doctoral dissertation Crowe later wrote at the Gregorian University in Rome, 'Conflict and Unification in Man: The Data in the Writings of St Thomas Aquinas' (1953).

After defending his doctoral dissertation, Crowe extended his initial interest in Lonergan's ideas, and they soon became the prime focus of his scholarly labor. As we now look back on that labor from the vantage point of 2003, we see that for the past fifty years Crowe has analyzed those ideas, traced their emergence and evolution in Lonergan's intellectual history, compared them with the ideas of others, drawn out their implications, developed them further, employed them to address a broad range of epistemological, moral, religious, and systematic theological issues, and fostered their availability to diverse audiences. He

1 'The Concept of *Verbum* in the Writings of St Thomas Aquinas,' *Theological Studies* 7 (1946) 349–92; 8 (1947) 35–79, 404–44; 10 (1949) 3–40, 359–93. Subsequently republished as *Verbum: Word and Idea in Aquinas*, ed. D.B. Burrell (Notre Dame: University of Notre Dame Press, 1967); 2nd ed., ed. F.E. Crowe and R.M. Doran, *Collected Works of Bernard Lonergan*, vol. 2 (Toronto: University of Toronto Press, 1997).

has pursued these tasks through teaching courses and supervising dissertations during twenty-seven years as a professor of theology, giving public talks, guiding group research projects, co-founding (with Robert Doran) Toronto's Lonergan Research Institute, guiding the establishment of no fewer than nine other Lonergan centers around the world, collecting and cataloguing all of Lonergan's writings and editing many of them for publication or republication, co-editing (again with Robert Doran) the projected twenty-four volume *Collected Works of Bernard Lonergan*,[2] and writing books and articles of his own with such regularity that his bibliography now numbers close to 200 items – roughly half of them produced since he 'retired' from teaching in 1980. In sum, the acuity, depth, lucidity, cumulative magnitude, and fecundity of Crowe's labor on and for Lonergan's ideas are such that today he is widely recognized as the world's foremost Lonergan expert.

In 1989, Crowe published *Appropriating the Lonergan Idea*,[3] a collection of twenty-two papers that I was privileged to edit. The papers were divided into two groups. Those of the first group, entitled 'Exploring,' were devoted to articulating diverse aspects of Lonergan's work. The papers of the second group, entitled 'Expanding,' were devoted to extending Lonergan's work and using it to address a range of particular issues.

In 2000, Crowe published *Three Thomist Studies*,[4] a second volume I was honored to edit. It consisted of three previously published investigations of Thomas Aquinas, two of them multi-part, and all of them profiting from Crowe's reading of Lonergan.

Developing the Lonergan Legacy is the third of Crowe's books on which I have worked as editor. Its publication reflects three conclusions reached by several people, not least of all a group of manuscript assessors for the University of Toronto Press. First, there is widespread and continuing interest among both scholars and the wider public in such matters as the character of human knowing and choosing, the ultimate criterion of good and evil, the meaning and destiny of human life, and characteristically Christian stances on these issues. Second, Lonergan

2 *Collected Works of Bernard Lonergan*, ed. F.E. Crowe and R.M. Doran (Toronto: University of Toronto Press, 1988–).

3 *Appropriating the Lonergan Idea*, ed. Michael Vertin (Washington: Catholic University of America Press, 1989).

4 *Three Thomist Studies*, ed. Michael Vertin (Boston: Lonergan Center of Boston College, 2000).

has something uniquely worthwhile to say on such matters. Third, Crowe's stature as Lonergan scholar, the location of the present collection midway between an introduction to Lonergan's thought and a highly specialized monograph, and the previously unpublished status or relative unavailability of many papers in the collection – all these factors suggest that the collection might be found valuable not only by Lonergan specialists but also and more broadly by philosophers, theologians, scholars in other disciplines, teachers, pastors, students, and perhaps even some general readers.

In both structure and content, the book is more like the first of the aforementioned volumes than the second. It comprises twenty papers plus a complete list of Crowe's writings to date. Fourteen of the twenty papers have already appeared in print, but six are published for the first time here. The twenty are divided into groups labelled 'Studies' and 'Essays' respectively.

The eight papers of the first group, 'Studies,' are *historical* in the sense that they focus more or less on Lonergan himself and certain features of his writings. They discuss his vocation as a Christian thinker; the history of his early work on the topic of foundations, and of his lifelong work on the topic of history; the genesis and ongoing context of his book *Insight: A Study of Human Understanding*;[5] elements of his ideas about religion, the historicity and inculturation of religious meaning, and communication; and the resources in his writings for addressing certain questions raised by feminism.

The twelve papers of the second group, 'Essays,' develop and apply Lonergan's work in different directions. Six are *theoretical* in the sense that their aim is to elaborate or illustrate particular points of explanatory philosophy or theology: John Henry Newman and theology in our day, the radical basis of interdisciplinary dialogue, the nuances of 'authentic subjectivity,' the role of insight in the realm of law, the learning function of the church, and a new divine attribute. And six papers are *existential* in the sense that their immediate concern is with various facets of living well and with Jesuit ideas about the latter: the Ignatian Spiritual Exercises, the character of Jesuit spirituality, our solidarity with the Holy Spirit as we pray, why God requires us to

5 *Insight: A Study of Human Understanding* (London: Longmans, Green, 1957; 5th ed., ed. F.E. Crowe and R.M. Doran, *Collected Works of Bernard Lonergan*, vol. 3, Toronto: University of Toronto Press, 1992).

die, how to live our everyday human-animal lives, and charting the future.

It remains that all twelve essays, as well as all eight studies, at root are clearly motivated by Crowe's deep concern for the concrete intellectual, moral, and religious welfare of his readers, of all those whom his readers might influence, and ultimately of the entire human community. That is to say, this volume manifests Crowe himself as richly deserving an epithet of praise that he is wont to apply to his mentor. Crowe, like Lonergan, is preeminently a '*pastoral* theologian.'

It is my happy task to conclude this Introduction with several expressions of gratitude.

First, I thank the editors of the following journals and the publishers of the following books for permission to reprint material that previously appeared in the form indicated by the respective introductory notes to the chapters mentioned: *Communication and Lonergan: Common Ground for Forging the New Age*, for chapter 4; *The Jurist*, for chapter 14; *Lonergan and Feminism*, for chapter 7; *Review for Religious*, for chapter 12; *The Thomist*, for chapter 19; and *Searching for Cultural Foundations*, for chapter 8.

Second, I thank the Social Sciences and Humanities Research Council of Canada for its generous financial support of this project.

Third, I indicate my deep appreciation to Daniel Monsour for his extremely careful proofreading of the manuscript at various stages, and for his meticulous checking and updating of the notes.

Finally and most importantly, I offer Frederick Crowe my profound thanks for the elegant written expressions of luminous meaning and holy value that he provides in this volume, and for the inspiring incarnate expressions of the same that he has long provided by his life.

Michael Vertin
St Michael's College
University of Toronto
31 October 2003

Author's Preface

The Preface to the first volume of my collected essays and lectures (*Appropriating the Lonergan Idea*) could be repeated almost word for word in this new volume fourteen years later. Again, there are essays exploring the thought of Bernard Lonergan; again, there are essays applying this thought in areas he did not touch, or at least in ways he did not so apply it.

But for all the uniformity of their reference to Lonergan they deal also with a scattering of topics, and readers of this volume may wonder what idea in Lonergan inspired such a motley collection. The answer is that there was no such idea, not at least an idea with a specific content. With a few exceptions the papers responded to requests to speak on particular topics. The invitations therefore predetermined the general theme, and my contribution had to be fitted into a wider program.

Still, I believe there is another angle from which a unity may be seen, a unity not of content, but of programming, the unity namely of the eight functional specialties. Wittingly to pursue any one of the eight confers on that one a unity borrowed from all eight.

I believe those specialties implicitly or explicitly guided Lonergan even before he formulated them. At the end of his *Verbum* articles, referring to the work of Rousselot, Peghaire, and Hoenen, he said, 'All that was needed was to put together what had lain apart.'[1] I would venture a similar statement in regard to his use of the functional specialties: in 1965 he put together what had lain apart. And as this pattern without

1 'The Concept of *Verbum* in the Writings of St Thomas Aquinas,' 10 (1949) 391.

use of the term 'functional specialization' guided his earliest work, so also it guided my study of his thought.

Which of the eight functions, therefore, do these essays represent? That varies a bit with varying emphasis, reflecting also my own growth in understanding of Lonergan's thought and familiarity with it. In my first contact the aim was simplicity itself: to understand. I remember well the years 1947–1950 when he was our teacher and I would pester him with questions. Understanding of course is the aim of the second specialty. And it remains in my old age as the basic need. If at last we come to some understanding, say, of his 'intelligible emanation,' that very success (or semblance of it) opens up the question of understanding his relation to Thomas Aquinas, which in turn leads to the question of his position and role in ongoing thought.

As for the other specialties I am content to leave them for other commentators. In particular I have not stressed critical judgment. Perhaps a similar modesty may be recommended to his readers. One sees in titles phrases like 'Lonergan: A Critical Study of His Epistemology'; not so often 'Lonergan: An Attempt to Understand His Epistemology.'

But understanding supposes data. Always there is the basic need of work at the lower level of simple research; and in my own case this grew more important with the multiplication of materials, so that when a question was raised my instinct was to ask what Lonergan has to say on that point. 'What does he mean?' supposes always 'What did he say?' The double privilege I enjoyed – early association with Lonergan himself, and easier access to the materials of research – reinforced this pattern. At present, then, the handiest categories to describe my work are research and interpretation.

So what has changed are not the functions themselves but the proportion of time and thought given the different functions. In 1947, the question 'What does he mean?' loomed large. That remains always a question, but in 1967 with the multiplication of materials (especially unpublished materials) the question 'What does he say?' loomed larger than it did: there was now a small mountain of research to be done. In 1997, applications to current questions would be more in order.

One such application, however, as a reader for the University of Toronto Press has pointed out, is almost missing: I have little to say on Lonergan's economics, and some of what I do say is misleading. Not that there should have been included a chapter on Lonergan's economics, an area I little understand. But there are occasions in these twenty chapters when I might have highlighted his interest and achievement in that field. There is even the misleading reference to economics as an interest in Lonergan's later years, as if he had not been at work on the question back in 1941–44.

One other paragraph could also be repeated almost word for word in this new volume from that of fourteen years earlier: my debt to Michael Vertin. A Latin tag comes to mind: *bis repetita placet.* Only the *bis* has now become *ter:* not just twice but three times I have had the pleasant duty of thanking Michael. Editing cannot entirely escape a measure of tedium, especially when the editor has projects of his own to pursue, as is the case with Michael. My unlimited thanks to him. Thanks also to the editors of the books and journals that authorized this reprint of previous publications. And I add my own special thanks to Daniel Monsour, whose office is next door to mine at the Lonergan Research Institute: rarely does so much work get done so quietly as it does in that office.

Frederick E. Crowe, SJ
Lonergan Research Institute of Regis College
Toronto School of Theology
7 October 2003

Frequently Cited Works

The footnotes to the papers in this volume frequently cite certain works of Bernard Lonergan, and certain journals and standard reference works as well. To simplify the footnotes, citations of these works omit some bibliographical details and sometimes also employ abbreviated versions of the titles. A list of these works, indicating the abbreviated titles where pertinent, and providing full bibliographical details, follows below. The first section is organized more or less chronologically, according to dates of original composition; the second, alphabetically.

Certain Works of Bernard Lonergan

'Gratia Operans'	'St Thomas' Thought on *Gratia Operans*,' *Theological Studies* 2 (1941) 289–324; 3 (1942) 69–88, 375–402, 533–78.
Grace and Freedom	*Grace and Freedom: Operative Grace in the Thought of St Thomas Aquinas*, ed. J.P. Burns (London: Darton, Longman & Todd; New York: Herder and Herder, 1971). Ed. F.E. Crowe and R.M. Doran, *Collected Works of Bernard Lonergan*, vol. 1 (Toronto: University of Toronto Press, 2000).
'Verbum'	'The Concept of *Verbum* in the Writings of St Thomas Aquinas,' *Theological Studies* 7 (1946) 349–92; 8 (1947) 35–79, 404–44; 10 (1949) 3–40, 359–93.
Verbum	*Verbum: Word and Idea in Aquinas*, ed. D.B. Burrell (Notre Dame: University of Notre Dame Press, 1967). 2nd edition, ed. F.E. Crowe and R.M. Doran, *Collected Works of Bernard Lonergan*, vol. 2 (Toronto: University of Toronto Press, 1997).

Insight	*Insight: A Study of Human Understanding* (London: Longmans, Green, 1957). 5th edition, ed. F.E. Crowe and R.M. Doran, *Collected Works of Bernard Lonergan*, vol. 3 (Toronto: University of Toronto Press, 1992).
Understanding and Being	*Understanding and Being: An Introduction and Companion to* Insight, ed. E.A. Morelli and M.D. Morelli (New York and Toronto: Edwin Mellen Press, 1980). 2nd edition, revised and augmented by F.E. Crowe et al., *Collected Works of Bernard Lonergan*, vol. 5 (Toronto: University of Toronto Press, 1990).
Topics in Education	*Topics in Education*, ed. F.E. Crowe and R.M. Doran, *Collected Works of Bernard Lonergan*, vol. 10 (Toronto: University of Toronto Press, 1993).
Collection	*Collection: Papers by Bernard Lonergan*, ed. F.E. Crowe (New York: Herder and Herder, 1967). 2nd edition, ed. F.E. Crowe and R.M. Doran, *Collected Works of Bernard Lonergan*, vol. 4 (Toronto: University of Toronto Press, 1988).
Papers 1958–1964	*Philosophical and Theological Papers 1958–1964*, vol. 1, ed. R.C. Croken, F.E. Crowe, and R.M. Doran, *Collected Works of Bernard Lonergan*, vol. 6 (Toronto: University of Toronto Press, 1996).
Papers 1965–1980	*Philosophical and Theological Papers 1965–1980*, vol. 2, ed. R.C. Croken and R.M. Doran, *Collected Works of Bernard Lonergan*, vol. 17 (Toronto: University of Toronto Press, 2004)
De Verbo incarnato	*De Verbo incarnato*, 3rd edition (Rome: Gregorian University Press, 1964).
De Deo trino	*De Deo trino*: vol. 1, 2nd edition (Rome: Gregorian University Press, 1964); vol. 2, 3rd edition (Rome: Gregorian University Press, 1964).
The Way to Nicea	*The Way to Nicea*, translation by Conn O'Donovan of *De Deo trino*, vol. 1, part 1 (London: Darton, Longman & Todd; Philadelphia: Westminster, 1976).
Doctrinal Pluralism	*Doctrinal Pluralism* (Milwaukee: Marquette University Press, 1971).
Method in Theology	*Method in Theology* (London: Darton, Longman & Todd; New York: Herder and Herder, 1972).

Philosophy of God, and Theology	*Philosophy of God, and Theology* (London: Darton, Longman & Todd, 1973). In *Papers 1965–1980* (2004) 157–218.
A Second Collection	*A Second Collection: Papers by Bernard Lonergan*, ed. W.F.J. Ryan and B.J. Tyrrell (London: Darton, Longman & Todd; Philadelphia: Westminster, 1974).
A Third Collection	*A Third Collection: Papers by Bernard Lonergan*, ed. F.E. Crowe (New York: Paulist Press; London: Geoffrey Chapman, 1985).

Certain Standard Reference Works

AAS	*Acta Apostolicae Sedis*
DS	Denzinger, Henricus, and Adolfus Schönmetzer, eds, *Enchiridion symbolorum definitionum et declarationum de rebus fidei et morum*, 36th edition (Barcelona: Herder, 1976).
NEB	*The New English Bible* (New York: Oxford University Press, 1976).
NRSV	*The Holy Bible*, New Revised Standard Version (New York: Oxford University Press, 1989).
RJ	Rouët de Journel, Marie-Joseph, ed., *Enchiridion patristicum*, 25th edition (Barcelona: Herder, 1969).
TS	*Theological Studies*

Part One

STUDIES

Chapter 1

Lonergan's Vocation as a Christian Thinker[1]

1 A Vocation within a Vocation

A first point is obvious and simple, but too easily ignored or forgotten. It is this, that Lonergan's vocation as a Christian thinker is a vocation within a vocation. His first vocation was to be a Christian, that is, to be an authentic human being and an authentic follower of Christ. Within that horizon and retaining its dominant orientation, he found his particular vocation to be a Christian thinker. This hierarchy of calls he himself fully recognized and pointed out now and then as a reminder to his readers and audiences. He knew that a theologian is a believer before he is a theologian. To quote a more formal statement: '... theology as a whole functions within the larger context of Christian living, and Christian living within the still larger process of human history.'[2]

This simple and obvious fact is easily ignored. The cause lies partly in ourselves. We are so fascinated by monumental works like *Insight* and *Method in Theology* that we imagine Lonergan was born with a

---

1 Originally presented on 28 January 1995 at a Lonergan conference in Milan. Translation published as 'La Vocazione di Lonergan Quale Pensatore Cristiano,' trans. Saturnino Muratore, *Rassegna di Teologia* 37 (1996) 313–31.

2 *Method in Theology* 144. Or, again, 'Theology stands to religion, as economics does to business' ('Belief: Today's Issue,' in *A Second Collection* 97). We need a study that would gather together and interpret the many scattered references in Lonergan to human living. This would be valuable in itself, and it might blunt objections to his views on experience, for I suspect that 'experience' in the wider sense (as contrasted with the technical sense of the *experience-understanding-judgment* triad) would overlap, and almost coincide with, his view of human living.

vocation to write them. The cause (I do not say 'fault') lies partly in Lonergan, because only occasionally in the years of his public career did he have occasion to declare his humanity and his Christianity. What is habitual operates without noise or fanfare: we do not, as we talk, keep repeating, 'I am talking'; nor do we, writing as a Christian, keep repeating, 'I am writing as a Christian.'

We must therefore remind ourselves from time to time that he was an infant born and nursed in a Catholic home, that he was a pupil who began school, like everyone else, in the primary grades, that he was a boy who served at the altar in his parish church, that he was a youth who received a religious vocation and became a Jesuit novice, all this when he was still quite ignorant of Bañez and Molina, of Hegel and Marx, and had not yet received and responded to his vocation as a religious thinker. That primary vocation was fundamental, and when conflict threatened to arise between primary and secondary vocation, it was the primary that remained dominant.

The threat of conflict was not, however, a lasting concern. At least from 1933 till the last work he did fifty years later, his primary and secondary vocations worked in conscious harmony. Moreover, even in his early years there was for the most part a healthy if unconscious symbiosis; for there were certain preliminary requirements for carrying out his thinker's vocation, there were conditions that had first to be fulfilled, and these too are part of what was provided in his primary vocation.

One condition, one requirement, was a dedication to work; and on this point the young Lonergan had to undergo a minor conversion. 'Minor' – not therefore one of the three great conversions, religious, intellectual, or moral, though perhaps to be subsumed under moral. The fact is, the boy Bernard had, in his early or mid teens, become a loafer. He had to be converted from leading a rather lazy life to the kind of life his second vocation would require, the kind the world knows him to have led, namely, a life of unremitting application to the intellectual problems of the time.

A corollary, or perhaps just an explicitation of this, is perseverance in one's work. 'To learn thoroughly is a vast undertaking that calls for relentless perseverance. To strike out on a new line and become more than a weekend celebrity calls for years in which one's living is more or less constantly absorbed in the effort to understand, in which one's understanding gradually works round and up a spiral of viewpoints with each complementing its predecessor and only the last embracing the whole field to be mastered.'[3] Again: 'Only through deliberate decision do people dedicate themselves to lives of scholarship or science, and only through the continuous renewal of that dedication do they achieve the goals they have set themselves.'[4] These statements, made in his mature years, describe his own fidelity to the intellectual vocation, but it was the kind of fidelity made possible by an underlying vocation that preceded his call to the life of a thinker.

When did conversion to a life of persevering work occur? Surely when he was a novice or junior at Guelph, Ontario. It is hard to imagine him going through the rigorous self-examination of the novitiate without realizing that he had been, as he said later, loafing, and hard to imagine him thrust into the vast field of the classics without a stir of ambition to conquer that world. From the time he made the Spiritual Exercises of St Ignatius, there would be, we can safely surmise, a dedication to work, whether it be washing pots and pans in the kitchen or studying Sophocles in the quiet of the library. And the commitment of his vows would be a context and a model for perseverance in whatever work he was given or called to do.

But a dedication to work is not yet a call to the intellectual apostolate, and I doubt that this vocation had become clear to him at Guelph in his first four years as a Jesuit. In any case there was not yet the corresponding and required mission from his religious order. On the contrary, in those early years his order was more inclined to exploit his talents for immediate practical purposes than to give him long-range preparation for a higher mission. In his juniorate years, besides being beadle for a time (the rector's 'go-between' with scholastics) he was appointed to teach Latin and Greek to the novices, and mathematics to his fellow-juniors. As for his own classical studies, he was largely self-taught, at least in the second year of his juniorate. His professors in his first year were adequate, but not so in the second; so he did what he could on his own, learning one-tenth, he was to say, of what he might have learned with proper teaching.[5]

3 *Insight* (1957) 186 [(1992) 210].

4 *Method in Theology* 122.

5 That he was an idler during his years as a student at Loyola College, Montreal (1918–22), we know from his own admission. Whereas in primary school the Christian Brothers at Buckingham had kept his nose to the grindstone, the Jesuits, he said, taught him to loaf. There is more information on these matters in the first chapter of

2 Discovering His Intellectual Vocation

When did his intellectual vocation emerge and become a responsibility he would carry on his conscience for the rest of his life? I believe it was during his years in England, where he was sent for his studies in philosophy, that this occurred. If Guelph gave him his spiritual character, England gave him his academic. Partly, I surmise, it was a matter of observing the English Catholic scene at close hand. For one thing so many of the Catholic thinkers were converts, and had learned their intellectual standards outside the church. Certainly, he recognized the inferiority of the Catholic schools in that country. He had found much to admire in the Catholics of England, but he was not blind to their situation:

> The English Jesuits make no bones about admitting that academically their schools cannot compete with such places as Eton or Harrow ... And their patrons, if good Catholics, accept the situation. As M. Gilson is reported to have remarked recently: I gave my children a Catholic education, but it was a great sacrifice.[6]

More directly, it was his work for a university degree that taught him the kind of intellectual standards that were set in the academic world outside the church. At the University of London, in contrast with Loyola College, he had to work his hardest (as he did also as a boy under the Christian Brothers, who provided an exception to the general rule).

His work at the University of London was in the Greek and Latin classics, in French, and in mathematics. He did not labor at the philosophy that was taught at Heythrop College, for that was a joke: 'anyone ... with any brains was getting a university degree; that was his main concern.'[7] Still his brilliance in philosophy led his professors to expect

---

my book *Lonergan* (Collegeville, MN: Liturgical Press, 1992) 5, 11; notes 10 and 18 there both refer to letters Lonergan wrote his Provincial Superior, John L. Swain, 5 May and 24 May, respectively, 1936.

But this period of idling was short and soon overcome. There is a certain analogy here with St Teresa of Avila, who for a period was inclined to gossip and idle parlor talk, but when converted became a great spiritual leader.

6 Letter of 24 May 1936, to John L. Swain.

7 Pierrot Lambert, Charlotte Tansey, Cathleen Going, eds, *Caring about Meaning: Patterns in the Life of Bernard Lonergan* (Montreal: Thomas More Institute, 1982) 8.

a future for him in that field. Father Bolland, his professor and prefect of studies, said as much to him when he was leaving Heythrop,[8] and this was possibly the first inkling of a mandate from his order that would correspond to what he increasingly felt to be his vocation. At any rate it is highly likely that he returned to Canada in 1930 with a somewhat clearer vision of what he wanted to do. What is certain, however, is that the next three years would show him how rocky the road to attainment of that vision could become and how discouraging his prospects were of following the vision.

3 Conflict and Resolution

A letter of 1935[9] shows how high and distant he had set his aim, but it reveals also how little hope of pursuing it he found in the next three years. Those years, 1930–33, were a period known as regency (common to Jesuit scholastics), between his philosophy studies and the theology to come. It was an interval that would test Lonergan severely. Despite the satisfaction there was in guiding young minds, and despite the enduring friendships he formed in those years, it was a trying time: days filled with prefecting, with moderating this or that student society, with overseeing their publications, with a full schedule of teaching, teaching too that did not extend his intellect or scholarship, but most of all, difficulties with his religious superiors and a lack of sympathy for the ideas that were taking shape in his fertile mind.

Still, he did not lose heart entirely. During the summer of 1933, when the three years were over, and during the first months of his theology in Montreal, he returned to the reading and study that regency had severely limited. 'I read St Augustine's earlier works during the summer before theology and found him to be psychologically exact. I then put together a 25,000 word essay upon the act of faith.'[10] Some scrap pages found among his papers seem to be part of this essay. They show evidence of Newman's influence, and Lonergan seemed set to do whatever he could with whatever opportunities were given him, as he began theological studies at the College of the Immaculate Conception in Montreal.

8 '*Insight* Revisited,' in *A Second Collection* 264.

9 January 1935, to Henry Keane, his Provincial Superior at the time, one whom he obviously admired and respected.

10 Ibid.

But after two months of theology at that college there came what was certainly a major turning point in his career. Due to factors that are merely accidental to us but were providential for his future, he was suddenly transferred to theology in Rome. In three interconnected ways this was an extremely important event for Lonergan. First of all, it was in Rome that his vocation became quite clearly and distinctly specified: this I conclude from that same letter of January 1935. Secondly, he received, what is so necessary in an order like his and what had been lacking up to now, a kind of official mission or mandate to the intellectual apostolate. Thirdly, there was a symbolism in the move that was almost sacramental in its effect on the young Lonergan. There was a great uplifting of his spirits. He saw his transfer to Rome as a 'vote of confidence' after a long period of being resigned to disappointment. It was not necessarily a matter of higher standards in the theology at Rome, though later when he taught in Montreal he had high praise for the intellectual atmosphere of Rome's theological schools. It was more a matter of a symbolic gesture, as well as a concrete endorsement of his hopes.[11]

At any rate during these four years in Rome he wrote and wrote. Several of his papers of that time survive, along with that most revealing letter of 1935 to his Provincial. From these scattered indications we can reconstruct the immediate context of the career of the next forty-five years that was soon to begin: his study of grace in Thomas Aquinas; his study of cognitional theory, again in Thomas; his Latin theology of grace, of the incarnate Word, of the Trinity; his monumental *Insight*; the long road to *Method in Theology*; his lectures of the 1960s and 1970s; his deep interest in the human sciences; and the work of his last years on economics.

4 Lonergan's Intellectual Vocation: Early Response

These biographical details are of absorbing interest to me, for I spend my life in their study, but my audience will surely ask for more substantial thinking on my part, and more discussion of Lonergan's ideas. So what exactly was his vocation as a Christian thinker? What did he

11 Ibid. He was to be a professor of philosophy. This was later changed to theology, and that of course has its importance, but the decisive thing was a mission from his religious superiors that corresponded to his personal vocation, adding concrete opportunity to vision and general orientation.

contribute to the intellectual treasury of the church, and what did he leave behind him as a legacy?

There is continuity here with his primary vocation, for his intellectual vocation also was an apostolic one. It derived from his deep Catholic faith and his religious commitment in the Jesuit Order. There was a need to be met, and the subject of the need was first of all the church. Later Lonergan would turn his attention to ecumenism, and especially to the wider ecumenism of the world religions. But his initial drive came from the need of his own church, which he saw as far behind the times in many respects. That defined the need and by the same token defined his response: his vocation was to do his part to bring the church to the 'level of the times.' It was a phrase he had found in Ortega y Gasset, a phrase that in the original Preface[12] of *Insight* would define the aim of that book with great precision, and would indeed define the goal of his life work from beginning to end.

Implicit in the aim of bringing the church to the level of the times, was a philosophy of history and development – a governing idea already in his early writings. We can be sure that he owed much to Newman under that heading, perhaps also to Darwin, whose 'chance variation' he would replace with the fundamental concept of emergent probability. We know also that in this early period it was Hegel and Marx that engaged his attention, rather than Thomas Aquinas and Kant. Further, the unpublished papers that survive from 1937–38 deal largely with a philosophy of history.[13] And when he would choose a Thomist text as a kind of motto for a paper of April 1935, it was not a text on insight into phantasm that caught his eye, but the principle of growth which he found implicit in intellect as potency:

> [O]ur intellect progresses from potency to act. But everything that progresses from potency to act arrives first at an incomplete act, one that is intermediate between potency and act ... Now an incomplete act is

12 Written in the summer of 1954, published thirty-one years later in *METHOD: Journal of Lonergan Studies* 3/1 (March 1985) 1–7; see 4. On his vocation in the context of the church's need, see the already quoted letter of January 1935: 'I do care enormously about the good of the church.'

13 File 713, available in the Lonergan Archives, Lonergan Research Institute, Toronto. [Besides '*Pantôn anakephalaiôsis*' (see below, note 15), another important paper from File 713 has now been published as well: 'Analytic Concept of History,' *METHOD: Journal of Lonergan Studies* 11 (1993) 5–35 (ed.).]

imperfect science, through which things are known indistinctly and with a certain confusion.[14]

This guiding principle, found at the head of Lonergan's '*Pantôn anakephalaiôsis*' essay,[15] was the first great principle Lonergan learned from Thomas. The date is 1935, ten whole years prior, so far as I can ascertain, to his discovery of Aquinas on insight into phantasm – though the famous text on insight was only one question earlier in the *Summa*, 1, question 84, article 7. That is odd, but it is even odder that, again so far as I have ascertained, Lonergan did his doctoral dissertation on *gratia operans* in Thomas Aquinas without coming across that key text of the *Pars prima*.[16]

Implicit in the principle of development was the role of tradition. We are pygmies standing on the shoulders of giants, a piece of wisdom that Lonergan would find concisely expressed in Leo XIII's *vetera novis augere et perficere*. So it was that two basic components of the grand strategy of later years appear in his study of the Thomist *verbum*: the *vetera* without which each generation would have to start all over again as Neanderthal man, and insight, the creative factor in the *augere et perficere* that would mark the *nova*.[17] Thus, as the late 1930s were the period of his general intellectual vocation, so the late 1940s were the period specifying the means that would define his strategy. For what the times demanded was an *organon* adequate to the need. The *organon* would be found in human self-appropriation, and the key step in self-

---

14 *Summa theologiae* 1, q. 85, a. 3, c.

15 Published fifty-six years later in *METHOD: Journal of Lonergan Studies* 9/2 (October 1991) 134–72.

16 *Summa theologiae* 1, q. 84, a. 7, c. The oddity increases when we believe, as I have argued elsewhere [in the essay '*Insight*: Genesis and Ongoing Context': see chapter 3 of the present volume], that his earliest writing was an implicit discovery of the act of insight. It is a salutary reminder that even great minds arrive slowly at their contributions.

17 Lonergan began his study of the Thomist *intelligere* (understanding, insight) in 1943 ('*Insight* Revisited,' in *A Second Collection* 266–67; see also *Caring about Meaning* 51, 98) and published the results in five articles in *Theological Studies*, 'The Concept of *Verbum* in the Writings of St Thomas Aquinas,' 1946–49 (subsequently republished as *Verbum: Word and Idea in Aquinas* [1967, 1997]). It was in 1953 that he completed *Insight*, and he regarded his two great works of the decade, 1943–53, as exemplifying respectively the *vetera* and the *nova*.

appropriation was insight. With that discovery Lonergan was on the way to his personal contribution to the task of bringing the church to the level of the times.

5 Meeting the Need: The Grand Strategy of an *Organon*

Nowhere, as far as I know, has Lonergan described the spectacular event in his experience that was the discovery of insight.[18] Spectacular it must have been, yet we have to remember that it was just one step in a complex development, and the further steps would have the effect of putting it in a wider context and so giving it less striking importance. In any case it is important to note at this point that the whole thrust of Lonergan's contribution is in a sphere remote, or at least at one remove, from the spectacular. It is self-appropriation rather than self-expression; it is method rather than the product of method; it is an *organon* rather than the use of the *organon*; it is Toynbee's withdrawal rather than his return. As critics complained during his lifetime: He has been a long time sharpening his knife, it's time he used it to cut something.

Perhaps Toynbee's terms come as close as any to a concise description of Lonergan's contribution. It is a matter of withdrawal and return, a forty-year withdrawal for the sake of a return which could in the end be all the more spectacular in proportion as the interval of withdrawal was creative, but which must be left to another generation to accomplish. That exaggeration conceals a valid and fundamental point, that Lonergan's great legacy was not a position on grace or Christology or the Trinity or epistemology or metaphysics. His contributions to particular questions like those have not yet been appreciated, but his great contribution was not to be made under such headings. It was to be mainly at one remove from them. It was to be in the area of what he called method, of what I think is better described as an *organon*. The *organon* that we call Aristotle's served for two thousand years; Bacon's *novum organum* has been influential for over three

18 He did describe, implicitly but graphically, his discovery of the 'two quite different realisms' (*Insight* [1957] xxviii, [1992] 22). He speaks explicitly of his discovery of the eight functional specialties, though he plays down the drama of the discovery (*Caring about Meaning* 59; see my *Lonergan* 106). But we are left in the dark as to what kind of experience it was to catch onto insight in Thomas (*Summa theologiae* 1, q. 84, a. 7) and in Aristotle (*De anima* III, 7, 431b 2 – a text Lonergan quotes on the title page of *Insight*).

hundred years; Lonergan's *organum novissimum* was his great life work, but it is for other generations to assimilate and apply it.[19]

The need for this approach is simply the impossibility of dealing in any other way with the unmanageably large quantity of material that confronts the arts and sciences and scholarship today. What else can one do with it? The content of knowledge, Lonergan said on beginning *Insight*, 'is so extensive that it mocks encyclopedias and overflows libraries.'[20] Leonardo da Vinci was the last person in history, I am told, for whom it was possible to be a *uomo universale*. From his time on, even with Michelangelo, the age of specialization would set in, the splintering of the disciplines would accelerate, and to do what Thomas Aquinas had done in the thirteenth century would become simply impossible.[21] It would be impossible a priori: it was not a matter of awaiting a genius who could get it all together, it is a matter of the impossibility of such a genius. So what can we do? Lonergan's answer in *Insight* was simplicity itself: 'our primary concern is not the known but the knowing.'[22] Prolong that simple remark into the full range of human consciousness and intentionality and you have defined the strategy of the Lonergan *organon*. A famous remark of Bacon's says that we conquer nature by submitting to her law.[23] That applies to the simplest tasks such as the use of a waterfall to grind grain. It applies par excellence to the kind of *organon* Lonergan created. Aristotle's was a matter of logic; Bacon's added experimental science and inductive

---

19 On the sequence of *organa* leading up to Lonergan, see my *Method in Theology: An Organon for Our Time* (The 1980 Pere Marquette Theology Lecture, Marquette University Press, 1980), reprinted as chapter 1 in *The Lonergan Enterprise* (Cambridge, MA: Cowley Publications, 1980).

20 *Insight* (1957) xviii [(1992) 12]. Also: 'An age of research has kept enriching us with ever further monographs ... This flood tide of scholarly diligence yields a vast multiplicity. Yet if we ask how the multiplicity is to be reduced to unity, we are presented with peculiar problems' ('Theology and Understanding,' in *Collection* [1967] 137, [1988] 128–29).

21 Joan Kelly Gadol, 'Universal Man,' *Dictionary of the History of Ideas* (New York: Charles Scribner's Sons, vol. 4, 1973) 437–43 (quoted at 443). I treated this point in my lecture 'Linking the Splintered Disciplines: Ideas from Lonergan' [see chapter 13 of the present volume].

22 *Insight* (1957) xviii [(1992) 12].

23 James Collins, in *A History of Modern Philosophy* (Milwaukee: Bruce Publishing Co., 1954), reports this as follows: 'Man must obey nature before he can command it' (p. 67, in his discussion of 'The New *Organon*' of Bacon).

discovery; but Lonergan's is found not in logic but in the logician, not in experimental science but in the experimental scientist, and not only in them but in philosophers and theologians and all who give themselves to the cultivation of what is human. That *organon* is most effective, therefore, which discovers the fundamental operations and so the natural laws of human spirit; that *organon* is most adequate which discovers the full range of operations and the full extent of the exigencies of human nature.[24]

I cannot set forth, even in outline, the structure and operation of Lonergan's *organon*. Nor do I need to do so, for the four-leveled structure of experience, understanding, judgment, decision is well enough known; well known too are the operations that are proper to each level. But it is not generally recognized how flexible the *organon* is, and how adaptable to the richness of human experience and history. So I will mention three factors of extreme importance that are often overlooked, leaving us with a mutilated *organon*.

First, this structure is a two-way street. One may ascend the levels from experience to values in the way of achievement, but equal in importance, indeed more fundamental and chronologically prior, is the descent in the other direction, the way of heritage, from love through values, truth, and understanding to a more mature and perceptive experience.[25]

---

24 That is why the discovery of insight was so important; for discovery of insight creates a new problem for judgment, that is, for the affirmation that something is. The positing of 'is' in its turn creates a new problem for dogma, for saying that the Son 'is' consubstantial with the Father (and even for saying 'God is'). And the problem of dogma is central to the whole great conflict today between a historical consciousness that easily slides into relativism and a conservatism that easily hardens into a dead immobility, guarding fossils in the history of our human race.

25 The idea of levels of consciousness as a two-way street came up repeatedly in Lonergan's lectures from 1974 on. For example, see 'The Dehellenization of Dogma,' in *A Second Collection* 32, 'The Subject,' ibid. 76–77, 79–80, 82, 'The Absence of God in Modern Culture,' ibid. 106, 107–108, 'Natural Knowledge of God,' ibid. 126, 'The Future of Christianity,' ibid. 160–61, 162–63, 'The Response of the Jesuit as Priest and Apostle in the Modern World,' ibid. 180–81, and 'Philosophy and Theology,' ibid. 196–97. Of course, it was almost fully explicit in the two phases of theology in *Method in Theology*. I employed this idea to structure my book *Old Things and New: A Strategy for Education* (Atlanta: Scholars Press, 1985), using the expressions 'the way of achievement' and 'the way of heritage.' The child, Lonergan maintains, has the content of the levels in a compact form in affectivity; as it grows in mastery of its heritage, the levels

A second additional factor is the role of community, where once again Lonergan's views and his extensive writings on community are widely ignored. For the way of heritage is totally contained within community, is possible only in community, is rendered actual only in community. Even the way of achievement, where individuals must develop their own personal understanding, judgment, and set of values, even this way requires the community of pupil and teacher in the schools, and the collaboration of scientists and scholars in the academic community.[26]

A third addition to an integral view is found on the historical side of development. The levels of consciousness give us a structure, but the history of the individual and the history of the human race are a record of what happens within the structure. Here we have room for all the differentiations of consciousness that pertain to the human race: the artistic, the scholarly, the theoretic, the philosophic, the religious, the mystic. Here too are the various degrees in which we become authentic human beings or fail to become authentic, the various responses or failures to respond to the conversions proper to a fallen human race – intellectual, moral, religious.[27]

Lonergan's *organon* is truly wide-ranging, all-embracing. It takes account of the stable structure of consciousness as well as of its fluctuations through time and history, of the individual as well as the community, of the fully developed subject and the underdeveloped, of our sin history and our grace history.

6 The *Organon* at Work in Theology

I have said that I cannot set forth this integral *organon* in detail, but per-

---

become distinct, and integration with the way of achievement is possible (*Dialogues in Celebration* [Thomas More Institute, 1980] 310–11, in an interview with Lonergan). For purposes of education, indeed for human everyday living, and especially for the harmony of praxis and knowledge, we are only half human if we neglect this way of heritage and limit ourselves to the way of achievement.

26 I have collected a number of texts from Lonergan in my pamphlet *Bernard Lonergan and the Community of Canadians: An Essay in Aid of Canadian Identity* (Toronto: Lonergan Research Institute, 1992) 6–18 (in note 20, p. 18, read *A Third Collection* rather than *A Second Collection*).

27 On differentiations of consciousness and the various conversions, see the Index to *Method in Theology*.

haps an equivalent result can be obtained by seeing it at work in one instance of its application. Lonergan's method is not merely for theology; rather, it is a method that 'would be relevant to any human studies that investigated a cultural past to guide its future.'[28] However, let me follow the theological path, which is more familiar to me. Further, let me do that, not through a somewhat abstract exposition of theology's eight functional specialties, but through a concrete illustration of the problem that confronts the twentieth-century theologian, the same problem that makes a twentieth-century Leonardo da Vinci impossible.

When I started theology almost fifty years ago, we brought three handbooks with us to every lecture in dogmatic theology: Merk's *Novum Testamentum*, Denzinger's *Enchiridion symbolorum*, and Rouët de Journel's *Enchiridion patristicum*. They were handbooks, desk manuals, the distillation of the work of thousands of scholars putting in hundreds of thousands of hours of study. (This applies to Merk too, if you think of him, not as publishing the word of God, but as providing a critical apparatus.) Such handbooks are indispensable. They reduce the mountains of material in a hundred encyclopedias to a measure that students of theology can handle. But what is the theological function of such handbooks? Theology is certainly not reducing encyclopedias to handbooks in order to spoon-feed students, and in any case what would you have when you finished but a baby encyclopedia? And how do the handbooks relate to one another? How does the content of the handbook relate to the act of publishing it? What relation has the content of Denzinger to the content of Merk?

That is where Lonergan's theological method has its point of application. What are Merk, Denzinger, and Rouët de Journel from his viewpoint? They belong to the specialty of research, and as research they relate with perfect clarity to the seven other theological specialties. We are no longer overwhelmed by the enormous quantity of theological material, for we realize that our control is not directly of the vast quantity of materials but of the process that produced them, and that the unity of the process is controlled by the unity of the *organon*

28 'Bernard Lonergan Responds,' in *Foundations of Theology: Papers from the International Lonergan Congress 1970* (Dublin and London: Gill and Macmillan, 1971) 233. Cf. *Method in Theology* 364–67, *A Second Collection* 210–11, and *Caring about Meaning* 57. See also chapter 13 of the present volume, and Frederick Crowe, *The Lonergan Enterprise* (Cambridge, MA: Cowley Publications, 1980).

that the theologians themselves embody. That is where we take control of the process, through control of the knowing that guides the process, provided we know what knowing is. I return to Lonergan's simple remark on beginning *Insight*: Our concern is not the known but the knowing.

'Control' of the *vetera* unfolds then in the three steps of research, interpretation, and history. Merk relates to *The Interpreter's Dictionary of the Bible* as research to interpretation, and research relates to interpretation as the data of experience to the level of understanding. Newman relates to the schools of Antioch and Alexandria as history to interpretation, and history relates to interpretation as the level of judgment does to the level of understanding. The decrees of Nicea and Chalcedon relate to Thomas Aquinas as doctrines to systematics, and these to one another as the levels of truth and understanding, unfolding now in the reverse direction of theology's second phase. Pastoral theology relates to Thomas Aquinas as communication to systematics, and these to one another as application to truth, again in the direction of mediated theology.

I have not mentioned the two specialties of dialectic and foundations, and with good reason. For these two specialties are so much Lonergan's own creation that it is hard to find examples in past or current theology that fit exactly. And that points directly to two specific tasks we face in bringing the church to the level of the times: the task of dialectic, and the development of new foundations.

When the first part of Lonergan's *De Deo trino* was translated as *The Way to Nicea,* he gave it the subtitle, *The Dialectical Development of Trinitarian Theology*. The pattern of the church's way to Nicea was dialectical, but what was a pattern of doctrinal development from Tertullian and Origen to Nicea is bound to be a pattern still today.[29] Today, the field of theology bristles with questions without answers, whose answers will be worked out in a dialectic similar to that of the third and fourth centuries, where the guidance of Lonergan's method will

29 That is a simple corollary of the fact that God is infinite mystery, theology must be open to indefinite development, and without the beatific vision developing doctrines cannot be demonstrated from premises. This suggests great caution in labeling stages in the development as heretical. If we said today what Tertullian and Origen said in their time, we would be heretics; but Tertullian and Origen were not heretics; not even Arius was a heretic till he refused to accept the judgment of the great church.

serve, not only to keep us on the orthodox way, but also to prevent too hasty an attribution of heresy to those engaged in the dialectic.

And that makes it even more important to develop the fifth functional specialty, foundations. Lonergan's shift from deductive theology (premises in scripture, conclusions by logical process) to foundations not in propositions but in the theologian, is a time bomb waiting to explode. There are few who realize its importance and its implications.[30]

7 Lonergan's Place in the Universe of Thought: Was He 'Scientific'?

Is Lonergan a scientific thinker? Naturally, that depends on what you mean by 'scientific.' This is an area made to order for academic imperialists, who decree that their work is scientific, and any work that does not satisfy their criteria is unscientific.[31]

But fundamentally it really does not matter who usurps the label 'scientific.' What matters is who develops human potentiality to the full. That means attending to the human operations involved: experience, understanding, judgment, decision, love. Further, if we agree that from the time of Leonardo da Vinci a 'uomo universale' has been impossible, it means attending also, within the framework of human operations, to the different patterns of consciousness – the common-sense pattern, the artistic, the theoretic, the philosophic, the religious. Thirdly, if we are to assign scientific value to the various disciplines, we need a vantage point from which to survey them, in themselves

---

30 This brings us to a sharp line of demarcation between two schools of thought on the extent to which theology is open to anyone. In Lonergan's view anyone can take part in the mediating theology of the first four functional specialties. Even an unbeliever can work on New Testament manuscripts, and only rarely and indirectly will faith be required to determine a correct reading. Similarly, unbelievers can work on interpretation and history, though more and more as they advance from function to function will their results be likely to differ from those of believers. With dialectic, however, believers and unbelievers come to a dividing of their ways, and with foundations they part company. Theology becomes theology 'in oratione recta,' not just a matter of what Matthew said, or what Mark meant, or what the history of Matthew's relation to Mark is, but a matter of what I myself hold.

31 Beginning his *Method in Theology* (p. 3), Lonergan wrote: '... today the English word, science, means natural science. One descends a rung or more in the ladder when one speaks of behavioral or human sciences. Theologians finally often have to be content if their subject is included in a list not of sciences but of academic disciplines.'

and in relation to one another. What will that vantage point be, and how shall we attain it?

What we need is a term that overarches three areas of study: first, empirical or natural or exact sciences; next, human sciences; and thirdly, human studies or scholarship. It is useless to ask physicists to evaluate emotion, and useless to ask psychologists to evaluate poetry: as specialists they are incompetent in other disciplines; they can at best only flounder and at worst only indulge their imperialist ambitions. Further, our overarching term should be one that commands respect from the whole academic community. What will it be, this term that regards the disciplines from a vantage point and commands respect from all of them?

There is a hint in a remark on Sophocles, made, I believe, by Matthew Arnold: 'He saw life steadily and saw it whole.' And there is a clear clue in a frequently quoted statement of Aristotle's, from whom I trace a trajectory to Lonergan. Speaking precisely in our context of the variety of disciplines, Aristotle has this to say.

> Our discussion will be adequate if it has as much clearness as the subject-matter admits of, for precision is not to be sought for alike in all discussions, any more than in all the products of the crafts ... We must be content, then, in speaking of such subjects [where there is 'much variety and fluctuation of opinion'] and with such premises to indicate the truth roughly and in outline ... and to reach conclusions that are no better. In the same spirit, therefore, should each type of statement be received; for it is the mark of an educated man to look for precision in each class of things just so far as the nature of the subject admits; it is evidently equally foolish to accept probable reasoning from a mathematician and to demand from a rhetorician scientific proofs.[32]

My English translation of Aristotle has him speak of what an educated person will expect: 'it is the mark of an educated man (in Greek, *pepaideumenos*) to look for precision in each class of things just so far as the nature of the subject admits.' Can we too speak of the educated person or the cultivated person as one who can appreciate the work of the natural scientist, the human scientist, the scholar, the philosopher, the

32 *Nicomachean Ethics* I, 3, 1094b 11–27.

theologian? Can we so include them in our Sophoclean vantage point that all have their function and value, so that 'science,' if restricted to one discipline, ceases to be the idol of academe and the university?

I think we can. I have said that a Leonardo da Vinci is impossible today, a priori impossible. No one can speak with the authority of an expert on mathematics, empirical science, economics and other human sciences, philosophy, and theology. But there is the intermediate state of one who had learned enough of them all, not to be familiar with their content, but to be familiar with their procedures, and so to speak of them in a way that would command respect. And perhaps that is the nearest we can come to a Leonardo da Vinci as we enter the twenty-first century, just half a millennium after his time.

The instrument I propose for such education, such cultivation of the whole person, is, of course, the *organon* provided by Lonergan. It would do for the cultivated mind and heart in general what Aristotle's *pepaideumenos* did for mathematics and rhetoric, or for mathematics and ethics. The eight functional specialties would do for all the fields and departments of a university faculty what Aristotle did for two or three of them.[33] Let the term 'science' be usurped then by one branch of human cultivation, and not the most important branch either. What we will aim at is the cultivation of mind that enables us to see arts and sciences, all the sciences, empirical and human, and not just human sciences but human studies in their full range, to see them all and judge them from a holistic viewpoint, to see the life of the mind steadily and see it whole.

And when we have achieved that aim, when we have done in our century and in our own way what Leonardo did in the fifteenth and in

33 There is an extremely interesting set of parallels in the ways that Lonergan extends an Aristotelian strategy and perhaps sublates it in a higher viewpoint. One instance is fcund in their use of retortion. As a way to handle skeptics Aristotle said, Get them to say something, and then you have them. Lonergan's famous self-involving retortion argument (anyone who disputes experience, understanding, and judgment must use the three levels in order to make his objection) is just Aristotle carried a few steps further. Another instance is found in their sets of programmatic questions: Aristotle has his set, Lonergan extends it significantly. A third instance is the present one. Aristotle thinks of educated persons as able to judge in regard to mathematics and rhetoric (and ethics). Lonergan extends this to envisage persons who fully appropriate themselves, and are thus able to judge in regard to the eight areas of the functional specialties. The three instances are parallel. (See also above, note 28.)

his way, what Thomas Aquinas did in the thirteenth, what Augustine did in the fifth – when we have done all this we may remember that our intellectual vocation is a vocation within a vocation. Then we may return to human and Christian living, at peace with our conscience and our church, as having done what Lonergan did: use his talents to the maximum in his effort to bring the church to the level of the times.

Chapter 2

From Kerygma to Inculturation: The Odyssey of Gospel Meaning[1]

The general theme of this workshop is meaning and mystery. Meaning and mystery, I would say, is an almost perfect pair of words to take us to the center of Bernard Lonergan's life and work. For mystery was at the heart of his religion, meaning informed his mind as he studied the problems of theology, and religion and theology pretty much define his life and work. He lived and worked, in the beautiful and illuminating phrase of *Method in Theology*, in 'the ongoing contexts within which mystery is adored and adoration is explained.'[2] Or, to expand that a little with another quotation from the same source, 'Man's response to transcendent mystery is adoration. But adoration does not exclude words.'[3] And we remember that it is in language or words that 'meaning finds its greatest liberation'[4] and 'becomes most fully articulated':[5] that is, it is in the words of theology that adoration is explained.

If I am right, if these two words, meaning and mystery, circumscribe Lonergan's life and work, there results a certain difficulty when we would contribute to this workshop through research, interpretation and history on the Lonergan *corpus* of writings: the difficulty, namely, of determining what to leave out. Is there anything in Lonergan that does not fall under one of these two headlines? Well, in one of his own

1 Originally presented at the thirteenth annual Lonergan Workshop, Boston College, 16–20 June 1986, where the general theme was 'Meaning and Mystery.' Not previously published.

2 *Method in Theology* 345.

3 Ibid. 344.

4 Ibid. 70.

5 Ibid. 112.

crisp phrases, You do what you can. Doing what I can, I leave out entirely the topic of mystery to speak only of meaning. Further, I restrict my discussion of meaning to two headings: historicity and inculturation. Both are fairly specific and will enable me to say something determinate in the time I have, but they are also key words that will unlock much of Lonergan's thinking on religious and theological meaning.

They are also linked to one another in a close relationship, having to do with the migrations of gospel meaning across the boundaries of space and time. For historicity relates to the meaning of the original gospel, the kerygma, the preaching of the apostles, and raises the question of recovering that meaning as we move farther and farther in space and time from our gospel origins. Inculturation, on the other hand, relates to present preaching, and raises the question of communicating the gospel meaning now to the many peoples with their many cultures in our world of the approaching twenty-first century. Thus, historicity and inculturation take us on the odyssey of gospel meaning from the time, place and culture of the Lord Jesus to all the times, places and cultures envisaged in the command to preach the gospel 'to the whole creation.'[6]

1 Historicity

What, then, is historicity? I take this definition from Lonergan's *Doctrinal Pluralism*: 'Historicity means – very briefly – that human living is informed by meanings, that meanings are the product of intelligence, that human intelligence develops cumulatively over time, and that such cumulative development differs in different histories.'[7] Thus, western peoples differ from eastern, as Europe does from China; the western peoples of the 1500s differ from the western peoples of the 1900s; and the western peoples of the 1900s differ among themselves according to their different histories.

It is not just a matter of the obvious differences: those of styles of dress, or manners of eating, or gadgetry in kitchen and livingroom. Much more basically it is a matter of different ways of thinking. Peoples of the plains do not think the same way as mountain peoples, or

6 Mark 16:15.
7 *Doctrinal Pluralism* 7–8.

citizens of a mighty power the same way as those of smaller nations, and these differences affect their imagery and enter deeply into their psyche. Both English and Americans have a great sense of humor, but English humor is not always American humor, and if you want your English comedy to succeed in the United States, you had better attend to that. There are differences, great differences, even within the West, and still more do we in the West differ from eastern peoples: 'Oh, East is East, and West is West, and never the twain shall meet.'

Of course they do meet at some profound level, the very deepest levels of human nature. Kipling realized that – it was his main point – and we shall notice this too with regard to the gospel. But the differences are also profound, and the notion of historicity brings them to our attention. If we attend only to what is the same in human nature, as happened during the long reign of classicism, we get a lop-sided essentialism in which a human being is defined as a rational animal, and the definition, being essential, applies to everyone: old or young, saint or sinner, genius or moron. We have to add to that a new attention to differences, and with it a whole new way of thinking and valuing, of realizing that differences are a product of time and place and culture, and appreciating the worth of differences. In sum, then, and for present purposes, historicity means that every human product is time-conditioned, place-conditioned, culture-conditioned. It bears the mark of its origin in a particular milieu: its meaning and value are discovered in reference to that milieu.

Now, this concept is to be completely generalized to include also the whole religious sphere on earth. All our religious ideas too, religious expressions, acts of worship, religious precepts – they too are human products, and hence conditioned by their origin in a particular milieu. I do not say they are *merely* human products, but only that they are *also* human products and so subject to the law of historicity. The obvious and helpful instance is that of the Hebrew and Christian scriptures. We think of them as the word of God, and rightly so; but if we think of them *only* as the word of God, and not *also* as the product of human heart and human mind and human pen, then our interpretation is going to be quite inadequate. The scriptures are an especially helpful instance, for by now the church has come to accept their historicity and interpret them according to their human authors. But at the same time the victory was recent, to be dated perhaps with the 1943 encyclical of Pius XII, recent enough then for us to remember the blood, toil, tears and sweat that went into this victory, and so to realize better the point at issue.

The paradigm instance is not, however, the scriptures: it is one of greater, far greater importance to our faith, and one that may be the field of even sterner battles, with even more blood, sweat and tears to be shed. It is the instance of our Lord and Savior, Jesus Christ. He too comes under the general law of historicity, and it is in seeing this that we will realize the full impact of the notion.

In the creed, then, which we recite each Sunday or maybe daily, we declare our faith in God the Father almighty, and in the only Son who became human for us. Now for long ages we have stressed the generic side of that humanity. That the Son of God became human, fully human, was clear enough, but how did we interpret that fact? It meant for most of us that he assumed human nature, that is, universal human nature, the human nature common to all of us, human nature conceived then in the somewhat abstract way of classicism. This way of conceiving the matter was and is true, so far as it goes; but it goes only halfway, and we must add the other half.

The Word was indeed made flesh, but the flesh was Jewish, not African or Polynesian. Jesus was born in the fulness of time, the Lord of universal history, but his birth occurred also at a particular date in history: it was when Herod was king and Augustus emperor. He was taught to pray to the one God of all tribes and peoples, but the images of his prayer were those of the Hebrew Psalms, not the Amerindian images of the Great Spirit. He could and would heal Jew or Gentile, Canaanite or Roman, but he would use his own spittle for the healing in a rite we find offensive and unhygienic. He went round teaching, and he spoke with full authority, but his speech was in the strange Aramaic tongue, and its imagery puzzles us even in translation. In short, he was a Jewish boy with a Jewish mamma: he grew up to be a Jewish rabbi who did not have our table manners, who would be baffled by our baseball madness, who would not understand our theology.

We have to generalize completely the law of historicity. Not only our literature but also our sacred books, not only our sacred books but also the Lord Jesus: all are subject to this general law of being human. We have also to generalize the application of the law to Jesus. It was not only in the social and cultural areas that his thinking was time-conditioned, but in the religious area as well. His world was a world peopled by evil spirits, it was structured in three storeys, it would end with the stars falling from heaven – and this world shaped the expression of his religious thinking.

It is time now to come to the point, that is, apply this to the church and her tradition. If historicity marks our scriptural sources, if it characterizes the very founder of our religion, then a fortiori it marks the church and all her works throughout all her history: the dogmas in which she has expressed her faith, the institutional forms she has assumed throughout the centuries, the ritual and ceremonies she has elaborated, the paths taken by her saints, and the accounts her mystics have given of their experiences. In our long history the Greek church has thought one way, the Latin church another, and the Assyrian church a third. Benedict has followed one path of discipleship, Francis of Assisi a second, and Loyola a third. In all our sources and in all our wealth of tradition we have been time and place and culture-conditioned.

Many of you will think that I have been laboring the obvious, and I will grant that it is obvious enough to you. But it is not obvious to all: it is a new development in our religious thinking. We had long thought of our doctrines – to take that example – as if they fulfilled the requirements of Vincent of Lerins, as if they had been held everywhere and always by everyone: 'quod ubique, quod semper, quod ab omnibus.' Newman showed how simplistic that thinking was: it had to be complemented with historical thinking, for to live is to change. But there are many in the church who have not yet learned what Newman had to teach, or even what Pius XII, with greater authority, taught in his encyclical on the scriptures. Or, if they reluctantly admit, after Pius XII, the historicity of the scriptures, and reluctantly admit with Newman the element of change, they will insist that the change came to a term in certain fixed formulations – classicism. There is no way they will admit that we can reformulate in a better way for our time the great dogmas of our faith. Dogmatic formulation is eternal truth: it states what was given once for all, and it states it once for all: the formulation itself is permanent.

There is a fixation here that will be loosened only by charity and understanding. We have to exercise the charity given us and try to promote the achievement of understanding with a view to forming a reasonable judgment, a judgment that takes account of what is legitimate in the notion of permanence without making fossils of our doctrines, and that takes account of what is legitimate in the notion of historicity without yielding to relativism. The onus of promoting understanding falls more directly on those of us who would combine historicity with permanence, for we are like the householder who would bring forth from the treasury new things and old. Those, on the other hand, who would deny historicity are householders content with what they have, with the status quo: why should they try to explain a combination and integration they regard as simply invalid? But that is exactly the problem facing us once we have learned the lesson of historicity: integration. We have added the historicity of dogma to its permanence. How do we put them together?

The answer is long and complex and, since I must give it in a few words, let me first draw a picture – which, we are told, is worth ten thousand words when it is a good one. My picture is of a coin – call it gold – that in the time of Jesus, as we know from a certain gospel story, would bear the image of Caesar Augustus. Now suppose that on the death of Augustus the coin was melted down and recast with the image of Tiberius: and suppose that on the death of Tiberius it was melted down again and recast, this time with the image of Caligula: and so also through the reigns of later emperors – Claudius, Nero, Galba, and the rest. Surely, it is the same gold coin in every instance; but just as surely it appears under a different form, which can be greatly varied, in every recasting and reissue.

With that picture to guide us, we can follow the outlines of what I think to be Lonergan's answer to the problem of integration, or how to relate and hold in unity the permanence and the historicity of dogma. The pure gold, then, that remains always the same under different forms, is meaning, and in the crucial case of doctrines, the meaning of dogma. That meaning is not given apart from a verbal formulation, but 'the permanence attaches to the meaning and not to the formula.'[8] This will be incomprehensible to those philosophers who give absolute priority to language over meaning, but I cannot delay on that point: I must simply refer you to Lonergan's discussion of it in *Method in Theology*.[9] Next, there is the melting down and recasting. This translates into theological language as the reduction of the formula through horizon-analysis to its original intention (the meaning that is beyond words and prior to words) and the transposition of that intention into the language appropriate in another context (recasting an old meaning under a new form).

The matter needs far more study than we can give it here, but I will offer two aids to bring it somewhat out of the abstract realm into the concrete. The first is the claim that, basically, I am saying the same

8 *Method in Theology* 323.
9 Ibid. 254–57.

thing that Pope John XXIII said in his speeches of 1962 on the reason for calling a council. Twice in that historic year he explained the need and the reason. It was not, he said, to reiterate old dogmas: we don't need a council for that. It was to give new expression to the old dogmas, and this was no simple step like translating them from the Greek or Latin of their formulation, but it was to be a leap forward into modern times, using modern methods, and thinking according to modern patterns.[10]

Another way to make my point more concrete is to trace with Lonergan the odyssey of the gospel meaning of Christ the Lord. Christ was first conceived in a Palestinian context, within Palestinian horizons, as the Son of Man coming in the clouds to the Ancient of days. This was transposed in Paul's ministry to other horizons where Christ was conceived as the Lord of glory, 'the image of the invisible God' with 'primacy over all created things.'[11] That in turn was transposed at the Council of Nicea into the dogma that the Son is consubstantial with the Father, and this has been transposed in our time into language more meaningful to us by saying that the Son is God in the same sense as the Father is God.[12] One golden coin of meaning, but how different the form, the appearance, the expression. Or again, one Traveler in the human universe, but how different the many places he visits, and how differently he is perceived in those many places.

2 Inculturation

I have talked of the odyssey of gospel meaning, of the way we might follow its travels from the original kerygma through the last nineteen centuries. But the nineteen centuries are only the beginning: the odyssey continues into our time and into the future. That is the point made by John XXIII as he opened the Second Vatican Council. It is what I wish to discuss now under the heading of inculturation, and I start by noting that there are two new factors involved here, one more subjective, the other more objective.

The subjective factor is not of present concern, but let us notice it and pass on. It regards the emergence of personal responsibility for the

10 John XXIII, *AAS* 54 (1962) 791–92; 55 (1963) 43–45.
11 Colossians 1:15.
12 George Prestige, *God in Patristic Thought*, 2nd ed. (London: SPCK, 1952) 213.

odyssey of gospel meaning. That is to say, we are no longer reading a book written by someone else: we are writing our own. We not only contemplate history, we must change it. In the terms of Lonergan's two phases of theology, 'If one assimilates tradition, one learns that one should pass it on. If one encounters the past, one also has to take one's stand toward the future.'[13] There is a new demand then on the subject doing theology: he or she must exercise a personal responsibility for the formulation of meaning, and not simply try to understand a meaning given by others. This of course is, or should be, a matter of intense existential concern to the theologian, but it is not a particularly theological problem, not at least the one that concerns us here.

There is also an objective difference and it does create a new theological problem which everyone discusses today under the heading of inculturation. That is our present concern. It was not a problem that greatly occupied the young Lonergan: he was busy into the 1960s with the problem of transposition from the scriptures to the dogmas. But by 1965 a new element had become thematic in his thinking: the empirical notion of culture. To be sure, the seed had been planted much earlier by his reading of Dawson in 1930,[14] but the seed bore fruit only in the 1960s with the relativizing – I do not say, the entire abandonment – of the old classical notion of culture and the acceptance of the new empirical notion. Here is a clear and forthright statement of 1965:

> [B]y and large, classical culture has passed away. By and large, its canons of art, its literary forms, its rules of correct speech, its norms of interpretation, its ways of thought, its manner in philosophy, its notion of science, its concept of law, its moral standards, its methods of education, are no longer accepted.[15]

Now it happened that in this very year of 1965 Lonergan had already discovered the integral structure of a methodical theology. The two discoveries meet, mesh perfectly, and go into operation together in communications, a word almost interchangeable with inculturation and Lonergan's choice for the name of his eighth functional specialty. Together the two discoveries provide a powerful dynamism for what

13 *Method in Theology* 133.

14 '*Insight* Revisited,' in *A Second Collection* 264.

15 'Dimensions of Meaning,' in *Collection* (1967) 258–59 [(1988) 238].

will surely be a major task of the twenty-first century, the inculturation of the gospel among all those we read of in the *Book of Revelation*, that 'vast throng, which no one could count, from every nation, of all tribes, peoples, and languages.'[16] In our global village we can no longer narrow the scope of that apocalyptic vision or ignore the problem of inculturation it poses, as I think we have unwittingly done in the past. Lonergan's Chapter 14, on communications, does not use the word, inculturation, but that, very exactly, is what he is talking about, and I wish to sketch his idea before concluding.

I began by noting that the problem is partly the same as and partly different from the problem we met in historicity and transposition. It is partly the same, for we are still dealing with the many peoples of the world and their vast differences: that remains the underlying reality and presents the basic problem. But I went on to talk of the many resulting cultures as presenting a new problem, once they are recognized as valid cultures with a right to live on and have the gospel preached to them, so far as possible, in terms intelligible to them. This new problem we discuss under the heading of inculturation. It is one thing to move from a Palestinian to a classicist culture that is thought to be normative: it is another to move from that culture to a myriad of cultures, each of which is valid but none of which is normative for the human race. The transposition now is not from a single source to a single term, but from a single source through a relativized mediating culture to ten thousand terms in the mission field, a mission field – be it noted – which includes the whole world, the subcultures of our western cities as well as the ancient culture of India.

We are dealing at least to some extent with a new problem. How do you preach a gospel of Palestinian origin in a Korea that is not Palestinian and has little relation to Palestine? Or in the subcultures of Boston, subcultures that have just as little relation to the Palestine of Jesus? How do you teach dogmas defined by European councils to African peoples who do not think in a European way and do not wish to think in a European way? It is mixing oil with water: it is bringing the good news of the message that will save them along with the bad news of a culture that will destroy their own. And that is not the whole story, for those many cultures, often very ancient, which have meanings, values, and usages of their own, and are not to be jettisoned for imports from

16 Revelations 7:9.

Europe but are to be retained – these cultures must also in their turn become the bearers of the gospel message. But how? Does Lonergan give us any guidance on such questions as these?

On the main point he is brief but perfectly explicit. Those who preach the gospel, he says, must

> enlarge their horizons to include an accurate and intimate understanding of the culture and the language of the people they address. They must grasp the virtual resources of that culture and that language, and they must use those virtual resources creatively so that the Christian message becomes, not disruptive of the culture, not an alien patch superimposed upon it, but a line of development within the culture.[17]

To find a line of development within each culture, a line that fulfils the two conditions of being 'true to the kindred points' of gospel and culture, that is the missionary task of the twenty-first century.

Is there more to be said? Yes, but it is a long story. Let me just indicate some of the steps and headings. I would begin the narrative with chapter 17 of *Insight*, where we have the first thematic wrestling with the problem of communications. We would absolutely have to include chapter 11 of *Method in Theology*, where you have not only the foundational reality that allows for transcultural communication, but sections on the pluralism of expression and the pluralism of religious language. Then we would make a thorough study of that neglected chapter 14 on communications, and conclude with the last formal paper Lonergan delivered, 'Unity and Plurality,' published as chapter 15 in *A Third Collection*. Let me also conclude my lecture there, with a quotation from the second section, 'Pluralism and Theological Doctrines,' of that paper.

> ... to preach the gospel to all nations calls for almost as many apostles as there are distinct places and times, and it requires each of them to get to know the people to whom they have been sent, and to catch on to the manner and style and way of their thought and speech. There follows a manifold pluralism, but primarily it is a pluralism not of doctrine but of communications. It remains that within the realm of undifferentiated consciousness there is no communication of doctrine except through the

17 *Method in Theology* 362.

> available rituals, narratives, titles, parables, metaphors, modes of praise and blame, of command and prohibition, of promise and threat.[18]

Curiously, the preceding chapter is entitled 'Pope John's Intention.' It is there that Lonergan brings sharply to our notice the fact that Pope John did not want a reiteration of old dogmas at the Council: he wanted a leap forward. Twenty-four years have passed since John spoke those prophetic words. We are still very much tied to old formulations of our ancient faith. But the leap forward will come, if not in our century, then in the next. It was the concern of Pope John, as it must be the concern of us all, to go forward in continuity with what is valid in our past. I believe that what we can learn from Lonergan under the twin headings of historicity and inculturation will help us in that concern, to make a forward leap but to do so intelligently, prayerfully, vigorously, and securely.

18 'Unity and Plurality,' in *A Third Collection* 243.

Chapter 3

Insight: Genesis and Ongoing Context[1]

The title of my paper names for discussion two aspects of the book *Insight*. The second aspect, the book's ongoing context, is ultimately equal in importance to the first. However, it will not receive equal time in my talk today, the far larger amount going to the book's genesis. This first part I will therefore subdivide according to the chronology of Lonergan's life over a quarter of a century. First, there was the breakthrough of 1928 to 1929, a breakthrough of great creative potential, but not one he was ready then to exploit; it was at that time, I would say, something like a soul without a body. Then, there was the long buildup to 1949, a marshaling of forces for a major campaign. The two main forces were Thomism and modernity, and they were allied to a personal self-appropriation somewhat as neighboring nations are to a homeland, or the external to the internal. Thirdly, after this long withdrawal there was the return in strength of 1949 to 1953. I do not say 'triumphant' return, for there are no triumphs in the world of great ideas; there is only a slow permeation of society and culture, so that after a hundred years what was first dismissed as ridiculous becomes a commonplace of education. Still, triumphant or not, Lonergan's return was overwhelming for those striving to keep up with his thought. One could call it an explosion of built-up forces when, during those extraordinary four years, starting almost from scratch and teaching every year except one, he wrote *Insight: A Study of Human Understanding*.

1 Originally presented at the fourteenth annual Lonergan Workshop, Boston College, 15–19 June 1987, where the general theme was '*Insight*: Thirty Years After.' Previously published in *Lonergan Workshop* 8 (1990) 61–83.

1 The Creative Breakthrough: 1928–1929

I start the body of my paper by demolishing a myth. The myth is that Lonergan began his career as a Thomist, then went on to add modernity (the seven centuries after Thomas), and so came to write *Insight*. My thesis states that, on the contrary, the most basic ideas of the book were very largely in place in Lonergan's thinking while he was still a student at Heythrop College – five years, it seems, before he had read a line of Thomas Aquinas. This thesis requires a rethinking of his debt to Thomas – not a canceling of the debt but a rewriting of its terms. It requires a rethinking also of the way Thomism is related to modernity in their dual input to the content of *Insight*; that will be the problem in the next part of my paper, and it fascinates me, but all things in order, and the first part of my paper first.

Lonergan was in the philosophy program – I do not say, studied philosophy – for three years, from 1926 to 1929, at Heythrop College in England, the Jesuit seminary for philosophy there. During these years he did his first publishing, though it was only in the student journal, *Blandyke Papers*, and 'publishing' meant simply copying his essay by hand into a notebook left in the College reading-room, a notebook containing all the contributions for that month that had been duly refereed and accepted.

His first essay was 'The Form of Mathematical Inference,' accepted for the issue of January 1928. Now the astounding thing about this essay, his first publication appearing when he had just turned twenty-four, is the firm appropriation it shows already of the act of insight. Lonergan does not use that term, and he is a long, long way from the mastery and technical language of his later Thomist studies, but he has already pinned down in concrete examples the fertile relation of image to understanding – what he will later call insight into phantasm.[2]

He begins by distinguishing 'two kinds of inference, one sensible the other conceptual.'[3] Conceptual inference, I suppose, would be that of ordinary logic, but sensible inference is clearly a matter of insight into phantasm. The language used is revealing enough by itself. Sensible inference, he keeps saying, depends on 'visualization.'[4] Again, there is

2 'Verbum' (1946) 372 [*Verbum* (1967) 25, (1997) 38].

3 'The Form of Mathematical Inference,' *Blandyke Papers* 283 (1928) 127.

4 Ibid. 130, 132, 134, 137.

'a directly and intuitively apprehended relation,'[5] an apprehension 'in virtue of a generic image,'[6] what he at one point calls 'an intuition of the *vis cogitativa*'[7] – a term I will come back to.

This language, I say, is already revealing, but his examples and the way he uses them is even more so, for they are very much those of the *Verbum* study in 1946 and of the *Insight* book in 1953. Take the 32nd proposition of Euclid's first book, the one about the exterior angle constructed by producing the base of a triangle. We are to prove that this angle equals the sum of the interior opposite angles. Euclid does not argue, Lonergan writes, from the concept *triangularitate*;[8] rather, 'he dealt with the figure in the diagram.' Latent here, in the contrast between arguing from a concept and grasping an idea in a diagram, is the familiar contrast of his later Thomist studies between conceptualism and intellectualism.

The utterly conclusive evidence, however, is found in Lonergan's procedure when he would account for the universal validity of Euclid's proof. This is a matter of creatively disposing the lines and angles of the diagram, realizing the potential divisions, shuffling the data. Take a normal triangle, ABC, and search for the required proof. Eighteen years later the *Verbum* articles will say, on a related problem:

> Stare at a triangle as long as you please, and you will not be any nearer seeing that its three angles must equal two right angles. But through the vertex draw a line parallel to the base, and the equality of alternate angles ends the matter at once. The act of understanding leaps forth when the sensible data are in a suitable constellation.[9]

The procedure is exactly parallel in the *Blandyke Papers* when Lonergan would demonstrate the universal validity of Euclid's proof. Granted that we see the point in this diagram; how do we know the proof is valid for every diagram? 'Visualize this triangle,' Lonergan says. So we visualize the triangle, ABC, with its base produced (ABD), and a line BE drawn parallel to the side AC (Fig. 1). Now form, he goes on, 'a

---

5 Ibid. 128.
6 Ibid. 129.
7 Ibid. 131; see also 129.
8 Ibid. 133; an odd term – we would surely say 'triangularity.'
9 'Verbum' (1946) 362 [*Verbum* (1967) 14, (1997) 27–28].

kinetic generic image.' That is, 'imagine the line CB swinging round as on a pivot at B [Fig. 2 – one has to make the lines elastic]. Every instant we see a different triangle and in the infinity of triangles seen while CB moves from coinciding with AB to coinciding with BE, CB is always a transversal of parallels and therefore [the angle] ACB = [the angle] CBE in all these instances.'[10]

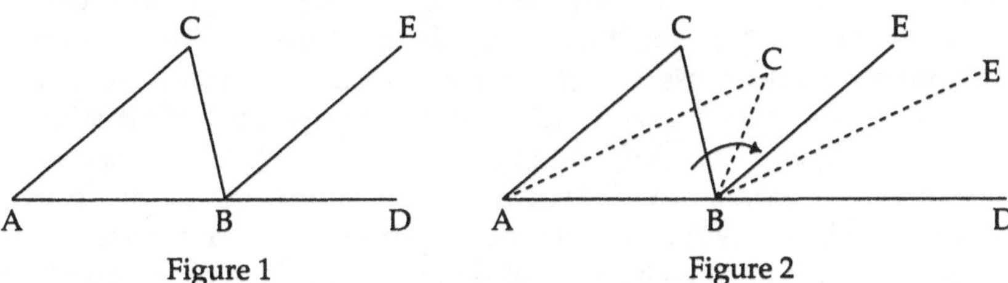

Figure 1

Figure 2

Lonergan now draws his modest conclusion: 'the diagram,' he says, 'is more important than ... is ordinarily believed.'[11] There is a line to remember. I nominate it as the philosophical understatement of the century: *the diagram is more important than is ordinarily believed.*

There is a great deal more to be mined from this 1928 paper, and much also, I am sure, to be criticized. But I have no doubt on the main point, namely, that we have here in its essential moment the section 'Insight into Phantasm,' of the *Verbum* article of 1946, and the basic idea of Chapter 1 of the book *Insight*.[12]

That alone is astonishing enough, but there is more to come. Lonergan writes at the end of this youthful essay: 'I do not think Card. Newman's illative sense is specifically the same as these concrete inferences but that question requires separate treatment.'[13] Indeed it is not the same; it is as different as direct understanding is from reflective, as different as concept is from judgment. And indeed it does require sepa-

10 'The Form of Mathematical Inference,' *Blandyke Papers* 283 (1928) 134. Figure 1 is from the typescript, prepared by Philip McShane, of Lonergan's handwritten essay. [Figure 2 is Crowe's own contribution (ed.).]

11 Ibid. 134–35.

12 I am by no means the first to recognize the importance of these essays in the *Blandyke Papers* as forerunner of later work. Thus, Desmond O'Grady recently remarked on this first paper of Lonergan's: 'His thesis was that mathematical principles are the fruit of insight into phantasm' ('"Verification": A Survey of Lonergan's Usage,' *METHOD: Journal of Lonergan Studies* 5/1 [1987] 13).

13 'The Form of Mathematical Inference,' *Blandyke Papers* 283 (1928) 136–37.

rate treatment, which is just what it receives one year later in an article called 'True Judgment and Science,' in the *Blandyke Papers* of February 1929. This is the work we must now consider.

'True Judgment and Science' is, then, from beginning to end a study of Newman's illative sense. It is also, in my view, the forerunner of Lonergan's second *Verbum* article (1947) and of his independent position in 1953 on judgment. My view might, I think, be established by analysis of the 1929 paper, but that would take time. The very nature of Newman's illative sense and of Lonergan's judgment make their basic identity more difficult to establish than the basic identity of visualizing Euclid's diagram with preparing an image for insight into phantasm. But there is a shorter, and indeed a more reliable route to the desired conclusion: it is Lonergan's own later statements of his dependence on Newman. He read the *Grammar of Assent* over and over at Heythrop College.[14] He says repeatedly that his reflective understanding has its anticipation in Newman's illative sense;[15] and Newman's way was surely that of appropriating his own cognitional processes. I think we can take it as evident, without need of detailed study of 'True Judgment and Science,' that in 1929 Lonergan was already well on the way to the appropriation of judgment that he describes in the second *Verbum* article[16] and in *Insight*.[17]

My basic thesis, then, is clear and simple, however imperfect my demonstration may have been: direct insight into phantasm in its essential moment had been appropriated by Lonergan in 1928, and reflective insight or reflective understanding in the following year of 1929. Further, as we shall presently discover, Lonergan seems to have had no immediate acquaintance at that time with the work of Thomas Aquinas.

2 Withdrawal and Build-up of Forces

In order to explore now the next twenty years of Lonergan's life and work, I ask what the options are for a brilliant young student with a

14 'Theories of Inquiry: Responses to a Symposium,' in *A Second Collection* 38; '*Insight* Revisited,' ibid. 263.

15 *Verbum* (1967) 47 [(1997) 60]; '*Insight* Revisited,' in *A Second Collection* 263, 273; *Understanding and Being* (1980) 133, 318 [(1990) 109, 351].

16 'Verbum' (1947) 35–79 [*Verbum*, chap. 2 (1967) 47–95, (1997) 60–105].

17 *Insight*, chaps. 9–10 (1957) 271–316 [(1992) 296–340].

brilliant new idea or pair of ideas. One option is illustrated in the life of David Hume, who had his great work, *A Treatise of Human Nature*, ready when he reached the greybeard age of twenty-six. This option is especially illuminating for us because it is the exact opposite of the way taken by Bernard Lonergan. Of course, the way taken by Hume was never a real option for Lonergan. The intrinsic possibility existed, latent in his student essays and in the potential of his fertile mind. But the extrinsic possibility did not exist: a Jesuit scholastic, even one fresh from philosophy, was in Lonergan's time only halfway through his assigned studies and did not do the kind of thing Hume did. Rather, he was first sent to teach young barbarians for three years, then to study an outdated theology for four more, and after that to renew his novitiate fervor in a year we call tertianship.

There was really no way, then, that the young Lonergan could have written at once his own treatise on human nature. And in fact he did not produce *Insight*, his counterpart to Hume's *Treatise*, till he was forty-nine years old, exactly the age at which Thomas Aquinas had finished all the work he was to do and gone to his reward. Now I am simply reporting facts here; I am not blaming the Jesuit system, or asserting that the twenty years that intervened before Lonergan started to write *Insight* were simply an empty interval, a kind of marking time before the forward march could begin again. I do not think they were empty years: I think they were years of tremendous growth. The course of development, however, is not easy to follow; for although there are extremely revealing documents, there are also great blank spaces. Still, that will add zest to an already fascinating study.

Let us get the problem clear. My thesis is that Lonergan did not begin his career as a neo-Thomist; he began with appropriation of his own cognitional structure in its two quantum leaps (thus, three essential levels), finding support for one of these leaps in Euclid and for the other in Newman. So the question arises, what was happening in Lonergan's mind during the next twenty years? In particular, what was he doing during the years which he spent, he says, 'reaching up to the mind of Aquinas?'[18] Of course, his cognitional theory existed only in embryo at Heythrop, and there was needed the full development of its internal resources, the operation of what he would later call the princi-

18 Ibid. (1957) 748 [(1992) 769].

ple of finality[19] and that of a self-assembling,[20] self-mediating[21] structure. But *Insight* is not a spider's web spun entirely from internal resources. There was an enormous input from external sources. That is what I want to explore in this section. I will do so under the headings of Thomism and modernity, the two external sources complementing the internal development and the self-appropriation. Thomism enters rather late, but its contribution can be determined more accurately, so I begin with that.

2.1 *Thomas Aquinas*

There can be no question of denying the great debt Lonergan owes to Thomas Aquinas. We have to take quite seriously his statement at the end of *Insight* that he spent 'years reaching up to the mind of Aquinas.' Our first step will be to ask what years he meant, and then to ask what he learned in this reaching up.

At the 1967 meeting of the American Catholic Philosophical Association there was a symposium on Lonergan's work and he was asked, politely but clearly: Since you were first a neo-Thomist and only later wrote *Insight*, did not your neo-Thomism predetermine the conclusions reached in that book?[22] Lonergan, equally polite if not equally clear, acknowledged his debt to Aquinas, but then went on: 'I just add, however, that my interest in Aquinas came late.'[23] It is here that politeness gets in the way of clarity. The clear statement would be: You have the order exactly opposite to the right one; my basic idea came first, and then Aquinas.

But at least we know his interest in Thomas came late. So how late, and when? I have a letter dated 3 March 1980, which is helpful here. Lonergan writes: 'my own work in [the] specialty [of research] was *Gratia operans* and *Verbum*, about eleven years of my life.' Eleven years, it happens, exactly separate the year 1938, when he began his doctoral dissertation on grace in Thomas, from the year 1949, when he finished the *Verbum* articles and turned to the writing of *Insight*.

19 Ibid. (1957) 444–51 [(1992) 470–76].

20 'Cognitional Structure,' in *Collection* (1967) 223 [(1988) 207].

21 'The Mediation of Christ in Prayer,' *METHOD: Journal of Lonergan Studies* 2/1 (1984) 1–20 [*Papers 1958–1964* 160–82].

22 'Theories of Inquiry,' in *A Second Collection* 37. I paraphrase the question.

23 Ibid. 38.

Did he have any direct acquaintance with Thomas prior to 1938? Not, apparently, at Heythrop College. For one thing, the textbooks there 'were ... Suarezian in conviction.'[24] The *Blandyke Papers* provide a more specific clue: here Lonergan attributes his insight into phantasm to the Thomist *vis cogitativa*.[25] This is quite simply an error, and could hardly have happened had he read Thomas on the question; but in fact, as his reference indicates, he was using secondary sources. The clinching evidence is provided by a letter of 22 January 1935 (to his Provincial Superior, Father Henry Keane), in which he says: 'I read St Augustine'[s] earlier works during the summer before theology [i.e., 1933] ... I then went on to study the *Summa* at first hand and began to suspect that St Thomas was not nearly as bad as he is painted.'

The picture now takes definite shape. In 1928, in all probability, he had not read Thomas, but he had seen some Thomist terms second-hand and had followed his sources, repeating their errors. Five years later he went directly to Thomas and began to read him with new understanding. I may add that just then he also came to know the work of Peter Hoenen and that of Joseph Maréchal, both of whom contributed to his cognitional theory and helped him to relate it to Thomist ideas. Another five years passed, and in 1938 he began his eleven years of research on Thomas, his period of reaching up to the mind of that thinker.

So what did he learn as he tried to reach up? It's all very well for him to say that the 'reaching had changed me profoundly,' and that 'that change was the essential benefit,'[26] but he must have learned something. What was it? His own statements give us a general idea, and I will suggest some specific ideas in the area of cognitional theory.

His dissertation, then, contends that a study of Thomas's thought on grace 'reveals him working into synthesis the speculative theorems discovered by his predecessors,' and adds that such a study 'brings to light the development of [Thomas's] own mind.'[27] The notion of synthesis would make an immediate appeal to Lonergan, and so would the notion of development. On publishing the dissertation a few years

24 Ibid. 263.

25 'The Form of Mathematical Inference,' *Blandyke Papers* 283 (1928) 129, 131.

26 *Insight* (1957) 748 [(1992) 769].

27 'The *Gratia Operans* Dissertation: Preface and Introduction,' *METHOD: Journal of Lonergan Studies* 3/2 (1985) 10 [*Grace and Freedom* (2000) 155].

later he enlarges both aspects, seeing the work of Thomas on grace in the context 'of a far vaster program,' which 'in point of fact no less than in essence ... was to lay under tribute Greek and Arab, Jew and Christian, in an ever renewed effort to obtain for Catholic culture that [most fruitful understanding] which is the goal of theological speculation.'[28] Then we read in the letter of 1980, on his eleven years of research: 'It is from the mind set of research that one most easily learns what Method is about: surmounting differences in historicity.'

Evidently, we are dealing with a complex question, one that moves us from the predecessors of Thomas, through Thomas himself and his development, to the historical consciousness that is the sign of the times seven centuries later. We have to do, in fact, with an ongoing context, as it is called in *Method in Theology*,[29] a context with prior and subsequent moments, a context in which tradition and innovation (the twin virtues he attributed to Thomas in his 1975 paper)[30] are in continual interchange with one another. Thomism did not end for Lonergan when he turned to the writing of *Insight*. Instead, it took on new meaning with each new aspect of modernity, and was sublated over and over as he carried it forward in his own development. Indeed, if we accept his later essays 'The Future of Thomism'[31] and 'Aquinas Today,' there is still an ongoing context for the ideas and work of Thomas Aquinas, and this suggests that we could profitably return to the role of Thomas when we have studied the parallel role of modernity in the genesis of *Insight*.

Meanwhile, however, there is the more specific role Thomas played in mediating between the embryonic ideas of the Heythrop years and the developed position of *Insight*. I want to say a word on that. The place to look is very obviously the *Verbum* articles, and out of the many specific ideas Lonergan got from that study of Thomas, I would select three as of special importance for *Insight*. The first is obvious enough: the dynamism of the mind, Aristotle's wonder that is the source of all science and all philosophy, the Thomist *intellectus agens*.[32] The second is

28 'Gratia Operans' (1942) 572–73 [*Grace and Freedom* (1971) 139, (2000) 143].

29 *Method in Theology* 312–14.

30 'Aquinas Today: Tradition and Innovation,' in *A Third Collection* 35–54.

31 'The Future of Thomism,' in *A Second Collection* 43–53.

32 *Verbum* (1967) 24, 47, 78, 80, 86–87, 174–75, and passim [(1997) 37, 60, 90, 91, 97–98, 184–85 and passim].

also obvious: cognitional structure, and the corresponding structure of reality. A key topic in Thomas would certainly be that of the *duplex operatio*,[33] the twofold operation of the mind, one pertaining to the formation of a concept, the other pertaining to the formation of a judgment. I can only guess how illuminating it must have been for Lonergan to come upon this idea, and how satisfying it must have been to find here a unifying theorem for his two Heythrop College papers.

The third idea is not at all obvious, but it has its own importance. Readers of *Insight* must have noticed two terms occurring like a refrain in that book: insight and formulation.[34] Possibly they came across them without reflecting much on their relation (as did the indexer, who failed to list this pair as such, though he provided some references for the corresponding pair 'Insight and concept'!). In any case the relation will be evident to students of the *Verbum* articles, for the key to the relation is the *emanatio intelligibilis*, the rational procession of inner word from understanding, of concept from insight, which is the central theme of those articles.[35] It is a question to me why Lonergan did not bother to explain the relation of insights and formulations by reference to the articles. I can only suppose that he felt his book was long enough already, and anyway he had at the beginning referred the reader to the *Verbum* study in a general way, as 'the parallel historical investigation.'[36]

2.2 *Modernity*

By modernity I mean nothing especially erudite, but just what came after Thomas in history, as seen in relation to Thomas. If Thomas, then, worked previous views on grace into synthesis, if in his vaster program he would lay under tribute Greek and Arab, Jew and Christian, if his way was to combine solid tradition with creative innovation, we have now to ask what the modern counterpart of all this is. What is solid in tradition as we approach the twenty-first century? Where today is the possibility of true creativity to be found? Who are to us what Greek and Arab were to Thomas? Such questions, explicit or implicit, surely occu-

33 Ibid. (1967) 4, 44, 51, and passim [(1997) 17–18, 57, 63–64 and passim].

34 *Insight* (1957) 6, 8, 31, 35, 79, 273, 275, and passim [(1992) 30, 33, 55, 59, 102, 298, 300, and passim].

35 'Verbum' (1946) 380–91 [*Verbum* (1967) 33–45, (1997) 46–59].

36 *Insight* (1957) xv [(1992) 9].

pied the mind of Lonergan throughout his career. Can we reach any answers to them at all?

At least the general orientation is perfectly clear. For all his love of Aquinas, Lonergan was relentlessly oriented to modernity. As he wrote in the original, unused Preface of *Insight*: 'But if I may borrow a phrase from Ortega y Gasset, one has to strive to mount to the level of one's time.'[37] For a start on what this level meant to Lonergan, we might run an eye down the Index of *Insight*, looking just for proper names. One will not find Capreolus there, or John of St Thomas; but one will find Adler, Bohr, Cassirer, Collingwood, Darwin, Freud, and so on. However, this is a very unsatisfactory answer to our question. 'Oriented to modernity' – who but a fundamentalist is not oriented to modernity? Again, a list of modern authors that does not include Newman or Dawson, though both of them influenced Lonergan profoundly, is woefully inadequate. In general we are in a state of *docta ignorantia* about the sources of Lonergan's *Insight*, and the book itself does not make our situation much more *docta*.

We have better clues, I feel, if we turn to the latter part of his life, the period from 1965 on. At this time he has three headings under which to speak of modernity or the new learning, and he uses them over and over in a way that suggest they have entered into his thinking as organizing ideas.[38] There is, first, a new notion of science – not just a new science, but a new idea of what science is – to replace the Aristotelian. There is a new scholarship to complement science – the sort of learning illustrated best by history and interpretation. And, thirdly, there is a new philosophy founded now on self-appropriation – philosophy, he says, has been invited 'to migrate from a basis in theory to a basis in interiority.'[39]

Now I would not say that these three factors were all working with equal efficacy when Lonergan was busy writing *Insight*, but they were working in some degree. The new notion of philosophy was quite explicit. The new sciences were well developed and the new notion of science was perhaps on the verge of formulation. The notion of scholarship, I would say, was not yet formulated, but certain elements of the notion were there in the discussion of common sense and interpretation. To these three generic headings one could add a study of more

37 'The Original Preface of *Insight*,' *METHOD: Journal of Lonergan Studies* 3/1 (1985) 4.

38 *A Second Collection*. See Index under 'Modern,' ' New,' etc.

39 *Method in Theology* 276.

particular ideas – higher viewpoints, world order, cosmopolis, finality, etc. – and thus come to a fair idea of what Lonergan meant by living on the level of the times.[40]

2.3 *Getting It All Together: Thomism, Modernity, Self-Appropriation*

We have now to try to organize, and not just juxtapose, the three sources of *Insight* I have been considering: Lonergan's self-appropriation from his Heythrop days, the later dominating influence of Thomas Aquinas, and modernity with all its unmanageable complexity.

In this situation one's mind runs first and naturally to metaphors. We could think of three streams joining up to make one river, but this is a mere mingling that hardly goes beyond juxtaposing. I earlier spoke of the self-appropriation at Heythrop as a soul without a body, but soul and body are connatural to one another: in what does the connaturality consist in our question? I have thought of an orbiting satellite with three forces combining to fix its route: the blast-off, earth's gravity, internal combustion; but the analogy of mere mechanical forces is not a proper explanation of cultural developments.

The nearest I can come to a proper explanation in Lonergan's own terms is to say, first, that modernity on its material side may be related to the other two factors, as diversified contents are related to a unifying structure. (Modernity on its material side does not include the new philosophy.) I would say, next, that self-appropriation is related to Thomism within the structure and as part of the structure, in the way subjective features are related to objective. Thomism, in this view, is related to modernity as a metaphysics providing a structure for the sciences. Of course, you have to think of Thomist metaphysics as an open, dynamic, integral structure, but why should you not think of it that way?[41] Turning now to the subjective aspect, I would say that Loner-

40 See also the work of David Tracy, who has studied especially the scientific revolution and the critical movement in philosophy in their influence on Lonergan's development: *The Achievement of Bernard Lonergan* (New York: Herder and Herder, 1970) 83.

41 On the integral character of Thomist metaphysics, one thinks of Gilson's thesis that Thomas added existence to Aristotelian essence. On its open and dynamic character, one thinks of Lonergan on consciousness as being 'like a concerto that blends many themes in endless ways' ('Religious Experience,' in *A Third Collection* 125), and of his attributing a similar character to Thomist thought (*Method in Theology* 30).

gan's interiority is related to both Thomism and the materials of modernity as the explicit formulation of their implicit source, that is, the formulation of what was immanently operative to make both of them possible: the dynamism that produced both Thomist metaphysics and the modern sciences.

Footnoting this presentation I would insist that we not play down the Thomist input to this last step. Certainly Thomist metaphysics had an anchoring effect on the ideas of Lonergan's *Insight*, but the *Verbum* articles revealed a measure of Thomist introspection too, and that double influence took Lonergan far beyond his Heythrop stage. Granted that he learned direct insight with the help of Euclid, and that he learned reflective understanding with the help of Newman, still it was his study of Thomas on *verbum* that enabled him to put the two together and complement them with all the apparatus of a fully elaborated cognitional theory.

I now have to leave a topic that needs far more explanation, but I wish before leaving it to stress again the positive side of the twenty years in question. It is easy to conjecture the David Hume that Lonergan might have been, and so to lament this period as almost total loss. But I believe providence was at work here; and though I do not use providence as a cover-up for human mistakes, my belief gives me an a priori expectation of finding a positive side, and so to search more hopefully for the hidden activity of this long period of Lonergan's withdrawal, the activity that was his remote preparation for the return in strength of 1949.

3 Return Engagement: The *Insight* Campaign

Insight was written, most of it, in the four years from 1949 to 1953, during which Lonergan taught theology at Regis College with only one year free, and that one not completely so. There was, however, a trial run a few years earlier, 1945–46, in the course of lectures entitled 'Thought and Reality,' at the Thomas More Institute in Montreal. Further, there were two sets of lectures while Lonergan was actually engaged in writing the book: one at Thomas More Institute again in 1950–51, under the title 'Intelligence and Reality'; the other at Regis College in 1952–53, under the simple (so it seems) title 'Insight.' We have notes on all three courses: Lonergan's own for the middle set of 1950–51, and the reports of two diligent students for the others.

Besides these more or less limited sallies, skirmishes before the battle, there is the actual typescript Lonergan wrote, with all its crossed-out paragraphs, its corrections and inserts, its marginal notations.[42] Sad to relate, hundreds of pages of early drafts of this or that paragraph or section were thrown out when Lonergan left Toronto for Rome. The archivist in me could weep over this lost evidence of a mind at work, but can also rejoice in the considerable materials we do have.

There is scope in these materials, I believe, for many a doctoral dissertation, but today the one point I wish to make, the point that is most germane to the general thrust of my talk, the point that leads directly into my final section on the ongoing history of *Insight*, is the fertility of Lonergan's development in this period, the rain-forest growth of the ideas sprouting in his mind. All I can do is illustrate this, and in the nature of the case my illustrations will have to be brief and simple.

First, one small indication that points to a quite phenomenal leap is the change in title from the 1945 lectures to those of 1950. The title for the first was 'Thought and Reality,' but for the second it was 'Intelligence and Reality.' The titles are accurate. The 1945 lectures begin in fact with science and metaphysics, and only in third place do they come to cognitional process. You remember the remark in the *Verbum* articles: 'logic might favor [starting from metaphysics] but, after attempting it in a variety of ways, I found it unmanageable.'[43] That sentence was probably written early in 1946, in which case Lonergan could well have been thinking of the fall lectures of 1945 as one of the attempts, which he found unmanageable, to give priority to metaphysics. The abandonment of those attempts, expressly asserted in the *Verbum* article, is implicit also in the change of title from 'Thought and Reality' to 'Intelligence and Reality': thought, science, the conceptual product organized in a metaphysics, is implicitly contrasted here with intelligence and insight, the fertile origin of both science and metaphysics.

A second more particular example is found in the 'Canons of Empirical Method.' A reviewer has said of them: 'Mill's "Methods" ... will

---

42 Lonergan's typescript was not the one that went to the publisher. This good copy was done almost entirely by Beatrice Kelly, of Montreal, who had been a student of Lonergan at a Thomas More Institute course of lectures, and volunteered for this immense task. The history of this achievement should also be written some time, but meanwhile readers of *Insight* will be immensely indebted to Ms. Kelly for her contribution. Full credit must also be given to Bernard's loyal brother, Gregory Lonergan, who typed some of the final chapters.

43 'Verbum' (1946) 392 [*Verbum* (1967) 45–46, (1997) 59].

appear ... puerile by comparison.' But the canons did not leap full-grown from Lonergan's forehead into Chapter 3 of *Insight.* The 1950 lectures do not know of six canons of empirical method; instead they speak of 'Two basic principles.'[44] One is the principle of 'exclusion,' and this becomes the canon of selection of the book; the other is the principle of 'relevance,' and this becomes, not the canon of relevance, but (more or less) the canon of parsimony of the book.

A third example is found in an early Table of Contents for *Insight,* drawn up while the book was still partly in the planning stage, but fortunately kept by Lonergan, and recently reproduced from the Archives and published.[45] It lists as titles for the last five chapters (then numbered IV to VIII in Part II): 'The Dialectic of Philosophy,' 'Elements of Metaphysics,' 'Elements of Ethics,' 'Elements of Natural Theology,' and 'The Structure of History.' 'The Dialectic of Philosophy' became 'The Method of Metaphysics'; the next three titles are easily related to those of the book; but what did Lonergan plan under the title 'The Structure of History'? One would give much for a documented answer to that question.

4 The Ongoing History of *Insight*

The picture I have drawn of *Insight* as Lonergan wrote it is that of a work in progress. It is an unfinished work, not simply in the sense that he set out to write a method for theology, and had to stop halfway through, go to Rome, and teach theology there without a developed method; but in the sense that it never would be finished, never could be finished, never should be finished, because it objectifies the very mind itself at work. So it is that we find Lonergan changing positions as he wrote.

We touch here on the paradox of all thinkers of stature: they are bound to be guided throughout life by a great idea, and thus to show a strong thread of continuity; but they are bound likewise to respond to the fertility of their own minds, to grow by leaps and bounds in their thinking, and thus to provide evidence also of considerable change and possibly even of radical discontinuity. What, then, if the guiding principle is not so much a great idea or system of ideas, but the very dynamism itself of the mind at work? Will not the paradox become

44 'Intelligence and Reality' 7.

45 'An Early Table of Contents for *Insight,*' *Lonergan Research Institute Bulletin* 1 (1986) 3.

even more acutely experienced? And is not this what we have in Bernard Lonergan?

Thus, there is evidence that the two great ideas of his Heythrop days continued to dominate his thought throughout life, evidence too that appropriation of his own dynamic intentionality, brought to bear on extensive reading, continued to create a rain-forest growth of products in his mind, products that ranged widely, anchored no doubt by Thomist metaphysics and the transcendental precepts derived from the dynamism of intentionality. But what of discontinuity? This calls for serious study, and serious evaluation of the results of our study. My research reveals changes that were not just the deeper intelligence of a higher viewpoint, or the strategic intelligence of a moving viewpoint, both of which he explains in *Insight*, but what appears at first glance to be a quite radical changing of his mind on quite basic points. How we are to evaluate this is a second question, but let us take the two in order.

I have in mind one single but very central example. It is this. In the 'Intelligence and Reality' lectures of 1950–51 Lonergan set up the potency-form-act structure for his metaphysics, but he did so in three triads instead of two. That is, there is conjugate potency, form, and act, just as we have it in *Insight*. There is also substantial potency, form, and act, again as we have it in *Insight*, though there it is named 'central.' But then – and here is the rub – we have what he calls 'group' potency, form, and act. This term is not found in *Insight*, so we seem to have here a major and quite radical change in Lonergan's thinking: a key notion completely abandoned. It will turn out, I think, that appearances here are somewhat deceptive. Still, the change is striking indeed. It will be worth our study, both for its own sake and for the light it sheds on a relentlessly inquiring mind.

The first step is to see how central and basic this notion of group potency, form, and act is in 1950–51, and thus to underline the gravity of any change of position that may have occurred under this heading. It is clear, then, that in 'Intelligence and Reality' Lonergan puts the group type of potency-form-act on a footing of full equality with the other two types. The same data, he says, can be understood in three complementary ways; hence there are three complementary types of form relevant to understanding a single proportionate being. 'Anything we can know about proportionate being' will fall under what he calls these nine 'terminal categories.' He has a section to which he gives the heading 'Inevitability of distinction between Substantial,

Conjugate, and Group.'[46] The clinching phrase occurs when he calls the nine elements the 'Invariants of possible scientific developments.'[47] We remember well the insistence in *Insight* on the invariance of experience, understanding, and judgment, and so we are confident of finding group potency-form-act brought forward into that work. It is disconcerting, to put it mildly, to find that it is not brought forward, at least in those terms.

That is the negative side of the picture. But there is a positive side to show that the change is not as radical as it at first appears. In fact, all the elements that three years earlier had been organized under the concept of group potency-form-act are found again in *Insight* and occupy an important place in the hierarchy of the book's ideas. Thus, the 1950 lectures tell us that we can consider data as instances, and then we come to substantial potency; we can consider data as similar, and come to conjugate potency; or we can consider data as in a concrete situation, and here we come to group potency.[48] These ideas are surely familiar enough to readers of *Insight*. If we turn now to form as it is conceived in the lectures, we learn that conjugate forms are known by understanding their relations,[49] where data admit systematization, where the questions are, Why? How?[50] Next, 'Substantial forms are concrete and intelligible unities of instances of conjugates';[51] here the data reveal the concrete unity and identity that enable us to investigate, to verify, to apply a theory to instances, and the question is, What is it?[52] Then what, thirdly, is group form? It is emergent probability,[53] where the data of a concrete situation do not admit systematization, and the questions are, How often? What is likely? What is to be expected?[54] Again, readers of *Insight* will find these ideas familiar. So we come to act, and learn that substantial act is existence, conjugate act is 'event, occurrence, performance, operation,' and group act is functioning, the 'totality of occurrences as actually realized.' It requires a group potency as 'the minimum set of

46 'Intelligence and Reality' 25.
47 Ibid. 26.
48 Ibid. 23.
49 Ibid. 24.
50 Ibid. 23.
51 Ibid. 24.
52 Ibid. 23.
53 Ibid. 24.
54 Ibid. 23.

substantial and conjugate potencies, forms, and acts that has to be postulated to account for functioning through emergent probability.'[55] This is all very much the language of *Insight*.

It is clear enough, then, that the underlying ideas of group potency-form-act are carried forward into *Insight*. Indeed, they are extremely illuminating for the structure of Chapter 15 of that book. This chapter is entitled 'Elements of Metaphysics,' and we remember that the first two sections set forth in six pages the six elements: potency, form, and act in their two types, central and conjugate. Then the chapter goes on for fifty pages to talk about explanatory genera and species, about limitation and finality, about development and genetic method. You may have wondered, as I did, what on earth Lonergan was doing. What he was doing is clear from the 'Intelligence and Reality' lectures: he was trying to work into his system the materials he had earlier treated under the heading of group potency-form-act. The second-last paragraph of his concluding summary is extremely helpful. There have been introduced, Lonergan says, the 'notions of central and conjugate potency, form, and act.' He explains them again in a summary manner. Then he continues:

> From the different modes of understanding concrete things and abstract laws, there follows the distinction between central and conjugate forms and, as a corollary, the distinctions between central and conjugate potency and between central and conjugate acts. From the structural unification of the methods by generalized emergent probability, there follow the structural account of the explanatory genera and species and the immanent order of the universe of proportionate being. Such are the elements of metaphysics.[56]

The mystery, it turns out, is not so mysterious after all. We still have the nine items of 'Intelligence and Reality,' but they are not listed as nine; they all pertain somehow to the elements of metaphysics, but six of them retain that title, the other three come in as a 'structural account of the explanatory genera and species and the immanent order of the universe of proportionate being.' What had seemed a radical about-

55 Ibid. 24.
56 *Insight* (1957) 486 [(1992) 510–11].

face turns into a further grappling with a great idea and a most illuminating glimpse of a mind in development.

There is still a puzzle, the real one. How could Lonergan refer to group potency-form-act as providing three of the nine invariants, talk about the inevitability of the distinction between substantial, conjugate, and group, and not use this terminology in *Insight*? We are dealing now with the puzzle, not of the metaphysical elements, but of a human mind at work. This is the really fascinating problem, with serious implications for evaluating Lonergan's results. If in 1950 group potency, form, and act are declared invariant along with the central and conjugate types, but then in 1953 are not listed with them as invariant, must we not be suspicious of the invariance also of experience, understanding, and judgment, and so of the consequent metaphysics of proportionate being? I approach this question with a sense that we are sharing with Lonergan in his most rigorous grappling with a profound idea.

My first remark is that calling the cognitional structure of experience-understanding-judgment an invariant comes to us initially, and remains with us permanently, as a challenge. It is indeed Lonergan's position, based on his own grasp of its inevitability. But to his readers it is initially a challenge: Revise it if you can. Can you propose a revision that doesn't attend to data? Can you offer an explanation of the data without understanding them? Can you expect anyone to accept your explanation unless you ground it in evidence? The invariant character of the three-tiered structure stands or falls with our inability to get round those three questions, but it stands or falls for each of us personally as we face the questions personally.

In actual fact, though hackles were raised on this point when *Insight* first came out, I think that stage has passed. Intelligent people, after all, can get hold of this point rather quickly, and are not about to be caught in an open contradiction between their objective position and their performance in stating that position. I believe that by and large opponents have now passed to a second stage, which I would name the 'So what?' attitude. This says in effect: 'Fine, I can't dispute your position without using what you call experience, understanding, and judgment; but where does that take you? I see no significant advance in philosophy as a result.' This stage, I believe, will last a great deal longer, for to go beyond it involves a real self-appropriation, not just an advertence to a contradiction between content and performance; but those who cannot even discover in consciousness their own acts of understanding are a long way from the self-appropriation that is the source of Lonergan's philosophy.

My second remark is made to those who accept the invariance of experience, understanding, and judgment, and see it, not as a constricting regulation, but as a creative opening. The remark is this, that the present challenge is to continue Lonergan's grappling with the materials of group potency-form-act, and see whether we can so refine our understanding of them as to bring this idea too to the privileged status of an invariant. I suggest that, as Lonergan brought his cognitional structure and consequent metaphysics to the point where he could challenge opponents, 'Revise it if you can,' he was working to bring his group potency-form-act to that stage also. He felt, it seems, as he was writing Chapter 15, that he was not quite ready yet to issue a challenge on the invariance of the idea. It's our task, I would say, to see what we can do with it. But given the difficulty of getting hold of that tremendous chapter, I don't see any prospect for an immediate answer.

Conclusion

It is time to conclude. The picture I have given you – so I said as I began my fourth section – is that of a work in progress. Lonergan had two extremely basic ideas as far back as 1929, but he did not stop there: he had already advanced them enormously in 1949. Nor was 1949 a stopping-point. He did not have *Insight* all worked out in that year, but throughout the next four years he was continually advancing his positions. Which means, I contend, that the advance has to continue beyond 1953, and not only beyond 1953 but beyond 1983 and subsequent generations. We and those later generations owe it to Lonergan and to this amazing volume, not to stop where he did, but to accept the invitation which is one of the volume's main messages: that is, to appropriate in ourselves the dynamism which is of the same nature as that which produced this volume, one which will inevitably carry us past this volume.

Only, I remember Kierkegaard poking fun at his contemporaries who would, he said, go beyond a point they had not quite reached. So I suggest that in our effort to go beyond *Insight*, we make sure we have reached the point we would transcend, namely, that of really understanding the book. Most of us will find that this will keep us busy for a good part of our lives. It should at least have the salutary effect of moderating any excessive self-confidence in our criticism.

Two images will summarize my conclusion. Part of it regards future development, and here I think of Tennyson: 'all experience is an arch' through which I look forward to 'that untravell'd world, whose margin fades/For ever and for ever when I move.' But the image of the arch does not convey the dynamism of the past; and part of what I have tried to say regards the enduring, if changing, influence of the past on the present. Here I need another image, and the one that comes to mind is rather that of a wave that rolls in from the ocean and washes over me; I move farther up the beach, only to find that the returning wave follows and washes over me again. This symbolizes the ongoing context of a classic. What Lonergan had learned from Thomas Aquinas by 1946 was not yet what he had learned from him by 1953, and that in turn was sublated by what Thomas meant for him in 1983. Something similar, all due proportion being maintained, can be said about the ongoing context of *Insight*. What it meant when we first read it in 1957 was not yet what it meant after *Method in Theology* came out in 1972; and what it meant in 1972 is nowhere near what it will continue to mean for us as the years roll on toward that untraveled world whose margin fades forever and forever as we move.

Chapter 4

The Spectrum of 'Communication' in Lonergan[1]

This article is an omnium-gatherum of ideas in Bernard Lonergan that relate, either centrally or tangentially, to the topic of communication. It therefore has to be sketchy on those ideas singly, but may provide an overall framework in which more detailed studies can be located and related to one another.

That does not mean that the article will attempt a synthesis of Lonergan's views. It remains simply a collection, from end to end of the spectrum, of points that seem to be relevant. Still, even an omnium-gatherum should show some order, based on an external principle if not on the intrinsic analysis of communication itself. So I propose to divide my article into five parts, on the basis of two simple divisions: the division between divine and human reality, and the division between what is interior and what moves out to others.

First, then, communication in divine interiority (part 1); then, the two aspects of human communication, one interior to each of us (part 2), the other moving out of oneself to communication with others. This latter aspect, as most directly related to communication in its normal sense, requires more elaboration, so I preface it by some philosophic points (part 3). Then, in the longest section of my article, I discuss communication with others in the context it has for Lonergan's own discipline of theology, namely, the crosscultural (part 4). I conclude with a shorter section on communication between God and humankind (part 5).

1 Previously published in Thomas J. Farrell and Paul A. Soukup, eds, *Communication and Lonergan: Common Ground for Forging the New Age* (Kansas City, MO: Sheed & Ward [now an imprint of Rowman & Littlefield, Lanham, MD], 1993) 67–86.

1 Communication within God

Lonergan's views on communication within God suppose the common Catholic doctrine on the Trinity, gradually developed in the early centuries, and magisterially set forth for the Christian West in the fifth-century creed, *Quicumque*. Further, on the ontological aspect of communication his views are the commonly held theology of his church: the Father communicates being, power, all the divine attributes, to the Son; and Father and Son communicate them to the Spirit. What is not communicable is personal identity. The Father's fatherhood cannot be communicated to the Son, and so too with the other distinctive personal notions; but this incommunicability is so little opposed to the communication of the divine attributes that it is in fact required for their communication.[2]

What is more characteristic of Lonergan's trinitarian theology (and more controversial) is the addition of the conscious factor. The three in God are not only persons in an ontological sense, they are also conscious subjects in a psychological sense: conscious not as we are conscious, only on the higher levels of our being, but in every aspect of their being.[3]

Now this bears directly on communication within God. The ontological incommunicability of the person does not preclude conscious communication in the fullest sense among the persons. For within God there are intersubjective relations among the three, and their intersubjectivity is as much a part of their conscious life as their being and knowledge and willing and other aspects of their divinity. That is, each of the three is conscious of the divine being, and of the divine self that that person is – and also conscious of, and consciously related to, each of the other two. Lonergan adds that, insofar as 'I' and 'Thou' signify the most perfect possible interpersonal relations, we can understand those terms as applicable also to the divine three.[4]

In summary: communication among the three divine persons is full

---

2 *De Deo trino*, vol. 2, 3rd edition (1964) 171–73. (Original work published 1957.)

3 Ibid. 186–93.

4 Ibid. 196. Lonergan speaks here of what he will say 'infra' – which I take to mean the section on *perichoresis* 205–208. Note, however, that when one is thinking in terms of the psychological analogy of *Dicens, Verbum, Amor*, it is only the Father who utters a Word. That Word, of course, expresses all that is, the divine being and the three in God; it is an '*affirmatio infinita*' (204).

and complete in what are called the absolute perfections of God (being, knowledge, power, and so on), but the relative properties that maintain personal distinctions (fatherhood, sonship) are not communicated. To this standard doctrine Lonergan adds his special focus on consciousness: communication among the three is fully conscious, conscious in the community of the divine being, conscious in the community of interpersonal relations.

To those who fear that three Gods would result from this, Lonergan's answer is simple: as one essence and one divinity is possessed by all three, and thus there is but one God yet so as to leave the three distinct in their possession of the one essence and one divinity, so there is one divine consciousness possessed by all three, and thus there is but one conscious God yet so as to leave each person distinct in the possession of the one consciousness.[5]

My presentation has been necessarily brief, but I thought it important to note this aspect of Lonergan's views on communication, partly because his trinitarian theology is tied in with the whole range of his thinking, partly because the example brings out at once a main feature and orientation of his thought, and the direction of his progress beyond traditional Scholasticism: in a phrase he himself has used, the progress from substance to subject, illustrated in the religious sphere when 'being in Christ Jesus' advances from 'the being of substance' to 'the being of subject.'[6]

2 Communication within the Human Being

Communication within God, in both its ontological and conscious aspects, is essentially interpersonal communication within one being. But on the human scene, however much we strive for and achieve unity with others, interpersonal communication essentially relates one being to another being. That external relationship must be central in our study, but I would draw attention first to a communication that is internal to the individual human being, one that is less commonly

5 Ibid. 192–93.

6 '*Existenz* and *Aggiornamento*,' in *Collection* (1967) 249–51 [(1988) 230–31]. There is a more humdrum daily advance with the 'emergence of consciousness in the ... dream, where human substance yields place to the human subject' ('A Post-Hegelian Philosophy of Religion,' in *A Third Collection* 208).

associated with communication in the modern sense, one that relates level to level in the multiform constitution of a human person, and one in which Lonergan may make a distinctive contribution.

A human being is a unity constituted by many levels: physical, chemical, biological, sensitive, intelligent, rational, affective. Each successive level is viewed as a higher integration of activities that would be merely a coincidental manifold on the lower level. Thus, the wonder that is observed in a child falls outside the system of laws that govern its sensitive life; and recurring acts of wonder would be only a coincidental manifold in the context of sensitive life, but they become systematic in the higher integration of intelligent life. Further, there is interaction between levels, and a principle of correspondence that merits the name of communication, when what is merely coincidental on a lower level (say, the child's recurring wonder) is brought under law through a systematizing form on the next higher level.[7]

Thus, we are material beings, so the laws of physics apply to us, and we fall from a height as stones do. There is a chemistry in the human body, so oxygen burns in our lungs as it does in the laboratory. There is a biological level on which, like other living things, we obey the laws of cellular formation. But in Lonergan's view of emergent probability, lower levels have a finality toward the higher, and the higher take over and subsume the lower within their own finality.[8] Maybe we would be justified in speaking of an ontological communication here on these lower levels, but it is in the conscious realm with its several sub-levels – sensitive, intelligent, reasonable, affective – that the question of communication especially and properly arises.

In this conscious realm correspondence goes far beyond that of, say, chemistry and biology in the human body. There is operative now the factor of intentionality, a conscious interior dynamism that works spontaneously to lift us from level to level. This factor is seen most vividly in the questions that continually arise to propel us beyond the slow torpor of ontological finality. Data of the sensitive and imaginative life are met by this dynamic intentionality with the question, 'What?' or 'Why?' or 'How often?' The result is an idea, or more often a number of alternative ideas – or when the idea is pursued, a coalescing cluster of ideas. These in turn are met by our dynamic intentionality with the question, 'Is it so?' Are our ideas all wrong? Or, is perhaps

7 *Insight* (1957) 532 [(1992) 555].
8 *Insight*. See Index under 'Emergent probability.'

one of them right? The result is a judgment on the fact of the matter, and our judgments grow incrementally to give us a view of a situation, only to be met again by our dynamic intentionality with the requirement that we act: 'What is to be done?' More specifically, 'What am I to do?' And, most comprehensively, 'What are my values?' 'To whom do I commit myself in love?'

We should not think of this higher integration, correspondence, and communication as simply an upward progress from level to higher level. It is equally a communication from higher to lower. Indeed, it is fundamentally that, for we begin life and develop consciously in the ambience of loving trust rather than on the basis of data examined and understood. In virtue of that loving trust we adopt almost unconsciously a view of life and our world, a set of beliefs and judgments, understanding of which follows much later to make our experience mature and perceptive. In the mature person, then, there can be various communications of level with level, in either the upward or the downward process, or a mixture of the two. There is continual two-way traffic all along the route, or between two points on the way, or between a point as reached in the upward progress and the same point as reached in the downward movement.

All this is familiar enough in itself, but I am not aware that it has been examined in relation to communication studies, and I believe it would add to them a dimension not generally appreciated. Let me therefore illustrate some of its latent richness in a more specific point that Lonergan makes about communication between sensitive and intelligent levels.

The levels are quite distinct, and their distinction is seen in the difference between human and animal activity. 'When an animal has nothing to do it goes to sleep. When a man has nothing to do he may ask questions.'[9] Now these two distinct levels are found in human beings, in psychic and intellectual activity. The intellectual level is quite distinct, with its own dynamic factor (the 'operator,' in Lonergan's terms): 'on the intellectual level the operator is concretely the detached and disinterested desire to know. It is this desire, not in contemplation of the already known, but headed towards further knowl-

9 *Insight* (1957) 10 [(1992) 34]. See also (1957) 185 [(1992) 208–209]: '... animals, safely sheathed in biological routines, are not questions to themselves. But man's artistry testifies to his freedom. As he can do, so he can be what he pleases. What is he to be? Why?'

edge, orientated into the known unknown.' This occurs on a higher level than the psyche. Nevertheless, the 'principle of dynamic correspondence calls for a harmonious orientation on the psychic level, and from the nature of the case such an orientation would have to consist in some cosmic dimension, in some intimation of unplumbed depths, that accrued to man's feelings, emotions, sentiments.'[10]

In a later work Lonergan speaks of this correspondence in terms of 'internal communication.' The context is the role of the symbol in linking organic and psychic levels with the higher. There is a need, he says,

> for internal communication. Organic and psychic vitality have to reveal themselves to intentional consciousness and, inversely, intentional consciousness has to secure the collaboration of organism and psyche. Again, our apprehensions of values occur in intentional responses, in feelings: here too it is necessary for feelings to reveal their objects and, inversely, for objects to awaken feelings. It is through symbols that mind and body, mind and heart, heart and body communicate.[11]

I leave this part of my article reluctantly, having room only to mention the array of omitted questions: the relation of understanding to the image, the function of reflection in relation to concepts and to the whole range of experience, the role of symbol as affect-laden image, and so on. Further, these notions on 'internal communication' seem especially pertinent to the problem to be seen later (Part 4.1) of the unity of consciousness in Jesus. Further still, it may be that they will not only widen the categories of communication theory, but will also be analogous to, or even a paradigm for, our communication with one another, and thus more directly affect what we may call the 'external communication' to which we now turn.

3 Human Interpersonal Communication: Philosophic Points

Far the most important area of study in Lonergan and communication regards the transmission of divine revelation from one cultural group

---

10 Ibid. (1957) 532 [(1992) 555]. Lonergan relates this to the nonrational element in Rudolph Otto's *Idea of the Holy* (Oxford: Oxford University Press, 1958 [original published 1923]). Lonergan's own work is not so much a study of that element as a framework in which to locate it and relate it to total human activity.

11 *Method in Theology* 66–67.

to another, and this will get the lion's share of my attention (a long fourth part), but as background for it I need some philosophic points on communication: the ontological unity of the human race, the priority of intelligence over language, the dynamics of expression, a view on intersubjectivity.

3.1 The Ontological Unity of the Human Race

I mention, to begin with, a curious view Lonergan expressed in an early essay to the effect that what is first is a kind of universal human being, and what comes second is the individuation of this into subsistent persons. The essay, written when he was a student and never published in his lifetime, developed at length the theme of human solidarity, and in this context we find such statements as these.

> [Man] is not simply an individual ... Philosophically, man is one universal nature in regard to what he is, and man is many merely in virtue of the modality of his being, in regard to the way he is. Man is one in virtue of his form, and he is many merely in virtue of matter ... Man as these many particulars is contingence and materiality; man as a universal nature is an intelligible essence and a limited aspect of the divine essence ... the difference between men is less real than the unity of men.[12]

Lonergan does not seem to have pursued this line in later life, but neither, as far as I know, did he repudiate it. In fact, it may be echoed in his remark in *Insight* on 'the concrete universal that is mankind in the concrete and cumulative consequences of the acceptance or rejection of the message of the Gospel.'[13] And there is a quite remarkable counterpart to this ontological solidarity in the psychological and intersubjective solidarity, which we will presently notice (Part 3.4 below).

3.2 The Priority of Intelligence

The priority of intelligence over language is a qualified position taken in response to the view 'that the meaningfulness of language is essentially public and only derivatively private.' In two ways Lonergan is

12 'Pantôn Anakephalaiôsis,' *METHOD: Journal of Lonergan Studies* 9/2 (1991) 151.
13 *Insight* (1957) 743 [(1992) 764].

prepared to acknowledge the role, and even admit the priority in a restricted sense, of expression. 'First, I do not believe that mental acts occur without a sustaining flow of expression. The expression may not be linguistic. It may not be adequate. It may not be presented to the attention of others. But it occurs.' He will go further. 'Secondly, I have no doubt that the ordinary meaningfulness of ordinary language is essentially public and only derivatively private. For language is ordinary if it is in common use. It is in common use ... because all the individuals of the relevant group understand what it means.' Thus 'children and foreigners come to learn a language ... by learning how it ordinarily is used, so that their private knowledge of ordinary usage is derived from the common usage that essentially is public.'[14]

Originally, however, and in the unqualified sense, that is not the case.

> Thirdly, what is true of the ordinary meaningfulness of ordinary language is not true of the original meaningfulness of any language, ordinary, literary, or technical. For all language develops ... developments consist in discovering new uses for existing words, inventing new words, and in diffusing the discoveries and inventions. All three are a matter of expressed mental acts ... Unlike ordinary meaningfulness, then, unqualified meaningfulness originates in expressed mental acts, is communicated and perfected through expressed mental acts, and attains ordinariness when the perfected communication is extended to a large enough number of individuals.[15]

To understand this view we must go back, I believe, to the 'insight into phantasm' that was one of Lonergan's earliest and most original contributions but is still so widely ignored. The basic question seems to be whether mental acts exist or are just occult entities. But their existence can be discovered only through appropriation of one's own interiority; and the mental act that is most likely to claim our attention, and to be 'discovered' in interiority, is the act of insight that Lonergan describes so vividly at the beginning of Chapter 1 of *Insight*, illustrating it with the 'Eureka!' of Archimedes.[16]

---

14 *Method in Theology* 254–55.
15 Ibid. 255–56.
16 *Insight* (1957) 3–6 [(1992) 27–31].

3.3 *The Dynamics of Expression*

Against this background I can be brief on my next heading, the dynamics of expression, set forth in Chapter 17 of *Insight*. The context is interpretation, the presupposition of interpretation is the occurrence of expression, and so Lonergan has a section on 'Levels and Sequences of Expression.'[17] He would classify modes of expression in terms of meaning, and so discusses 'distinctions ... between (1) sources, (2) acts, and (3) terms of meaning.'[18] Next, levels of expression depend on 'the sources of meaning both in the speaker or writer and in the hearer or reader.'[19] But with his strong sense of the historical, Lonergan cannot leave the matter in this somewhat static aspect.

> Besides levels of expression, there also are sequences. Development in general is a process from the undifferentiated to the differentiated, from the generic to the specific, from the global and awkward to the expert and precise. It would simplify enormously the task of the interpreter if, from the beginning of human speech and writing, there existed and were recognized the full range of specialized modes of expression. But the fact is that the specializations had to be invented, and the use of the inventions presupposes a corresponding development or education of prospective audiences or readers.[20]

Perhaps I may leave here a topic that is likely to be studied more thoroughly in other contributions to this volume, but a word of caution is in order. It would be easy to take an impoverished view of expression as coldly instrumental, forgetting poetry, song, laughter, and other everyday modes of expression. One has to watch, therefore, in this Chapter 17 of *Insight*, for references to literary modes, to the incidental and even the accidental factor, to elementary patterns of experience, to the aesthetic, dramatic, and practical, to the mystical, to nonexplanatory meaning, to the application of the canon of residues in this field, to 'dynamic constellations of the writer's psyche,'[21] to such

---

17 Ibid. (1957) 568–73 [(1992) 592–95].
18 Ibid. (1957) 569 [(1992) 592].
19 Ibid. (1957) 569 [(1992) 592].
20 Ibid. (1957) 571–72 [(1992) 594].
21 Ibid. (1957) 590–91 [(1992) 613].

statements as the following: 'Expression not only is an instrument of the principal acts of meaning that reside in conception and judgment but also a prolongation of the psychic flow from percepts, memories, images, and feelings into the shaping of the countenance, the movement of the hands, and the utterance of words.'[22] Again, to quote from *Method in Theology*: 'With Giambattista Vico, then, we hold for the priority of poetry. Literal meaning literally expressed is a later ideal and only with enormous effort and care can it be realized, as the tireless labors of linguistic analysts seem to show.'[23]

3.4 *Views on Intersubjectivity*

All this touches directly on intersubjectivity. That topic is surely vital to a theory of communication, but for my purpose a few simple points will suffice.

Chapter 17 of *Insight* supposes, of course, the basic possibility of intersubjective communication for its theory of expression and interpretation, but Lonergan goes much further than that. Parallel to our first point on the ontological unity of the human race, he has views on a primordial psychological unity of persons.

> Prior to the 'we' that results from the mutual love of an 'I' and a 'thou', there is the earlier 'we' that precedes the distinction of subjects and survives its oblivion. This prior 'we' is vital and functional. Just as one spontaneously raises one's arm to ward off a blow against one's head, so with the same spontaneity one reaches out to save another from falling. Perception, feeling, and bodily movement are involved, but the help given another is not deliberate but spontaneous. One adverts to it not before it occurs but while it is occurring. It is as if 'we' were members of one another prior to our distinctions of each from the others.[24]

Further, there is communication on this level. Lonergan, drawing on the work of philosophers and phenomenologists, lists some of the

22 Ibid. (1957) 592 [(1992) 615].

23 *Method in Theology* 73. The most extensive presentation of Lonergan's ideas on poetry, drama, and other forms of art, is in the ninth of his lectures on education, given at Xavier University, Cincinnati, 1959, now published as *Topics in Education*, volume 10 of *Collected Works of Bernard Lonergan*.

24 *Method in Theology* 57.

ways in which feelings are communicated: 'community of feeling, fellow-feeling, psychic contagion, and emotional identification';[25] and he goes on to speak of intersubjective communication of meaning, comparing the meaning of a smile with linguistic meaning.[26] The sociologists too make their input with their stress on the social origin of one's awareness of self, along with personalists who 'have urged that the notions of "I" and "you" emerge as differentiations of a prior "we" or "us."'[27]

Lonergan, however, separates himself from those phenomenologists who maintain, on the basis of their cognitional theory, that we know other persons only intersubjectively. His own cognitional theory allows him to escape this limitation.

> I would point out that, just as we pass from consciousness of the self as subject to an objectification of the self in conception and judging, so too we pass from intersubjectivity to the objectification of intersubjectivity. Not only do we (two subjects in a subject-to-subject relation) speak and act. We speak about ourselves; we act on one another; and inasmuch as we are spoken of or acted on, we are not just subjects, not subjects as subjects, but subjects as objects.[28]

One very important point in the philosophy of communication has been omitted: interpretation, the counterpart of expression. But that enters deeply into Lonergan's theology, and so I transfer discussion of it to the fourth part of my article.

4 Communication in the Theological Context

To turn to communication in Lonergan's special field of endeavor is to shift attention from individual relationships to the relationship of generations distant in time from one another, or to the relationship of groups distant in cultural ways from one another. If this seems to some a very abrupt change of direction, the reason may be that they think of

---

25 Ibid. 57–59.

26 Ibid. 59–61.

27 'Prolegomena to the Study of the Emerging Religious Consciousness of Our Time,' in *A Third Collection* 56.

28 'Natural Knowledge of God,' in *A Second Collection* 131.

Lonergan as focused on the individual rather than on the community. The truth is that from beginning to end of his career it was the community that was central. His seeming concentration on the individual was more a withdrawal in a grand strategy of withdrawal and return. Obviously the present volume is not the place to debate that question, but this prefatory paragraph may help eliminate much misunderstanding.

Of quite central interest to this volume, however, is the last chapter (14) of Lonergan's *Method in Theology*, called simply 'Communications.'[29] The views expressed there have a clear and very pointed reference to our present topic, but they are the result of a long development and clarification, and my present task is to see how he arrived at them.

4.1 From Jesus to Gospel

We have to go back, then, to what is to be communicated. This, for Lonergan the theologian, was the revelation given by God, and for Christians the revelation given by God in the Son: 'Long ago God spoke to our ancestors in many and various ways by the prophets, but in these last days he has spoken to us by a Son.'[30] '... no one knows the Son except the Father, and no one knows the Father except the Son and anyone to whom the Son chooses to reveal him.'[31] Our study of communication in Lonergan the theologian must begin therefore with the message of Jesus.

The Christian position on this question is dominated by the doctrine of the human knowledge Jesus had, the Catholic position adds the doctrine of what is called the beatific vision, and Lonergan's position adds his cognitional theory.[32] In this theory 'vision' is considered an unhappy choice, for it suggests ocular experience, and a view of human knowledge analogous to ocular vision. Lonergan spoke rather of the ineffable knowledge Jesus had, and of the struggle it was to make the ineffable effable (I take some liberty with English here, in order to have two words that correspond to Lonergan's Latin pair, *ineffabilis* and *effabilis*).

29 *Method in Theology* 355–68.

30 Hebrews 1:1–2.

31 Matthew 11:27.

32 *De Verbo incarnato*, 3rd ed. (Rome: Gregorian University Press, 1964), Thesis 12a: 'De scientia Christi' 332–416. (Original was published in 1960.)

To understand the ineffable knowledge of Jesus we must go to analogy, for by hypothesis this knowledge is beyond properly human understanding. Lonergan finds an analogy in the Thomist agent intellect, or in the notion of being we all have, a notion that encompasses everything in anticipation but nothing in determinate categories.[33] Analogy is partly the same and partly different. In this case there is difference in that we operate in pursuit of the goal, with a desire to 'see' God, where Christ operated from the attained goal, struggling to communicate to others what he had received. But there is a similarity in that his knowledge and mine, each in its own way, is all-encompassing. Similarity too in that the vision of God gave Jesus no actual knowledge that was expressible. He had to win this slowly; he labored to express what was first given him in an inexpressible form.[34] I suggest, for an idea of this labor, the struggle that mystics like Teresa of Avila had in expressing what is not communicable in human terms except by metaphor for the mystic or by analogy for the theologian.

Jesus then was faced with the first great problem in Christian communication. How much he was aware of it, and what the terms in which he might be able to describe it are good questions, but from my viewpoint the problem is located, as a special case, within the area of internal communication dealt with earlier (Part 2). At any rate Jesus did achieve the needed measure of internal communication, and did go on to communicate divine revelation to his followers, in terms he and they could understand, in 'effable' language. They in turn communicated it to their world in teaching and preaching, in writing and worship, in a 'way,' as the *Acts of the Apostles* several times puts it.[35] And so the revelation given Jesus by God the Father passed on to the church of Palestine.

That church, however, was to embrace all nations: 'Go into all the world and proclaim the good news to the whole creation.'[36] And there the problem of communication emerged in a new form, for those nations were an extremely heterogeneous multitude. The new problem existed from the time the 'message' left Palestine and was preached to the Greco-Roman world; but it became formulated in a precise man-

33 Ibid. 337–38, 405–406.

34 Ibid. 405–412.

35 E.g., Acts, 9:2, 19:9, 19:23.

36 Mark 16:15.

ner, and so became consciously a problem only with the rise of historical consciousness in our time, roughly in the last two centuries. The church fathers and the medieval Scholastics could dip into the scriptures and transfer a text across the centuries without a clear sense of the vast chasm that separated their culture and manner of thinking from that of the earliest church. Today that is no longer possible.

Lonergan came to grips with the problem in two steps: the problem of moving from the early church to the doctrines of the later church, and the problem of moving from these doctrines to our contemporary world in its irreducible plurality. His early theology is concerned with the first step, and one could say that his later work, *Method in Theology*, is focused on the second, since he makes it the topic of his final chapter and the crowning phase of theology: communications, he says, 'is a major concern, for it is in this final stage that theological reflection bears fruit.'[37]

Logically, both steps were contained in a discovery he made in the early 1930s.

> In the summer of 1930 I was assigned to teach at Loyola College, Montreal, and despite the variety of my duties was able to do some reading. Christopher Dawson's *The Age of the Gods* [1933] introduced me to the anthropological notion of culture and so began the correction of my hitherto normative or classicist notion.[38]

But it is quite unlikely that Lonergan saw at once the full implications of this discovery; the German Historical School seems to have been a factor here, and that influence came later, when he was teaching in Rome: 'The new challenge came from the *Geisteswissenschaften* ...'[39]

4.2 From Gospel to Doctrine

The correction of his 'hitherto ... classicist notion' was introduced first into the transition from the sources to conciliar and Catholic doctrines. There is no simple path from one to the other. The sources are not like Euclid's elements of geometry, which may offer a problem to under-

37 *Method in Theology* 355.
38 '*Insight* Revisited,' in *A Second Collection* 264.
39 Ibid. 277.

standing but present no special problem of interpretation: 'while there is a task of coming to understand Euclid, there is no task of interpreting Euclid ... while there have been endless commentators on the clear and simple gospels, there exists little or no exegetical literature on Euclid.'[40] With the scriptures then there is a problem of interpretation, and it exists in principle; for they are written not in the systematic order which puts axioms and theorems first and their consequences and applications later, but in the commonsense order which puts immediate applications and relevance first, and is little concerned with going back to axioms and theorems.

There is a parallel in the origin of the sciences. Thus chemistry (to take an example Lonergan used over and over) began in daily life with the infinite variety of materials encountered there by everyone, with what is first for us. In the course of history, it arrived at the systematic presentation of the periodic table, which, however remote from experience, can be made basic, a first in itself, in teaching the science. For Lonergan the history of Catholic thinking from scripture to church doctrines was analogous to the history of chemistry from everyday materials to the periodic table.[41] And the problem of interpretation (that is, of communication between the centuries, of the early church speaking to us, and of our hearing the early church) is focused on that history and its justification.

Lonergan struggled with this first problem for some twenty years or more, and especially during his twelve years teaching in Rome, when he was confronted more directly with the problem of the *Geisteswissenschaften*.[42] We may take as basis for discussion his course of 1958–1959 at the Gregorian University, *De intellectu et methodo*.[43] There is a transition from one manner of thinking in the sources of church doctrines to another quite different manner of thinking in the doctrines themselves. A gap has opened: in Lonergan's Latin-Greek term, a *chasma*. We leap across the gap, and the question is how to justify the leap.

Through ten pages, single-spaced and legal-size, Lonergan struggles with the answer.[44] We do not reach our foundations and justify the

---

40 *Method in Theology* 153–54.

41 *Verbum* (1967) 61–62 [(1997) 74].

42 '*Insight* Revisited,' in *A Second Collection* 277.

43 '*De intellectu et methodo*' (Notes taken by students of lectures in theology course, Gregorian University, 1959).

44 Ibid. 16–25.

leap by the external form of the words we use. Here one may surely think of the 'fundamentalists,' for whom words do serve as foundations. And not through manipulation of concepts and judgments – one thinks now of the 'conceptualists,' adversaries in the *Verbum* articles Lonergan had written some years earlier[45] – for that works only with a given system. Lonergan had already rejected deduction as a means of transition, and returns to it again to declare it helpless when questions arise that the system cannot account for – precisely the situation when there is a leap from one way of thinking to another.

His own solution does not surprise us. It is to go behind the words, behind the concepts and judgments, and appeal to intelligence itself and its threefold formation through understanding, science, and wisdom.[46] A long discussion follows of wisdom and the way it lies deeper than words and concepts. Wisdom was a key concept in Lonergan's early writings. Later, individual wisdom yielded to a collective wisdom gained through dialectic and foundations. But in both the individual and collective approaches the goal is true judgment, the truth of the transposition of doctrines from one culture to another.

We can round off discussion of communication in this first step with a point Lonergan makes in his 1962 lecture 'Hermeneutics'[47] and repeats in Chapter 7 of his *Method in Theology*. About half the lecture is devoted to the first two of the basic questions for dealing with a text that requires interpretation: (1) understanding the text, and (2) judging how correct one's understanding of the text is. Given Lonergan's cognitional theory, there is no special problem here. It is the role of 'scholars' – we anticipate here his later distinction between scholarship, a matter of learning and erudition, and science, a matter of principles and laws[48] – to become familiar with the commonsense expressions of another age and culture. As we gradually come to understand our own language by years of experience of its use, so scholars gradually come to understand the language of another time by years of experience with its monuments, artefacts, language, relics.

The real problem emerges in the third of the basic exegetical tasks,

---

45 *Verbum* (1967) [(1997)]: in Index, see 'Conceptualism.'

46 'De intellectu et methodo' 16.

47 'Hermeneutics' (unpublished lecture, 1962; available at the Lonergan Research Institute, Toronto).

48 *Method in Theology* 233–34.

when scholars try to state the meaning of the text and communicate their findings to us. Lonergan devotes the second half of his lecture to this.[49] On the face of it the problem may seem fabricated: if the scholars know the meaning of a text and want to tell the rest of us what it is, why don't they just go ahead and tell us? But a moment's reflection reveals the problem. What language are they going to use? Not the language of the documents they study, for that is the language needing interpretation in the first place: if they use that, we are no further ahead than if we read the documents ourselves. But they cannot simply turn to our modern language either, for by hypothesis there is a gap between the text and ourselves, between the language of the text and our language. Our initial problem was how to make and justify the leap over that gap, and simply to turn from the language of the documents to our own leaves us no better off than patristic and medieval exegesis was.

We may turn to Chapter 7 of *Method in Theology* for a definitive treatment of the question. Here, in the context of this third problem, three cases are distinguished. 'The exegete qua exegete expresses his interpretations to his colleagues technically in notes, articles, monographs, commentaries.' In this case, exegetes will use all the instruments provided by research: grammars, lexicons, and so on. They will also relate their work functionally to previous work in the field. Secondly, the 'exegete also speaks to his pupils, and he must speak to them in a different manner. For notes, articles, monographs, commentaries fail to reveal the kind of work and the amount of work that went into writing them. That revelation only comes in the seminar.'[50]

Neither of these first two cases presents the real problem, which is how to speak to those who are neither scholars (at least in the relevant field) nor in training to be scholars: the problem, in other words, of how to speak to the rest of us. Lonergan brings his categories of description and explanation to bear on this.[51] Following the practice of reliable scholars at the descriptive stage, he would have the biblical theologian respect the originality of each of the inspired authors.

> He [the biblical theologian] will appear to be happy to proceed slowly, and often he will follow the ways of beginners. His descriptions will con-

49 'Hermeneutics' 9–16.
50 *Method in Theology* 170.
51 Ibid. 171–73.

> vey a feeling for things long past; they will give the reader an impression of the foreign, the strange, the archaic; his care for genuineness will appear in the choice of a vocabulary as biblical as possible; and he will be careful to avoid any premature transposition to later language, even though that language is approved by a theological tradition.[52]

Finally, he will be wary of general presentations of the divine plan running through history.

To this basic procedure Lonergan would add his own specific contribution.

> What is needed is not mere description but explanation. If people were shown how to find in their own experience elements of meaning, how these elements can be assembled into ancient modes of meaning, why in antiquity the elements were assembled in that manner, then they would find themselves in possession of a very precise tool, they would know it in all its suppositions and implications, they could form for themselves an exact notion and they could check just how well it accounted for the foreign, strange, archaic things presented by the exegetes.[53]

4.3 *From Doctrine to the Living Word*

So much for the first step, the theological problem of hearing an ancient word in our time. That, however, is only half the battle, as we discover when Lonergan lines up the two phases of theology. 'If one is to harken to the word, one must also bear witness to it. If one engages in *lectio divina*, there come to mind *quaestiones*. If one assimilates tradition, one learns that one should pass it on. If one encounters the past, one also has to take one's stand toward the future.'[54] And that presents new problems which Lonergan dealt with rather late in life.

I have said that, in logic, the problem of a further transmission of the message we have ourselves received should have surfaced simultaneously with the problem of receiving the message. If interpretation of the faith of the early church is a problem precisely because the early church expressed its faith in a way of thinking that is foreign to us,

---

52 Ibid. 171.

53 Ibid. 172–73.

54 Ibid. 133.

then presumably there will be a similar problem when we go on to express Catholic doctrine in the equally foreign categories of the various particular cultures of the world.

Lonergan, however, came to that second problem later. Even in 1954, two decades and more after reading Dawson[55] (1933), when he had been teaching theology fourteen years, it hardly bothered him. That year he could write of systematic theology that

> it bestows upon one's teaching the enviable combination of sureness of doctrine with versatility of expression. Finally ... it is fixed upon one's intellectual memory. So we find that non-Catholic clergymen, often more learned in scripture and the fathers, preach from their pulpits the ideas put forward in the latest stimulating book or article, while the Catholic priest, often burdened with sacerdotal duties and administrative tasks, spontaneously expounds the epistle or gospel of the Sunday in the light of an understanding that is common to the ages.[56]

It was only later that Lonergan came to appreciate the problems presented in this second step of communication, and then he realized that there was a parallel here with the scholarship needed to understand the documents of antiquity. Just as the exegete must become familiar with the artefacts, the monuments, the writings, of the culture he is investigating, so the missionary must become familiar with the culture of the people being evangelized. As the theological community must labor to overcome the gap between antiquity and the doctrines of the church today, so the pastor or missionary must labor in the reverse order to overcome the gap between church doctrines and the culture or subculture of the pastoral or mission area.

That is the focal point of Lonergan's final chapter in *Method in Theology*, 'Communications.' The chapter may seem to lack direction, and we may wonder why he rambles on about ontology, society, state, church, Christianity today, redemption, social science, and the rest. But all this is integral to his position, and it reveals what his fundamental view of communication is. In that view, the solidarity of the human race across space and time, the very idea with which he began to write

---

55 Christopher Dawson, *The Age of the Gods* (London & New York: Sheed & Ward, 1933). (Original work published in 1928.)

56 'Theology and Understanding,' in *Collection* (1967) 133 [(1988) 125].

some forty years earlier, the ontological solidarity which finds a psychological counterpart in spontaneous intersubjectivity – this is a basic supposition. If we go on to think of society constituted by meaning, and of meaning having many different expressions in the many nations that make up the church, then we have the framework for his more specific views on communication.

These he expresses as follows.

> The Christian message is to be communicated to all nations. Such communication presupposes that preachers and teachers enlarge their horizons to include an accurate and intimate understanding of the culture and the language of the people they address. They must grasp the virtual resources of that culture and that language, and they must use those virtual resources creatively so that the Christian message becomes, not disruptive of the culture, not an alien patch superimposed upon it, but a line of development within the culture.[57]

But we are not out of the woods yet. As the route from gospel to doctrines had its specific problem, so also does the route from doctrines to their communication in a particular culture. Doctrines are necessary; they have 'the function of explaining and defending the authenticity of the church's witness to the revelation in Christ Jesus.'[58] But they are not the primary thing. That privilege belongs to the gospel; and how to relate gospel, doctrines, and preaching the gospel to all nations is the present question.

Several times in the period after *Method in Theology* Lonergan took his lead in this matter from the views on a pastoral council expressed at the time of the Second Vatican Council by M.-D. Chenu.[59] We may refer to an unpublished lecture, 'A New Pastoral Theology,' given in Toronto in 1973 and a year later in New Haven,[60] and a published one, 'Pope John's Intention,' given in Boston in 1981.[61] Negatively, we should not reduce 'pastoral' to the application of doctrine, and reduce

57 *Method in Theology* 362.

58 'Unity and Plurality: The Coherence of Christian Truth,' in *A Third Collection* 245.

59 Marie-Dominique Chenu, 'Un concile "pastoral,"' in *La parole de Dieu*, vol. II: *L'évangile dans le temps* (Paris: Cerf, 1963). (Original article published in 1963.)

60 'A New Pastoral Theology' (Unpublished lecture, New Haven, 1974).

61 'Pope John's Intention,' in *A Third Collection* 224–38.

that application to the tactics of classical oratory.[62] It is quite inadequate to begin from doctrines, abstracted in the first place from the living word, and attempt to flesh them out again into living speech.[63] If pastoral 'means no more than the logical application of universal norms to particular cases, there is no need for a pastoral council or ... pastoral theology.'[64]

Positively, something more is needed, and 'that something has to be found in what escapes the universal, in the individual and the personal, in the concrete community and the ongoing process of history.'[65] As philosophy has now to 'take its stand on the inner experience of the individual and from that basis proceed to an understanding of human process, human community, human history,'[66] so theology must become existential, taking its stand on the subject who lives the reality that is expressed in doctrines. It must be worked out in relation to authentic Christian experience that is alive, that as shared is intersubjective, as shared by many is community, as transmitted is historic, and so on.[67] In this way the leap forward that Pope John[68] desired his pastoral council to take would lie in 'the enrichment of the technical formulation by the vital, the personal, the existential.'[69]

Lonergan is complex, but his various statements hang together. Especially worth noting is the grounding in the same way of the two major steps we are studying in this fourth part. We saw that exegetes, to communicate what they have learned through scholarly research, must turn to their interior: 'If people were shown how to find in their own experience elements of meaning, how these elements can be assembled into ancient modes of meaning, why in antiquity the elements were assembled in that manner, then they would find themselves in possession of a very precise tool ...'[70] With slight changes this could be said of our preaching the gospel today: 'If we could find in

62 'A New Pastoral Theology,' see page 7 of the MS.

63 Ibid. 8–9.

64 Ibid. 17.

65 Ibid.

66 Ibid. 18.

67 Ibid. 15–16.

68 Pope John XXIII, 'Concilium oecumenicum Vatican II sollemniter inchoatur,' *AAS* 54 (1963) 791–92; 'Allocutiones ... IV,' *AAS* 55 (1964) 44.

69 'Pope John's Intention,' in *A Third Collection* 227.

70 *Method in Theology* 172.

our own experience elements of meaning in our faith, see how these elements could be assembled in the language of the people we wish to evangelize, knowing their culture well enough to understand why what we preach in their language is faithful to the gospel, then we would possess a very precise tool ...'

This long section has focused on the theological problem of communication between cultures. The basic supposition is the solidarity of the human race – solidarity across space but especially across time, for ours is a historic, communitarian religion. Something was given us once for all, and it was given long ago and far away: its transmission and reception is a classic problem of communication.

5 The Two-way Communication of God and Humankind

I have talked of the divine interior communication of the three in God, of the communication internal to the many-leveled entity that a human being is, of the external communication of human being with human being and especially of culture with culture, of the theological problems presented in the move from Jesus to gospel, from gospel to doctrines, and from doctrines to preaching the gospel. There remains the important question, all-important to each of us, of the mutual communication of God and humankind.

It is customary to speak of God's self-communication. 'Self' may be understood here to denote a person; and then we think of each of the three, not communicating the selfhood which that person is (for that is incommunicable, both within God and externally), but entering into the intimate and loving relationship which in human affairs makes the other the *dimidium animae meae* (half of my soul), and in divine–human communication constitutes a union and a sharing that is incomparably greater. But 'self' may be used impersonally, as when we speak of the thing itself. In this sense one may think of the divine nature itself as being communicated to the human race, always remembering that the divine nature is not a lifeless, unconscious thing, but the fulness of understanding, truth, love, peace, the consciousness that is internal 'experience.'

This second sense is found in Lonergan's theology of grace, most succinctly in the little work, *De ente supernaturali*.[71] Here the first thesis

71 *De ente supernaturali* (Montreal: College of the Immaculate Conception, 1946; text available at the Lonergan Research Institute, Toronto).

states that there is a created communication of the divine nature, or a created principle of those operations in which the creature may attain to God as God is in the divine being. The second thesis states that this created communication of the divine nature exceeds the grade of being of any creature whatever and is simply supernatural. All this, of course, is a fairly straightforward Scholastic rendition of 2 Peter 1:4, where we are said to share in the divine nature.

The first usage of 'self' also is found in Lonergan's theology, along with the term 'self-communication,' but with the caution of the theologian, he states that it is the divinity (not the selfhood) that the divine self communicates. Thus, 'there is a threefold personal self-communication of divinity to humanity ... in Christ the Word becomes flesh ... through Christ men become temples of the Spirit ... in a final consummation the blessed know the Father.'[72] Again, 'the self-communication of divinity in love ... resides in the sending of the Son, in the gift of the Spirit, in the hope of being united with the Father.'[73]

Much more personal to Lonergan (and possibly unique, for I have not noticed it in other authors) is the way he integrates this doctrinal position into his theology of the trinitarian relations. In standard Catholic theology there are four real relations within God: Lonergan finds in the economy of salvation four divine graces par excellence, and he correlates the four graces with the four trinitarian relations in a one-to-one correspondence.

Thus sanctifying grace is a created participation in the relation we call active spiration of the Spirit, and so has a special link with the Holy Spirit within us. Likewise, the great virtue of charity is a created imitation of the relation we call passive spiration, and so it links us to Father and Son as principle of the Spirit. The grace of the incarnation is a created participation of fatherhood, and so is found in the Son. And the light of glory is a created participation of sonship, and so is found in the vision the blessed have of the Father.[74] This seems to me an extraordinary suggestion, with manifold implications. Lonergan offers it rather tentatively. I am not aware that he pursued it at any time in later life, but again there is no evidence that he dropped it.

One final point. Communication between God and humankind is

72 'Mission and the Spirit,' in *A Third Collection* 26.

73 Ibid. 31.

74 *De Deo trino*, vol. 2 (1964) 234–35.

mutual. One may speculate that Ignatius Loyola's *Spiritual Exercises* influenced Lonergan as it has influenced countless Jesuits. Here the crowning contemplation has the purpose of attaining love, and Ignatius prefaces the exercise with the remark that 'Love consists in a mutual communication between the two persons.'[75] So if God communicates with us from the divine side, we must ask what kind of communication there is from our side with God.

It is a matter of adoration and prayer, beginning with that 'orientation to transcendent mystery' which is 'the primary and fundamental meaning of the name, God,'[76] moving to a 'response to transcendent mystery [in] adoration,'[77] and culminating in a 'withdrawing from the world mediated by meaning into a silent and all-absorbing self-surrender in response to God's gift of his love.'[78]

Whether or not theologians experience this withdrawal, and to what extent they should speak of such personal experience, are questions on the border between religion and theology. What is clearly a theological question is the relation of religion and theology, and this Lonergan indicates with laconic brevity: 'Man's response to transcendent mystery is adoration. But adoration does not exclude words ... [W]ords, in turn, have their meaning within some cultural context ... Accordingly ... the worship of God and ... the religions of mankind stand within a ... context and ... generate the problems with which theologians attempt to deal.'[79]

Keeping to my purpose of showing the spectrum of passages in Lonergan relevant to communication, I can do no more than indicate his position on the intersubjectivity of God and the human race. It is an area that would surely repay study but would require a piecing together of many scattered observations. Still, theologians are believers before they are theologians, and so was Lonergan. It was not his style to speak of such matters, but it is known how important to him his prayer life was, how in early years he had to struggle with prayer, how in later years it became a joyful experience.

---

75 Ignatius Loyola, *Spiritual Exercises*, trans. G.E. Ganss, in G.E. Ganss, P.R. Divarkar, E.J. Malatesta, and M.E. Palmer, eds, *Ignatius of Loyola: The Spiritual Exercises and Selected Works* (Mahwah, NJ: Paulist Press, 1991) 176, no. 231 in the numbering that is standard for all editions.

76 *Method in Theology* 341.

77 Ibid. 344.

78 Ibid. 273.

79 Ibid. 344.

But he knew that the duality of believer and theologian can give rise to conflict. The prayer of Thomas Aquinas at the end of his life 'became so intense that it interfered with his theological activity. But earlier there could have been an alternation between religious and theological differentiation, while later still further differentiation might have enabled him to combine prayer and theology as Teresa of Avila combined prayer and business.'[80] In such a way the limited communication of mind with Mind that the theologian enjoys becomes the believer's full communication of heart with Heart, when *cor ad cor loquitur* (heart speaks to heart).

80 'Unity and Plurality,' in *A Third Collection* 242.

Chapter 5

'All my work has been introducing history into Catholic theology'

(Lonergan, 28 March 1980)[1]

Back in 1977, Lonergan remarked, 'The whole problem in modern theology, Protestant and Catholic, is the introduction of historical scholarship.'[2] Three years later he summarized his own lifework under that heading, declaring, 'All my work has been introducing history into Catholic theology.'[3] At the same time he set that work within the wider context of the Second Vatican Council: 'The meaning of Vatican II was the acknowledgement of history.'[4]

All three remarks were made in conversation, and survive on tape-recordings. They have a value like that of headlines in respectable newspapers: on the subjective side they focus our attention, perhaps even startle those less familiar with Lonergan; and on the objective side they bring a mass of confused data to a point, distill the very essence of the matter, something that can easily escape us in an hour-long lecture. My quotations may not startle anyone attending this workshop, but they are still useful to bring into focus what certainly has to be a major element in the Lonergan legacy, and to sharpen our overall view on what he was doing with his life.[5]

---

1 Originally presented at the 20th annual Lonergan Workshop, Boston College, 21–25 June 1993, where the general theme was 'The Legacy of Lonergan.' Previously published in *Lonergan Workshop* 10 (1994) 49–81.

2 *The Question as Commitment*, ed. Elaine Cahn and Cathleen Going (Montreal: Thomas More Institute, 1977) 103.

3 *Curiosity at the Center of One's Life: Statements and Questions of R. Eric O'Connor*, ed. J. Martin O'Hara (Montreal: Thomas More Institute, 1984) 427.

4 Ibid. 426.

5 Of course these brief 'headline' remarks omit the illuminating details, but that loss turns to the advantage of the secondary writer, who can fill them in and thus have something to contribute to a workshop such as this.

Well, that is one side of the story. I once read a headline claiming that we are becoming a nation of headline readers. If that is not to be the case in Lonergan studies, we have the task of discovering what the headline means. When it means the events of a lifetime, and we have an hour in which to detail them, we must set limits to our task. My limits are those of a historical sketch. I will chart the course of this lifelong work, note transition points in the development of Lonergan's thought as the problem emerged ever more clearly, mark off the main steps in the history of his work on history.

A sketch has to be selective, so I reduce this long history to six steps. The first three deal with the period in which he had not fully adverted to the need, and take us up to about 1959. The fourth step is full advertence, the turning point when he discovered the real problem and began to take tentative steps toward a solution. And the fifth and sixth deal with the two main features of his final position, when he had got it all together, insofar as it was given to him to do so in one lifetime.

To expand that table of contents a little, I locate the first step in the period 1933 to 1938, when Lonergan's interest was in the history that happens. The next is that of his doctoral dissertation, 1938–40, in which he begins his work on the history that is written, but confines the question to the history of speculative development. The third step turns from speculative to dogmatic development. The effort is to structure theology according to the two ways of analysis and synthesis, with the history of dogmatic development guided by the analytic process; and this reached its full development in his Trinitarian theology around 1957.[6]

Then there is a great leap forward in the late 1950s and the early

6 The boundaries of Lonergan's focus on the analytic-synthetic structure are 1946, when he was teaching theology in Montreal and wrote the notes *De ente supernaturali* (unpublished, Lonergan Archives, Toronto) in the synthetic order, and 1964, when he was teaching in Rome and published the two volumes of *De Deo trino*, one a work of analysis and the other a work of synthesis. But 1964 really falls in the next period; he had been moving out of the analytic-synthetic orbit since 1959 with his course *De intellectu et methodo*, and indeed had recorded his doubts on its adequacy in his 1954 article 'Theology and Understanding' (*Collection* [1967] 121–41, [1988] 114–32; see the section on 'Contemporary Methodological Issues,' [1967] 135–41, [1988] 127–32 [the title for the section appears only in the 1988 edition]). An interesting point: the first edition of volume 1 of *De Deo trino* (1961) was subtitled *Pars analytica;* the second edition (1964) was subtitled *Pars dogmatica*. To be noted also: Lonergan, in finding the analytic-synthetic pair inadequate, did not repudiate it (see his 'Christology Today: Methodological Reflections,' in *A Third Collection* 96 n. 10).

1960s, when Lonergan came to realize how important was the challenge of the German Historical School. This involved a radical change in his approach, so radical that I would make the realization itself a distinct step, quite apart from his efforts in this period to find a solution, though these also deserve our attention.

The fifth step is the discovery of differentiations of consciousness as the subjective key to development in theology and so to history in that field, and this is the work of the late 1960s.[7] The final step is the objective counterpart of differentiations of consciousness: stages of meaning in human development, subjective in each of us, but objective in the history that happens. (So we return to the theme of step one, but with a greatly enriched view of what happens in human development.) Lonergan's final word on this culminating step, I would say, is given in the paper of 1977–78, 'Philosophy and the Religious Phenomenon.'[8]

As you can see by now, Lonergan's introduction of history into Catholic thought starts with its introduction into his own thinking. His work was to make history intelligible in the context of a theology that was strong on tradition, and first of all intelligible to himself. This meant learning, and learning is a slow advance in tentative steps. So we do not expect to find Lonergan saying in 1928, 'All my work will be to introduce history into Catholic theology.' His idea of the task at hand evolved through forty years and more, and the outcome can hardly be understood except in terms of the massive manoeuvring of his forces during all those years.[9]

---

7 Differentiations of consciousness is a term with a long and complex history in Lonergan, and it is difficult to decide where to stop the flow to examine progress. As we shall see, 1962 introduces the term in the present context, but the step is hardly completed before *Method in Theology* was written in 1971. A useful marker: 'Natural Knowledge of God' in 1969, defining undifferentiated consciousness and listing some differentiations in the new technical sense (*A Second Collection* 131–32). But there are anticipations long before; see Appendix C.

8 See note 68 below.

9 I take occasion here to justify the procedure of this paper, which is to study the history of Lonergan's thinking on history rather than to start from his final position, build on it, relate it to current theology, and so on. There is a partial justification in the theme of the workshop: Lonergan's legacy. Immigrants to a new land work hard to give their children a better life, only to find sometimes that the third generation has little appreciation of the sacrifices made on their behalf; the same could happen in Lonergan studies. A better justification is the light which the genesis of a position throws on the position itself: the light that *Insight* brings to *Method in Theology*, that *Verbum* brings to

It should be understood, however, and is worth an explicit declaration, that we are dealing with a steady flow rather than with discrete building blocks. There is no sharp boundary between phase and phase of Lonergan's evolution. We do not cross Rubicons, rather we explore unmapped territory, reaching plateaus that enable us to see what we have traversed, sometimes following inadequate directions and retracing our steps, and so on. Thus stages of meaning, which assume new importance in 1977–78, were elaborated in *Method in Theology*, anticipated in the levels and sequences of expression of *Insight*'s Chapter 17, and have their roots in the writings of the 1930s (File 713 of the papers in the Lonergan Archives). Again, differentiations of consciousness are broached already in the three categories of *Insight*: common sense, theory, and interiority. And so also in other questions. But we have to stop the flow of history at certain points if we are going to give a manageable account of it.

A final introductory point: our interest is not in historical details but in the general structure of history. The question will not be of the type, which letters of Ignatius of Antioch are genuine? Or who drafted *Pascendi* for Pius X? The purpose will rather be to take an X-ray of history.[10] Our interest will be in the upper blade of empirical method rather than in the lower blade of particular data.[11] All through the phases of his development, then, Lonergan was concerned, and we will be concerned in following his progress, with a theoretical compo-

---

Insight, that the unpublished writings of File 713 of the Lonergan papers bring to Lonergan's apprenticeship to Thomas Aquinas (I borrow the term from William Mathews). There is a third reason, perhaps the real one, that we all do what we can, and I am more at home in Lonergan's history than in bringing his thought to bear on current problems.

10 A phrase Lonergan used to describe his work in *The Way to Nicea* viii: 'But the reader must be warned that we do not propose to add to erudition by research, or to clarify interpretation by study, or to enrich history with fresh information. Such functional specialities we presuppose. Our purpose is to move on to a fourth, to a dialectic that, like an X-ray, sets certain key issues in high relief to concentrate on their oppositions and their interplay.'

11 One could speak, as Lonergan did at first, of the a priori, which has a legitimate use in any field of investigation (the a priori of possibilities), but the a priori seems sometimes to be rejected on principle (though how that is done without using an a priori premise I do not know), so it is better to use Lonergan's term of the upper blade. (His usage can be found through the index of such books as *Insight*, or *Understanding and Being*, or *Topics in Education*.) The alternative to the upper blade he called 'the principle of the empty head' (*Method in Theology* 157).

nent that combines with concrete data to mediate insight: the scissors action of empirical method.

1 The History That Happens, 1935–1938

A first and basic distinction must be made between the history that happens and the history that is written about what happened. Both of these were part of Lonergan's thinking from the 1930s, and remained part of his thinking forty years later. But in 1938 the history that happens was the focus, and in 1978 it was the history that was written. Furthermore, when he spoke in 1968 of 'the task of doing genuine history,' a task that 'confronts contemporary Catholic theologians with the most basic and far-reaching of problems,'[12] he did not mean the history that happens; we do not, except in a minimal sense, 'do' the history that happens. He meant the history that is written.

Nevertheless, the history that happens was a major question in Lonergan's own early thinking, probably because of the influence Hegel and Marx had on him in this largely undocumented period.[13] It remained a topic of major importance throughout his life. References in *Insight* to the same pair of thinkers indicate this, and his 1973 statement that Chapter 20 of *Insight* presents the whole idea of the structure of history affirms it clearly enough.[14] The most rewarding context in which to study this is the human good: 'at the present time it would seem that the immediate carrier of human aspiration is the more con-

---

12 'Belief: Today's Issue,' in *A Second Collection* 96. See also the quotation in my first paragraph, where the question is of introducing *historical scholarship*, again the history that is written.

13 A letter Lonergan wrote to his Provincial Superior, Henry Keane, 22 January 1935, speaks (p. 5) of this influence; we hope to publish this letter in the biography being written by William Mathews. In another letter to Keane, written 10 August 1938, Lonergan reveals his hope of studying the 'essential branch of philosophy' that philosophy of history is, though it is 'not yet recognised' as such. Both letters are extant in the Lonergan Archives, Toronto.

14 '*Insight* Revisited,' in *A Second Collection* 272. The structure is the familiar triad of progress, decline, and redemption, which are to be understood as operating not consecutively but simultaneously: we are always progressing, always declining, always being redeemed. See *Topics in Education* 69, on 'intellectual development ... sin ... redemption': 'in the concrete all three function together. They are intertwined. They do not exist in isolation, but they have to be described separately before they can be considered together.'

crete apprehension of the human good effected through such theories of history as the liberal doctrine of progress, the Marxist doctrine of dialectical materialism and, most recently, Teilhard de Chardin's identification of cosmogenesis, anthropogenesis, and christogenesis.'[15]

2 The *Gratia Operans* Dissertation

As time went on, the history that is written engaged Lonergan's interest more and more, and it is this history that he came eventually to regard as the real problem. The very term 'historical scholarship' that appears in my first paragraph is evidence of that, and all the rest of my paper will confirm it.

The first step in the long journey was taken in Lonergan's doctoral dissertation. I would not say that he knew he was taking such a step. He knew he was dealing with history; he knew that historians must exercise their understanding – the enemy at this stage is historical positivism; but he was still twenty years from experiencing and measuring the impact of the German Historical School. What he was specifically concerned with, as the subtitle shows, is the speculative development of thought on operative grace from Augustine to Thomas Aquinas.[16] The study had to be historical, but without surrender to positivist principles, as if historical inquiry were conducted 'without a use of human

15 'The Transition from a Classicist World-View to Historical-Mindedness,' in *A Second Collection* 7, a paper of 1966. See also the 1976 paper 'Questionnaire on Philosophy,' on liberal progress, Marxist dialectical materialism, and religious conversion (*METHOD: Journal of Lonergan Studies* 2/2 [1984] 14–19 [*Papers 1965–1980* (2004) 366–70]). The place of Christ in history would have been a key factor in Lonergan's new Christology, had he lived to write it. Around 1963–64 with this in mind he began a work with the unlikely title *De bono et malo* – unlikely, unless one understands his structure of history as progress, decline, and redemption.

16 'Gratia Operans: A Study of the Speculative Development in the Writings of St Thomas Aquinas. Being a thesis undertaken under the direction of the Rev. Charles Boyer, S.J., towards partial satisfaction of the conditions for the Doctorate in Sacred Theology, Rome, Gregorian University, 1940' (Lonergan Archives, Toronto). The thesis, considerably revised, was published in four articles in *TS* 1941–42, and the articles in turn were published in book form in 1971 as *Grace and Freedom: Operative Grace in the Thought of St Thomas Aquinas*. The introductory pages to the dissertation, all-important for Lonergan's methodology, were not published till 1985 – see the next note. [The thesis and the book were subsequently brought together and published in 2000 as vol. 1 of *Collected Works of Bernard Lonergan*, under the same title as the book published in 1971 (ed.).]

intelligence.' Lonergan would find a middle course. 'That middle course consists in constructing an a priori scheme that is capable of synthesizing any possible set of historical data irrespective of their place and time, just as the science of mathematics constructs a generic scheme capable of synthesizing any possible set of quantitative phenomena.'[17]

The a priori of 1940 is the upper blade of empirical method of 1953, and the search for this kind of understanding marks all Lonergan's work. The scheme in question here is 'the general form of the speculative movement on the nature of grace from St. Augustine to St Thomas.'[18] This will follow the general form of any speculative development, which oscillates between general and particular in the following way. We have an insight on a specific point; we generalize it and make it the whole explanation; we learn it is insufficient for a complete explanation, so we go behind it to a more general factor; we make this in its turn the whole explanation, only to discover that it too is insufficient by itself; we go back to our first insight, the specific one, but now we make a synthesis of the general and specific, and have a better approximation to a complete explanation.[19]

There are parallels in more familiar territory. For example, in a religious order silence is seen to be a good thing for a life of prayer, so a rule is laid down: Let there be silence. Then there's a fire in the house, and considerable damage is done because people kept silence too rigidly. So a specific rule is added: Let there be silence except when the house is on fire. And so on. For another example, in the church we might start with the people of God, the *laos*. But with this alone we get the disorders Paul talks of in *1 Corinthians* 14. So it seems good to have leaders, those who oversee the operation, those who preside, elders who make decisions, and so on. This side may develop over two millennia, but eventually it too is found to be insufficient. And so on, once again.

Parallels from daily life are not as clear-cut as the form of speculative development, but they make the point in a rudimentary way, and enable us to avoid the heavy weather of Lonergan's doctoral dissertation. He could not take our easy way out, for he was dealing with

17 'The Gratia Operans Dissertation: Preface and Introduction,' *METHOD: Journal of Lonergan Studies* 3/2 (1985) 11 [*Grace and Freedom* (2000) 156].

18 Ibid. (1985) 13 [(2000) 158].

19 Lonergan's own words are quoted in Appendix A.

actual history, a concrete case of speculative development; but using this constant form of the dialectic of particular and general discoveries, he was able to find an intelligible order in the work of theologians like Augustine, Abelard and Bernard Clairvaux, Peter Lombard, Philip the Chancellor, Alexander of Hales and Albert the Great, and Thomas Aquinas (the latter in two distinct phases of his development).[20]

3 The Form of Dogmatic Development

When Lonergan chose to work on Thomas Aquinas for his doctorate, it was more or less predetermined that the relevant field of history would be that of speculative development. But when he was assigned to teach theology, the context changed, and it was almost predetermined now that the relevant field of history would be that of dogmatic development. At any rate in the next step, as I read his history, we have the form of dogmatic rather than of speculative development.

The conceptual tool he uses now is easily traced to Aristotle and Aquinas. In the more dialectical form of speculative development, the previous step, one suspects the influence of Hegel and Marx to be operative still, but for the pair of analysis and synthesis, with their inverse orders, with their interlocking and their mutual conditioning, it is Aristotle and Thomas who are the teachers.

Lonergan liked to illustrate this pair of concepts in the field of chemistry. Analysis begins with what is immediate: chairs, lights, paper, whatever. So, if one 'followed the history of the development of the science'

> one would begin from common material objects, learn the arts of qualitative and quantitative analysis, and very gradually advance to the discovery of the periodic table and the sub-atomic structures. But one might

20 'The Gratia Operans Dissertation: Preface and Introduction,' *METHOD: Journal of Lonergan Studies* 3/2 (1985) 35–39 [*Grace and Freedom* (2000) 182–90]. Note that what went forward between Augustine and Aquinas in the theology of grace is part of the history that happens. But Lonergan's reflections on how to understand that history and his use of an upper blade to make it intelligible come under the heading of the history that is written. This twofold consideration applies over and over in the history I am sketching: Lonergan is often dealing with the history that happens, but I am more concerned, at least after the first section of my paper, with the history that is written.

> begin at the other end with pure mathematics, then posit hypotheses regarding electrons and protons and neutrons, work out possible atomic and then molecular structures, develop a method of analysis, and finally turn for the first time to real material things.[21]

But there is an example of analytic process in Aristotle himself that illustrates the process simply and effectively. Someone comes to you. Why did he come? To get some money. Why did he want money? To pay a debt. Why did he wish to pay the debt? To be just. Why be just? And so on, till we reach the ultimate notion of the good.[22] If, however, we were teaching ethics, we would invert Aristotle's order, start with the ultimate notion of the good, work out the human and social good, find justice as a division, and the payment of debts as a subdivision.

Lonergan used this pair from 1946 to 1964 as providing the ideal structure for theology – ideal, for he did not get round to using it everywhere himself. He did, however, structure his whole Trinitarian theology according to this idea, proceeding by analysis from the three consubstantial persons to the divine relations, from the relations to origins, from origins to processions, from processions to the psychological analogy. Turning to the synthetic order, and starting from the fundamental idea of the psychological analogy, he systematically derived the notions of processions, relations, and consubstantial persons – the inverse of the analytic order.[23]

The focus of Lonergan's interest at first was clearly the synthetic side. See, for example, his *De ente supernaturali* of 1946, a synthetic work on grace, and his *De Deo trino*, where the second, synthetic volume was written first (*Divinarum personarum conceptio analogica* in the first edition of 1957). But gradually, as time went on, his interest turned to the analytic. That is of some importance for the present study, for the analytic way was the temporal way, the way of actual historical development in the church, while the synthetic way was outside time, the way

21 *Verbum* (1967) 62 [(1997) 74].

22 *Posterior Analytics* I, 24, 85b 30–35; Thomas Aquinas, *In Aristotelis libros ... Posteriorum analyticorum* 1, lectio 38, n. 334 (Turin: Marietti, 1955) 288. Aristotle actually speaks not of what is good, but of what is right.

23 This rather cryptic outline is found in the 1954 article we saw earlier ('Theology and Understanding,' in *Collection* [1967] 129–30, [1988] 122). It summarizes some six hundred pages of the later two-volume work *De Deo trino* (1964).

of logical simultaneity.[24] It follows that analytic process is slow. Thus, the laboratory experiments in chemistry that Lonergan speaks of recapitulate in a short time what took thousands of years in actual development. The swift steps Aristotle took in the laboratory of his mind to reach the notion of the good took several thousand or maybe several million years of cultural development in the actual history of the human race. And similarly, the Trinitarian theology that Thomas Aquinas arranges with such apparent ease in the synthetic order took twelve centuries to reach the point where his synthesis was possible.

All this is rather dull stuff compared to the exhilaration we feel in dealing with liberation theology, religious experience, inter-religious dialogue, hermeneutics of suspicion, and so on. Maybe so, and maybe Lonergan was a dull theologian for the first half of his life. But some of us who were teaching theology in the 1950s can testify to the extraordinary power this analytic-synthetic pair had to reduce to some order the extremely chaotic mass of material a teacher of dogmatic theology had somehow to handle.

As for Lonergan's personal history, unless we understand that first half of his career, we are likely to find the most flagrant contradictions between what he said earlier and what he said later, and so to dismiss him as incoherent. For example, right up to 1964, he has theology begin, not with data as in the empirical sciences, but with the truths of faith: 'non a datis sed a veris incipit.'[25] Within three years he seems to have abandoned this and to be holding the exact opposite. Thus in his 1967 paper, 'Theology in Its New Context,' he says, 'theology was a deductive, and it has become largely an empirical science. It was a deductive science in the sense that its theses were conclusions to be proven from the premisses provided by Scripture and Tradition. It has become an empirical science in the sense that Scripture and Tradition now supply not premisses, but data.'[26]

---

24 The analytic member is also called the way of discovery, the way of reduction to causes, the way of certitude, and the temporal way. The first four are found in *Divinarum personarum conceptio analogica* (Rome: Gregorian University Press, 1957) 20; the fifth, the temporal way, is added in *De Deo trino*, vol. 2 (1964) 33. The contrasting synthetic way is also called the way of composition, or the way of teaching (thus, in *Divinarum personarum* 21), to which the 1964 work adds the way of probability and the way of logical simultaneity (*De Deo trino*, vol. 2, 33–34).

25 *De Deo trino*, vol. 2 (1964) 20.

26 'Theology in Its New Context,' in *A Second Collection* 58.

But before we assert a flat contradiction, it would be good to examine in what sense he is using the word 'theology' in each case. In fact, as he said at the Florida conference of 1970, in reply to a question on this very point, 'behind the shift there is a greatly enlarged notion of theology.'[27] The 'theology' of 1964 was restricted to and practically coincident with systematics, with doctrines as basis, and theology in that sense still begins from truths, in 1993 as in 1963. The 'theology' of 1972 begins with research, true enough, and therefore from data, not truths; but research, which was not considered part of theology in 1964, has become in the 'greatly enlarged notion of theology' an intrinsic part.

Lonergan himself did not see a break with his former position, but rather a development in continuity with it. The synthetic side represented by Thomas Aquinas still has its place in the functional specialties, namely, in systematics. The analytic side is taken out from under dogmatic theology, and set free to develop according to its own nature, but it also has its place in the functional specialties, namely, in the first four or five.[28] The synthetic way, which claimed the lion's share of attention in 1946, is now just one functional specialty in eight.

4 The Real Problem Emerges

When Lonergan was called to Rome in 1953 to teach at the Gregorian University, there was unhappiness in many quarters. Regis College didn't want to lose him from Toronto, and Lonergan himself, deep in what was meant to be a book on method in theology, was pessimistic about finding leisure in Rome to finish it. I myself wrote to the General of the Jesuits, to the effect that a theologian of Lonergan's calibre should be allowed to stay where he could work in peace. The General replied that if Lonergan were really of the calibre I claimed, it would do him good to come to Rome.

I don't want to make that long-suffering General into another Caiphas, but in fact he prophesied for the people. It did do Lonergan good to go to Rome and encounter challenges there that we at Regis

27 'Bernard Lonergan Responds,' in Philip McShane, ed., *Foundations of Theology: Papers from the International Lonergan Congress 1970* (Dublin: Gill and Macmillan, 1971; Notre Dame: University of Notre Dame Press, 1972) 224.

28 'Aquinas composed his *Summa Theologiae* in the *via doctrinae*; see the *Prologus*. It corresponds to the functional specialty, *Systematics*, of my *Method in Theology*. The *via inventionis* would cover the first four or perhaps five previous specialties' ('Christology Today,' in *A Third Collection* 96 n. 10).

College were not likely to present to him. The challenge, to simplify the matter, came from the German Historical School,[29] and it came via the six hundred students he had to face daily in the classroom. That is his own account,[30] given in headlines again and needing qualification, for he was already moving on his own, maybe more slowly, to meet the challenge.[31]

In any case there was, during those twelve years Lonergan spent teaching in Rome, a stubborn wrestling with new ideas and something of a quantum leap in his own thinking.[32] I venture to be even more

29 Simplified, because the full list is longer; for example 'Time and Meaning' has this: 'the contribution to thought worked out in the nineteenth century by German philosophers, German historians, German students of languages, German students of literatures ... the *Geisteswissenschaften,*' in *Bernard Lonergan: 3 Lectures* (Montreal: Thomas More Institute [1975]) 30; reprinted in *Papers 1958–1964* (1996) 95. But Lonergan regularly focussed on the German Historical School.

30 In 1970 he was asked about his growing interest in meaning after *Insight,* and replied: 'Well, it was being sent to Rome and having to deal with students from northern Italy and France and Germany and Belgium who were totally immersed in continental philosophy – I had to talk meaningfully to them, and it involved getting a hold of the whole movement of the *Geisteswissenschaften*' ('An Interview with Fr. Bernard Lonergan, S.J.,' in *A Second Collection* 220). A little more formally three years later: 'The new challenge came from the *Geisteswissenschaften,* from the problems of hermeneutics and critical history, from the need of integrating nineteenth-century achievement in this field with the teachings of Catholic religion and Catholic theology. It was a long struggle that can be documented from my Latin and English writing during this period and from the doctoral courses I conducted *De intellectu et methodo, De systemate et historia,* and eventually *De methodo theologiae.* The eventual outcome has been the book, *Method in Theology*' ('*Insight* Revisited,' in *A Second Collection* 277). See also *Caring about Meaning: Patterns in the Life of Bernard Lonergan,* ed. Pierrot Lambert, Charlotte Tansey, Cathleen Going (Montreal: Thomas More Institute, 1982) 105: 'I was learning all the time myself; I was moving into the European atmosphere in which phenomenology was dominant.' In some defence of the students Lonergan had in Montreal and Toronto, I should say that we did pepper him with questions, but our questions were more likely to concern *scientia media* or *actuatio finita per actum infinitum;* we were not excessively concerned with phenomenology or with the German Historical School.

31 Chapter 17 of *Insight* is revealing here, along with such remarks as: 'Prior to all writing of history, prior to all interpretation of other minds, there is the self-scrutiny of the historian, the self-knowledge of the interpreter' (*Insight* [1957] xxix, [1992] 23).

32 Charles Hefling has dealt largely with the problem I am attacking, in his article 'On Reading The Way to Nicea,' in Timothy P. Fallon and Philip Boo Riley, eds, *Religion and Culture: Essays in Honor of Bernard Lonergan, S.J.* (Albany: State University of New York Press, 1987) 149–66. I do not know at this date how much my pondering of the question owes to my earlier reading of Hefling – and I could make a parallel remark about my debt to many others who have written on Lonergan.

specific, to narrow down the critical period that I am calling the fourth step, and locate it in the four years 1959 to 1962. So much is happening then that to deal with this short period alone will require the longest part of my paper.

I choose 1959 for the start, partly because the course Lonergan taught that year, *De intellectu et methodo*, puts the problem of history more clearly than any previous work of his that I know, partly because in his education lectures of that summer he declared, 'It is at the present time that the full impact of the development of the historical sciences during the past century is hitting theology, and theology has not thought its way through the problems yet,'[33] a remark that I take as implicitly autobiographical: only now is Lonergan feeling the impact, and he has not yet thought his way through the problem.

The year 1962 is less clear-cut as marking the emergence of a new approach and the outcome of the period of wrestling, since so much went on in 1963 and 1964 before what we call the great breakthrough to functional specialties in 1965; but 1962 saw the crucial differentiations of consciousness beginning to emerge as an explanatory factor in development, and so many new avenues had opened by that year that it is not wholly arbitrary to make it a turning point and give it special significance in Lonergan's evolution.[34]

So, let me first address the problem of history as it presented itself to Lonergan in 1959, and then the situation in 1962 when the elements and shape of a solution were beginning to emerge from the chaos.

The work to study for 1959 is the course *De intellectu et methodo*, given at the Gregorian University in the spring term of that year.[35] The focal concern in at least the first half of that course was the difference between the sources of theology and theology itself, and the way we move from one to the other. How do we make the transition from the conceptuality, say, of Palestine, to that, say, of medieval Scholasticism? How maintain continuity in making the transition? How bridge the

33 *Topics in Education* 247.

34 For easier reference to what occurred during these formative four years, I list in Appendix B below the main pieces in the picture.

35 We have a very good set of notes on this course, 72 pages, legal-size, single-spaced, with a monitum, '... notae ... collectae et ordinatae ... ab aliquibus auditoribus ex his tantum quae in scholis colligi potuerunt'; we owe the notes to Francesco Rossi de Gasperis and P. Joseph Cahill. The course of the following year, *De systemate et historia*, is also important, but we have better documentation for *De intellectu et methodo*.

ever widening gap as theological systems take us further and further from our sources?[36] It's the problem of what we call the historicity of the human race, the problem of the mark of time on our social arrangements and cultural achievements, the mark of time on all human thinking and activity – the mark of time therefore on scripture, creed, and dogma, all of which, however divine they be, are also human products.

Naturally, Lonergan sees no solution in simply clinging to the terms of scripture and tradition (we may think here of fundamentalism), no solution either in mere manipulation of concepts and judgments (we may think here of conceptualism). He goes behind words and concepts in his habitual appeal to intelligence itself and its threefold formation through understanding, science, and wisdom. His twofold way of analysis and synthesis is invoked.[37] A key factor is wisdom,[38] but wisdom is something we only gradually acquire, so it does not offer an easy way out, any more than an appeal to book or authority. The solution has to lie in growing up to meet the problem.

This is vintage Lonergan, and a good foundation as far as it goes. But it is equally a foundation for tracing any development, be it in chemistry, ethics, philosophy, whatever; more is needed to meet the specific problem of the historicity of scripture, creed, and dogma. Lonergan tackles this specific question in a detailed analysis of two quite different ways in which we experience, conceive, think, judge, and know: the symbolic mode, illustrated most simply in the case of two persons who smile at one another, and the theoretic mode, illustrated best historically in the achievements of the Greek *logos*.[39]

The problem is now clear to Lonergan. He has posed it openly and faced it squarely enough with the resources at hand, namely, the two modes of thinking and knowing and acting which he contrasts here. Quite clearly these derive from the common sense and theory of *Insight*. It is more important, I think, that Lonergan has recognized the locus of the solution and is on the way to the differentiations of consciousness that are not yet a theme in *Insight*,[40] that become a

36 Student notes 11–25.

37 Ibid. 6–8, 12–13, 27–28.

38 Ibid. 18–22.

39 Ibid. 31–36.

40 That statement is provocative, in view of what chapter 17 of *Insight* has to say, but I believe it can be defended; see Appendix C below on early approaches to differentiations of consciousness.

theme in 1962, and then in *Method in Theology* are seen as the key to development.

What effected the change to the later meaning and use of differentiations of consciousness? A chief mediating factor is the concept of worlds. It surfaced along with that of horizon in the 1957 lectures on existentialism,[41] it makes an appearance in *De intellectu et methodo* in 1959,[42] and it becomes a central theme in the 1962 course at the Gregorian University, *De methodo theologiae*. The worlds are set out in a series of antitheses: the sacred world over against the secular (*profanus*), the interior world against the external, the visible world against the intelligible.[43]

The antitheses are of special importance in *De methodo theologiae*, one might even say that this notion structures the whole course.[44] They are important too as we look forward, for they parallel the differences, not to say oppositions, we shall find to obtain between differentiations of consciousness. Indeed, change a word here and there, and you could say the theme of the course is differentiations of consciousness rather than the antithetic worlds. In any case, there is the closest relationship: the differentiation of the worlds, Lonergan says, is according to the dynamism of consciousness, the structure of consciousness, the technical evolution of consciousness.[45]

Lonergan, I believe, is moving toward a more thematic treatment of differentiations of consciousness. The movement is well advanced in a lecture he gave later that same summer of 1962 at Regis College, Tor-

41 A week of lectures at Boston College, July 1957. Extant are Lonergan's notes for the course, a tape-recording of the lectures, and a transcription of the recording (Lonergan Archives). [Subsequently published in 2001 as chaps. 9–14 of *Phenomenology and Logic*, vol. 18 of *Collected Works of Bernard Lonergan*.]

42 Student notes 34–35.

43 See 8–11 of the student notes of the course *De methodo theologiae*: 60 pages, legal-size, single-spaced, with the monitum again, 'Notae desumptae ab alumnis.' Also available are the tape-recording and transcription of the parallel lectures of the institute 'The Method of Theology,' Regis College, Toronto, August 1962.

44 Thus, following 8–11 describing the antitheses, 11–14 reflect on the antitheses, 15–18 set out the problematic founded on the antitheses, and the rest of the notes labor over the problematic. The summer institute adds lectures on hermeneutics and history that were not part of the Latin course. Note that both the course and the institute lectures have operations of the subject for a starting point, and they go on from there to discuss the worlds of the subject.

45 Student notes 11. Also 9 on the opposition of the sacred and secular worlds: 'Cuius oppositionis radix est in ipso *dynamismo* conscientiae humanae.'

onto, and the Thomas More Institute, Montreal: 'Time and Meaning.' I will therefore close off our fourth step with some account of that lecture, which happens also to provide a rather good statement of the problem of history.

The approach now is through Piaget and his notion of differentiation, grouping, and grouping of groups. But the grouping of groups runs into the same problems we considered in the antithetical worlds. For example, the two worlds of common sense and theory 'do not admit this grouping of two lower groups into one single higher group. One has to shift from one to the other. There are fundamental oppositions between these two worlds and by illustrating that, we'll have a first fundamental division of field of distinct types of development.'[46] So it is not directly the differentiations of consciousness that give us types of development; it is the worlds. But there is still the closest relationship between the two: 'the four spheres [namely, those of common sense, theory, interiority, and religion] ... may be differentiated in consciousness.'[47] In fact, Lonergan oscillates between the objective and subjective throughout this lecture; the turn to the subject, so often employed to characterize his later work, is not yet fully achieved.

I remarked earlier on the very clear statement of the question that 'Time and Meaning' gives us. Let me conclude our fourth step with that. 'I want ... to offer a sketch of the way in which meaning develops ... And when I speak of a sketch of the way in which meaning develops, I mean some sort of thread or highway that will perhaps be of some use in relating what appear ... to be totally unrelated ways of understanding human life and its significance.'[48] Lonergan clarifies this positive goal by contrast with two mentalities to be excluded: the romanticist and the classicist. The latter is more familiar: 'The interest of the talk may ... be taken ... as opposed to an abstraction, to a cult of

46 'Time and Meaning,' in *Bernard Lonergan: 3 Lectures* (1975) 44 [*Papers 1958–1964* (1996) 112].

47 Ibid. (1975) 48 [(1996) 116]. Further, Lonergan speaks now of the 'undifferentiated consciousness' of the primitive (1975) 51, (1996) 118. Once there were differentiations of common sense (*Insight* [1957] 180, [1992] 203), but then the word had not acquired its technical sense; when that occurs, Lonergan will use 'brands' for the varieties of common sense (*Method in Theology* 276). See also the 1962 seminar notes, *De argumento* ... (note 50 below).

48 'Time and Meaning,' in *Bernard Lonergan: 3 Lectures* (1975) 29 [*Papers 1958–1964* 94–95].

the universal, the ideal, the norm, the exemplar, with the result that one never really apprehends things in their particularity.' But on the other side, the interest of the talk may also be taken 'as opposed to a romanticism which knows the concrete, the singular, the individual, the personal, the historical, but does so at the expense of any overall view and results in a sort of fragmentation, compensated by enthusiasm, that is lost in detail.'[49]

This has been a long and rather confused section, and even then I had to omit several topics and pass over a good deal of the data.[50] But a sketch is a sketch, and I have to leave these four years, 1959 to 1962, with the monitum that they merit the closest scrutiny as a unit in Lonergan's development.

5 The Upper Blade for History: Ordered Multiplicity in Differentiations of Consciousness

There is a long way to go in our fifth step: the introduction of research, interpretation, and history into the intrinsic structure of theology; the

49 Ibid. (1975) 30 [(1996) 95].

50 Topics omitted: meaning and interpretation, horizons and conversions, mediation (which becomes a prominent theme in 1963), foundations (which appears in *De methodo et intellectu*, 1959, and will be a topic in 1964), the question of method itself, and so on.

Another datum of the time is Lonergan's outline for a presentation at a faculty seminar of the Gregorian University and the Biblical Institute, *De argumento theologico ex sacra scriptura* (Spring 1962), which talks of transition from one context to another, asks what makes it possible, and responds that it seems to be the transcendence of truth ('Videtur transcendentia veri,' 3), which allows it to be transposed from context to context. He illustrates this with the transposition a doctor makes of a patient's report, or the transposition a judge makes of witnesses' testimony (the same examples of doctor and judge are used, with expanded treatment, in *De methodo theologiae* 49).

Of special interest here is Lonergan's list of the ways in which scripture can be viewed and become thematic (as language, encounter, event, word of God – seven ways in all), and of four contexts in which a theologian may work (dogmatic-theological, human life ...).

The transcendence of truth and the possibility of its transmission will remain a rock in Lonergan's theology (see Appendix D below), but I would say it is a precondition and presupposition of transposition from context to context. It is even a positive factor, but it is not the immediate and specific factor in the transition. That will be found in the ordered multiplicity of differentiations of consciousness, with their ordering in stages of meaning.

creation of dialectic and foundations to replace the old appeal to proof-texts; the rethinking of doctrines and systematics so that what was once theology *tout court* is now restricted to two specialties out of eight; the addition of communications, to give the handing on of the message equal importance with receiving it; and, most directly relevant to the present purpose, the thematizing of differentiations of consciousness and of their role in the development of theology.

Much of this was achieved, at least on the broad scale, with what we call the breakthrough of February 1965, but it seems the next six years were needed to work it all out to the satisfaction of Lonergan's rigorous mind.[51] He once remarked that with the reading of Dawson's *The Age of the Gods* in the early 1930s there began 'the correction of my hitherto normative or classicist notion' of culture.[52] No doubt the correction began then, but it was still a long road to his 1966 paper 'The Transition from a Classicist World-View to Historical-Mindedness.'[53] I see a similar pattern and struggle in the move from analysis-synthesis to the eight functional specialties.

Is the point at issue growing obscure? Let me recall our headline: 'All my work,' Lonergan said, 'has been introducing history into Catholic theology.' Introducing history into theology, so we are in the world of meaning. Introducing history, so we are in the world of developing meaning. History in Catholic theology, so we have a starting point in a Palestinian culture and a terminal point in any people whatever who await the preaching of the gospel: Palestine, the Greco-Roman world, the Middle Ages, modern times with its innumerable peoples around the globe and its innumerable subcultures within our great cities.

Historically, the problem arose in its general form with the German Historical School, and it soon received its specific theological applica-

51 I think here of Dorothy Sayers's trinity of the artist (first outlined at the end of her play *The Zeal of Thy House*, 1937, then expanded into a whole book, *The Mind of the Maker* [New York: Meridian Books, 1956]): the creative idea, the laborious task of working it out in words or symphony or stone, the reception the work of art inspires in the observer. Lonergan had his creative idea in 1965, and had carved it in words by 1971; the third step, I suppose, is ours to take. On the breakthrough of February 1965 see *Caring about Meaning* 59.

52 '*Insight* Revisited,' in *A Second Collection* 264.

53 'The Transition from a Classicist World-View to Historical Mindedness,' in *A Second Collection* 1–9.

tion among Protestants of the German-speaking world. For most Catholics, however, the impact of the German Historical School was still a century away. Their problem was posed rather in works like Newman's on the development of doctrine, and it became acute with the definition of the Immaculate Conception in 1854 and of papal infallibility in 1871. There had been a change in doctrine; how do you account for it? What made it happen? How do you justify it? Attempts to go beyond Newman took various forms: at one end of the spectrum an excessively logical attitude that would turn the whole *Summa theologiae* of Thomas Aquinas into dogma, at the other an excessively mystical view of development that dispensed with rational justification.

Lonergan began with full reliance on Newman – that is my memory of the years 1946–50 when he taught me. Insofar as something more than Newman was needed, he found it in the analytic member of the twofold way. This is not to be reduced to the bare logic of conclusions theology: the difference is in understanding. We have 'The Assumption and Theology' of 1948 to illustrate that in the concrete, we have 'Theology and Understanding' of 1954 to give it a wider theological application, and we have the 'Questionnaire on Philosophy' of 1974 for a general statement.[54] In the last-named work, when urging that young philosophers become generalists in the world of thought, Lonergan said:

> [I]t cannot be stressed too strongly that the mediation of the generalists is intelligent rather than logical: by logical mediation I understand the process from universal concepts to particular instances as just instances; by intelligent mediation I understand the process from understanding the universal to understanding the particular.[55]

The same paper speaks of the harm that results when theologians, in deriving the dogmas of the church from scripture, give an ultimate role to logic. Logic works within a given universe of discourse, but other universes of discourse are always possible, and to pass from one to another is beyond the competence of logic. He continues:

54 'The Assumption and Theology,' in *Collection* (1967) 68–83, [(1988) 66–80]; 'Theology and Understanding,' see note 6 above; 'Questionnaire on Philosophy,' see note 15 above.

55 'Questionnaire on Philosophy' 32–33 [*Papers 1965–1980* (2004) 383].

> We reach the notion of method when we ask how does one effect the transition from one universe of discourse to another or, more profoundly, how is there effected the transition from one level or stage in human culture to another later level or stage or, vice versa, from a later to an earlier level or stage. Obviously the operations involved in such transitions are not ruled by the logic of clear terms, coherent propositions, rigorous inferences. Quite different, though quite common, types of operation have to be considered and considered just as explicitly as the logical operations that from Aristotle to Hegel were thought to control legitimate mental process.[56]

That restates in other terms the problem we already saw in *De intellectu et methodo* and in 'Time and Meaning.' It adds a helpful clarification by its contrast with logic. Moving from one universe of discourse to another, we need more than logic. What do we need? What is it that makes developments possible in doctrines and theology? Chapter 12 of *Method in Theology* undertakes to tell us.

We need, of course, 'exact historical investigation' to 'determine the starting-point, the process, the end-result of any particular development'; and to 'determine the legitimacy of any development' we need to 'ask whether or not the process was under the guidance of ... conversion.' But these are not the fundamental questions. There is a deeper issue, and that 'deeper issue is the more general question that asks how is it that developments are possible? How is it that mortal man can develop what he would not know unless God revealed it?' Lonergan continues: 'The basis for an answer to this question lies in what I have already referred to as the differentiation of consciousness.'[57]

This is a new concept of development, miles apart from both the narrowness of logic and the surrender of reason to authority. It needs a thorough study with Chapter 12 of *Method in Theology* at the

---

56 Ibid. 24 [375].

57 *Method in Theology* 302. And, a few years later: 'So there emerges the question of doctrinal pluralism. Its real basis, I believe, is the multiple differentiation of consciousness possible at the present time and often needed to master issues in theology' ('Theology and Praxis,' in *A Third Collection* 197–98). And, after a few more years: 'Differentiations of consciousness justify or lead to the discovery of previously unnoticed implications in the sources of revelation' ('Unity and Plurality: The Coherence of Christian Truth,' in *A Third Collection* 250 n. 8).

center,[58] but I think I can take a shorter route by examining a lecture given two years after the completion of *Method in Theology*, where he takes up the question again and, in my view, breaks new ground.

The lecture in question is 'Variations in Fundamental Theology.'[59] Its point of departure is volume 46 of *Concilium*, which has Fundamental Theology as its theme. It runs through the difficulties fundamental theology encounters today, quoting the various contributors to the volume. Coming to theological pluralism, Lonergan refers to Rahner on the contrast between an earlier time when 'their medieval heritage had given Roman Catholic theologians a common and to some extent unambiguous language'and the present time when we have no common language.[60]

It is in this context that we find what we are looking for. Lonergan remarks, casually enough, that the 'scattering of views I have illustrated may, perhaps, be given some unity by referring to my *Method in Theology*.'[61] But on Rahner's point in particular he has this to say:

> For Rahner's puzzlement over the swarm of disparate theologies that resist precise classification and so escape theological judgement, we may offer a set of larger containers, namely, the ordered multiplicity of differentiations of consciousness and their diversification by the presence or

58 What I just quoted from chapter 12 is a kind of thesis. In good Scholastic style Lonergan explains the terms of the thesis with a list of the differentiations of consciousness (*Method in Theology* 303–305). Because these same differentiations 'also characterize successive stages in cultural development' (305) he outlines those stages; first in the move from the scriptures (symbolic apprehension) to theological and church doctrines (305–12); then (314–18) in the three developments by which he regularly characterizes the modern thinker: 'his science and his conception of science, his history and his conception of history, his philosophy and his conception of philosophy' (317). Turning to the development of doctrines (319–20) he feels obliged to state his Catholic position on the permanence (320–24) and the historicity (324–26) of dogmas, before taking up pluralism and the unity of faith (326–30), and concluding with what is more of an appendix, some pages on the autonomy of theology (330–33).

59 [*METHOD: Journal of Lonergan Studies* 16/1 (1998) 5–24; *Papers 1965–1980* (2004) 240–58] The second in a series of the four Larkin-Stuart lectures given at Trinity College, Toronto. First delivered in November 1973, it was presented a second time with slight changes at New Haven in 1974; the key phrase 'ordered multiplicity' was lost in the second version.

60 Ibid. 19 [253].

61 Ibid. 24 [258].

> absence of religious, moral, or intellectual conversion. Such broad genetic differences can serve to mark off frontiers that contain conceptually disparate views.[62]

This is a fundamental statement for the purpose of my paper, and the phrase 'ordered multiplicity of differentiations of consciousness' is a key to the most radical concept of development of doctrine since Newman's book on that subject. We are talking about theological differences, we locate them as genetic differences, we ascribe the diversity to differentiations of consciousness,[63] we group the diverse theologies under 'larger containers,' we unite them in an ordered multiplicity. There is a third option, then, that escapes the two extremes I mentioned: a logical development that would make dogmas of all the conclusions of Thomas Aquinas, and a mystical approach that surrendered reason to the unsearchable.

6 Stages of Meaning as the Ordering Principle

We now have 'the ordered multiplicity of differentiations of consciousness' as the key factor not only for development of doctrine but also for unity in the pluralism of communication. But if a series is ordered, there is an ordering principle: that is good Thomist doctrine. So what is the ordering principle here? Can we take the question one step further in that direction?

Late in life Lonergan seems to have thought so, and I will come to his final position presently; but there is earlier background in what he has to say on the origin of differentiations. How do they arise? Some

---

62 Ibid.

63 I doubt that Lonergan ever tried to draw up a complete list of differentiations of consciousness. *Method in Theology* names ten: the child's move into a world mediated by meaning, the world of common sense, orientation to the transcendent, the development of symbols, arts, literature, the emergence of systematic meaning, post-systematic literature, the emergence of method, the development of scholarship, the development of post-scientific and post-scholarly literature, the exploration of interiority (303–305). A simpler list is found in *Philosophy of God, and Theology*: religious, linguistic, literary, systematic, scientific, scholarly, self-appropriation (57; *Papers 1965–1980* [2004] 209). Elsewhere, after distinguishing four differentiations (scientific, religious, scholarly, modern philosophic), he adds a note to say, 'Our listing ... is not intended to go beyond the needs of this paper' ('Unity and Plurality,' in *A Third Collection* 250 n. 12), a remark that may caution us in interpreting other lists.

information on that should be helpful in the effort to reduce them again to an 'ordered multiplicity,' and I believe we have a rich source on this in the 'Patterns of Experience' of Chapter 6 in *Insight*. The wealth of that chapter is not forgotten when Lonergan comes to the sources of pluralism in Chapter 12 of *Method in Theology*, but it is compressed into a couple of lines while other factors are added.[64]

I believe, then, that there is potential for the ordering of the multiplicity of differentiations in a study of their origins. Statements like the following are instructive: 'the intelligibility proper to developing doctrines is the intelligibility immanent in historical process. One knows it, not by a priori theorizing, but by a posteriori research, interpretation, history, dialectic, and the decision of foundations.'[65] It is in historical process that differentiations arise, and it is there that we may grasp their intelligibility. Again, when Lonergan introduced the phrase 'ordered multiplicity,' he referred us to *Method in Theology*, and by speaking of 'broad genetic differences' gave us a clue what to look for there. How are 'broad genetic differences' rendered intelligible in *Method in Theology*? It seems to be done through an analysis of the stages of meaning, which are certainly related genetically: 'just as the second stage comes out of developments occurring in the first, so the third stage comes out of developments occurring in the second.'[66]

Further, I believe that, in linking the ordered multiplicity of differentiations of consciousness with stages of meaning, we are on the track of something very important for what Lonergan calls his lifework of bringing history into theology. To start with, the idea has roots deep in his earliest work on history, where already he had developed a theory of stages correlated with what we would now call differentiations of

64 *Method in Theology* 326: 'There are three sources of pluralism. First, linguistic, social, and cultural differences give rise to different brands of common sense' (on this see Appendix E below, where there are some data from chapter 6 of *Insight*). Secondly, there is undifferentiated consciousness and there are its differentiations. Thirdly, there is conversion and its presence or absence.

The word 'pluralism' perhaps points more clearly to the fact that we are not dealing just with developments of the past, but are also concerned with applications in the pluralist world of the present and on into an indefinite future. In fact, much of this section 11 of *Method in Theology* deals with preaching the gospel to all nations with their enormous differences.

65 *Method in Theology* 319.

66 Ibid. 94.

consciousness.[67] Then *Method in Theology* provides the materials for a new integration of history and meaning. To cap the series we have what I consider to be Lonergan's definitive position in the paper 'Philosophy and the Religious Phenomenon,' found in File 725 among his papers, and to be dated, from evidence in the text, in early 1978 or late 1977.[68]

There is no need to present the paper in detail, but it had two parts, the second part had two concerns, and the second concern 'was with the ordering of the differences due to developments'[69] – exactly our question. Further, Lonergan in his own view is taking a step forward: after referring to his earlier work, he now feels that he can present his case 'in a less abstruse approach.'[70] Let me quote. 'The issue in hand is the need of some account and ordering of the various contexts in which, first, religious living occurs and, secondly, investigations of religious living are undertaken.' The account will be a dialectic in which two sets of terms are involved: 'the terms whose meaning shifts in the course of time and ... the terms that denote the factors bringing about such shifts in meaning.'

The first factor is clearly identified and subdivided at once: 'The terms whose meaning shifts are social contexts and cultural contexts,' the former illustrated by 'family and mores, community and education, state and law, economics and technology,' the latter by 'art, religion, science, philosophy, history.'[71] The second factor ('terms that denote the factors bringing about such shifts') is found in four stages of meaning: 'the linguistic, the literate, the logical, and the methodical.'[72]

---

67 The stages were naturally different all those forty years ago. See in Appendix F below an excerpt from the unpublished paper (c. 1937–38) 'Philosophy of History.'

68 'Philosophy and the Religious Phenomenon,' *METHOD: Journal of Lonergan Studies* 12/2 (1994) 125–46 [*Papers 1965–1980* (2004) 391–408].

69 Ibid. 143 [408]. For discussion of the question see 138–43 [404–408].

70 Ibid. 138 [404]. Lonergan does not clarify for us the relation of his 'ordered multiplicity' of 1973 to his 'less abstruse approach' in the present paper, but it is clear that he is not repudiating differentiations of consciousness as explanatory for development: he still calls on this idea in a paper of 1982, 'Unity and Plurality' (see the quotation above, note 57). My description of stages of meaning as 'the ordering principle' is an attempt at the desired clarification.

71 'Philosophy and the Religious Phenomenon,' *METHOD: Journal of Lonergan Studies* 12/2 (1994) 138 [*Papers 1965–1980* (2004) 404].

72 Ibid. 139 [404–405]. The text has simply 'stages'; I supplied 'of meaning' from *Method in Theology*, remembering always how comprehensive the term is.

This appears from a summation a page later, where he speaks of 'headings of social arrangements' and 'areas of cultural interest,' and then of 'four stages diversifying the scope of social and cultural initiatives.'[73] Stages diversifying the social and cultural are surely to be identified with the factors bringing about shifts in the meaning of social and cultural terms. And, obviously, an underlying cause of the shifts, these stages are the more fundamental of the two factors.

This analysis is now applied to religion.

> [W]ithin these varying social and cultural contexts ... religion discovers itself, works out its identity, differentiates itself from other areas, and interacts with them. But in its linguistic stage religion will manifest itself as myth and ritual. In its literate stage it becomes religion of the book, of the Torah, the Gospel, the Koran. In the logical stage it may reduplicate itself with the reflection on itself that would end dissension by dogmatic pronouncements and would seek overall reconciliation by systematic theologies. In the methodical stage it confronts its own history, distinguishes the stages in its own development, evaluates the authenticity or unauthenticity of its initiatives, and preaches its message in the many forms and styles appropriate to the many social and cultural strata of the communities in which it operates.[74]

The analysis that applies to religion in general is now illustrated by the history of Christianity, which 'began and spread through the words and deeds of Christ and his apostles. But by the end of the second century there had emerged an élite that studied the scriptures and read Irenaeus ... Hippolytus ... Tertullian ... Clement and Origen.'[75] So we have the transition from the linguistic to the literate stage. This literate stage leads 'into the logical stage' and a focus on truth. Of course, this did not await the third stage: one can find 'brief formulas of faith embedded in the New Testament,' that is, in the first stage itself, but the 'apologetics and controversy' of the second stage, as it were, forced the issue. So we have the several various councils with their condemnation of the several various heresies.[76]

73 Ibid. 140 [406].
74 Ibid. 140–41 [406].
75 Ibid. 141 [406].
76 Ibid. 141 [407].

The next transition is from uttering the truth to reaching some understanding of it. The trend began early but 'became the occupation of a large and ongoing intellectual community in medieval Scholasticism. The inspiration of Scholasticism was Anselm's faith seeking, though hardly attaining, understanding. Its schoolmaster was Abaelard's *Sic et non*. Its achievement was the collected works of Aquinas.' The promise, however, of its 'spontaneous method, stemming from the practice of *lectio et quaestio*,' was not fulfilled: it 'was led astray by the ineptitude of Aristotle's *Posterior Analytics*.' In this situation, Lonergan locates the Reformation and Council of Trent.[77]

True, the Reformation 'remained faithful to the Greek councils and so was committed to a logical stance and, in time, to a Scholasticism of its own.' Nevertheless

> Protestant insistence on scripture kept open a door. Through that door in due course there entered into scriptural studies the application of new, nineteenth-century methods to historical investigation and textual interpretation. So there came to light the differences between the mind of the scriptures and the mind of the councils, and there followed doubts that conciliar dogmas could be attributed to divine revelation.[78]

Lonergan finds three surrenders to this problem of the differences between scripture and the councils: 'nineteenth-century Liberal Protestantism ... early twentieth-century Modernism' and the movement 'in the wake of the Second Vatican Council when even Catholic theologians find the definition of Chalcedon questionable and wish to change both our traditional understanding of Christ and our profession of faith in Christ.'[79]

Perhaps it is time for a resume. The task was to incorporate the infinite riches of history without surrendering to relativism, to acknowledge history but to retain doctrines and systematics. A good summary of the problem was quoted from 'Time and Meaning': we want a thread to guide us through history, to enable us to avoid both the rigidity of classicism and the chaos of romanticism. There is the multiplicity of history to welcome, but there is the ordered multiplicity that comes

77 Ibid. 142 [407].
78 Ibid. 142–43 [408].
79 Ibid. 143 [408].

from an upper blade of empirical method. The upper blade, the ordering principle, is provided by a theory of the stages of history.

The problem, then, is the one that so many theologians have tried to deal with in the last hundred years: to combine changing history and permanent dogma, to have a view of things that is broad enough and deep enough and strong enough to allow one to acknowledge history and retain traditional faith. If Lonergan is found to have finally got it all together, to have succeeded in integrating history with doctrine and system, it will certainly be due to his twofold analysis: his analysis of the human mind and heart when it is thinking, understanding, judging, deciding, and his analysis of the human mind and heart when it is changing, developing, growing, responding to challenge.

Appendix A: Excerpt from Lonergan's Doctoral Dissertation*

First, the specific theorem is adverted to and analyzed: it is seen to explain something.

Second, the specific theorem is generalized: all parallel differences are considered and coordinated.

Third, its implications are worked out and there will be a tendency to give it the systematic significance of alone constituting the solution to the whole problem.

Fourth, the insufficiency of the specific theorem to account for the whole problem leads to the discovery of the generic theorem.

Fifth, the generic theorem is analyzed, generalized, has its implications worked out.

Sixth, there is a tendency to make the generic theorem serve as the full solution of the problem ...

Seventh, the insufficiency of the generic theorem is adverted to and there follows the rediscovery of the specific theorem in a new setting. This gives the synthesis of generic and specific theorem.

'The Gratia Operans Dissertation: Preface and Introduction,' *METHOD: Journal of Lonergan Studies* 3/2 (October 1985) 32–33. [*Grace and Freedom* (2000) 180].

Appendix B: Sources for Step Four, 1959–1962†

(For unpublished works see Lonergan Archives, Toronto)

De intellectu et methodo, 1958–59, documented in typed notes of Francesco Rossi de Gasperis and P. Joseph Cahill, and in some of Lonergan's own notes.

'Method in Catholic Theology,' *METHOD: Journal of Lonergan Studies* 10/1 (Spring 1992) 1–26, a paper before the Society for Theological

* See note 19 above.

† See note 34 above.

Studies, Nottingham University, April 1959 [*Papers 1958–1964* (1996) 29–53.]

Topics in Education, lectures at Xavier University, Cincinnati, August 1959, on the philosophy of education. [Vol. 10, *Collected Works of Bernard Lonergan* (1993).]

De systemate et historia, graduate course, Gregorian University, Rome, 1959–60, documented in the handwritten notes of Francesco Rossi de Gasperis and in some of Lonergan's own notes.

'The Philosophy of History,' lecture at Thomas More Institute, Montreal, 23 September 1960. [*Papers 1958–1964* (1996) 54–79.] (This lecture is not to be confused with the unpublished paper of the 1930s 'Philosophy of History,' mentioned in note 67 above.)

De Deo trino: Pars analytica, 1st edition (Rome: Gregorian University Press, 1961).

'The Origins of Christian Realism,' lecture at Regis College, Toronto (repeated elsewhere), 8 September 1961. [*Papers 1958–1964* (1996) 80–93.]

De argumento theologico ex sacra scriptura, notes for a faculty seminar, Gregorian University and Biblical Institute, Rome, May 1962.

De methodo theologiae, graduate course, Gregorian University, 1961–62.

'The Method of Theology,' 2-week institute covering the same ground as the previous entry, Regis College, Toronto, July 1962; tape-recording and transcription available.

'Time and Meaning,' *Bernard Lonergan: 3 Lectures* (Montreal: Thomas More Institute Papers, 1975) 29–54; lecture, Regis College, Toronto, 16 September 1962, and Thomas More Institute, Montreal, 25 September 1962. [*Papers 1958–1964* (1996) 94–121.]

'History' and 'Philosophy of History,' papers in the Lonergan Archives, Batch IX, File 7, sheaves a, e, f; to be dated, it seems, in the early 1960s.

Appendix C: Early Approaches to Differentiations*

Chapter 17 of *Insight* speaks of levels and sequences of expression (section 3.3), and declares, 'Development in general is a process from the

---

* See note 40 above.

undifferentiated to the differentiated' ([1957] 571, [1992] 594). But the focus is more on the levels of consciousness than on its differentiations, and when we come to the natural place for the latter to appear, the question is more of differentiations in writing than in consciousness: advertising, literary writing, scientific writing, philosophic writing ([1957] 568–71, [1992] 592–93). Further the term most favored is not differentiation but classification: 'It is a distinction that grounds not an actual but a potential classification' of levels and types of expression ([1957] 571, [1992] 594). Again, 'Because the classification is potential rather than actual ...' ([1957] 571, [1992] 594). And again, '... the problem of working out types of expression ... is to be met, not by assigning some static classification that claims validity for all time, but by determining the operators that relate the classifications relevant to one level of development to the classifications relevant to the next' ([1957] 572, [1992] 595).

Chapter 6 of *Insight* speaks of 'the differentiation of common sense' ([1957] 180, [1992] 203), but in the sense of the later 'brands' of common sense; the very fact that he uses the word here for varieties of common sense shows it has not yet acquired its technical meaning, for then common sense will be characterized as undifferentiated.

Topics in Education (lectures of 1959) provides more data on Lonergan's usage. But his usage has not yet jelled, and we have to keep our eye always on the context. In *Topics in Education* the immediate context is the human good, first as object, then as the developing subject. The human good as object divides into two chapters, first the invariant structure (Chapter 2), then differentials and integration (Chapter 3). Integration is achieved on four levels (73–78): undifferentiated common sense, differentiated common sense, classicism which is the pure development of intelligence, the Greek achievement, and fourthly, historical consciousness (a term, incidentally, receiving here what may be its first thematic treatment). Now the third level, classicism, 'involves the differentiation of consciousness' (75). Again, education is a differentiation of consciousness (116), and in Nicea there is a transition from the compact symbolic consciousness of the New Testament 'to a more enucleated theological consciousness expressed in the Greek Councils' (57–58).

How evaluate all this? I would say that 'differentiation' (like 'experience') is a term with a general sense that has a very wide application, that in this general sense it was at first applied both to the varieties of common sense and to common sense itself as a mode of knowing, that in both *Insight* and *Topics in Education* it has this general and rather fluid sense, but that later it became quite technical and was reserved for differentiations that went beyond common sense, which is now designated as undifferentiated. But the question needs more thorough research than I have given it here.

Appendix D: Positive Theology and Doctrines*

The transcendence of truth and the possibility of its transmission were central questions in Lonergan's long struggle to relate positive or historical theology to the traditional speculative or systematic theology of the type created by Thomas Aquinas. High points in the struggle are recorded in 'Theology and Understanding' (see note 6 above) in *Collection* (1967) 137–39 [(1988) 128–30]; *De constitutione Christi ontologica et psychologica* (Rome: Gregorian University Press, 1956) 42–43 [*The Ontological and Psychological Constitution of Christ*, vol. 7 of *Collected Works of Bernard Lonergan* (Toronto: University of Toronto Press, 2002) 76–79]; 'Method in Catholic Theology' (see Appendix B) 16–21; *De intellectu et methodo* (see notes 6 and 35 above) 13, 48, and 58–65 passim, especially 64; *De methodo theologiae* (see note 43 above) 48–60; *De Deo trino*, vol. 1 (1964) 5 note 1.

The last-named work begins to differentiate the functions of theology in a way that will be fully worked out in *Method in Theology* (see note 7 above), but the more difficult question was the relation of history to doctrines. Lonergan's earlier work stressed their interlocking characters (see especially 'Method in Catholic Theology') but he had not found a view that would release historical theology from its domination by dogma and allow it to grow according to its own nature. Nor could he effect this release till he had created the functional specialties of dialectic and foundations to join phase one, theology in indirect discourse (what Matthew said, what Athanasius said, etc.) to phase two, theology in direct discourse (what the theologian affirms). Without dialectic and foundations, historical theology 'becomes lost in the wilderness of universal history' ('Method in Catholic Theology,' *METHOD: Journal of Lonergan Studies* 10/1 [Spring 1992] 21 [*Papers 1958–1964* (1996) 51]) and falls prey to out-and-out historicism.

---

* See note 50 above.

All the pieces of the puzzle fell into place at once on that February day of 1965 when *Method in Theology* took sudden shape in Lonergan's mind. It must have been a 'eureka' experience of the first order.

Appendix E: Origin of Differentiations of Consciousness*

Chapter 6 of *Insight*, under the heading of patterns of experience, gives a good deal of background for the later and more precise notion of differentiations of consciousness.

Contrasting the infinite potentiality of human offspring with the fixed patterns of the animal, Lonergan remarks that the 'initial plasticity and indeterminacy' of the human child grounds 'the later variety' ([1957] 189, [1992] 213). And he adds quite a list of the factors that produce the variety: 'the locality, the period, the social milieu' ([1957] 187, [1992] 211); or again, the variation will depend 'upon native aptitude, upon training, upon age and development, upon external circumstances, upon ... chance' ([1957] 186, [1992] 209); or, still again, in the drama of life, each person will find and develop 'the possible roles he might play' ([1957] 188, [1992] 212); and yet again, 'the stream of sensitive experience is a chameleon' ([1957] 186, [1992] 209), while 'aesthetic liberation, artistic creativity, and the constant shifting of the dramatic setting open up vast potentialities' ([1957] 191, [1992] 214).

Some of these factors suppose certain differentiations to be already achieved, but it is easy to reduce them to originally given factors like locality, natural aptitude, and potentiality.

Appendix F: Excerpt from Philosopy of History†

Now the possibility of philosophy leads us to distinguish between two phases in human progress: the automatic stage in which there is a constant succession of brilliant flowerings and ultimate failures; the philosophic stage in which the historical expansion of humanity has its

* See note 64 above.

† See note 67 above.

ultimate goal in a sound philosophy that not only is sound but also is able to guide the expansion effectively.

Next, the actual course of human events divides this division once more into two sections. Hence we have:

A. The world prior to the discovery of philosophy, that is, up to Socrates, Plato and Aristotle.
B. The failure of philosophy to fulfil its social mission, that is, from Plato to the Dark Age.
C. The automatic cultural expansion following upon the Dark Age and continuing up to the present. It has had sound philosophy but no social consciousness of the social necessity of philosophy.
D. The future.

'Philosophy of History' (unpublished manuscript of the 1930s) 101–102.

Chapter 6

Lonergan's Universalist View of Religion[1]

The work under study in the fall 1994 issue of *METHOD: Journal of Lonergan Studies*, 'Philosophy and the Religious Phenomenon,' is one of a series of papers, some published, some unpublished, that Lonergan wrote on the topic of religion in the last years of his life.[2] Like most of the series, this paper maintains quite explicitly 'a universalist view of religion.'[3] That universalism, as Lonergan conceived it, is the central

1 Previously published in *METHOD: Journal of Lonergan Studies* 12/2 (1994) 125–46.

2 Other examples in *A Third Collection* are: 'Prolegomena to the Study of the Emerging Religious Consciousness of Our Time' (55–73); the three 'Lectures on Religious Studies and Theology' (111–65); and 'A Post-Hegelian Philosophy of Religion' (202–23).

Earlier papers that touch on religion, for example several in *A Second Collection*, are clear on the universal salvific will of God: 'Theology and Man's Future' 139, 146; 'The Future of Christianity' 155; 'The Response of the Jesuit as Priest and Apostle in the Modern World' 174. However, these papers do not use the term 'universalist.'

The term occurs in *A Third Collection*: 'universalist ... concern' in 'Prolegomena to the Study of the Emerging Religious Consciousness of Our Time' 69, and 'universalist movement' in 'The Ongoing Genesis of Methods' (the third of the series on 'Religious Studies and Theology') 159. Also note the idea in 'A Post-Hegelian Philosophy of Religion' 217–18.

The paper 'Faith and Beliefs' (see note 19 below) refers to the universalist aspect of faith: 1–2, 14–15 of the autograph MS (*Papers 1965–1980* [2004] 32, 42–43). 'Sacralization and Secularization' (a lecture at Trinity College, Toronto, November 1973; repeated with considerable revision, St. Thomas More Lectures, New Haven, February 1974; published in *Papers 1965–1980* [2004] 259–81) is on religion from beginning to end, and refers to various religions; but the argument does not call for a position on the universalist question.

3 'Philosophy and the Religious Phenomenon,' *METHOD: Journal of Lonergan Studies* 12/2(1994) 135 (*Papers 1965–1980* [2004] 401).

theme of my article; but I need a preface to determine exactly what Lonergan meant by the 'religion' of which he takes such a view, and I need a sequel for his position on the closely connected question of Christianity in the context of universalist religion. The result is something like a sandwich, with much more space given to the difficult first and third sections (especially the third), and much less to the relatively clear central theme.

1 Religion

What, then, does Lonergan mean by 'religion' in the present context? It is not any of the institutional religions with their expressed beliefs and codes of conduct, their rituals and customs. As numerous passages to be cited will show, that is exactly what is not universal. Rather, it is all superstructure and, while 'religion' is regularly and legitimately used for the superstructure, Lonergan would go behind it to an infrastructure that is to be understood in reference to his sharply defined use of 'experience' – and in the present case, 'religious experience.'

Experience is used, by Lonergan and everyone else, in a very general sense of knowledge: a person of experience is one who 'has long been engaged in some trade or profession, some art or craft, and has come to possess a full and balanced knowledge of the ins and outs of his way of life.'[4] But Lonergan has his own technical sense, in which experience is an element in the compound of experience, understanding, and judgment, three constituents which together result in knowledge. To get back to pure experience in this sense, we must go behind questions and ideas with regard to the data, go behind description of the data, go behind even the word 'experience,' for all that is superstructure.[5]

Religious experience is conceived in this same precisely defined sense. Lonergan refers to the work of William Johnston, who 'advances to an area that, as experience, is common to East and West, morally uplifting, cosmic in orientation but, when interpreted, takes on the distinctiveness of diverse traditions'; advances, that is, to an infrastructure that has not yet been 'incorporated within an interpretative suprastruc-

4 'Prolegomena to the Study of the Emerging Religious Consciousness of Our Times,' in *A Third Collection* 57.

5 Ibid. Lonergan would agree that, except in the early life of the infant, experience is rarely, if ever, 'pure,' and would not in any case be observable in the pure state.

ture.'[6] He also refers here to the work of Raimundo Panikkar, and in a later paper returns to Panikkar's view that if we want a theology 'that has its ground free from the influence of particular places and times, particular cultures and viewpoints, we have to have recourse to the wordless prayer of the mystics representing the world religions.'[7]

Can we form a more positive view of this religious experience? There is language for it, in Christianity as in other religions, and I will collect some of the descriptions Lonergan uses, but with the reminder that in using language we are on the level of superstructure, and are merely pointing to an infrastructure that ceases, as soon as it is named, to be pure religious experience.

The *locus classicus* for Lonergan's views on religion and religious experience is Chapter 4 of his *Method in Theology*, entitled simply 'Religion.'[8] But, since this chapter is strikingly different from what he published fifteen years earlier in *Insight* on the notion and existence of God (Chapter 19, 'General Transcendent Knowledge'),[9] and seems, if we know only *Insight* and *Method in Theology*, to have come out of the blue, it may be helpful to indicate its antecedents.

Religious experience was, in fact, an integral part of Lonergan's theology before the publication of either *Method in Theology* or *Insight*. His early attitude may seem rather negative, but that is explained by the context: his opposition to a modernist view that opposed religious experience to dogma.[10] A more positive view is found in the *Verbum* articles of the late 1940s,[11] and soon after entered his theological

6 Ibid. 67.

7 'A Post-Hegelian Philosophy of Religion,' in *A Third Collection* 218. The question of pure experience now becomes the question of pure religious experience: does it occur? Since, as we shall see, it is the pure gift of God, we can hardly deny the possibility. If God wishes to give the pure gift of love 'without an intellectually apprehended object' (see text below, at note 66), who is to say, 'You can't do that; the gift must be historically conditioned'? It is true that any objectification of the gift, even internal to oneself, any attempt to express the gift is historically conditioned; but differences here do not disprove a pure common experience, except in a philosophy that makes language prior to internal acts – certainly not Lonergan's position.

8 *Method in Theology* 101–24.

9 *Insight* (1957) 634–86 [(1992) 657–708].

10 For example, *The Way to Nicea* 129–30, where Lonergan opposes a 'disjunction between religious experience ... and hellenistic ontology' (see the whole section, 127–37). Also see *Insight* (1957) 733 [(1992) 756].

11 *Verbum* (1967) 92 [(1997) 102–103]. Also see note 34 below.

method as a structural element. Thus a letter of 1954 puts the matter in this brief formula: religious experience is to theology and theology is to dogma as potency is to form and form is to act.[12] This succinct and very precise statement makes religious experience an essential element in Lonergan's theological thinking. An article written around the same time relates the abstract formula of the letter to the history of Christian thought. The documents of tradition, it says, are the product of a mind 'that conceived and judged not in the objective categories of Scholastic thought but in the more spontaneous intersubjective categories of ordinary human experience and ordinary religious experience.'[13]

Up to this time, however, Lonergan's interest was focused on theology within the Roman Catholic church. It was almost certainly the Second Vatican Council that widened the range of his interests; for he speaks, as stemming from that council, of the church's 'concern with ecumenism, with non-Christian religions, and with the atheist negation of religion.'[14] One surmises that his own concern had the same origin. At any rate, from 1967 on there is recurring mention of religious studies in their relation to the human enterprise and to theology in particular.[15] The universalist theme begins to be considered not just in relation to Catholic doctrines, but in relation to empirical studies of religion.[16] On the latter point, 'Theology and Man's Future' is explicit: 'Finally, there is the theological doctrine that God grants all men sufficient grace for their salvation. This doctrine is relevant to religious studies; it makes them studies of the manifold ways God's grace comes to men ...'[17] It is

12 Letter of 5 May 1954, to F.E. Crowe. I have substituted words for Lonergan's mathematical symbols.

13 'Theology and Understanding,' in *Collection* (1967) 136 [(1988) 127 (original publication, *Gregorianum* 35 [1954] 630–48)]. One may mention also a paper, 'Openness and Religious Experience,' that Lonergan wrote a few years later: see *Collection* (1967) 198–201 [(1988) 185–87]. Also see note 20 below.

14 'Theology and Man's Future,' in *A Second Collection* 138, a paper of October 1968. This same trio of new interests was listed the previous year in 'Theology in Its New Context,' in *A Second Collection* 62. A curious result of coming simultaneously to these new concerns is that Lonergan, leaping in one bound to both ecumenism and the wider ecumenism, concentrated on the latter and never gave the same attention to relations between churches that he gave to relations between religions.

15 'Theology in Its New Context,' in *A Second Collection* 62–63. See also 'The Absence of God in Modern Culture,' ibid. 107; 'Theology and Man's Future,' ibid. 138; etc.

16 'Theology and Man's Future,' ibid. 146; 'The Future of Christianity,' ibid. 156.

17 'Theology and Man's Future,' ibid. 139.

in this period too that more attention is paid to Christianity in relation to 'the other world religions.'[18] A very useful work in which the several features of this new direction are set forth is the unpublished paper 'Faith and Beliefs.'[19]

I shall return to these papers when I deal directly with the universalist theme. At the moment I simply note that Chapter 4 of *Method in Theology* does not appear suddenly out of nowhere but had been in preparation since Vatican II, and further that it has antecedents that go back some twenty-five years.[20] This gives a better perspective from which to examine what *Method in Theology* has to say on religion and religious experience.

I begin with a statement found not in Chapter 4 but in Chapter 13: 'an orientation to transcendent mystery ... provides the primary and fundamental meaning of the name, God.'[21] Here we have the two poles: God

---

18 'The Future of Christianity,' ibid. 155–63.

19 'Faith and Beliefs' was a lecture at a plenary session of the American Academy of Religion, October 1969 (there is an inaccuracy in the program listing of the title), with Wilfred Cantwell Smith and Herbert Richardson as respondents. Extant in the Archives are Lonergan's autograph MS of 23 pages, and what seems to be a retyping by William Shea (13 pages, single-spaced), the latter with a transcription from the tape-recording of the discussion between Lonergan and Smith (pp. 13–15). My references will be to the autograph. It has been published in *Papers 1965–1980* [2004] 30–48.

I should add here that, while the various references in notes 14 to 19 do indicate a new focus in Lonergan's interest in world religions and an increased concern to take account of what God is doing through them, we may not conclude that he had no interest at all in such questions before the Second Vatican Council. In fact, his interest goes back at least to 1954, when he discovered Mircea Eliade (letter of 5 May 1954, to F.E. Crowe).The discovery occurred in time for him to insert a footnote in *Insight* ([1957] 549, [1992] 572) before it went to the printer; references to Eliade are regular from that time on; see two examples in note 53 below.

20 I would assign an important mediating role to 'Openness and Religious Experience.' Written for a 1960 congress, when Lonergan's Latin theology had nearly reached its term, it still precedes the new interest generated by Vatican II.

The paper was requested, and Lonergan's short response (just a series of headings, his opening remark suggests) provides clues on the relation of nature and grace. It relates the enlargements of human consciousness to the pure desire to know and speaks of the ultimate enlargement 'when the subject knows God face to face' (*Collection* [1967] 200, [1988] 186–87). It declares the fundamental place religious experience holds in the process that is 'man's making of man' and in the philosophy that reflects on the process (*Collection* [1967] 201, [1988] 187). However, it does not take up religious experience directly.

21 *Method in Theology* 341.

and the religious subject. But we also have the mediating factor, which is located not in experience of God but in orientation to transcendent mystery. We shall see presently that Lonergan does not speak of religious experience as 'experience of God' or make God an object of ordinary experience. Still less does this orientation to mystery make God an object in the sense of 'anything that is intended in questions and known through correct answers, anything within the world mediated by meaning.'[22] On the contrary, orientation to transcendent mystery 'is the principle that can draw people out of that world and into the cloud of unknowing.'[23] What is immediately called for is not thought or words: 'Man's response to transcendent mystery is adoration.'[24]

Still, 'withdrawal is for return,' and we can reflect on our prayer.[25] For 'adoration does not exclude words.'[26] There are the words that describe the experience: 'a conscious dynamic state of love, joy, peace, that manifests itself in acts of kindness, goodness, fidelity, gentleness, and self-control'; 'it is an experience of mystery ... the mystery evokes awe ... the gift of God's love is an experience of the holy.'[27] 'Ordinarily the experience of the mystery of love and awe is not objectified. It remains within subjectivity as a vector, an undertow, a fateful call to a dreaded holiness.'[28] There is another set of words by which we name God, whether it be that word 'God' with which most of us associate from childhood our religious experience, or words like 'absolute intelligence and intelligibility, absolute truth and reality, absolute goodness and holiness,'[29] with which some of us try to relate God to the words and meanings and ways of thinking that philosophy has taught us.

Such in brief is Lonergan's view of religion and religious experience, expressed by a Christian, and held in virtue of a Christian faith. It is not his main purpose here to provide a language in which to speak to non-Christians, but he does attempt, I believe, to use terms that would

22 Ibid.
23 Ibid. 342.
24 Ibid. 344.
25 Ibid. 342.
26 Ibid. 344.
27 Ibid. 106.
28 Ibid. 113. Also see 240–41: 'It [religious conversion] is revealed in retrospect as an under-tow of existential consciousness, as a fated acceptance of a vocation to holiness, as perhaps an increasing simplicity and passivity in prayer.'
29 Ibid. 116.

get behind Christian language to something common. By definition that is impossible: what is common is God's pure gift and what it does to human consciousness; and as we cease to reflect on this, as our experience approaches the purity of its infrastructure, it becomes wordless. Still, we must talk, even the mystics do that (if only in obedience to a spiritual director), and so we continue to attempt the impossible.

There is another avenue besides language to explore. As pure experience is wordless, so there is a wordless human intentionality that reveals itself more radically in performance than in terms and concepts, and we can set religion in that context. This common way of performing appears in the very effort we make to talk to one another. If we do not make that effort, there is no problem to discuss; if we do make it, we implicitly acknowledge something common in our performance.

At any rate Lonergan relates his view to the innate dynamism of human consciousness which carries us from level to level in a pattern I have already indicated in speaking of knowledge as a compound. There is the level of experience (in Lonergan's technical sense), with the dynamism producing questions for intelligence and issuing in ideas and concepts. This lifts us to the next level, where the dynamism produces questions for reflection and leads to judgments and knowledge. The same insatiable dynamism next asks questions for deliberation leading to a choice of values and decisions. (I have used words to describe our common intentionality, but intelligence, which is not bound by words, can discern what I am doing, and others may find in their own performance what I describe in those words.)

The goal sought in all its activity by the dynamism of human consciousness is self-transcendence, but there are steps in its attainment: for example, 'cognitional self-transcendence in his judgments of fact and moral self-transcendence in his judgments of value.'[30] The steps are not always taken without the shattering experience of conversion, especially the third step.

> Intellectual conversion is to truth attained by cognitional self-transcendence. Moral conversion is to values apprehended, affirmed, and realized by a real self-transcendence. Religious conversion is to a total being-in-love as the efficacious ground of all self-transcendence, whether in the

30 Ibid. 45.

> pursuit of truth, or in the realization of human values, or in the orientation man adopts to the universe, its ground, and its goal.[31]

Lonergan distinguishes capacity for self-transcendence – revealed in the spontaneity of our questions for intelligence, for reflection, and for deliberation – and the realization of the capacity. 'That capacity becomes an actuality when one falls in love': love of intimacy, love of all the members of our human race, love of God.

> Being in love with God, as experienced, is being in love in an unrestricted fashion. All love is self-surrender, but being in love with God is being in love without limits or qualifications or conditions or reservations. Just as unrestricted questioning is our capacity for self-transcendence, so being in love in an unrestricted fashion is the proper fulfilment of that capacity.[32]

Thus, we are in the grip of two complementary forces. On one side there is the gift of God's love,[33] the effect of which, prior to all images and reflection, is orientation to mystery, the response to which is adoration. On the other side there is the spontaneous intentionality of human spirit, starting from experience, asking endless questions, and seeking a good beyond criticism, intentionality therefore as human capacity for religion, reaching up toward love of God.

I do not wish to overload this first section with detail, but two further points deserve attention: the relation of the exact empirical sciences to religion, and the relation of religious experience to Chapter 19 of *Insight*.

The first question is raised by present media interest. Someone orbits the earth and returns from 'space' to report that he did not find God out there; others carry physical science to the limit and report that they did find God there. From Lonergan's viewpoint the first statement has more validity, but the second is of greater interest. We do not expect to find God in space travel, but neither should we appeal to the sciences,

31 Ibid. 241; see also 104–106 on cognitive, moral, and total self-transcendence. To be noted: religious conversion is not conversion to a church, or even to a religion, but to God.

32 Ibid. 105–106.

33 'That fulfilment is not the product of our knowledge and choice. On the contrary, it dismantles and abolishes the horizon in which our knowing and choosing went on and it sets up a new horizon in which the love of God will transvalue our values and the eyes of that love will transform our knowing' (*Method in Theology* 106).

natural or human, for a doctrine on God. Science works with data, and there are no data on God. As for deductions from the data, the situation has changed since the time of Aristotle, who introduced no logical break between knowledge of this world and knowledge of ultimate causes. While modern science 'still speaks of causes, what it means is not end, agent, matter, form, but correlation.' Correlations are verified within this world. Modern science 'is knowledge of this world and only of this world. It proceeds from data and to data it adds only verifiable hypotheses. But God is not a datum of human experience ... Again, between this world and God there is no relationship that can be verified, for verification can occur only between data ... there are no data on the divine itself.'[34] In other words metaphysics is not just 'meta' as another part of a book; it is 'meta' as a new genus in thought:

> [T]here are defects of intelligibility in the existing world, and those defects are universal. They cannot be eliminated by any possible development of science in the ordinary sense, that is, science that does not go on to raise metaphysical questions. There is no technique or method of obtaining from physics or chemistry or biology or any other similar science an answer to the question, Why should there be anything at all? A thing is, in fact, because it is a virtually unconditioned; its conditions have been in fact fulfilled. You can explain it provisionally by saying that *this* is because *that* is. But why is *that*? As long as you stay within the limits of the world of your experience, you do not get beyond the virtually unconditioned, beyond that which happens to be because its conditions are fulfilled.[35]

I cannot develop the point here, but it had to be made, for a confusion of physics and metaphysics leaves a gap in human knowledge that invites a gnosticism of pseudo-explanation. As Lonergan wrote in

---

34 'Belief: Today's Issue,' in *A Second Collection* 94–95. See also ibid. 107, in 'The Absence of God in Modern Culture': 'The divine is not a datum to be observed by sense or to be uncovered by introspection'; and 120, in 'Natural Knowledge of God': '... there are no data on the divine. God is not among the data of sense and he is not among the data of human consciousness.'

This is said, however, of ordinary experience and ordinary religious experience. Lonergan seems to have held from early on that in the mystics there is 'an awareness of God' and, though his terminology was not fully worked out at the time, I would equate this with the later use of 'experience.' See *Verbum* (1967) 92 [(1997) 102–103] and the *Verbum* Index on 'Awareness.'

35 *Understanding and Being* (1980) 300–301 [(1990) 243–44].

Insight of an analogous situation: 'It is through this gap that there proudly march the speculative gnostic and the practical magician.'[36] I doubt that we have much to fear today from the practical magician. We are far too pragmatic, too sophisticated, to rely on practices we know will not work: we are not about to revert to alchemy. Gnosticism is another matter: ideas are ersatz in origin and, if taken for knowledge, provide a truth that is too cheaply purchased. When verification is in the nature of the case impossible, what gnostics claim to verify will turn out to be a god reduced to the dimensions of science. That is impossible with the God of Chapter 19 of *Insight*, but this can be understood only in understanding the difference between the 'is' of affirmation and the verification procedures of science.[37]

---

36 *Insight* (1957) 542 [(1992) 565].

37 This is a long story in Lonergan's thought, involving his early metaphysics. In terms of potency, form, and act of existence (the components of any being that is proportionate to our understanding), what is intelligible is the *quidditas rei materialis*, with form as directly intelligible, potency intelligible only as limit to form, and existence intelligible only in its dependence on a necessary being (*De ente supernaturali: Supplementum schematicum* [Toronto: Regis College edition available in photocopy, 1973; ed. Frederick E. Crowe, Conn O'Donovan, Giovanni Sala] 64; originally notes for students, 1946). See also *Verbum* (1967) 193 [(1997) 200]: '... contingent existence is not intelligible in itself but only in its relation to the necessarily Existent ...' More fully in 'A Note on Geometrical Possibility,' in *Collection* (1967) 107–108 [(1988) 102].

Now this pattern is found in scientific thinking: 'by verification the scientist knows contingent existence, by theories he knows essences and forms, and by appealing to instances he acknowledges matter as well as form and existence' ('Isomorphism of Thomist and Scientific Thought,' in *Collection* [1967] 146, [1988] 137). But the Being whose essence is to be is not proportionate to our understanding, and so a different kind of intelligibility is operative in the transition from this world to its Creator; see *Understanding and Being* (1980) 300–301 [(1990) 243–44] (just now quoted in our text).

On the difference between verification and true knowledge of what is, see 'Questionnaire on Philosophy,' *METHOD: Journal of Lonergan Studies* 2/2 (October 1984) 25–26 (*Papers 1965–1980* [2004] 376):

> [V]erification falls short of proof: for in verification the argument runs, not from affirming the hypothesis to affirming its implications, but from affirming the verified implications, to affirming the hypothesis. Such an argument is cogent if and only if the hypothesis in question is the only possible hypothesis; and proof of such unique possibility commonly is not available.

This explains the rather cryptic remark in 'Natural Knowledge of God': 'I should like to see greater attention paid by certain types of analytic philosophy to the notable gaps between an observation and a process of verification and, on the other hand, true and certain knowledge' (*A Second Collection* 125).

This leads directly to my second point, which can be made very briefly. It concerns the relation of religious experience to Chapter 19 of *Insight*. In my view they are in direct continuity, with the continuity that exists between believer and philosopher in their search for God, with the continuity that a mystery loved as God's gift has with a mystery humanly understood to be mystery. 'Why is there something and not nothing?' the philosophers ask.[38] This is not a question on the intelligibility of data, it is a question on the intelligibility of 'is'; and that raises the question of God and points to mystery. This is the same mystery to which we are oriented in religious experience, and when the two are found in one person, the philosophic mystery becomes the intellectual component of the religious mystery: their identity is realized in consciousness.[39]

2 Lonergan's Universalist Position on Religion

In this central section I examine Lonergan on the fact of a universalist faith and religion, the extent of the fact (just how universal is his 'universal'?), and the grounds for asserting the fact, which divide into the a priori of Lonergan's own tradition and the a posteriori of the empirical evidence. The three topics are not always distinguished in his discus-

38 Often quoted from Martin Heidegger, and attributed to him as source (for his discussion, see the first chapter of his *An Introduction to Metaphysics*, 'The Fundamental Question of Metaphysics' [New Haven and London: Yale University Press, 1959] 1–51); but Étienne Gilson traces the question to Leibniz (see his *God and Philosophy* [New Haven: Yale University Press, 1941] 138–39, and *Elements of Christian Philosophy* [New York: Doubleday & Co., 1960] 164–65; in neither work, however, does Gilson give the precise location). In Leibniz's writings, the question 'Why does something exist rather than nothing?' occurs in §7 of *Principles of Nature and Grace, Founded on Reason* (see Gottfried Wilhelm Leibniz, *The Modalology and Other Philosophical Writings*, trans. R. Latta [London: Oxford University Press, 1898] 415). Lonergan surely had this fundamental question of metaphysics in mind in his own formulation, 'Why should there be anything at all?' (just now quoted in our text, from *Understanding and Being* [1980] 300, [1990] 244).

39 My language here is philosophic but the process described is an everyday one. As *Insight* has it: '... because it is difficult to know what our knowing is, it also is difficult to know what our knowledge of God is. But just as our knowing is prior to an analysis of knowledge and far easier than it, so too our knowledge of God is both earlier and easier than any attempt to give it formal expression' (*Insight* [1957] 683, [1992] 705). The point is made again twenty years later in *Philosophy of God, and Theology* (1973) 55–56 (*Papers 1965–1980* [2004] 208).

sion, and some overlapping is therefore involved in ours. Pedagogically I have found it simpler to begin with the grounds, for they determine the full extent of 'universal.'

Lonergan himself, in 'Philosophy and the Religious Phenomenon,' describes two approaches to the universalist position.[40] One is the familiar Roman Catholic doctrine (it was gradually made clear and explicit in the 1800s and is accepted without question in the 1900s) that since God wills everyone to be saved,[41] then everyone is given sufficient grace to be saved.

In what does that grace consist? That is the question. Lonergan argues that it includes love, and in this way he ties it to his anthropology (intentional dynamism, self-transcendence realized in love). But his argument is brief in the extreme. At first he simply said, 'it is difficult to suppose that grace would be sufficient if it fell short of the gift of loving God above all and loving one's neighbor as oneself.'[42] Two years later he expands the argument slightly.

> [A]ccording to the thirteenth chapter of the first epistle to the Corinthians, charity is necessary for salvation. Again, by common consent, charity is sufficient for salvation. But, as theologians argue from the first epistle to Timothy ... God wills all men to be saved. Accordingly, he wills to give them all the necessary and sufficient condition for salvation. It follows that he gives all men the gift of his love, and so it further follows that there can be an element in all the religions of mankind that is at once profound and holy.[43]

But Lonergan, as far as I know, never felt it necessary to develop this

---

40 'Philosophy and the Religious Phenomenon' 135 (*Papers 1965–1980* [2004] 401).

41 1 Timothy 2:4.

42 'The Response of the Jesuit as Priest and Apostle in the Modern World,' in *A Second Collection* 174. Lonergan admits that the 'common opinion of theologians that God gives everyone sufficient grace for salvation' does not include the further step of equating this grace with the gift of charity (unpublished question sessions at the Lonergan Workshop, Boston College, 1977, page 19 of transcript by Nicholas Graham). Sometimes he does not look for a theological argument, but simply turns to the empirical approach: 'That this grace does include ... the gift of God's love, may be inferred, I think, from Prof. Heiler's account of the seven areas common to all the high religions' ('The Future of Christianity,' in *A Second Collection* 155).

43 *Philosophy of God, and Theology* 10 (*Papers 1965–1980* [2004] 170).

argument, and in 'Philosophy and the Religious Phenomenon' he seems simply to suppose '...that those God wills to save will be given the charity described in the thirteenth chapter of the first letter to the Corinthians ...'[44]

The appeal to the divine universal salvific will is straightforward Roman Catholic doctrine. This supplies the real ground for Lonergan's personal adherence to the universalist position, but he could not suppose it to have cogency for others. As he said in his 1969 address to the American Academy of Religion, after asking whether 'universalist' should not extend beyond the world religions, 'As a theologian ... I must expect an affirmative answer; but as a mere theologian, I must leave the factual answer to students of the history of religions.'[45] We shall turn now to the empirical data, but it is good at this point to remind ourselves that basically he writes as a Christian to Christians, not as an ecumenist to non-Christians. From that perspective we have to take 'universal' as meaning just what it says, understanding always that we are talking of what is inmost and vital in the 'religion' of the religions, that is, of what lies behind superstructure and is religious experience as it comes in its purest state as the gift of God.

Lonergan's second approach, however, borrows from empirical studies of the many religions, to which he will add his own observations from time to time. With some caution he would appeal to Friedrich Heiler, who had 'listed seven features common to all the high religions ... I feel that he would recognize at least a rough equivalence between his seven features and what I have said of being in love with God.'[46] The caution is emphasized and the attitude made more specific a year later: 'For present purposes it will be best to regard Prof. Heiler's position not as an exhaustive empirical statement on the world religions but as an ideal type or model, that is, neither a description nor an hypothesis but a heuristic and expository device open to all the additions and modifications that empirical investigation may dictate.'[47]

44 'Philosophy and the Religious Phenomenon' 135 (*Papers 1965–1980* [2004] 401).

45 'Faith and Beliefs' 14 (*Papers 1965–1980* [2004] 42).

46 'Theology and Man's Future,' in *A Second Collection* 146.

47 'Faith and Beliefs' 22, n. 7 (*Papers 1965–1980* [2004] 40–41 n. 25). This parallels very exactly Lonergan's use of Arnold Toynbee on history, namely, caution in accepting Toynbee's empirical side, with esteem for his 'ideal types' as tools of thought: 'Toynbee thought he was contributing to empirical science. Since then, however, he has recanted. But, I believe, his work remains a contribution not to knowledge of reality,

Heiler continues to be quoted on the seven common areas,[48] but in 'Prolegomena to the Study of the Emerging Religious Consciousness of Our Time' Lonergan turns for support on the empirical side to Panikkar and Whitson,[49] and in the paper we are studying now he simply appeals to them and others without developing the point.[50]

Generally, in referring to these empirical studies, Lonergan has in mind the high world religions, but sometimes he goes a good deal further. Thus, in 'Faith and Beliefs' he first set forth his position 'that a basic component of religious involvement among Christians is God's gift of his love,' then went on to argue 'that the same may be said of religious involvement in all the world religions, in Christianity, Judaism, Islam, Zoroastrian Mazdaism, Hinduism, Buddhism, Taoism' (appealing again to Heiler), and finally adds the rather startling question: 'But may one not extend this view to the more elementary forms of religion? Can one not discern in them the harvest of the Spirit that is love, joy, peace, kindness, goodness, fidelity, gentleness, and self-control (Gal 5, 22)?' We have seen his answer: as a theologian, yes; as a mere theologian, he leaves the matter to students of the history of religions.[51]

On other occasions, however, he does not leave the matter there.

---

not to hypotheses about reality, but to the ideal types that are intelligible sets of concepts and often prove useful to have to hand when it comes to describing reality or to forming hypotheses about it' ('Dialectic of Authority,' in *A Third Collection*, 10; also passim in that volume – see the Index, under 'Toynbee').

48 In *Method in Theology* 109; also in the late paper 'A Post-Hegelian Philosophy of Religion' (1980), in *A Third Collection* 217.

49 *A Third Collection* 55–73; see esp. 65–70. But Lonergan's acceptance of Panikkar is qualified. In a paper of 1973 ('Variations in Fundamental Theology,' Trinity College, Toronto; repeated with changes, 1974, St Thomas More Lectures, New Haven), he states that 'the preverbal and, indeed, preconceptual foundation of theology proposed by Fr Panikkar [intends to be a common starting point. Insofar as one starts from it and moves towards Christ it] corresponds to the foundational reality in chapter eleven of *Method*, a reality conceived by Christians in terms of St Paul's statement: "God's love has flooded our inmost hearts through the Holy Spirit he has given us" (Romans 5:5)' (*METHOD: Journal of Lonergan Studies* 16/1 [1998] 24; (*Papers 1965–1980* [2004] 258).

I have not noticed a similar qualification in Lonergan's use of Whitson, and perhaps Robert Doran (see note 99 below) is right in suggesting that I could stress their agreement more than I do.

50 'Philosophy and the Religious Phenomenon' 135–36 (*Papers 1965–1980* [2004] 401).

51 'Faith and Beliefs' 12–14 (*Papers 1965–1980* [2004] 40–42).

Indeed one might say that he strikes out on his own and casts his net beyond all religions to include the human race, as when he remarks that 'Christians ... can become so devoted to the Christian cause as to forget its subordination to the cause of mankind.'[52] Or when he makes God's gift of his love the basis for a universalist faith, and says of the latter: 'It does not presuppose any specific set of historical conditions. It can be bestowed on the members of any culture at any stage in its development'.[53] Or, finally, when he includes the 'unlearned' among those brought to God by love,[54] for this category applies to persons in their individuality more than does the category 'the members of any culture at any stage in its development.'

We may further note, returning to the religions, that Lonergan applied to them in a positive way the text 'By their fruits you shall know them.'[55] Thus he states (though rather tentatively): 'I am inclined to interpret the religions of mankind, in their positive moment, as the fruit of the gift of the Spirit, though diversified by the many degrees of social and cultural development, and distorted by man's infidelity to the self-transcendence to which he aspires.'[56]And so he could speak

---

52 'The Future of Christianity,' in *A Second Collection* 158.

53 'Faith and Beliefs' 15–16 (*Papers 1965–1980* [2004] 43). See also 'Sacralization and Secularization' 16 (15 in 1974 MS; *Papers 1965–1980* [2004] 269): 'Religions of the infrastructure [that is, those tied more closely to the world of immediacy] can, in principle, be as authentic and genuine as any, for I do not suppose that the grace of God is refused to certain stages in the unfolding of human culture yet granted to other stages.' Some years earlier Lonergan had appealed to the work of Eliade to suggest the 'possibility of mystical experience in the most primitive peoples, and of its having an influence on society' (*Topics in Education* 56–57). Indeed, he saw Eliade's work as pointing to a common humanity in us all: 'One can turn to the liturgists and the historians of religion to search, with Mircea Eliade, for a crosscultural language that is prior to manmade languages and independent of them' ('Dimensions of Meaning,' in *Collection* [1967] 263 [(1988) 242] – a lecture of 1965).

54 'This complete being-in-love ... is the efficacious reality that brings men to God despite their lack of learning or their learned errors' ('Natural Knowledge of God,' in *A Second Collection* 129).

55 Matthew 7:16. See 'Philosophy and the Religious Phenomenon,' *METHOD: Journal of Lonergan Studies* 12/2 (1994) 135 (*Papers 1965–1980* [2004] 401).

56 'The Response of the Jesuit as Priest and Apostle in the Modern World,' in *A Second Collection* 174. See ibid. 'Theology and Man's Future' 139: when we recognize God's will to save all, religious studies become 'studies of the manifold ways God's grace comes to men ...'; and 146: 'God gives all men sufficient grace for salvation. Nor is his grace without fruit.'

quite positively of the good in all religions: 'an element ... profound and holy.'[57]

A concrete instance of this, and a good index of his position, is his repeated reference to the statue of the Buddha: 'So you can have an experience of God's gift of his love ... It's an experience that you can see on the face of the Buddha.'[58] And, asked about the external expression of God's gift of his love: 'Did you ever see a statue of the Buddha?'[59] And again, 'anything affirmed is thereby objectified, and any objectification is a withdrawal from the ultimate solitude of the mystical state. The alleged atheism of the Buddhist may be, perhaps, the expression of non-objectivized experience.'[60] And yet again, 'The posture and, above all, the features of the Buddha at prayer radiate a serenity that reveals what might be meant by authenticity attained.'[61]

On infidelity to God's gift see also *Philosophy of God, and Theology* 54 [207]: 'No doubt, such experience [religious] takes many forms. No doubt, it suffers many aberrations. But it keeps recurring. Its many forms can be explained by the many varieties of human culture. Its many aberrations can be accounted for by the precariousness of the human achievement of authenticity.'

That aberrations occur among Christians too is a sad truism. But see 'Sacralization and Secularization' on primitive religions as more open 'to palpable idolatry and superstition, to orgiastic and cruel cults, even to the ritual murder of human sacrifice' (1973 MS: 16, 1974: 15; (*Papers 1965–1980* [2004] 269).

57 *Philosophy of God, and Theology* 10 (*Papers 1965–1980* [2004] 170); the context is the familiar one of God's salvific will for all. 'Accordingly, he wills to give them all the necessary and sufficient condition for salvation. It follows that he gives all men the gift of his love, and so it further follows that there can be an element in all the religions of mankind that is at once profound and holy.'

58 Interview with Lonergan, recorded and transcribed by Richard Renshaw (to whom our thanks), 18 January 1973, p. 10.

59 Interview of some professors and students from McMaster University, 6 February 1973, p. 10 of the transcript made by Nicholas Graham.

60 'Religious Commitment,' in Joseph Papin, ed., *The Pilgrim People* (Villanova, PA: Villanova University Press, 1970 [but the congress was held in 1971]) 62. On Buddha Lonergan refers to Ernst Benz and Friedrich Heiler, both in Mircea Eliade and Joseph M. Kitigawa, eds, *The History of Religions: Essays in Methodology* (Chicago: University of Chicago Press, 1959).

61 'Religious Experience,' in *A Third Collection* 123. Add a reference in the Question Sessions of the Boston College Lonergan Workshop, 1977, p. 10 in the transcript by Nicholas Graham. Also a most interesting connection that Lonergan makes in a list of what he would call the creative minority: 'the saints and mystics who, like the statue of Buddha, place before our eyes the spirit of prayer and adoration' ('Reality, Myth, Symbol,' in Alan M. Olson, ed., *Myth, Symbol, and Reality* [Notre Dame and London: University of Notre Dame Press, 1980] 34).

3 Christianity in the Context of Universalist Religion

It is one thing to say that religion as inner experience is a universal phenomenon, to go so far even as to claim that all institutional religions are of God; it is another to say that one of these particular institutional religions has a universal claim on the human race; it is a third to adopt both of these positions at once. That is the situation in which many Christians seem to find themselves today; their universalist view of religion, in the sense described for Lonergan, seems to be in conflict with counterclaims from the side of their own particular religion.

Jesus is the one mediator between God and the human race;[62] there is no other name under heaven given to us by which we may be saved;[63] we are to go out to the whole world and preach the good news to every creature;[64] in former times God spoke through prophets and in varied ways, now at the endtime God has spoken through the Son.[65] What is one to make of these claims if the universal salvific will of God is fulfilled through the gift of divine love to everyone, Christian and non-Christian, in world religions and in primitive religions, in reference to institutional religions or independently of institutions?

There is question here of what is called, in the terms commonly used, the absoluteness or the uniqueness of Christianity, or again, its finality as something not to be surpassed, or its normativity as criterion for judging other religions. This question, arising early in the twentieth century, took on new life recently and has been vigorously debated for a decade. Lonergan's active career was at an end before that happened, and as far as I know, he never took this question up expressly. He did, however, leave a wealth of material on the basis of which a 'Lonerganian' statement, in distinctively Lonergan terms, might be cautiously ventured. I will make a limited attempt in that direction; but first let me highlight some of the material that provides a basis for it.

I have multiplied these references, because it is clear that Lonergan felt a deep affinity with the Buddha, and one wonders why. Perhaps the theme of nonviolence would be worth studying here, for Lonergan abhorred the violence prevalent at this time in his church.

62 1 Timothy 2:5.

63 Acts 4:12.

64 Mark 16:15.

65 Hebrews 1:1–2.

3.1 Background Material

If we start with the love of God as the basic factor in all religion, the first thing to notice is that this does not of itself include knowledge of God.

> God's gift of his love is God's free and gratuitous gift. It does not suppose that we know God. It does not proceed from our knowledge of God. On the contrary I have maintained that the gift occurs with indeed a determinate content but without an intellectually apprehended object. Religious experience at its root is experience of an unconditioned and unrestricted being in love. But what we are in love with, remains something that we have to find out.[66]

This is fundamental Lonergan doctrine for all religious people and for all religions: we love an Unknown and need to find out what or whom we love.

It is not enough to find this out and give expression to it in the privacy of one's own interiority. We need also to give external expression to what we discover and come to believe. Thus, for Lonergan the gift of love is an inner word, and there is a need in human nature for a corresponding outer word by which we can communicate with one another. This need unfolds under three headings, though he did not always distinguish them. There is the need the community has to express for itself the religious experience its members share, and the need those members have individually to express to themselves their experience. There is, secondly, the need God has to speak a public word to accompany the personal gift of divine love. And thirdly, there is the need that God speak such a word as will manifest the full, unlimited extent of the divine love.

To start with the first heading, the community need for an outer

---

66 *Philosophy of God, and Theology* 50–51; see also pp. 38, 54 (*Papers 1965–1980* [2004] 204, 193, 207). The same idea is found in *Method in Theology*: 'God's gift of his love is free. It is not conditioned by human knowledge; rather it is the cause that leads man to seek knowledge of God' (283; see 340–41). And remarkably, it is found thirty years earlier in the articles on grace: 'The first act [of operative grace] does not presuppose any object apprehended by the intellect; God acts directly on the radical orientation of the will' (*Grace and Freedom* [1971] 124 [(2000) 128]; original publication in 1941–42).

word arises directly from our social nature, from the dominant role community plays in the life of even the most individualistic people: this need is found in religion too. That is, God's gift is given to many, but the many are one social body; its members need each other; they communicate; they share their interiority; they support one another; an outer word enables individual members to check their experience and its expression against that of others, and enables the community to build up a tradition for itself.[67]

The same point may be made in the context of religious conversion. Conversion 'occurs in the lives of individuals.' But 'it is not so private as to be solitary.' The many who are converted individually, and individually receive God's gift of love and the Spirit, 'can form a community to sustain one another in their self-transformation, and to help one another in working out the implications, and in fulfilling the promise of their new life.'[68]

---

67 The point is often repeated. *Method in Theology* 118–19 is the familiar locus, but it builds on what had been said earlier. For example, in 'Theology and Man's Future': 'Deeply hidden, intensely personal, this love [of God] is not so private as to be solitary. The Spirit is given to many, and the many form a community. The community endures over generations, spreads over different nations, adapts to cultural changes. It acquires a history of its origins, its development, its successes and failures, its happy strokes and its mistakes. Its failures and its mistakes becloud its witness, but they argue not for abolition of religion but for its reform' (*A Second Collection* 146). Lonergan agrees with Augustine that our hearts are restless till they rest in God. 'But what it is to rest in God is not easily known or readily understood. Though God's grace is given to all, still the experience of resting in God ordinarily needs a religious tradition for it to be encouraged, fostered, interpreted, guided, developed' (ibid.). Again, Christians who receive God's gift 'need one another to come to understand the gift that has been given them, to think out what it implies and involves, to support one another in their effort to lead Christian lives ... to be members of one another, to share with one another what is deepest in ourselves, to be recalled from our waywardness, to be encouraged in our good intentions' (ibid., 156–57, in 'The Future of Christianity'). And yet again, we need an outer word to balance the mystical and organizational aspects of human living (ibid. 157–59), to overcome the 'loveless isolation of individuals' (ibid. 159), to know what's happening in the gift we have received (*Caring about Meaning: Patterns in the Life of Bernard Lonergan*, ed. Pierrot Lambert, Charlotte Tansey, Cathleen Going [Montreal: Thomas More Institute, 1982] 235). And one last quotation: 'Without the visible mission of the Word, the gift of the Spirit is a being-in-love without a proper object; it remains simply an orientation to mystery that awaits its interpretation' ('Mission and the Spirit,' in *A Third Collection* 32).

68 'Theology in Its New Context,' in *A Second Collection* 65–66.

If we substitute more general terms wherever Lonergan uses Christian language, all that has been said would apply to any religion and especially to any of the world religions. There are of course the religious hermits, but hermits derive their way of life from a parent religion and live it on the margin of the parent. When Thomas Merton felt the need to live in his hermitage, he worked out a very rational relationship to the mother house, including even procedures for going there to take a shower. Lonergan's position, then, rests on what is basic in human nature, and has at least potential application to all religions.

My first heading had to do with an outer word by which any religious-minded community might express for itself its relation to God. My second heading has to do with God speaking an outer word of revelation to a community, by whatever means that might be done. Lonergan understood this through the analogy of a man and woman in love: as they need to express their love for one another, so God and a human community need to express openly their love for one another.

> If a man and woman were to love each other yet never avow their love, then they would have the beginnings of love but hardly the real thing. There would be lacking an interpersonal component, a mutual presence of self-donation, the opportunity and, indeed, the necessity of sustained development and growth. There would not be the steady increase in knowledge of each other. There would not be the constant flow of favors given and received, of privations endured together, of evils banished by common good will, to make love fully aware of its reality, its strength, its durability, to make love aware that it could always be counted on.[69]

---

69 'The Response of the Jesuit as Priest and Apostle in the Modern World,' in *A Second Collection* 173–74. See also *Method in Theology* 112–13: 'When a man and a woman love each other but do not avow their love, they are not yet in love. Their very silence means that their love has not reached the point of self-surrender and self-donation. It is the love that each freely and fully reveals to the other that brings about the radically new situation of being in love and that begins the unfolding of its life-long implications.' And ibid. 283: 'For being-in-love is properly itself, not in the isolated individual, but only in a plurality of persons that disclose their love to one another.' Likewise in the McMaster interview (note 59 above): a man and a woman who 'never avow their love ... are refusing themselves the development that that love could have if they were interacting and acknowledging their relation with one another' (7).

An analogy, of course, proves nothing. Its role is to serve understanding, not to establish a truth. Here it serves our understanding of God's reason for entering into the human world with a human word to take part in the human enterprise: 'words ... are the vehicles of meaning, and meaning is the stuff of man's making of man. So it is that a divine revelation is God's entry and his taking part in man's making of man.'[70]

Does this second aspect likewise apply to all religions? It seems that Lonergan is open to understanding it that way: 'There is a personal entrance of God himself into history, a communication of God to his people, the advent of God's word into the world of religious expression. Such was the religion of Israel. Such has been Christianity.'[71] Now to say that 'Such was the religion of A and B' is to speak of a type of religion that may be exemplified not only in A and B but also in C and D, and so on.

Another remark suggests the same conclusion: 'God's gift of his love has its proper counterpart in the revelation events in which God discloses to a particular people or to all mankind the completeness of his love for them.'[72] A 'particular people' could be the people of any religion, and 'all mankind' could be reached either through particular revelations to each religion, or through one revelation made to one religion but meant for the whole human race. As far as these statements go we might conclude either to one word of God spoken for everyone, or to various words of God spoken, one for Judaism, another for Islam, another for Hinduism, and so on.

Nevertheless, Lonergan was definite on what is specifically Christian.

> What distinguishes the Christian ... is not God's grace, which he shares with others, but the mediation of God's grace through Jesus Christ our Lord ... In the Christian ... God's gift of his love is a love that is in Christ

---

70 'Theology in Its New Context,' in *A Second Collection* 62. The theme of God's entering the human world to take part in the human enterprise is a familiar one in Lonergan: faith 'is admitting the possibility and acknowledging the fact that God could and did enter into the division of labor by which men come to know ...' ('Belief: Today's Issue,' ibid. 97). See also *Method in Theology* 119, to be quoted immediately in the text.

71 *Method in Theology* 119.

72 *Method in Theology* 283; the passage continues: 'For being-in-love ...,' as quoted in note 69 above.

Jesus. From this fact flow the social, historical, doctrinal aspects of Christianity.[73]

We come then to our third heading, to find the ultimate differentiating factor of Christianity pinpointed in Lonergan's address to the Catholic Theological Society of America (1977). The context was his familiar defense of the role of dogma, and his advice on what to do when old dogmatic formulas seem to have lost their meaning.

Personally I should urge that in each case one inquire whether the old issue still has a real import and, if it has, a suitable expression for that import be found. For example, at Nicea the real import was whether Christ, the mediator of our salvation, was a creature. Today many perhaps will be little moved by the question whether we have been saved by a creature or by God himself. But the issue may be put differently. One can ask whether God revealed his love for us by having a man die the

---

73 'The Future of Christianity,' in *A Second Collection* 156. On the face of it, Lonergan seems here to make Christ the mediator of grace for Christians only. But that is certainly not the position of his Christology, where Christ is called *fons omnis gratiae* and *mediator omnis gratiae;* see Lonergan, *De Verbo incarnato* (1964) 325: 'Gratia capitis est gratia Christi qua caput corporis sui mystici; ideoque est gratia secundum quam Christus est mediator, fons omnis gratiae ... Christus est mediator omnis gratiae quia dilectio Patris erga Filium aeternum extenditur (1) in Filium qua hominem, unde gratia Christi sanctificans, et (2) mediante Filio in filios adoptionis.' ['The "grace of the Head" is Christ's grace as Head of his mystical body, and so it is on the basis of this grace that Christ is the mediator, the fountain of every grace ... Christ is mediator of every grace because the Father's love towards the eternal Son is extended (1) to the Son as man (hence the sanctifying grace of Christ) and (2) to sons by adoption, by the mediation of the Son.'] The same mediation is found in Lonergan's Trinitarian theology; see his *De Deo trino* vol. 2 (1964) 239.

What Lonergan's view takes for granted is that mediation starts with God the Father, whose infinite love is the primary mediating agent. The present point was set forth in detail in 'The Mystical Body of Christ' (unpublished 'Domestic Exhortation'), a talk that Lonergan gave to his religious community, Toronto, November 1951. The pattern here corresponds to that of 'Theology and Praxis' (to be quoted at once in my text), where the meaning of the question whether we were saved by a creature or by a divine Son is found in the Father.

On what is distinctive of Christianity see also 'Bernard Lonergan Responds' (*Foundations of Theology: Papers from the International Lonergan Congress 1970*, ed. Philip McShane [Dublin: Gill and Macmillan, 1971; Notre Dame: University of Notre Dame Press, 1972] 233); *Philosophy of God, and Theology* 67 (*Papers 1965–1980* [2004] 217–18); and 'Sacralization and Secularization' (17 in 1973 MS, 16–17 in 1974; *Papers 1965–1980* [2004] 269–70).

> death of scourging and crucifixion? Or was it his own Son, a divine person, who became flesh to suffer and die and thereby touch our hard hearts and lead us to eternal life?[74]

This is a radical shift on the question of the divinity of Christ. Instead of focusing on Christ himself, our mediator with God, we focus on God showing in the sending of the Son the divine love God has for us, and showing it in the most heart-rending way by delivering up the only Son to death. Christ is seen as God's Isaac, with God's love the analogue for Abraham's obedience. But where a higher voice from heaven intervened to spare Abraham's Isaac, there is no higher voice to overrule God's love and save the divine Isaac. So God 'did not spare his own Son, but surrendered him for us all.'[75] And 'that is God's own proof of his love towards us.'[76] Here, in regard to this ultimate act of God, Lonergan comes to ultimate clarity on what is distinctive of Christianity.

Equally clear, and in no need of proof-texts, is his own personal adherence to Christ, and indeed to his Roman Catholic faith. Clear too is his position on the loyalty Christians and Catholics owe to their tradition. Some of his sharpest critiques are reserved for fellow-Catholics who seem to hedge their bets on the Council of Nicea and the divinity of Christ.[77]

There is no doubt either about his position on the universal import of Christianity.[78] A good index is his position to the end on the church's mission to preach the gospel. The last chapter of *Method in Theology* dealt with the church's mission to all peoples. A decade later his position was unchanged. In a paper of 1981, he wrote on the church's call 'to leap forward in its apostolic mission by preaching to mankind the liv-

---

74 'Theology and Praxis,' in *A Third Collection* 198. To be noted: God did not choose the cross for Jesus in arbitrary cruelty; the cross has its own mysterious rationale – but that is another matter.

75 Romans 8:32.

76 Romans 4:8; see 1 John 4:8–9.

77 One may note the curiosity that in *A Third Collection* one of the most outspoken papers on universalist religion (chap. 5) happens to be followed by a paper with an equally outspoken critique of fellow-Catholics on their Christology (chap. 6).

78 I speak of 'import,' choosing that neutral word instead of the 'claims' that a unique, normative, absolute, unsurpassable religion might make on the world. This is not to repudiate those claims, but rather to assert that a Lonerganian position will view the whole problem from a different perspective.

ing Christ.'[79] A year later, he wrote on the diversity of apostles needed 'to preach the gospel to all nations.'[80]

All this sounds rather uncompromising. Still it is not the whole story.

3.2 Christianity and Other Religions

So what should be our position on Christianity and other religions? There is an immediate practical question, and there is an ultimate factual question of the divine overarching purpose.

The immediate practical question regards our *modus operandi* in carrying out the church's mission. We are not to ride roughshod over the beliefs of others; we are to dialogue with the other religions, and not necessarily in our own terms. Speaking of the lack of a common style of religious thinking, and of the long-term approach to such a common style, Lonergan has this to say:

> [A]t the present time specific discussion of emerging religious consciousness has to proceed on the basis of some convention. If it is not to be merely generic, it has to adopt the formulation of some particular tradition at least as a temporary or momentary convention. Commonly this could be the formulation of the group that is carrying on the discussion or the one most relevant to the material being discussed.[81]

When Christianity is to provide the terms of discussion, we will speak of God's love flooding out hearts. But presumably Judaism, Islam, Hinduism, Buddhism, and other religions could be asked on parallel occasions to provide the terms, and then we must hold ours in abeyance.

There are scattered remarks in Lonergan on the way interdisciplinary and ecumenical and interreligious discussions should be carried on. They need to be brought together and studied in relation to his triad of dialectic, encounter, and dialogue. The move from conflict of statements to encounter of persons would be of particular importance for the present question, and not to overload this article with detail, I

79 'Pope John's Intention,' in *A Third Collection* 237.
80 'Unity and Plurality: The Coherence of Christian Truth,' ibid. 243.
81 'Prolegomena to the Study of the Emerging Religious Consciousness of Our Time,' ibid. 70.

suggest simply that what Lonergan has to say of the encounter of person with person might be adapted to the encounter of religion with religion. 'Encounter ... is meeting persons, appreciating the values they represent, criticizing their defects, and allowing one's living to be challenged at its very roots by their words and by their deeds.'[82]

But we have not yet tackled the real question of the ultimate divine purpose. To be open to dialogue is not to say it's all one with God whether we are Christian or Hindu; rather, it is to try to discover the divine purpose in its widest compass. To deal with that question I need to go back to still more general considerations, for it is not primarily a question of religions and their relationship, still less of their competing claims, but one of God's direction of universal history.

To begin, then, at the beginning, the matter is more in God's hands than in ours. Writing at the end of Chapter 20 of *Insight*, Lonergan offered this ray of hope to anyone laboring in the search for religious truth: 'Nor will he labor alone ... for the realization of the solution and its development in each of us is principally the work of God who illuminates our intellects ... who breaks the bonds of our habitual unwillingness to be utterly genuine ...'[83] This remark is not a bit of piety dragged in irrelevantly. Those who were privileged to attend Lonergan's courses on divine providence and grace will recognize it as intrinsic to and deeply representative of his thinking. Now such an orientation affects our question in a fundamental way. For to know that the matter is mainly in God's hands leads us to ask what the divine economy is for the running of the universe, and that question both checks a tendency to attribute excessive importance to our own responsibility and opens an avenue to a more humble exercise of the responsibility proper to our secondary role.

There is, first, the divine economy of the gift of the Spirit, inseparably linked with the gift of God's love. There is a huge and inexplicable gap here in the work of a great many theologians, who can discourse at length on religion and the religions without so much as a single mention of the Spirit, thus effectively ignoring half the divine input and ruling out of court half the available data.

---

82 *Method in Theology* 247.

83 *Insight* (1957) 730 [(1992) 751]. A similar point is made in the homely context of one's personal spiritual life: 'When you learn about divine grace you stop worrying about your motives; somebody else is running the ship' (*Caring about Meaning* 145).

The matter cries out for attention; for the Spirit is real, is really sent into the world, is really present among us, has a mission on earth as really distinct as the person of the Spirit is really distinct in the Godhead; and the potentiality of this divine fact for a theology of religion is disregarded by all except a minority of theologians.

Complementary to God's initiative in giving the Spirit, a fully awakened Christian sensitivity refuses to believe that billions of people, separated by thousands of miles and thousands of years from a gospel preacher, are to be condemned for not believing in Christ. In line with Lonergan's view I would maintain that through the Spirit given them they belong already to God's family.[84]

This does not eliminate the need of preaching the gospel. If God, in giving the Holy Spirit to the human race, nevertheless judged it necessary to send the Only-begotten to be one of us, then we have the strongest possible ground for continuing to preach the gospel, the ground namely of the very example of God. But equally if God can give the Spirit of Love, and yet with infinite patience keep the 'divine secret ... in silence for long ages,'[85] leaving millions of us without the gospel, then we seem to have two excellent clues to the working of divine providence, and two excellent directives on our manner of cooperating with the divine purpose in the exercise of our limited responsibility.

Our reflections have taken a fairly definite direction. The first two aspects of the divine economy, the mission of the Spirit as inner gift

---

84 Ten years ago I expressed my concern at the way theologians of religion neglect the role of the Spirit: *Son of God, Holy Spirit, and World Religions: The Contribution of Bernard Lonergan to the Wider Ecumenism* (Toronto: Regis College Press, 1984). This lecture was reprinted as chapter 19 in Michael Vertin's edition of my papers and articles, *Appropriating the Lonergan Idea* (Washington: The Catholic University of America Press, 1989) 324–43; see esp. 339 n. 26. My suggestion (ibid. 335–36, 339 n. 26) that 'anonymous Spiritans' is preferable in Christian conversation to 'anonymous Christians' (both may be found offensive by non-Christians) has a basis in Lonergan: 'there is a notable anonymity to this gift of the Spirit ... What removes this obscurity and anonymity is the fact that the Father has spoken to us of old through the prophets and in this final age through the Son' ('The Response of the Jesuit as Priest and Apostle in the Modern World,' in *A Second Collection* 174–75). But only when we know as we are known (1 Corinthians 13:12) will all obscurity and anonymity vanish; meanwhile we are anonymous members of the family of the Father from whom every family takes its name (Ephesians 3:15). Maybe 'God's anonymous children' would come nearer the truth than either of the other two expressions.

85 Romans 16:25.

and of the Son as outer word, call now for a third: the working out of the divine economy in human history, and this in the whole of human history. We have not only to try to understand this working out in the long ages of the past: we have also to ask how much we can conjecture about its working out in the long ages that possibly still await us in a future that is largely contingent. To attempt a view of history in its universal scope and sweep, and within the rationale of a divine economy for the universe, sounds to the non-theologian like hubris. Theologians, however, recognize this kind of thinking as their calling, and here, I believe, is where Lonergan has a profound contribution to make, though he has left us only scattered elements of a theory, not a comprehensive and elaborated view.

The focus is no longer the possibility of salvation for all; that is now taken for granted, and as a question is relegated to the margins (as part of our religious living, of course, it is in no way marginal). Neither is the universalist claim of Christianity, or the claims of any other religion, the focus of discussion. From the perspective that I consider Lonerganian, the relevant question is, What is God doing in the divine economy, that extends over all ages, of the twofold mission? What was God doing in past ages? What is God doing now? What can we discern of the possibilities the future holds and of the actualities God's intentions may have already determined for us? Some total view of history seems called for: what does Lonergan contribute under that heading?

In a first approach to his thought we can discern two ways of attempting an overall view of history. The first is the familiar trio of progress, decline, and redemption. This he calls the structure of history, but I would modify that term, for there is a kind of structure also in the sequences of history which I will come to in a moment. So I suggest that we speak of synchronic and diachronic structures. The structure of progress, decline, and redemption is synchronic, not sequential. Though emphases may vary in some sequence, we are always progressing in some degree, always declining, always being redeemed.[86]

86 For Lonergan's very early work on the history that happened (as distinguished from the history that is written) see his 'Analytic Concept of History,' *METHOD: Journal of Lonergan Studies* 11/1 (1993) 5–35. This essay (found after his death in File 713 – see note 87 below) certainly belongs to the period 1937–38 which some thirty-five years later he mentions in '*Insight* Revisited' as the time of his early interest in the topic (*A Second Collection* 271–72). In the same paper (272) he speaks of chapter 20 of *Insight* as

That familiar synchronic view is paralleled in the field of religions by the simultaneous presence among us of the many religions, each with its fidelity to the Spirit present in them, each with its infidelity to the promptings of the Spirit.

The other way to attempt an overall view is to study sequences in history: sequences in meaning and expression, in social institutions and culture, in all that pertains to human living, and this, whether it be question of progress or question of decline. For the human race, or some part of it, can advance, when the emphasis is on progress, from level to level of meaning; and equally the human race, or some part of it, can decline when the emphasis is evil from bias to bias, until a rich heritage has been squandered.[87] There is a structure here too, certainly in the sequences of progress, and even in the disintegrating sequence of decline, and so I propose that we call this the diachronic structure of history.

In the context of this diachronic structure the question of Christianity and world religions arises in a new way. God has seen fit to allow –

---

presenting the whole idea, and it seems that at one point in writing the book he planned to call chapter 20 'The Structure of History' (*Insight* [1992] 802, editorial note *r*). The three-membered structure runs through his work; it returns in *Method in Theology* 52–55, in 'Questionnaire on Philosophy' (*METHOD: Journal of Lonergan Studies* 2/2 [1984] 33; *Papers 1965–1980* [2004] 383), and elsewhere; but the creative work goes back to his student days.

On progress, decline, and redemption as concurrent see Lonergan's *Topics in Education* 69: '... in the concrete all three function together. They are intertwined. They do not exist in isolation.'

87 The data on the diachronic structure of history, like those on the synchronic, begin in the unpublished papers Lonergan wrote as a student and kept in a file numbered 713 and called 'History' (now in the Lonergan Archives); for example, in the paper entitled 'Philosophy of History' (not to be confused with a 1960 paper that has a similar title). More data are found in chapter 17 of *Insight*, in 'Levels and Sequences of Expression' ([1957] 568–73, [1992] 592–95). Likewise in *Method in Theology*, in 'Stages of Meaning' (85–99). But these few references are only high points in a long list of references, among which the paper 'Philosophy and the Religious Phenomenon' is not least in importance.

For the sequences in the disintegrating order of decline see 'The Role of a Catholic University in the Modern World': 'besides the succession of higher syntheses characteristic of intellectual advance, there is also a succession of lower syntheses characteristic of sociocultural decline' (*Collection* [1967] 116, [1988] 110). Also see *Insight* (1957) 231 [(1992) 256] on 'the successive lower viewpoints of the longer cycle' of decline; and *Method in Theology* on the steps by which a 'civilization in decline digs its own grave with a relentless consistency' (55). But again the references are legion.

and promote – the simultaneous existence of many religions; has God a 'plan' also for sequences in the various roles of the various religions? Are some transient, and others meant to endure to the end, if there is to be an end? What is the rationale of the appearance at a particular time of the Judaic religion, of the birth, when Augustus was emperor of Rome and Quirinius governor of Syria, of Jesus of Nazareth? Was the appearance of Jesus 'timed' not only in relation to Augustus and Quirinius, but also in relation to the stage of development reached by the world religions?

In the wide context of such questions one could attempt to insert and interpret the scattered remarks and essays Lonergan has given us on the economy of salvation history and on the mission of Christianity: what he wrote in his student days on restoring all things in Christ;[88] what he wrote of the fulness of time in which Christ came;[89] what he wrote 'on the concrete universal that is mankind in the concrete and cumulative consequences of the acceptance or rejection of the message of the Gospel';[90] what he was preparing in his unfinished work on the historical causality of Christ;[91] his views on the diversity of Eastern,

88 'Pantôn anakephalaiôsis: A Theory of Human Solidarity ...' (the full title is much longer), *METHOD: Journal of Lonergan Studies* 9/2 (October 1991) 139–72. The MS (also found in File 713) is dated very exactly 'Dominica in Albis 1935' (28 April).

89 'It was at the fulness of time that there came into the world the Light of the world' (*Insight* [1957] 742, [1992] 764 – one should read the whole long paragraph). See also 'Finality, Love, Marriage': '... only when and where the higher rational culture emerged did God acknowledge the fulness of time permitting the Word to become flesh and the mystical body to begin its intussusception of human personalities and its leavening of human history' (*Collection* [1967] 21, [1988] 22).

90 *Insight* (1957) 743 [(1992) 764].

91 Charles Hefling, in his lecture at the Lonergan Workshop, Boston College, 23 June 1993, drew attention to two short lines in *De Verbo incarnato* : 'Ulterius desideratur consideratio de causalitate historica quam Christus homo manifeste exercet' ['There is need for a further consideration of the historical causality that Christ the man manifestly exercises.'] Found on page 416 of the 1964 edition as Scholion 2 to Thesis 12, this statement appeared also in the editions of 1960 and 1961, under the same heading, 'De potentia Christi hominis.' We know that a fourth edition was in preparation when Lonergan's career at the Gregorian University was cut short by lung surgery. Begun about 1963–64, the new work would have developed the account of the historical influence of Christ that was lacking in previous editions: so Lonergan told me in conversation in 1972. His unfinished work seems to be extant in Files 657 and 674 of his papers – some 300 pages revising his theology of the redemption and adding a section, 'De opere Christi,' that discusses the social agent, the historical agent, Christ as agent, Christ as historical agent, and so on.

Semitic, and Western religion;[92] his attempt in 'Philosophy and the Religious Phenomenon' to give 'some account and ordering of the various contexts in which ... religious living occurs and ... investigations of religious living are undertaken.'[93] And so on.

Besides collecting these and other particular questions, we would inevitably be led to background questions of great generality. For example, the question of the order of the universe. This was a key concept for Lonergan's Latin theology of the 'convenientia' of the incarnation. It would have to be rethought now to relate the role of the Holy Spirit to the order of universal history:[94] what is the 'convenientia' of the interior gift of the Spirit to God's people? How should we conceive the overarching order of a universe when we give equal attention to the presence of Son and Spirit? Theologians argue whether theology should be Christocentric or theocentric; but their neglect of the Spirit's role leads to the omission of a prior question: is a view that makes the Son the center of theology to be modified by a view in which Son and Spirit are equally central, as are the foci of an ellipse? Only then should we take up the question of relating this to a theocentric theology.

For another example, there is the question of contingency. For Lonergan there is no contingent decision of God without a created counterpart: only if the created universe exists is it true to say God creates. To put it starkly, as of now there is no tomorrow: if at midnight God so wills, tomorrow will come into existence as another today.[95] That is

---

92 See *Method in Theology* 114: 'Eastern religion stressed religious experience. Semitic religion stressed prophetic monotheism. Western religion cultivated the realm of transcendence through its churches and liturgies, its celibate clergy, its religious orders, congregations, confraternities. It moved into the realm of theory by its dogmas, its theology, its juridical structures and enactments. It has to construct the common basis of theory and of common sense that is to be found in interiority and it has to use that basis to link the experience of the transcendent with the world mediated by meaning.' See also 'Philosophy and the Religious Phenomenon,' *METHOD: Journal of Lonergan Studies* 12/2 (1994) 139–41 (*Papers 1965–1980* [2004] 404–406).

93 Ibid. 138 [404].

94 Both ideas, *ordo* and *convenientia*, may be studied in the little work *De ratione convenientiae eiusque radice, de excellentia ordinis ...*; this *Supplementum schematicum* was provided for his students the first year Lonergan taught Christology at the Gregorian University, Rome, 1953–54. It remains unpublished, but is scheduled to appear in vol. 16 of *Collected Works*.

95 The regular context for Lonergan's doctrine on God's contingent acts and the corresponding created entity is his Trinitarian theology of the divine missions. See his *De Deo trino*, vol. 2 (1964), Assertum XVII, 226: 'Divinae personae missio ita per divinam relationem originis constituitur ut tamen per modum condicionis consequentis ter-

no great problem; the problem arises when we realize the implication: that as of now, God has no will for tomorrow, or for anything else that is not. The problem arises more acutely in the Christian religion with the implication of what was really contingent on Mary's *Fiat mihi* to Gabriel,[96] of what was really contingent on the *Non quod ego volo, sed quod tu* of Jesus in the garden,[97] with the question of what alternatives were available to God had the responses been other than they were.

The problem arises personally and contemporaneously, in the context of our own limited secondary responsibility, with the question of what is really contingent for me on my decisions from day to day, and what is really contingent for the human race on the aggregate of our decisions. If God's 'plan' is already in place for us, that is, in the 'already' of our 'now,' then to that extent we are no longer free. And if God has a determinate 'plan' in place for Christianity and the world religions, then we will let be what must be. But suppose God has no such plan, suppose that God loves a slow-learning people enough to allow them long ages to learn what they have to learn, suppose that the destiny of the world religions is contingent on what we all learn and do – say, on Christians being authentically Christian, Hindus being authentically Hindu, and so on. Then responsibility returns to us with a vengeance, and the answer to the question of the final relationship of Christianity and the world religions is that there is no answer – yet.

To elaborate a Lonerganian theology of the divine economy working in human history would therefore be a long and difficult task,[98] and I do not know whether in the end enough data would be found for a comprehensive view. What I feel is the fascination of the question, the possibility that such a study would shake up very thoroughly the relation of Christianity to world religions, the hope that someone may yet be able to undertake the study. In any case it is a task for another occasion.[99]

---

minum ad extra exigat [The mission of a divine person is constituted by a divine relation of origin in such a way that it still requires, by way of consequent condition, an external term].'

96 Luke 1:38.

97 Mark 14:36.

98 The task would be complicated by genetic and dialectical factors in the history of Lonergan's thinking and personal development: we cannot simply juxtapose what he wrote in his student days and what he wrote as a seminary professor, or what he wrote as a seminar professor and what he wrote in his *Method in Theology* period.

99 I am grateful to Ovey Mohammed and Robert Doran, both of Regis College, Toronto, for reading my article in typescript and enabling me to eliminate some of its defects; those that remain are, of course, my own.

Chapter 7

The Genus 'Lonergan and ...' and Feminism[1]

A book on Lonergan and feminism is an instance of a genus, 'Lonergan and ...' The genus itself seems to merit some attention, especially since instances of the present kind are multiplying (Lonergan and hermeneutics, Lonergan and communications, and so on). It occurred to me that under that general heading I might make a contribution to this collection of articles, though I hope to offer some suggestions on the particular application as well.

In general, if 'X and Y' is the title of a study, and both X and Y are writers with something to say on a certain topic, the study may unfold quite simply. Let us say that X's doctrine of God and Y's doctrine of God are to be compared and evaluated. We collect the data from both authors, interpret each in the appropriate context, set each in the ongoing discussion of the question, point out strengths and weaknesses, see them in a complementary, genetic, or dialectical relationship, and perhaps argue for the superiority of one over the other. The task is fairly straightforward.

The case could be somewhat different when X is an author and Y is a topic. Then it may still be, in some cases, a relatively simple matter. X has something to say on the question Y, and our task is still one of collecting and interpreting the data, locating X in the movements of the time, evaluating his or her contribution, and possibly taking a position in regard to it. But it may also happen that X is a thinker of the generalist type, whose ideas have applications in areas that X never personally

1 Previously published in Cynthia Crysdale, ed., *Lonergan and Feminism* (Toronto: University of Toronto Press, 1995) 13–32.

studied, applications not only in Y but also in A, B, C, and so on without end. In that case we have the more difficult task of discovering the relevance of X's ideas to those new areas, and pursuing their 'application' (a tricky word, that) in ways X never attempted.

The latter is the particular subdivision of 'Lonergan and ...' that I wish to study. Lonergan certainly belongs to that class of thinkers (not very numerous) who have aimed at fundamental ideas, ideas of a type that should have wide-ranging implications, ramifications, applications, adaptations. It may indeed be possible to find in him explicit ideas on feminist questions; but I think that, independently of such good luck or careful research, we can still expect the fundamental character of his thinking to make it relevant to this volume. I will therefore first set forth the role of Lonergan as a generalist thinker, and ask what it means to 'apply' such a thinker to particular questions. Then, in a second part, I will use these general ideas to suggest what might be a profitable approach to some of the questions raised by feminism.

1 General Thought and Its Application: 'Lonergan and ...'

The crux of the matter is that Lonergan's thought is extremely general and fundamental (general because fundamental), that projects of the type 'Lonergan and ...' are to some degree particular, and that the transition from general to particular, if it is to advance our knowledge and understanding, requires further insights that will themselves be creative and hard won.

In other words, to 'apply' Lonergan to the particular case is not the simple and obvious matter of applying a yardstick to measure a new quantity.[2] It is not the automatic click of a computer which, given a set of premises, adds the conclusion: all men are mortal, Peter is a man, therefore ...; or, all women are mortal, Portia is a woman, therefore ... Such automatic results are most easily attained when the concepts used are hollow; but fill the concepts with meaningful content, and the matter is not so simple. For example, the mortality of Peter and Portia can be made the same only at the expense of hollowing out to some

2 Without venturing into etymology, I suggest that the simplest illustration of 'ply' for present purposes is 'plywood': one layer 'applied' to another. From that we could move to a yardstick being 'applied' to measure a length, then to standards in general being applied, and so to our usage in the present study.

extent the concept of mortality. In the concrete, I would say, the two mortalities are significantly different. Dying is a lifelong process, and the process goes forward differently in male and female. But let us take up these questions in proper order.

1.1 General and Particular

A word first, before we turn to the question of application, on the role Lonergan would assign to a generalist. A key passage is one where, in the context of the formation of philosophy teachers, he sets out the generalist ideal for philosophers: 'they must ... come to understand how arduous is their task. They are to be generalists.'[3] But that is only the beginning. In the turn to the particular (where all knowledge must in the last analysis find its referent), they cannot take the easy path of simply adding a conclusion to premises. Mediating this transition is a far more difficult matter.

> [I]t cannot be stressed too strongly that the mediation of the generalists is intelligent rather than logical: by logical mediation I understand the process from universal concepts to particular instances as just instances; by intelligent mediation I understand the process from understanding the universal to understanding the particular. The difference between the two is a difference in understanding: in logical mediation one understands no more in the instance than one did in the universal; in intelligent mediation one adds to the understanding of the universal a fuller and more determinate understanding of the particular case. The generalist that is just a logical mediator turns out to be an obtuse intruder; the generalist that is an intelligent mediator speaks not only his own mind but also the language of his interlocutor.[4]

In other words – to come at once to the point – if Lonergan has something significant to say on the most general topic of the human, and we

3 'Questionnaire on Philosophy,' *METHOD: Journal of Lonergan Studies* 2/2 (October 1984) 32 (*Papers 1965–1980* [2004] 382). It was an ideal that Lonergan himself regularly aimed at. For example, at the end of his long exposition in *Insight* of organic, psychic, and human development, he wrote, 'It has all been ... very general. It is meant to be so' (*Insight* [1957] 478 [(1992) 503]). There is a short note on his usage of 'general' and 'universal' in *Collection* (1988) 272 (note *d* to chap. 6).

4 'Questionnaire on Philosophy' 32–33 (*Papers 1965–1980* [2004] 383).

wish to 'apply' his general thought to the question of being female or male, we must achieve 'a fuller and more determinate understanding' of what it is to be female or male, and thus make the 'application' of the general to the particular – a process by no means simple.

1.2 'Application': Data Samples

There is no proper understanding without data. Thus, when Lonergan aimed in *Insight* at understanding understanding, he provided sample after sample of understanding in operation. Can we find parallel samples for understanding his view of the process from general to particular? I believe we can; and I will suggest four cases that seem to qualify, and a fifth that is rather special.

There is first the case of adding to the abstract science of 'classical' formulations the additional insights needed to make valid statements about the concrete. For example, you want to put an object into orbit around the earth: you can have all the science you want, in the classical sense of systematic laws, and you will not have enough for the task.

> To apply those laws to any concrete case one still has to have an insight into this concrete situation, an insight that enables one to select these laws rather than those, an insight that grasps what one has to measure in this situation to be able to apply the laws to it. One must have an understanding of the concrete situation to apply even perfect knowledge of physics to it.[5]

For a second sample, somewhat akin to the first, there is the way Lonergan came to see Toynbee's contribution to history. From the first he

5 *Understanding and Being* (1980) 83–84 [(1990) 70]. See also (1990) 353: there is 'a step between a scientific system and the solution of a concrete scientific problem. That step is the occurrence of an insight that selects which laws are relevant to this concrete situation, which elements in this concrete situation have to be measured, and with what degree of accuracy the laws are to be applied to these elements when we work out a solution, and so on. There's that mediating insight.'

The case of abstract science and the concrete is worked out more fully in *Insight* (1957) 46–53 [(1992) 70–78]. For present purposes, I note the statement that 'concrete inferences from classical laws suppose not only knowledge of laws and information on some basic situation but also an insight that mediates between the situation and general knowledge' ([1957] 51, [1992] 75).

was deeply impressed; but as his critical sense developed, he realized that Toynbee's work should be viewed 'not as an exercise in empirical method, but ... as a formulation of ideal types that would stand to broad historical investigations as mathematics stands to physics.'[6] You cannot create a physics out of a mathematics: you must add the insights of physics. Similarly, you cannot, from ideal types alone, write a history: you must add the insights needed for the particular case.

The procedure for using ideal types has some resemblance to the procedures of common sense, which is a third instance of transition from general to particular. Common sense understands in the same way as the scientific mind. It generalizes too, as science does, and with great abandon, but without the careful control that science exercises, and certainly without zeal for proper form. It 'applies' its general knowledge, but not by formal deduction: '... there is ... a flow of questions, and ... a clustering of insights ... but the cluster is not aimed at arriving at universal definitions and universal propositions that will bear the weight of systematic and rigorous deduction.'[7]

> It follows that where the scientist or the mathematician wants to lay down universal principles that hold in all applications, common sense deals with proverbs. What are proverbs? They are general rules that usually one will find worth while paying attention to. The truth of a proverb is not a premise from which you can deduce conclusions that are going to be found to be true in absolutely every case ... It is a piece of advice that is relevant to the processes of knowing.[8]

---

6 'Natural Right and Historical Mindedness,' in *A Third Collection* 178. Again, 'Toynbee thought he was contributing to empirical science. Since then, however, he has recanted. But, I believe, his work remains a contribution not to knowledge of reality, not to hypotheses about reality, but to the ideal types that are intelligible sets of concepts and often prove useful to have to hand when it comes to describing reality or to forming hypotheses about it' ('Dialectic of Authority,' ibid. 10).

In the well-known scissors action of empirical method, ideal types give no more than the upper blade of theory meeting the lower blade of data: it's a case again of the move from general to particular, with the qualification that we may have to add to or revise theory to get the scissors working. We could, I think, associate the role of models to that of ideal types; but there is some discussion of Lonergan's use of the term models, and I don't wish to get sidetracked into that.

7 *Understanding and Being* (1980) 107 [(1990) 88–89].

8 Ibid. (1980) 111 [(1990) 92]. Lonergan continues with a proverb that illustrates this very principle: 'For example, "Look before you leap" is the proverb that governs the point that usually you have to complete your habitual nucleus of insights if you want to deal

A fourth instance is the role of the sciences, natural and especially human, and of human studies, in mediating theology and philosophy to give meaning and value to a way of life. This case differs somewhat from the previous three. Not only does the concrete situation require further understanding, but the human sciences themselves have to be worked out to give that 'fuller and more determinate understanding' we need.

Three works of Lonergan illuminate this mediating process. First, there is his short essay 'The Example of Gibson Winter,' where the issue is the role of human sciences in developing a way of life, and in particular of inculturating the gospel.[9] A second essay is a paper he wrote for the International Theological Commission.[10] The issue is the same: the role of the human sciences in mediating a Christian way of life, specifically, a valid moral theology. The situation is analyzed to the extent of considering three cases. There are cases where the science is sufficiently clear, and moral precepts can be laid down. There are cases where the 'science is not sufficiently determinate to yield fully concrete applications,' and then Lonergan would advise 'a course of social experimentation.' And, finally, there are cases where the 'human science is itself open to suspicion. Its representatives are divided ideologically ... The notorious instance at the present time is economics.'[11] A third essay is his work in that very field of economics. So much did he feel this science to be in need of radical criticism that he devoted the last years of his life to its study.[12] I take that study as paradigmatic. Besides the

---

in exactly the right fashion with a situation that is a bit novel, a bit strange, not the sort of thing to which you are accustomed. And it is a good bit of advice: it hits off exactly the point that the nucleus has to be completed as soon as the situation ceases to be within the ordinary routine' ([1980] 111–12, [1990] 92).

The ascetical advice to do as Jesus would do provides a simple but classic instance of the way 'application' of common sense works. Jesus acted in a different way with Herod, Pilate, the Pharisees, Judas, Peter – the list goes on and on, and each case has the role of a virtual universal as soon as I consider it as model. But which of these 'universals' comes nearest to my present situation? How should I apply it, with what modification, etc.? Only a further insight into the concrete present situation will tell me that.

9 In *A Second Collection* 189–92. This essay is especially useful for the strategy and tactics employed. That is to say, Lonergan does not feel responsibility here for creating the sciences needed; he simply goes to those who are already expert in them.

10 'Moral Theology and the Human Sciences,' *METHOD: Journal of Lonergan Studies* 15/1 (1997) 5–18 (*Papers 1965–1980* [2004] 301–312).

11 Ibid. 5.

12 See *Macroeconomic Dynamics: An Essay in Circulation Analysis*, ed. F.G. Lawrence, P.H. Byrne, and C.C. Hefling, *Collected Works of Bernard Lonergan*, vol. 15 (Toronto: Univer-

value it has in itself, whatever that may be, it also illustrates the effort we must make for a fuller and more determinate understanding of the human sciences in general if they are to mediate between a theology-philosophy and a way of life.

I have given four samples of moving from a universal to the particular, taking 'universal' in a broad sense that includes the laws of classical science, the ideal types of human action, the generalizations of familiar proverbs, the mediating role of the human sciences between theology and human living – there is a family resemblance in what is required in all these cases. What do you need to move from the abstract laws of science to a particular engineering project? To move from ideal cases of human activity to a particular chapter of history? To use the common sense of your proverbs when you find yourself in an unfamiliar situation? To apply your theology and philosophy to a way of life? Always one adds to the understanding of the universal a fuller and more determinate understanding of the particular.

There is a fifth instance of a transition from general to particular. It is the move from transcendental to categorial, and the transcendental character of Lonergan's thinking makes this, of course, an area of special interest in a volume of the type 'Lonergan and ...'[13]

It has some resemblance to the previous instances, but notable dif-

---

sity of Toronto Press, 1999). Lonergan had given special attention to economics in 'Moral Theology and the Human Sciences.' Speaking of the radical critique from an independent base needed by some sciences, and illustrating it by Ricoeur's critique of Freud, he continued: 'the human science, economics, is in need of similar radical criticism.' In economic theory the main variants ('the traditional market economy, the Marxist-inspired socialist economy, and the new transactional economy constituted by the giant corporations') are all under the influence of an ideology, and what is needed in the first place 'is a pure economic analysis of the exchange process untainted by any ideology' (17). In this case there did not seem to be a Gibson Winter to provide guidance, and Lonergan felt compelled to enter the field of economics himself.

13 It is here that the difference between 'Lonergan on ...' and 'Lonergan and ...'comes to light. A study of 'Lonergan *on* the Community of the Swiss' might result in a single line, 'Lonergan has nothing on the community of the Swiss'; but a study with the title 'Lonergan *and* the Community of the Swiss' could exploit ('apply') for that instance all his rich thought on community. This difference illustrates the difference between mediating and mediated functions. In the first we are much more limited by what we find in research, while in the second we can be more creative. This remark, of course, and similar remarks throughout this essay are true not only of Lonergan, but also of other thinkers of his type.

ferences, most especially in the sense of 'general.' The other four all begin with determinate knowledge, the knowledge we have through classical science, the knowledge we have through common sense, the knowledge we have through ideal types, or through models, the knowledge we have through human sciences and scholarship. The transcendental notions are not knowledge in that sense at all; rather, they are purely heuristic, like the notion of being in Chapter 12 of *Insight*. Their application is not a matter of a determinate content becoming more determinate; it is a matter of a universal but indeterminate dynamism producing each and every determinate category. They are universal not in the way a universal concept is universal, but universal in the way a comprehensive intention is. To apply them is to move, not from object to object, but from subject to object, from the dynamic intentionality that is innate in the subject to the products and constructions that result from the free exercise of that intentionality.[14]

1.3 'Application': Difficulty of the Process

I have examined five samples of the move from generalist thought to particular cases. In the concrete the fourth comes closest, I think, to the topic of the volume *Lonergan and Feminism*; but the most wide-ranging, and the most powerful by reason of its comprehensive intentionality (not because of any alleged 'abstractness') is the fifth. There is, however, the same requirement, and the same basic difficulty, in them all: the fuller understanding that must be added.

The difficulty in the first three is to add 'the fuller and more determinate understanding of the particular case' that we spoke of. The fourth has the further difficulty of elaborating the relevant human sciences. The fifth has both these sets of difficulties, along with its own special difficulty of moving from the innate intentionality of the subject to

14 It is this property of the transcendentals, a property shared in due measure by the functional specialties of *Method in Theology*, that has led some friendly readers to ask whether the transcendental notions are not a bit thin. They are thin in determinate content; but, like the intellectual light of Thomas Aquinas, they have the whole of knowledge in their range of power: 'in lumine intellectus agentis nobis est quodammodo omnis scientia originaliter indita' (*De veritate*, q. 10, a. 6: 'in the light of agent intellect all knowledge is, in some way, originally given to us'). Light, perhaps, might be called thin; but to those who live in darkness, it is extraordinarily rich in what it enables them to see, in its potential content.

the objectified products and determinate knowledge of the things that are.

The question of that 'fuller and more determinate understanding of the particular case' deserves more attention in studies of feminism, since it will remain a personal difficulty for each of us even after the intermediate human sciences have been worked out. I will return to it in the second part of my article. Meanwhile I would recommend those working on the present question to undertake this kind of personal study in some less sensitive area, and thus become acquainted with the process and what it involves.

May I illustrate this by two efforts of my own? Some years ago I was persuaded to speak and write in application of Lonergan's thought to education. Lacking the specialization of educators, I still had long experience in being educated and contributed what I could from that personal experience.[15] More recently I felt compelled to write on Canadian identity and Lonergan's thought on community. Lacking again the demography, the political science, the critical history, and the other knowledge that a full treatment would require, I still had long experience in being Canadian. I asked myself what that meant to me and contributed what I could from that perspective.[16] These two forays into 'fuller and more determinate understanding of the particular case' have helped me see what is involved in the application of Lonergan to specific areas of thought, to show me how handicapped one is without the human sciences, but also to offer hope of making a limited contribution from the side of experience – though, as I will presently remark, in the area of feminist questions each of us has only half the experience needed.

So much for these two little chapters of autobiography. So much also for the general case of the move from general to particular, or for generalities on the application of a generalist position to concrete instances.

---

15 Frederick E. Crowe, *Old Things and New: A Strategy for Education* (Atlanta: Scholars Press, 1985).

16 Frederick E. Crowe, *Bernard Lonergan and the Community of Canadians: An Essay in Aid of Canadian Identity* (Toronto: Lonergan Research Institute, 1992). For this foray I blame no one. There were no invitations to lecture on the topic. There was only my conscience prodding me. My country was being torn apart, Lonergan had a great deal to say on what unites a community and what tears it apart, I had had more opportunity to study Lonergan's thought than most Canadians had, and it was on my conscience to bring that thought to bear on our national identity.

2 '... and Feminism'

My division is indicated by the subtitles 'Lonergan and ...,' for the first part, and '... and Feminism,' for the second. That is, first the general pattern for application of a fundamental idea; then, its actual use in questions of feminism.

In this second part, the two steps would normally be, first, study of what it is to be human in general (or for present purposes, what Lonergan thought it is to be human), and, second, study of what it is to be male or female in particular. But how to handle that first step without writing a treatise is a difficult question, which different contributors will answer in different ways. My own choice is to make certain assumptions, to describe them briefly (I will not say 'defend' them), and to proceed on that basis with my argument, leaving it to readers to determine how much the argument may suffer from a procedure they regard as faulty.[17]

My first assumption is a traditionally Christian one: 'There is no longer Jew or Greek, there is no longer slave or free, there is no longer male and female; for all of you are one in Christ Jesus.'[18] I take this passage to mean that in Paul's thought there is something, however one may define it, that makes us all one before God. If Paul himself is found to have relied on unexamined suppositions, I would fall back on a more general religious view of a loving God whose purpose it is to save the whole human race.

My other assumption is a more complex matter. I rely, as far as may be needed here, on Lonergan's position that we cannot revise our cog-

---

The role of the sciences, and the complementarity of sciences and personal experience, came home to me in a new light in a third exercise in *docta ignorantia* when I attempted to write on Lonergan and the life of the unborn. Here I could draw on neither sciences nor experience, but could only set out what seemed to be relevant ideas from Lonergan and ask others to determine their usefulness. See 'The Life of the Unborn: Notions from Bernard Lonergan,' in Frederick E. Crowe, *Appropriating the Lonergan Idea*, ed. M. Vertin (Washington: Catholic University of Toronto Press, 1989) 360–69.

17 I am grateful to Cynthia Crysdale, the editor of *Lonergan and Feminism*, for a careful critical reading of my article and in particular for alerting me to some objections feminist writers would have to my procedure. Working under the pressure of time, I cannot at the moment undertake a study of those objections; but I hope to make it possible at least to discern more clearly the differences in our views.

18 Galatians 3:28 (NRSV).

nitional structure without using that very structure: 'revision cannot revise its own presuppositions. A reviser cannot appeal to data to deny data, to his new insights to deny insights, to his new formulation to deny formulation, to his reflective grasp to deny reflective grasp.'[19] I say 'as far as may be needed,' for my interest here is determined by the kind of discussion that the volume *Lonergan and Feminism* undertakes. There is an unmediated intersubjective immediacy (say, of parent to parent at the burial of their child) which may bypass the structure and certainly is unaware of it, but we could not discuss that intersubjectivity in the style proper to this volume without using the structure. Objections may certainly be raised at this point, but it would seem that one cannot not raise them without providing data, interpreting the data, and arguing the point.

Still, this assumption needs more explanation, and the first thing needing explanation is the emotion with which men react to Lonergan's position. By 'men' I mean males. Women may react to the position too for their own feminist reasons; but I have noticed that men with no feminist agenda can become quite emotional about it. I suspect that this is due to a sense that they are being manipulated from outside rather than being counselled and helped to exploit their own inner resources. It would be interesting, if we could recover the history, to learn how ancient skeptics reacted to the strategy that refuted them simply by getting them to talk, to say something. Lonergan's strategy is an elaboration of that.

But the major point in my explanation is to take a broader view and get Lonergan's position into perspective. We should not take it for granted that there is a one-to-one correspondence between the attention he gave to any one aspect of cognitional and intentionality theory and the importance he attached to that aspect in the integral whole. Certainly, the four-leveled structure of human intentionality, as it rises from experience through understanding and judgment to values and decision, received a great deal of attention from him; certainly, it is central to the picture. But it is not the whole picture. Other very general and quite essential features have to be added, and in their context the seemingly rigid structure turns out to be a rather flexible instrument.

There is first the double movement along the structure: development from below upward, and development from above downward.

19 *Insight* (1957) 336 [(1992) 360].

Not only do we move up from experience to values, but we move in the other direction as well; and this movement is prior and more fundamental, for it begins at an early age in the affectivity of the infant.

> On affectivity rests the apprehension of values. On the apprehension of values rests belief. On belief follows the growth in understanding of one who has found a genuine teacher and has been initiated into the study of the masters of the past. Then to confirm one's growth in understanding comes experience made mature and perceptive by one's developed understanding. With experiential confirmation the inverse process may set in. One now is on one's own. One can appropriate all that one has learnt by proceeding as does the original thinker who moved from experience to understanding, to sound judgment, to generous evaluation, to commitment in love, loyalty, faith.[20]

I suggest that this prior and more fundamental form of development, from affectivity through values, judgments, and understanding to richer and more meaningful experience, puts a new light on what may seem a too cerebral (and is certainly a one-sided) use of a structure beyond revision. But this is an aspect of Lonergan's thought that we have hardly begun to study.

A second point, one that has received somewhat more attention but is still far from being exhaustively studied and even more from being fully exploited, is the role of feelings in being human, and indeed in knowing in a human way. This role is implicit in that whole development from above that begins in infancy, but there are also explicit statements that reveal the wider importance of feelings, in development from below as well as from above. One good example may suffice: 'Without feelings this experience, understanding, judgment is paper-thin. The whole mass and momentum of living is in feeling.'[21] We tend to associate this concern with the later Lonergan, but there is ample evidence for it in the earlier Lonergan too: many of us were simply slow to notice the data.[22]

---

20 'Natural Right and Historical Mindedness,' in *A Third Collection* 181.

21 'An Interview with Fr. Bernard Lonergan, S.J.,' in *A Second Collection* 221.

22 It is quite instructive from this point of view to compare the index entry for 'Feelings' in the first edition of *Insight* with that in the fifth and observe how many subentries have been added in the latter.

A third factor to broaden our perspective is the addition of what we may call the historical side of consciousness, in contrast with its ahistorical structure. The structure is a given that we all use, but the way we use it varies with all the richness of human differences and human history. Everyone operates at times in the commonsense pattern of consciousness, but besides that some of us develop a theoretic pattern, others an artistic pattern, many of us a religious pattern. Again, there are various conversions: many of us are given a religious conversion, perhaps most of us achieve a moral and a psychic conversion, and some few may become intellectually converted. Further still, there are stages of meaning that successively characterize the human race in its secular and in its religious development. All these variations can occur without prejudice to a given structure when that structure is so flexible an instrument.[23]

If these three factors, to which others may be added,[24] dispose the reader more favorably to the view that we can find a common basis for the discussions of this volume, *Lonergan and Feminism,* it remains to note that the complexities which they add to the discussion discourage any a priori or hasty analysis of the differences between tribes, classes, nations, cultures. So likewise they caution great care in assigning causes for the differences between men and women. It is conceivable that through natural disposition men and women are differently involved in the upward or downward movements of development, differently disposed toward the active intentionality of the subject or the feelings of the subject, differently affected by the various conversions, differently situated in the stages of meaning. It is equally conceivable that, if these differences exist, many of them owe more to education and conditioning than they do to a natural disposition, conceivable too that individual men and women, as well as groups and societies, vary in the extent to which they have overcome or are over-

---

23 Another instructive exercise is to examine the six canons of empirical method (chap. 3 of *Insight*) and ask whether they pertain to the historical aspect of consciousness or the structural. The first canon is obviously related to the structure, but the second is obviously related to the ongoing history of science, to what happens within the structure.

24 For example, the communal context of individual learning. The contribution of Cynthia Crysdale to the volume *Lonergan and Feminism* ('Women and the Social Construction of Self-Appropriation' 88–113) corrects a common misapprehension on this point. I am grateful to her for allowing me to read her essay in manuscript.

coming that education and conditioning. Such matters are not to be settled without study.

So we come to the difficult question of moving from what it is to be human to what it is to be male or female; and we must return to the sciences and human studies, and their indispensable role of mediating between generalist notions and feminist questions. I do not mean that we need the sciences in all the everyday events of everyday life. To take a simple example, I do not need any human science to tell me what to do when I see a child running dangerously close to a cliff: spontaneous intersubjectivity acts without stopping to invoke systems of thought. But that is in the world of immediacy, of pure immediacy, and we live only a very small part of our lives there. That very day I may wish to buy grapes for the same child, and find myself in the world mediated by meaning and motivated by value. Where were these grapes grown? Were they harvested by oppressed migrant workers? What stand will I take on the boycott of the oppressors? Inevitably we are drawn into a world where the human sciences and human studies play an essential role.

With adaptations the same is true of feminist questions, adaptations that are needed because any natural spontaneity there is between male and female was overlaid in former times by habits that were conditioned. Relationships between men and women that seemed natural then were actually natural only in the way the 'second nature' of a habit is, so that we really did not know what was natural and what was not. Today everything must be questioned. For example, I hesitate now to offer a courtesy that a few years ago would have been 'spontaneous.' Then there was no need for reflection to intervene; now I must reflect on the way my offer will be received. What will she think? What does she think I am thinking? We may soon get tied up in R.D. Laing's *Knots*, where human sciences could be rather helpful.

Leaving to others, however, the study of the relevant human sciences, I will concentrate on the further step that Lonergan introduced between 'classical' laws and concrete situations, one that I would introduce between the human sciences and concrete human situations. Just as classical laws need a fuller and more determinate understanding of the particular case, so also do the human sciences. Perhaps I can profit from my already mentioned forays into education and Canadian identity to say something on a parallel need and a parallel move for the present question. As we can accumulate years of experience as pupils without ever reflecting on what it means to learn, as I can live all my life in a country without ever reflecting on what my country means to me, so also we can live all our lives as male or female without ever reflecting on our experience of being one or the other, without trying to determine what it means to us to be male or female. I wish to offer some suggestions on how to repair this neglect.

A useful context in which to consider the question is that of substance becoming subject. This awkward phrase is recurrent in Lonergan, it has a profound meaning, it is directly relevant to the present question, and thus it is worth exploring. We are familiar with the shift in orientation of modern thought that is called the turn to the subject: from metaphysical categories like act and potency, form and matter, we have turned to meaning and value, consciousness and subjectivity, and the like. 'In contemporary philosophy there is a great emphasis on the subject, and this emphasis may easily be traced to the influence of Hegel, Kierkegaard, Nietzsche, Heidegger, Buber.'[25] Lonergan epitomizes this development as moving from substance to subject: 'by speaking of consciousness, we effected the transition from substance to subject. The subject is a substance that is present to itself, that is conscious.'[26]

What we have to note about this pair of words is that it does double duty: 'from substance to subject' can refer to a shift in philosophic thinking, but more properly it refers to the existential development in which a substance becomes a subject.[27] Thus, at the most elementary level there is 'the emergence of consciousness in the fragmentary form of the dream, where human substance yields place to the human subject.'[28] At

25 'The Subject,' in *A Second Collection* 69–70. In a note to this passage Lonergan writes as follows: 'One should, perhaps, start from Kant's Copernican revolution, which brought the subject into technical prominence while making only minimal concessions to its reality. The subsequent movement then appears as a series of attempts to win for the subject acknowledgement of its full reality and its functions.'

26 *Topics in Education*, chap. 4, sect. 1.3; the quoted passage is on p. 83. Lonergan originally gave these lectures at Xavier University, Cincinnati, in 1959.

27 There is a helpful parallel in *Insight* between cognitional process and the 'reciprocal notion' of world process: 'For it is not only our notion of being that is heuristic, that heads for an objective that can be defined only in terms of the process of knowing it, but also the reality of proportionate being itself exhibits a similar incompleteness and a similar dynamic orientation towards a completeness that becomes determinate only in the process of completion' ([1957] 444, [1992] 470). The 'reciprocal' pair in question here are the turn from substance to subject in *thought*, and the development from substance to subject in our existential *becoming*.

28 'A Post-Hegelian Philosophy of Religion,' in *A Third Collection* 208.

the other end of the spectrum on the religious level the same phrase characterizes the difference between the newly baptized infant, who is in Christ Jesus with the being of substance, and one who is advanced in the spiritual life and is in Christ Jesus with the being of subject.[29]

Now these examples show that there is not only a development from substance to subject according to the levels of intentionality, so that we emerge as subjects according to *degrees* of consciousness, but a development also from substance to subject in the way we are human, that is, according to the *differentiations* of our consciousness – and this not only according to the major differentiations, so that we emerge as religious subjects, or artistic subjects, but also according to the minor differentiations of class or nation or whatever. Thus, to take a sample case already used, I was born a Canadian citizen without any experience whatever of what it means to be a Canadian. My being Canadian was a being of substance. But when circumstances led me to reflect on what this meant to me I began to transform this being of substance into a being of subject. And to come finally to the point: I believe a similar transformation is needed to pass from being male or female with the being of substance to being male or female with the being of subject. The difference again is in the conscious attention to what we are.

In mere animals this transition does not occur. There is a physical development which breeders watch to determine when male and female characteristics have developed enough for their purposes, but the animal doesn't reflect on this, or consider the needs of its partner, or take any step toward transforming substance into subject. At the animal level in us a similar physical development occurs, and the question is whether it will occur with or without the transformation that turns substance into subject. No doubt a hundred influences are at work to promote or impede this transformation. No doubt, in stable times where the wisdom of a tradition operates in quasi spontaneity, the influence is on the whole beneficent. But if we are to live on the level of our times with the full realization of our potential, we are called to a more reflective appropriation of what we are, more especially in times that are as unstable as ours, with traditions that may be moribund and are in any case widely flouted.

There is, however, a very special difficulty for the human race when we come to reflect on our sexual nature: only half the experience of the

---

29 '*Existenz* and *Aggiornamento*,' in *Collection* (1967) 250 [(1988) 231].

race (roughly half – I simplify here the data of biology and psychology) is ours to reflect on. Men cannot reflect on the experience of being woman, nor women on the experience of being man. Fifty million French people can reflect on the experience of being French, but only twenty-five million of them can reflect on their experience of being male, and another twenty-five million on their experience of being female. This peculiarity, however, which seems to limit the value of the recommended reflection, can actually be turned to advantage through Lonergan's little-known idea of mutual self-mediation.

In 1963 he did extensive study of the notion of mediation, first in a summer institute entitled 'Knowledge and Learning' at Gonzaga University, Spokane, and at the end of the summer in a lecture at the Thomas More Institute, Montreal.[30] Mediation is a very general term, with applications in the mechanical, organic, psychic, and logical fields, as well as others. Mutual mediation is illustrated mechanically in a watch: 'The function of movement is immediate in the mainspring ... The function of control ... is immediate in the balance wheel ... The two functions mediate each other. The balance wheel controls itself and the mainspring. The mainspring moves itself and the balance wheel.'[31] Self-mediation is illustrated in the growth of an organism, and one can find it in the species as well as in the individual organism.[32] A further grade is seen in the self-mediation of consciousness, and a further one still in the self-mediation of self-consciousness. 'The animal mediates itself not only organically but also intentionally,'[33] and the inward displacement to consciousness 'gives rise to the 'we,' the intersubjective community.'[34] Then in the area of self-consciousness, we have in

30 'The Mediation of Christ in Prayer,' *METHOD: Journal of Lonergan Studies* 2/1 (March 1984) 1–20. In the first seven sections the editor, Mark Morelli, has 'integrated the two sources' (the Gonzaga University notes, and the Thomas More Institute tape-recording); the last section (on prayer) is from the tape alone (p. 19, n. 1). [Subsequently published in 1996 as chap. 8 (pp. 160–82) in *Papers 1958–1964*.]

31 Ibid. (1984) 4 [(1996) 165]. In the later edition the sentence fragments 'The function of movement is immediate in the mainspring ... The function of control ... is immediate in the balance wheel ...' do not appear; for an explanation of the differences in the two versions, see editorial note 1 on pp. 160–61.

32 Ibid. (1984) 6–7 [(1996) 167–68].

33 Ibid. (1984) 8 [(1996) 169].

34 Ibid. (1984) 9 [(1996) 170]. The later edition has '... the displacement gives rise to the group, to the "we."'

human development 'the mediation of autonomy,'[35] reaching its climax in the existential moment 'of finding out for oneself what one can make of oneself.'[36] 'Again, this disposing of oneself occurs within community and particularly within the three fundamental communities ... marriage ... state ... Church.'[37] 'Just as we extended the notion of mediation in the case of organisms to the perpetuation of the species, so we can say that the community mediates itself by its history.'[38]

I am afraid this is a rather hurried approach to the point I wish to make on the role of mutual self-mediation in human development. But the notion seems to me so significant not only for our common human development but also for our development as male or female that I could not omit it, yet I could include only in ruthlessly abbreviated form the broad context that gives it its full meaning. But we do what we can, and so with this abbreviated context I propose to set forth now what Lonergan means by mutual self-mediation. Perhaps it will be wisest to do so in his own words.

> [W]e remarked of existential decision that it occurs in community, in love, in loyalty, in faith. Just as there is a self-mediation towards autonomy, so there is a mutual self-mediation and its occasion is the encounter in all its forms (meeting, regular meeting, living together).[39]

Various illustrations are given:

> Meeting, falling in love, getting married is a mutual self-mediation ... There is a mutual self-mediation in the education of the infant, the child, the boy or girl ... There is a mutual self-mediation in the relationships of

35 Ibid. (1984) 9 [(1996) 170].
36 Ibid. (1984) 10 [(1996) 171].
37 Ibid. (1984) 10 [(1996) 172].
38 Ibid. (1984) 11 [(1996) 172]. The later edition has 'the organism' and 'in its history.'
39 Ibid. (1984) 13 [(1996) 174]. In the later edition the text reads: '... we remarked of existential decision that it occurs in community, in love, in loyalty, in faith. Just as there is a self-mediation towards autonomy, and a mutual mediation illustrated by the organism or the functional whole that is not just a machine, so there is a mutual mediation.' An additional sentence, taken from Lonergan's Gonzaga notes, is given in footnote 19: 'Its occasion is the encounter, the meeting, keeping company, living together.'

mother and child, father and son, brothers and sisters. There is a mutual self-mediation between equals ... between superiors and inferiors.[40]

The key word in these passages is 'encounter,' for this links mutual self-mediation at once with the dialectic that Lonergan worked out a few years later in *Method in Theology*, and makes of it, in fact, a very highly specialized case of dialectic. The functional specialties of research, interpretation, and history are concerned with the past but do not achieve an encounter with the past.

> They make the data available, they clarify what was meant, they narrate what occurred. Encounter is more. It is meeting persons, appreciating the values they represent, criticizing their defects, and allowing one's living to be challenged at its very roots by their words and by their deeds. Moreover, such an encounter is not just an optional addition to interpretation and to history. Interpretation depends on one's self-understanding; the history one writes depends on one's horizon; and encounter is the one way in which self-understanding and horizon can be put to the test.[41]

We have only to substitute present living people for a word and message coming to us in documents from the past, to see mutual self-mediation as the dialectic of husband and wife, of teacher and pupil, of brother and sister, the dialectic that is operative in almost any meeting of persons, the dialectic that makes illusory the happy ending of a certain old-style novel and shows the authentic realism of the modern novel which stops in the midst of process and leaves ambivalent situations unresolved.[42]

---

40 Ibid. (1984) 13 [(1996) 175]. There are slight variations in the later edition: 'Meeting, falling in love, getting married is a mutual self-mediation ... There is a mutual self-mediation in the education of children, of the infant, the child, the boy or girl ... There is a mutual self-mediation in the relationship of mother and child, father and son, and brothers and sisters. And there is mutual self-mediation between equals ... between superiors and subjects ...'

41 *Method in Theology* 247. (For more on the pertinence of the functional specialties not just to theology but to any sphere of scholarly human studies, see chap. 1 of the present volume, esp. n. 28.)

42 In his lectures on mutual self-mediation Lonergan makes a remark which I find highly suggestive for further study: 'The exploration of the field of mutual self-mediation is perhaps the work of the novelist.' He returns to the point a moment later: 'Mutual self-mediation proves the inexhaustible theme of dramatists and novelists'

So what does mutual self-mediation offer? I am not being facetious, though I make the point with a certain exaggeration, when I say that it offers what Churchill offered in the dark days of 1940: 'blood, toil, tears and sweat.' Mutual self-mediation is not an answer but the raising of a question. It is not a fact but an invitation. It is not an invitation to be but to become. If accepted it does not inaugurate a state but a process. It is not a sure-fire process but one fraught with uncertainty, ambivalence, false starts, repeated failures. It is an indefinitely ongoing process in which we are being continually challenged and continually responding or failing to respond, responding authentically or responding inauthentically. In brief, it has all the menace of the struggle for authenticity that dialectic is, and it offers no more guarantee of success than dialectic does.

> Human authenticity is not some pure quality, some serene freedom from all oversights, all misunderstanding, all mistakes, all sins. Rather it consists in a withdrawal from unauthenticity, and the withdrawal is never a permanent achievement. It is ever precarious, ever to be achieved afresh, ever in great part a matter of uncovering still more oversights, acknowledging still further failures to understand, correcting still more mistakes, repenting more and more deeply hidden sins. Human development, in brief, is largely through the resolution of conflicts ...[43]

But if mutual self-mediation is fraught with menace it also has the silver lining of promise. It is a continual self-making. As Lonergan kept repeating, 'We are self-completing animals,'[44] and we complete ourselves in a never-ending process and in relation to one another. As method 'is not just a list of materials to be combined in a cake or a medicine' but 'regards recurrent operations, and ... yields ongoing and cumulative results,'[45] so living and meeting and growing in relation to

---

('The Mediation of Christ in Prayer' [(1984) 13, (1996) 175, 176]; the later edition has 'To explore ...' and 'provides the exhaustible ...'). I believe there is no better way to obtain a real apprehension of his meaning than to examine novels and plays under this heading of mutual self-mediation, but to illustrate this is perhaps a separate task.

43 *Method in Theology* 252.

44 'Religious Experience,' in *A Third Collection* 127; 'Religious Knowledge,' ibid. 141; 'The Ongoing Genesis of Methods,' ibid. 154; 'A Post-Hegelian Philosophy of Religion,' ibid. 207; and passim elsewhere.

45 'Religious Knowledge,' ibid. 140.

one another is an ongoing series of attempts and successes and failures and renewed attempts.

If that is what mutual self-mediation is, we should not regard it suspiciously as simply a ploy to introduce a male fifth column into the meeting of men and women, or assume that it prejudices results by invoking a position worked out by male thinkers who were careful to exclude the possibility of revision. What it introduces is a method to uncover any fifth column and banish it from the scene. What it invokes is an open mind and a ready will. For the key word is encounter, and a chief positive supposition of encounter is that I may be wrong, that I have much to learn, that meeting others will challenge my self-understanding, that it opens up the possibility of growing together, that while failure is always possible so too are repentance after failure, fresh resolve, and renewed efforts.

All this, I venture to suggest, has a direct relevance to the kind of effort the volume *Lonergan and Feminism* makes. For it would add to the list of encounters that Lonergan uses in illustration (husband and wife, brother and sister, and so on) not just another instance but another kind of encounter. In inviting several men and several women to contribute, it looks beyond individual persons to a wider collaboration. Besides the mutual self-mediation that two persons may experience as a pair, it envisages the mutual self-mediation that each half of our human race may experience as a unit in relation to the other half. It is a symbol of encounter not only between nations, between churches, between university faculties and groups of every kind, but of encounter on a global scale between the race of men and the race of women. While it will not achieve the intimate partnership of husband and wife, that model can serve to inspire the partnership of the two halves of God's creation working out our human destiny, not in the parliament of a nation but in the worldwide parliament of men and women – Tennyson's 'Parliament of Man' transposed to the realities of a hundred years later.

In the measure that such attempts succeed, they will, it seems to me, add a new dimension to the Pauline vision in which we grow to the fulness of the body of Christ where there is neither male nor female. For all the emphasis on growing and becoming in relation to others does not alter the fact that what we ultimately become is ourselves – our authentic selves, to be sure, but nevertheless ourselves. That means becoming our authentic male selves and our authentic female selves; and it enriches the unity of spiritual fulness that Paul proclaims with the diversity of a material human fulness – the human fulness, that grows with human history, of being men and women. In any case, while we are on the way, our study must surely be not of feminism, and equally not of masculinism, but of both, and of each in relation to the other. Neither will it be just a study *of*, or a learning *about*, but an *encounter* in mutual self-mediation.[46]

46 I wish to thank Robert Croken for reading this article in typescript and helping me to clarify a number of points.

Chapter 8

Lonergan's Search for Foundations: The Early Years, 1940–1959[1]

The title of this volume, *Searching for Cultural Foundations,* suggests the aim of its chief contributors: the constructive work of laying foundations in specific areas of culture. It also obliges me to justify the contribution I am offering, for I have not attempted, and would not attempt, that kind of constructive work. Still, my justification need not be far-fetched. The other studies are all inspired by, and would carry forward, the seminal ideas of Bernard Lonergan. Now I know that their authors share the conviction that a basic task, still far from finished, is that of understanding Lonergan himself, that a developmental work such as this volume would be, is an effort in a sense to go beyond a point we have not yet reached. That is not fatal to the enterprise. On the contrary. Genuine progress is often an oscillation, maybe a dialectic, between going beyond our sources and returning to them for new inspiration. Thus, as this project may serve to force us back to our origins, so that return may contribute in its own way to the total enterprise. That, anyway, is my hope as I begin this study of Lonergan's early years, during which he was searching, in a way that gradually became more explicit, for his own foundations.

The material limits of my study should be stated. It covers the period from 1940, the date of Lonergan's dissertation, to 1959, the year in which he gave a course at the Gregorian University under the title *De intellectu et methodo,* and brought the question of foundations into sharp focus. There is good reason for regarding this year as marking a

1 Previously published in Philip McShane, ed., *Searching for Cultural Foundations* (Lanham, MD: University Press of America, 1984) 113–39.

half-way point, and some reason (beyond the personal one of pressure of time) for stopping the present study there. For not only has Lonergan's thought reached a kind of plateau, but the route he followed is relatively easy to trace; whereas documenting the next stage of the journey, especially through the crucial years from 1962–65, is more difficult. We should be clear at any rate that the foundations of 1959 are not yet those of 1972, as set forth in his *Method in Theology*. The early years offer contrast, then, as well as positive input; and to some extent I will be showing the influences Lonergan had to overcome in order to make his own creative contribution. I would not exaggerate that aspect, but it is well to realize at the outset that we have here the problem, recurring in any thinker of stature, of keeping in perspective the elements of continuity and discontinuity in his development.

Lonergan completed his dissertation, a study of the development of operative grace in the thought of Aquinas, in the spring of 1940.[2] The results of his positive investigations, considerably rewritten, were published soon after in *Theological Studies* and re-edited three decades later in book form.[3] But the original Introduction, whose main part is called – significantly, as we shall see – 'The Form of the Development,' was never published. David Tracy provided a welcome summary and evaluation in *The Achievement of Bernard Lonergan*;[4] a photocopy of the Introduction is available in the Lonergan Center of Research at various institutions;[5] and for several years, and with increasing interest, students of Lonergan have been making it the starting point of their inves-

2 '*Gratia Operans*: A Study of the Speculative Development in the Writings of St Thomas Aquinas,' Gregorian University, Rome, 1940, 338 pages. Breakdown in communications with Rome prevented the award of the doctorate until the academic year 1946–47.

3 'Gratia Operans' (1941–42); *Grace and Freedom* (1971). [More recently (2000), the articles have been republished, together with the 1940 dissertation, as *Grace and Freedom: Operative Grace in the Thought of St Thomas Aquinas*, vol. 1 of *Collected Works of Bernard Lonergan* (ed.).]

4 David Tracy, *The Achievement of Bernard Lonergan* (New York: Herder and Herder, 1970) 39–44.

5 On this continent, at Regis College, Toronto; Concordia University, Montreal; University of Santa Clara, Santa Clara. Overseas, at Dublin, Naples, Manila, Sydney, and Melbourne. There are 47 introductory pages, divided as follows: Preface, 1–2; Introduction, 2–9; 'The Form of the Development' (chap. 1), 10–47. But it has become customary to refer to the whole as the Introduction [*Grace and Freedom* (2000) 153–92].

tigations. Quite rightly, for it allows us a valuable glimpse of his early thinking on what theology is and how it should proceed.

For my own purposes it will be preface enough to say that this Introduction sets forth the aim of the dissertation, which is to be an historical study, and indeed an historical study of a speculative development; that it shows a concern for determining the objectives of such a study, especially those of an inductive method that is not positivist and of a scientific objectivity that rises above the hopeless disputes of the previous three centuries; and that the strategic device it proposes for achieving those objectives is a general theory of development which would function as an a priori, somewhat in the way mathematics does for the quantitative sciences. Readers will recognize here the beginning of a long wrestling with the notion of the a priori, in which the movement will be back from logical principles to heuristic structures and to the real principles found in the dynamism of human consciousness. Similarly, the notion of generalizing will have a history – presently we will refer to the general form of inference, and one remembers the later role of generalized empirical method – though again there will be an important modification: the addition of attention to the particular (meaning and interpretation, plurality of cultures, etc.).

But now to the point. The developmental law of the greatest possible generality will be stable; there will be 'a point of vantage outside the temporal dialectic, a matrix or system of thought that at once is as pertinent and as indifferent to historical events as is the science of mathematics to quantitative phenomena.'[6] The stability has a basis: 'the human mind is always the human mind.'[7] Here, stated with utmost simplicity, we find an orientation that will guide Lonergan throughout his career. We will be disappointed, however, if we look for detailed anticipations of later thinking. Lonergan's a priori at this time is quite prosaic: 'The general law is perfectly simple. The mind begins from the particular and works to what is most general; it then returns from the most general through the specific differences to the particular.'[8] It is true, the general law is made somewhat more complex here to deal with the data on grace, but it would be a digression to go into that now.

6 '*Gratia Operans*: A Study ...' (1940) 10 [*Grace and Freedom* (2000) 162]. Hence, the title of chapter 1, 'The Form of the Development' – clarified also by contrast with the title of chapter 2, 'The Data of Inquiry.'

7 '*Gratia Operans*: A Study ...' (1940) 6 [*Grace and Freedom* (2000) 157].

8 '*Gratia Operans*: A Study ...' (1940) 32 [*Grace and Freedom* (2000) 179].

What is relevant now and can be documented is that we are dealing already with an interest in foundations, and that the foundations are located where they will be thirty years later, that is, in the human subject, and rather more specifically at the moment, in the human subject's mind. But, when Lonergan has pursued foundations to that point, he is content and drops the search: he does not go on to an epistemology. An epistemology would, no doubt, result in an imbalance in a dissertation whose introduction was now long enough. In any case Lonergan's creative energies are not directed at this time to further exploration of that area, but rather to the complexification of his a priori and its application to the immense field of data on divine grace.

The next work to interest us is a short article on the nature and form of inference, published in 1943.[9] Its immediate aim: 'an empirical investigation of the nature of inference';[10] but it is conceived also as 'a first step in working out an empirical theory of human understanding and knowledge.'[11] That latter statement is bound to excite the historian of Lonergan's thought, but I draw attention to this essay for other reasons: it is another instance of a bent for generalized understanding, and it records an early concern for rigorous demonstration, the process 'from implier through implication to implied.'[12] This concern was later balanced by other factors but, as far as I know, never abandoned. Not in the polemic against conceptualism and its syllogisms, of which more presently. Not in *Insight*'s study of the non-logical paths of discovery. Not even in *Method in Theology*, which seems to do an about-face with its claim that 'objectivity is the first fruit of authentic subjectivity';[13] for in that work the subject 'still needs truth ... The truth he needs is still the truth attained in accord with the exigences of rational consciousness.'[14] Nor does the primacy accorded conversion dispense with the role of proof; only now it is clear that 'proof becomes rigorous

9 'The Form of Inference,' first published in *Thought* 18 (1943) 277–92; then as chapter 1 of *Collection* (1967) 1–15 [(1988) 3–16].

10 Ibid. (1967) 14 [(1988) 15].

11 Ibid. (1967) 15 [(1988) 16].

12 Ibid. (1967) 15 [(1988) 16]. In 'Finality, Love, Marriage,' *TS* 4 (1943) 477–510, published the same year therefore as 'The Form of Inference,' there is a long paragraph discussing and applying various types of implication. See 'Finality, Love, Marriage,' in *Collection* (1967) 28 n. 34 [(1988) 28–29 n. 34].

13 *Method in Theology* 292.

14 Ibid. 242.

only within a systematically formulated horizon,' and that it is conversion that establishes the horizon.[15] These remarks, inserted out of context, may help us maintain a proper perspective on a difficult question. To be noted, finally, in the 1943 work: inference is not affirmation (Newman's influence here surely). That is implied in the last paragraph where both induction and deduction are distinguished from 'the more ultimate process from sense through intellection to judgment,'[16] and it is made explicit some years later.[17]

The search for foundations takes a distinct step forward, though almost entirely in the cognitional field, a few years later in the series of articles on the concept of *verbum* in St Thomas Aquinas.[18] Like a great inland waterway, with branches and fingers reaching into remote areas, they penetrate the whole vast plain of cognitional theory. Omitting then the wrestling with the thought of St Thomas, and merely noting that Lonergan's contemporary purpose was to get behind a conceptualism that deals with terms, judgments, and syllogisms, to an intellectualism that studies the source of all these, we may quote his stated historical purpose: 'to understand what Aquinas meant by the intelligible procession of an inner word,'[19] and record his sense of 'intelligible process,' that 'an inner word not merely has a sufficient ground in the act of understanding it expresses; it also has a knowing as sufficient ground, and that ground is operative precisely as a knowing, knowing itself to be sufficient.'[20] Now the second article, appearing first in March, 1947, and then as the second chapter of the later book,[21] deals extensively with foundations under the heading of the critical problem. For we are talking about 'the reflective act' of understanding, which 'generates in judgment the expression of consciously possessed truth through which reality is both known and known to be

15 Ibid. 338. See also Lonergan's *Philosophy of God, and Theology* 12 [*Papers 1965–1980* (2004) 172]: '... proof ... presupposes the erection of a system ... but the system itself ... has its presuppositions. It presupposes a horizon.'

16 'The Form of Inference.' in *Collection* (1967) 15 [(1988) 16].

17 In 'The Assumption and Theology,' in *Collection* (1967) 76 n. 17 [(1988) 73–74 n. 17] (see note 49 below for information on original publication): 'it is not an implication as such but the affirmation of an implication that is true or false, certain or probable.'

18 'Verbum' (1946–49). The articles were published in book form, with an Introduction added by Lonergan, some twenty years later: *Verbum* (1967) [subsequently republished in 1997 as vol. 2 of *Collected Works of Bernard Lonergan*].

19 *Verbum* (1967) 215 [(1997) 222].

20 Ibid. (1967) 34 [(1997) 47].

21 Ibid. (1967) 47–95 [(1997) 60–105].

known,'[22] in which the issue is 'not knowledge as true or false but knowledge as known to be true or false.'[23]

Three headings are distinguished here: assent, criteriology, and epistemology, this latter not so named in the listing.[24] I delay on assent only to note that it is not just a synthesis of subject and predicate, but the positing of that synthesis as true[25] – assent therefore in Newman's sense, going beyond inference. Criteriology is the business of telling true judgments from false, 'measuring by a standard,'[26] which means a return from judgments to their sources. Those sources are found 'in sense and in intellectual light';[27] or, again, 'in sense and in naturally known principles.'[28]

Now an infinite regress is repeatedly rejected,[29] but 'naturally known principles' do raise the question of the 'nature' by which they are known; and, if that nature be the 'light' of intellect, then that light too must be studied. So we come to the section on wisdom[30] and to questions of epistemology. Wisdom is ultimate for Aquinas, for it 'validates even first principles themselves.'[31] The ontological explanation of this: we can make 'true affirmations of existence ... in virtue of our intellectual light, which is the participation of eternal Light.'[32] But epistemologically that is not enough, for the issue is not just knowing but knowing our knowing: 'intellectual knowledge is not merely true but also aware of its own truth.'[33] And here Lonergan finds a Thomist epistemology inchoate in the notion of intellect's reflecting on itself to know its own nature; 'and if it knows its own nature, intellect also known its own proportion to knowledge of reality.'[34]

---

22 Ibid. (1967) 48 [(1997) 61].
23 Ibid. (1967) 59 [(1997) 71].
24 Ibid. (1967) 60 [(1997) 72–73].
25 Ibid. (1967) 59 [(1997) 71].
26 Ibid. (1967) 60 [(1997) 72].
27 Ibid. (1967) 64–65 [(1997) 77].
28 Ibid. (1967) 65 [(1997) 77].
29 Ibid. (1967) 56, 67, 70 [(1997) 68–69, 79, 82].
30 Ibid. (1967) 66–75 [(1997) 78–87].
31 Ibid. (1967) 68 [(1997) 80].
32 Ibid. (1967) 74 [(1997) 85–86].
33 Ibid. (1967) 75 [(1997) 86].
34 Ibid. (1967) 75 [(1997) 86]. More on the relation of ontology and epistemology, ibid. (1967) 87 [(1997) 98]. See also '*Insight*: Preface to a Discussion,' in *Collection* (1967) 160 [(1988) 150], on ontological cause and cognitional reason (this was a paper read to the American Catholic Philosophical Association at its 1958 meeting).

The next section, 'Self-knowledge of Soul,'[35] is Lonergan's deepest penetration here of this question of grounding our knowledge in its ultimate cognitional basis. The key point: with certain restrictions 'we may say that the light of agent intellect is known *per se ipsum*'[36] – not known as an object is known, but known in illuminating objects and making them known,[37] and so going beyond Aristotle's agent intellect[38] but also replacing the Augustinian 'vision of eternal truth.'[39] Thus far we have Aquinas as guide; but Lonergan feels we must carry Aquinas forward to an epistemological position based on 'a development of understanding by which we come to grasp just how it is that our minds are proportionate to knowledge of reality,' namely, through 'a grasp of the native infinity of intellect.'[40]

The *Verbum* articles then, though their direct concern is the thought of St Thomas, are a significant stage in Lonergan's own search for foundations. The phrase, 'ultimate ground' occurs and is used in an ontological sense, but with implicit extension to the epistemological.[41] And the concern is clearly Lonergan's own. After what may seem a pejorative reference in the first article to 'the epistemological bog,'[42] he makes a point of bringing out the inchoate Thomist epistemology, expressly tries to go beyond it, and would heighten the 'echo in a modern mind.'[43] Thus, he sees the modern critical problem as one not 'of moving from within outwards' but 'of moving from above downwards, of moving from an infinite potentiality commensurate with the universe towards a rational apprehension that seizes the difference of subject and object in essentially the same way that it seizes any other real distinction.'[44] His own epistemology in simplest summary: 'We know by what we are; we know we know by knowing what we are.'[45]

But I would note that it is only a 'stage' in his search; even in the search for cognitional foundations, it is only a stage. It will take time

35 *Verbum* (1967) 75–88 [(1997) 87–99].
36 Ibid. (1967) 80 [(1997) 91].
37 Ibid. (1967) 80 [(1997) 91].
38 Ibid. (1967) 79, 83 [(1997) 90–91, 94–95].
39 Ibid. (1967) 83 [(1997) 95].
40 Ibid. (1967) 85 [(1997) 96].
41 Ibid. (1967) 74 [(1967) 85–86].
42 Ibid. (1967) 7 [(1997) 20].
43 Ibid. (1967) 87 [(1997) 98].
44 Ibid. (1967) 88 [(1997) 98–99].
45 Ibid. (1967) 88 [(1997) 99].

and effort to move out of the Thomist context, replace Thomist language, refine the Thomist solution, and move fully into the twentieth century. The metaphor of light, useful though it be, will give way in *Insight* to direct appropriation of interiority, of 'the dynamic orientation of intelligent and rational consciousness,' that is, the notion of being.[46] The knowledge of light *per se ipsum* will be replaced by a self-authenticating grasp of the virtually unconditioned. The native infinity of intellect will likewise yield to the unrestricted objective of intelligence, to the permanently self-transcending nature of a consciousness that never ceases to ask questions, that can be known empirically to be oriented to the All, and to suppose by its very activity the intelligibility of the All. But intellect as a faculty, and wisdom as its highest realization, make a slow exit. They emerge again after *Insight*, to disappear almost completely only in the post-1965 regrouping of forces for the writing of *Method in Theology*.[47] There is work to be done also on the subjective conditions of knowing. And maybe most fundamental, though elusive and hard to document, is a mentality that seems to change subtly at this time. I mean that there is, in 1947, almost a hint of proving antecedently that we can know. Deduction is expressly excluded, but there is 'a sort of reasoning' which is 'a development of understanding'[48] in the way intellect knows its capacity to know. Such language, I think, would be alien in *Insight*. In fact, we may be surprised to learn, the critical problem gets rather short shrift in that work.

I pause, on the way to *Insight*, to notice two relevant articles. The symposium paper 'The Assumption and Theology'[49] is an instance of the actual founding of a dogma in the sense which foundations would then have had for Lonergan, and it shows the principles by which he would provide those foundations. Unquestioned is the given starting point: 'a divine revelation which already is in the order of truth.'[50] But

46 *Insight* (1957) 370 [(1992) 394–95].

47 See note 144 below. A point to be kept in mind, in relation to Lonergan's continual insistence on human development, is the slow growth of wisdom; see, for example, 'The Natural Desire to See God,' in *Collection* (1967) 89 [(1988) 86]: 'wisdom is the cumulative product of a long series of acts of understanding' (this was a paper read to the Jesuit Philosophical Association at its 1949 meeting).

48 See *Verbum* (1967) 85 [(1997) 96].

49 'The Assumption and Theology,' first published in *Vers le dogme de L'Assomption* (Montreal: Fides, 1948) 411–24; then as chapter 4 of *Collection* (1967) 68–83 [(1988) 66–80].

50 Ibid. (1967) 76 [(1988) 74].

since the assumption of Mary is not explicit in our sources of revelation, we have to seek an additional principle. Lonergan defines it as 'a development of understanding, an opening of the eyes of faith, upon what had been long revealed but ... not ... apprehended.'[51] So he tries to do here with the data of the New Testament what Jesus himself had done for the two disciples on the way to Emmaus with the Old Testament data.[52] It is a matter of the 'implication' of scripture,[53] 'grasped as human understanding ... penetrates the economy of man's fall and redemption and settles our Lady's place in it.'[54] On the question of foundations, then, I would say that this is the classical type of theology, but brought forward by Newman's notion of development, and further refined by Lonergan's view of the act of understanding. I have no doubt that it is still valid, but also by the standards of *Method in Theology* it is a long way from being complete.

The other article is 'A Note on Geometrical Possibility,'[55] dated 1950. We may note the rather extrinsic point that Lonergan refers to Forder's book on *The Foundations of Euclidean Geometry*,[56] and himself speaks of 'the problem of consistency of foundation propositions'[57] – an indication of his familiarity then with foundational language. But what I find more interesting is the application of such language to possibility and intelligibility, for we think of it more commonly in the context of actuality and truth. Thus, 'the ground of possibility is intelligibility,'[58] and so likewise 'knowledge of possibility rests on knowledge of intelligibility.'[59] It is true that Lonergan is speaking of 'true judgment of possibility,' with the two groundings it may have, the consequent ground of known actuality and the antecedent ground of known intelligibility.[60] Still, grasp of intelligibility seems to have this peculiarity that no further positive input is required to know it. At any rate this article sug-

51 Ibid. (1967) 72 [(1988) 71].
52 Ibid. (1967) 73 [(1988) 71].
53 Ibid. (1967) 75 [(1988) 73].
54 Ibid. (1967) 82 [(1988) 80].
55 First published in *The Modern Schoolman* 27 (1949–50) 124–38, and then as chapter 6 of *Collection* (1967) 96–113 [(1988) 92–107].
56 Ibid. (1967) 97 [(1988) 92].
57 Ibid. (1967) 97 [(1988) 93].
58 Ibid. (1967) 108 [(1988) 103].
59 Ibid. (1967) 111 [(1988) 105].
60 Ibid. (1967) 107 [(1988) 102].

gests to me the analogy of foundations. We know that Lonergan does not talk much of analogy as such, but does draw up, repeatedly, creative analogies: the analogy of being, of matter, of intelligence, of meaning, etc. So we might draw up an analogy of foundations: foundations of being and of knowing; in the former, of actuality and of possibility; in the latter, foundations of truth, of inference,[61] and also, presumably, of intelligibility.

So we come to *Insight*, dated more usefully in 1953 when, except for a few revisions, it was finished, than in 1957 when it was published.[62] We find that the focus has shifted now away from an earlier concern with epistemology to a concern with the nature and forms of knowing, and with its subjective conditions understood in a somewhat more existential sense. This I will explain in due course.

It is worth making the preliminary point that *Insight* as a work bears the general character of Lonergan's work: that is, it is itself an exercise in foundations, in the analogous senses just indicated. One can easily verify this in what we have seen him name 'criteriology.' I note three samples of his criteriology in action. The first is his writing style. One may take a few test pages (try [1957] pp. ix–xv, [1992] pp. 3–9) and see how often the phrase 'it follows' occurs there. The second might be a couple of his more famous formal arguments, that from latent to explicit metaphysics,[63] and that for the existence of God.[64] The third: his frequent reference to the role of the a priori, especially for the upper blade of the heuristic method. A large question, all this, but my sketchy paragraph may help us maintain an ever difficult perspective.

To turn from practice to the thematizing of it, I would say that a chief contribution of *Insight* to our question is its displacement of the critical problem, a displacement announced in the first paragraph of

---

61 'Syllogism ... is ... an instrument for exhibiting the grounds of a judgment on the conclusion' ('Theology and Understanding,' in *Collection* [1967] 125, [1988] 117).

62 The published form of 1957 differs from the typescript of 1953 mainly in having a new Preface and revisions to the mathematical and scientific examples of the first five chapters. The 1953 typescript is available at some of the Lonergan Centers of Research (note 5, above). [The original Preface now has been published in *METHOD: Journal of Lonergan Studies* 3/1 (1985) 3–7 (ed.).]

63 *Insight* (1957) 399–400 [(1992) 424–25].

64 Ibid. (1957) 672 [(1992) 695]. Lonergan does not, in 'The Form of Inference,' use the term 'syllogism' for arguments of the form, 'If A, then B; but A; therefore B.' Nor does he do so, as far as I know, in *Insight*.

the Introduction: 'In the first place, the question is not whether knowledge exists but what precisely is its nature.'[65] Rarely does an opening salvo find so unerringly its target, for in *Insight*'s analysis of what knowing is we have not only the positive foundation for an expanding correct knowledge but also the dialectical factor that can either lead to aberrations or, if recognized, enable us to account for and reverse the aberrations. The point is: 'in each of us there exist two different kinds of knowledge ... separated and alienated in ... rationalist and empiricist philosophies.'[66] The resulting duality does not mean we should reduce them to one in a kind of self-mutilation. 'The problem set by the two types of knowing is, then, not a problem of elimination but a problem of critical distinction. For the difficulty lies, not in either type of knowing by itself, but in the confusion that arises when one shifts unconsciously from one type to the other. Animals have no epistemological problems.'[67] Thus we have 'two quite different realisms ... [one] incoherent ... half animal and half human ... [the other] intelligent and reasonable.'[68] The whole of *Insight* can be read, it seems to me, as an extended effort to establish a coherent realism based on a proper recognition of the duality of our knowing. This lies behind the repeated statement that the real is being, that is, what can be intelligently grasped and reasonably affirmed – not, as might be thought by a naive realist, what can be seen or touched. If I may venture an opinion after years of mulling over these matters ('venture' – hoping it will not be taken for a shibboleth), I would say that, if one understands what Lonergan is after in proclaiming the real to be identical with being, one possesses the master key to *Insight*.

I spoke above of criteriology in action. But it can be set forth as a position too, on the basis of Chapters 9 and 10. To be noted: we are still in the first part of the book, on insight as an activity and not as knowledge; hence, the critical problem can hardly be an issue yet. What is at issue is where to find the measure of our knowledge. Thus, Chapter 10 speaks of judgment as resulting from the marshalling and weighing of evi-

65 Ibid. (1957) xvii [(1992) 11].

66 Ibid. (1957) xvii [(1992) 11–12].

67 Ibid. (1957) 253 [(1992) 278]. Robert M. Doran, *Psychic Conversion and Theological Foundations* (Chico, CA: Scholars Press, 1981) 59, refers to 'what *Insight* calls the polymorphism of human consciousness and identifies as the root of the foundational dilemma.'

68 *Insight* (1957) xxviii [(1992) 22].

dence, and asks: 'But what are the scales on which evidence is weighed?' The answer takes us to 'the grounding act of reflective understanding,' illustrated 'from the form of deductive inference'[69] as showing the meaning of the virtually unconditioned, but not to be identified with deduction at all: 'deductive inference cannot be the basic case of judgment, for it presupposes other judgments to be true.'[70] A further step takes us to the invulnerable insight that 'there are no further, pertinent questions.'[71] But to recognize that we have reached that stage we need a 'happy balance between rashness and indecision.'[72] So Lonergan concludes with what are essentially practical rules for judgment: give the questions a chance to arise; let the question we try to answer be in a familiar field; let the process of learning break the vicious circle in which judgment on any insight seems based on previous correct insights.[73] That is, the 'self-correcting process tends to a limit ... reaches its limit in familiarity with the concrete situation and in easy mastery of it ... [W]hile the limit is not marked with a label, still its attainment is revealed by a habitual ability to know just what is up.'[74]

This does not sound much like direct confrontation with the critical problem, and in fact it is not that. It is criteriological, in the sense of the *Verbum* articles. It is strategic. It takes us behind 'our conceptual distinction between correct and mistaken insights' to 'an operational distinction between invulnerable and vulnerable insights.'[75] But it does not and cannot, and neither can any criteriology or strategy, offer an ultimate rule, criterion, norm, standard, scale, for judging judgment simply and universally. 'Were there some simple formula or recipe in answer to such questions, then men of good judgment could be produced at will and indefinitely.'[76] What we can achieve is what Lonergan in Chapter 17 will call a 'proximate criterion' of truth.[77]

69 Ibid. (1957) 279 [(1992) 304–305].
70 Ibid. (1957) 281 [(1992) 306].
71 Ibid. (1957) 284 [(1992) 309].
72 Ibid. (1957) 285 [(1992) 310].
73 Ibid. (1957) 285–87 [(1992) 310–12].
74 Ibid. (1957) 286–87 [(1992) 312].
75 Ibid. (1957) 284 [(1992) 309].
76 Ibid. (1957) 285 [(1992) 310].
77 Ibid. (1957) 549 [(1992) 573]. In the notes on 'Mathematical Logic' (note 95, below) Lonergan tells us: 'The criterion of truth is analyzed ... in *Insight*, Chap. X, as a virtually unconditioned' (III/3).

The critical problem in the standard sense belongs, then, in Part Two of the book, which deals with insight as knowledge; and it does emerge in Chapter 11, to receive, I would say, rather quick riddance. The chapter has to do with what is called 'Self-affirmation,' but the point lies in the kind of self that is affirmed, namely, a self that is conscious empirically, intelligently, and rationally. Section 6, 'Self-affirmation as Immanent Law,'[78] offers a negative and a positive solution to the critical problem. First, there is the contradiction of self-negation, seen in the traditional device of getting the skeptic to talk. In Lonergan's formulation: the skeptic is involved in contradiction because he has no choice but to be conscious empirically, intelligently, rationally, once he chooses to talk.[79] The negative statement, then: rational consciousness can criticize everything else, but 'only on condition that it does not criticize itself.'[80] The positive counterpart is an operating reality and our appropriation of it. The reality can be given many names: a dynamism, an eros, a spontaneity, an inevitability, a necessity, an immanent Anagke. It can be seen as operative in the whole process from experience through understanding to judgment, as giving us no rest till we arrive at the realm of fact to which the dynamism committed us from the beginning. To write such lines (based on this section 6) is to try to give expression to an appropriation of the reality. Maybe it can be put more simply still:

> Behind that contradiction [of self-negation] there have been discerned natural inevitabilities and spontaneities that constitute the possibility of knowing, not by demonstrating that one can know, but pragmatically by engaging one in the process. Nor in the last resort can one reach a deeper foundation than that pragmatic engagement. Even to seek it involves a vicious circle; for if one seeks such a foundation, one employs one's cognitional process; and the foundation to be reached will be no more secure or solid than the inquiry utilized to reach it.[81]

---

78 *Insight* (1957) 329–32 [(1992) 353–57].

79 Ibid. (1957) 329 [(1992) 353–54].

80 Ibid. (1957) 332 [(1992) 356].

81 Ibid. (1957) 332 [(1992) 356]. The rest of chapter 11 speaks passim of this foundation as not subject to revision (see especially section 7, 'Description and Explanation,' [1957] 332–35, [1992] 357–59, and section 8, 'The Impossibility of Revision,' [1957] 335–36, [1992] 359–60). Section 6 would stand to these sections as the reflection that appropriates foundations does to the reflection that appropriates the security of the foundations.

The preceding paragraph is a statement of Lonergan's epistemology, of his solution to the critical problem as that problem is commonly posed, of the foundations he assigns for knowledge. It is a brief statement, as was the original, the section studied being only four pages out of nearly eight hundred, and the epistemology occupying only one page of the four. Why say more? Negatively, the opposite claim is self-destructive; positively, Lonergan's position rests ultimately on fact, not on talking about the fact. The need of talking arises when there is confusion about the nature of knowing or about the subject himself or herself, when there are biases, when there is flight from understanding. We can still call this a discussion of foundations, if we will, but only in an analogous sense.

We come, then, to discussion of subjective factors in knowledge, a feature of *Insight* that I did not attend to properly when I made the Index twenty-five years ago.[82] I bring it in now in reference to the remote criterion of truth, about which the reader may be wondering since my mention above of the proximate criterion. As defined it is simple enough. 'The remote criterion is the proper unfolding of the detached and disinterested desire to know.'[83] But far more complex is the actual unfolding: 'The subject becomes more or less secure or anxious about the genuineness of his inquiry and reflection, and further inquiry and reflection will in their turn be open to similar questioning. What is in doubt is the subject himself, and all his efforts to remove the doubt will proceed from the same suspected source.'[84]

It is worth the while to collect some of the data on this subjective side, for they anticipate *Method in Theology* to a quite remarkable extent. Thus, we read in the Introduction to *Insight*: 'Prior to all writing of history, prior to all interpretation of other minds, there is the self-scrutiny of the historian, the self-knowledge of the interpreter'[85] – surely a sentence that could be set without change in the Introduction to *Method in Theol-*

82 Compare the word 'Subject' in the Index of *Insight* and in the Index of *Understanding and Being*. Though the latter book edits lectures of 1958, covers the same ground as *Insight*, and is less than half the size, the references to the subject in its Index are far more numerous. I recall a remark of Philip McShane, when he had worked on the Index to *Method in Theology*, to the effect that an index reveals mercilessly the horizons of the indexer.

83 *Insight* (1957) 550 [(1992) 573].

84 Ibid. (1957) 551 [(1992) 574].

85 Ibid. (1957) xxix [(1992) 23].

ogy. Take another sounding in Chapter 6: 'common sense relates things to use. [But] ... who are we? ... an account of common sense cannot be adequate without an investigation of its subjective field.'[86] The chapter on judgment, too, can be reread with the same question to guide us: 'It is only when I go to the root of the matter and become efficaciously critical of myself that I can begin to become a reliable judge.'[87] To take but one more sounding, Chapter 14 on the method of metaphysics goes deeply into the question of the polymorphic human consciousness, and sees it as the source of diverse philosophies, of positions and counterpositions on knowing, objectivity and reality. A revealing pair of sentences: 'Metaphysics ... is not something in a book but something in a mind,'[88] and, 'the starting-point of metaphysics is people as they are.'[89]

A few notes now to relate *Insight* more accurately to Lonergan's other writings, and first its general relation to the *Verbum* articles. *Insight* makes much of its focus on the nature of knowledge, but we saw something quite a bit like that in the articles. The differences, I would say, are these. The articles talk of the nature of intellectual light, but *Insight* of the nature of our knowing, and then with a view to distinguishing two types of knowing. More important: the articles almost make the 'known' nature of light an antecedent ground for knowing that we can know, and this through a reasoning process, and that does not fit in *Insight*, which distinguishes more sharply, and abides by the distinction, between nature and existence of knowledge, and gives little time to either the existence or the possibility of knowing. Finally, both works appeal to what we are as a foundation, but the articles to what we are in virtue of a light proportionate to the universe, and *Insight* to what we are in virtue of a eros, an immanent Anagke, a commitment to the realm of fact.

A second note concerns Thomist wisdom. It appears in *Insight* but only in a historical overview of positions on being. Still, Lonergan is reluctant to abandon the term. To the two Thomist uses – the wisdom which is a gift of the Spirit, and the wisdom which is 'first philosophy ... as the knowledge of all things in their ultimate causes'[90] – he would

86 Ibid. (1957) 181 [(1992) 204].
87 Ibid. (1957) 293 [(1992) 318].
88 Ibid. (1957) 396 [(1992) 421].
89 Ibid. (1957) 397 [(1992) 422].
90 Ibid. (1957) 407 [(1992) 432].

add a third which our times require and we can piece together in cognitional terms from the works of Aquinas, an obvious reference to the *Verbum* articles. Thomist wisdom will continue to haunt Lonergan's work on foundations in his summer institute of 1957, and in his course *De intellectu et methodo* in 1959 and *De methodo theologiae* in 1962, to disappear almost completely, at least as a category under this name, in the *Method in Theology* of 1972.[91]

My third note relates *Insight* to its own second edition. I suppose that is the edition used by most of my readers, and they may have wondered why I did not mention the little section that appears under the title 'Foundations' on page 98 [(1992) 122]; and, even more, why I did not notice the references on pages 340–41 [(1992) 364] to the third constitutive level of knowing as 'both self-authenticating and decisive.' The reason in both cases is that those usages appear in the revised edition of 1958 but not in the first edition, and are almost certainly due to the Boston College lectures of 1957. For foundations is a theme in those lectures, and 'self-justifying horizons' almost is. I do not think that is the case in *Insight* (one learns to be cautious on those 300,000 words and more), though 'foundation' occurs in a passage quoted already,[92] and we read of 'limiting structures that carry their own guarantee,'[93] the equivalent of self-authenticating grasp of the virtually unconditioned.[94]

We come then to 1957 when Frederick Adelmann, of the Boston College Department of Philosophy, invited Lonergan to give a summer institute there, with a week of lectures on mathematical logic and a week on existentialism. Records of those lectures I find illuminating

91 *De methodo theologiae* was a course given at the Gregorian University in the spring of 1962; a good part of it is available, in notes taken by students (60 pages, legal-size), at the various Lonergan Centers; the same ground was covered in an 'Institute on the Method of Theology,' in the summer of 1962 at Regis College, Toronto. For my little history of 'wisdom' I refer the reader again to note 144 below.

92 *Insight* (1957) 332 [(1992) 356].

93 Ibid. (1957) 551 [(1992) 575].

94 Robert Doran, *Psychic Conversion and Theological Foundations*, (above, note 67) remarks (214, note 33 to his chap. 2): 'In *Insight*, Lonergan does not use the term, foundations, in this context [that of chaps. 11–13], but refers to cognitional theory as the *basis* for metaphysics, ethics, and theology.' On the matter of revisions of *Insight*, users of the first edition may have noticed that line 24, page 341, should have 'inflexibility' rather than 'flexibility' for the Kantian categories.

for the direction of his development at this time.[95] The first week offered five lectures: the general character of mathematical logic; the history of its development; the truth of its systems; the foundations of logic; and the relation of mathematical logic to Scholasticism. The third lecture not only assigns to the systems of logic 'the verbal type of truth that pertains to the analytic proposition,'[96] but would also grant them fragments of a form of factual truth, that is, factual truth of 'the provisional type.'[97] So lecture four, dealing with foundations, is dealing with the foundations of truths, and they are clearly stated. 'The subject in this self-knowledge [that is, that of *Insight*] is the foundation of logic; it is a foundation in the reality of the subject himself, and in every experiencing, intelligent, reasonable subject; it is a foundation in a reality and so it is beyond formulations ... of philosophic positions.'[98]

Lonergan goes on at once to extend the same foundations to other branches of philosophy. More clearly still in the next lecture: 'Hence, in the fourth lecture, I sought the foundations of logic in the subject's personal appropriation of his own empirical, intellectual, and rational consciousness; on this view the foundations of logic are by identity the solution of the epistemological problem, the foundations of metaphysics, the foundations of ethics, and the foundations of natural theology.'[99] Succinct and clarifying statements, these, locating foundations in the reality of the subject, and extending its foundational role over the range of philosophic disciplines.

Two notes on this week of lectures. The first: the reader will have noticed the verbal usage in my last quotation, where we have 'the foun-

---

95 A sheaf of 22 pages is available at the various Lonergan Centers, under the title 'Mathematical Logic. Notes for Lectures at Boston College, July, 1957.' They are numbered by lectures; thus 'III/3' means page 3 of lecture 3. For some help in relating mathematicians' interests to those of *Insight*, see Philip McShane, 'The Foundations of Mathematics,' chap. 2 of *Lonergan's Challenge to the University and the Economy* (Washington: University Press of America, 1980). Understanding and Being ([1980] 235–38, [1990] 191–93) has some remarks on the foundations of science. [Lonergan's notes for both sets of lectures, together with the texts of the lectures as reconstructed from tape recordings, were published in 2001 as volume 18 of *Collected Works of Bernard Lonergan* (ed.).]

96 'Mathematical Logic' III/4 [(2001) 153].

97 Ibid. III/5 [(2001) 154]. On the meaning of 'provisional' here, see *Insight* (1957) 306–307 [(1992) 331].

98 'Mathematical Logic' IV/6 [(2001) 160].

99 Ibid. V/1 [(2001) 162].

dations of metaphysics' but 'the solution of the epistemological problem.' This surely represents a deliberate and careful choice. Sciences that, methodically, are derivative have a foundation; but that from which they cognitionally derive cannot strictly have a cognitional foundation, and that is the field of epistemology; so we 'solve' the critical problem by appropriation of our knowing, but basically the knowing is self-authenticating. Our second note: there is a clarification on Thomist wisdom. Still holding wisdom to be 'ultimate and decisive' but still feeling the need to modify the Thomist account, Lonergan tells us that in *Insight* he tried to work out 'a genetic account' of wisdom.[100] We shall see him in 1959 study the genesis in some detail.

The lectures of the second week, on existentialism, bring to focus many scattered elements in previous work and make thematic the existential subject that will figure so largely in *Method in Theology*.[101] Actual lecture divisions are not clear in the records we have, but topical headings are: for example, 'On Being Oneself'; 'The Dilemma of the Subject'; 'Subject and Horizon'; 'Horizon and Dread'; 'Horizon and History'; 'Horizon as the Problem of Philosophy.' All these topics follow some historical lectures, mainly on Jaspers, Husserl, and Heidegger. Our locus of interest is the last heading of the lectures, 'Horizon as the Problem of Philosophy' (I suspect we should read '*the* Problem'). Here we find the following: 'The multiplicity of horizons as philosophic issue arises when we ask: Is some horizon the field, or is there no field? If some horizon is the field, how can it be determined?'[102] The distinction has been made, 'The field is *the* universe, but my horizon defines *my* universe.'[103] Lonergan, of course, opts for a field, so the problem does arise of determining this horizon-field and justifying it.

It is not a simple problem, for any answer 'arises within a stream of consciousness and so arises within what already is constituted as a horizon.' The horizon cannot then be justified by the realities which are known within that horizon and are regularly consonant with it; if it

100 Ibid.

101 Available at the various Lonergan Centers under the title 'Existentialism. Notes on Lectures at Boston College, July, 1957.' But there have been different 'editions'; for my references I use that of the Thomas More Institute, Montreal, 1957, but I have numbered the pages consecutively (1–28). [On the publication in 2001 of these notes and the reconstructions of the lectures, see above, note 95 (ed.).]

102 'Existentialism. Notes on Lectures at Boston College, July, 1957,' 27 [(2001) 213].

103 Ibid. 20 [(2001) 199].

could, every horizon would 'automatically be self-justifying.' This applies not only to objects known but equally to the subject known as object, for it becomes then one of the realities known within the given horizon. If neither the object known as object, or the subject known as object, can provide justification, that is, 'constitute a self-justifying horizon,' where shall we look? Lonergan's answer is the subject as subject: 'The prior reality that both grounds horizons and the critique of horizons and the determination of the field is the reality of the subject as subject.'[104]

These ideas surely flow into the revisions of *Insight* that were drafted in the spring of 1958 for the second edition. They just as surely flow into the abstract of the talk never actually given on 'Philosophic Differences and Personal Development.'[105] In fact, some lines of the latter are taken almost verbatim from the lectures on existentialism:

> A new higher viewpoint in the natural sciences ordinarily involves no revision of the subject's image and concept of himself, and so scientific advance easily wins universal and permanent acceptance. But a higher viewpoint in philosophy not only logically entails such a revision but also cannot be grasped with a 'real apprehension' unless the revision actually becomes effective in the subject's mental attitudes. So the philosophic schools are many ...

Interesting as these bits of history are, the main thing is the issue being debated, and the passage just quoted is clear enough on that: the issue is the subject and his conversion. Foundations then has emerged as a theme in 1957; so has the subject. It remains to add the theme of historical differentiation and to import these themes more fully into theology. This will be achieved in the work of 1959.

To go forward, however, to 1959 and the plateau I judge that year to represent, we need to go back to 1954 and an article I have omitted, 'Theology and Understanding.'[106] Historically, this is very significant for Lonergan's development. It shows the full measure of his debt to Aquinas in theological method, but also introduces the factors that will

---

104 Ibid. 28 [(2001) 214].

105 See *The New Scholasticism* 32 (1958) 97.

106 First published in *Gregorianum* 35 (1954) 630–48, and then as chapter 8 of *Collection* (1967) 121–41 [(1988) 114–32].

take him eventually so far beyond Aquinas. Two streams are meeting, but not yet in turmoil and still less unified. As for Aquinas, then, Lonergan's concern here is to rescue him from the 'conclusions-theology' where some were bent on locating him. The rescue operation is performed by the same means used in 'the Assumption and Theology,' namely, a concept of theology as understanding to be found in the Thomist works. The syllogism, says Lonergan, has two functions: it is 'an instrument for exhibiting the grounds of a judgment on the conclusion ... But it is also an instrument of developing understanding'[107] and this latter aspect in St Thomas is lost by those who read him as a conclusions-theologian. As for foundational ideas, Thomist wisdom plays its regular role for ultimate validation on the human side, and we need not go through that again. Objectively the whole depends on God's word: 'From revelation come the premises ... and on the truth of the premises rests the truth ... of their conclusions.'[108]

So far we do not seem to have advanced much beyond 'The Assumption and Theology.' But that changes in the latter part of the article, where there appears in thematic form a whole new world which had lain outside the Thomist horizon and will occupy Lonergan now for the next eighteen years. Still, the breakthrough is not trumpeted but introduced modestly enough as follows:

> Aristotelian and scholastic notions of science seem to me to be adequate for a formulation of the nature of speculative theology [notice the qualification: 'speculative' theology] both in itself and in its relations to revelation, to philosophy, and to the teaching authority of the church, still I should avoid the appearance of making exaggerated claims and so I should acknowledge the existence of contemporary methodological issues that cannot be dispatched in so expeditious a fashion.[109]

These issues are four in number: the patterns of human experience;[110] the relations between speculative and positive theology;[111] those between speculative theology and the empirical human sciences;[112] and

107 Ibid. (1967) 125 [(1988) 117].
108 Ibid. (1967) 131 [(1988) 123].
109 Ibid. (1967) 135 [(1988) 127].
110 Ibid. (1967) 135 [(1988) 127].
111 Ibid. (1967) 137 [(1988) 128].
112 Ibid. (1967) 139 [(1988) 130].

the way the issues of historical interpretation 'are complicated by the self-knowledge of the interpreter,' presenting us with 'all the complexities of the critical problem.' But here, as in *Insight*, one has to conceive the critical problem 'not as the easy question whether we know but as the real issue of what precisely occurs when we are knowing.'[113]

We come at last to *De intellectu et methodo*, a course offered to doctoral students in theology and philosophy at the Gregorian University, Rome, in the spring semester of 1959. It was reported rather fully in notes taken by students, to whom we can never be sufficiently grateful; for this course represents, as far as I know, the first documented thematizing of foundations as the problem occurs in theology.[114] It is still far enough from the 1972 position of *Method in Theology*, but does mark a clear and significant stage on the way.

We will be concerned with the first part of the notes, on the notion of the question,[115] and especially with the sixth and last section of this part, the one with the lion's share:[116] '*de problematibus fundamenti-historicitatis-separationis*.'[117] Let us run quickly through the approach. The first four sections deal mainly with the conditions for the existence of a question,[118] the historical series of questions,[119] the ordering of the answers,[120] and the series of such orderings.[121] Examples are drawn mainly from Trinitarian theology, and the problem to be tackled in the last section already appears in the example of divine missions. This notion is first in the ordering we call the *via analytica* (St Paul's notion of mission) but last in the ordering we call the *via synthetica* (no doubt a reference to St. Thomas in his *Summa theologiae*; see pages 8–10 of the notes). The fifth section[122] is on the criteria of any new ordering. Obviously owing something to the lectures of 1957, it declares the impossibility of

113 Ibid. (1967) 141 [(1988) 132].

114 There are 72 pages of notes, legal-size and single-spaced, available again at the Lonergan Centers. According to my sources, our chief benefactors are Francesco Rossi de Gasperis and P. Joseph Cahill, both students of the course.

115 *De intellectu et methodo* 1–25.

116 Ibid. 11–25.

117 Ibid. 1.

118 Ibid. 1–4.

119 Ibid. 4–5.

120 Ibid. 5–8.

121 Ibid. 8–10.

122 Ibid. 10–11.

transforming Scholasticism into a system like that of mathematical logic, but remarks that the attempt would nevertheless be very useful; for it would show clearly the futility of the eternally disputed Scholastic questions and the need for a new ordering of theology. It might also suggest the need to raise the problem of method. Lonergan's mind is naturally on method throughout the course.

Section six, then, regards the three problems that I translate as the problems of foundations, of historicity, and of estrangement.[123] Lonergan will presently explain them as the problem of *transition* from one ordering of doctrine or theology to another, the problem of *continuity* throughout the orderings, and the problem of the ever greater *systematizing* of an ordering, which means we are taken farther and farther from our sources. And he will add that they are not really three problems, but one problem of method with three aspects.[124] Still, he will set them forth singly,[125] and propose a solution in the same way.[126]

It is revealing that at this time Lonergan sees the problem of foundations as one of transitions. It means that for him theology is still 'classical' in regard to its sources, whose foundations are not called into question: what happens afterwards is what creates the problem. It is, indeed, a wider problem than that of theology. The whole history of philosophy and theology is a series of orderings and of transitions from one ordering to another. Further, there are various views on what we call 'perennial philosophy' or 'solid Catholic doctrine' (that is, teaching which extends over time, and presumably has achieved transitions without loss of continuity). Hence, faced with opposing views, we cannot avoid the task of choosing. But what will be the criterion of our choice? Thus do we come to the problem of foundations. It can be seen in particular when one studies development in a single author, say, Aquinas (no doubt Lonergan has in mind here the theology of grace

123 As reported in the notes, Lonergan uses both *separatio* and *chasma/chaos* (this in reference to Luke 16:26) where I translate *estrangement*. In the lectures of 1957 on *Existentialism* he spoke of the 'existential gap' between one's horizon on oneself and what one really is (p. 22 of the notes [(2001) 203]). The context is different but the idea of gap is the same. For our context, see the statement of *Method in Theology* 276: 'Scholarship builds an impenetrable wall between systematic theology and its historical religious sources.'

124 *De intellectu et methodo* 16.

125 Ibid. 11–16.

126 Ibid. 16–25.

studied in his own doctoral dissertation). Logically one cannot account for the differences: one would have to postulate many Aquinases. Lonergan would prefer to ask what the foundation was for Aquinas as he moved from one position to another. More generally, the problem is seen in the church's transition from one ordering of its doctrine to another while the dogmatic teaching nevertheless remains permanent. '*Quomodo fiet iste transitus et quibusdam criteriis eligetur nova ordinatio?*'[127]

The problem of estrangement is illustrated by the familiar example of the *homoousios,* introduced into church doctrine by the Council of Nicea in 325 and rejected as alien to tradition by the Arians and semi-Arians. St Athanasius did not deny the fact – the term *was* unbiblical, and hence alien to previous ways of talking – nor did he defend it as an ideal. But the constraint of the times made him defend it for the sake of the church's faith in the Son of God.[128] As for historicity, it is sufficiently illustrated by the example already seen and now repeated: divine missions as conceived by St Paul are not the same as divine missions as conceived by St Thomas Aquinas. There is then a leap, and the problem of foundations is to justify that leap.[129]

How are we to justify it? Pages 16–25 struggle with the answer. We do not justify it by the external form of the words we use: one may surely think of the 'fundamentalists' here, for whom words do serve as foundations. And not through manipulation of concepts and judgments (one thinks now of the 'conceptualists' – adversaries in the *Verbum* articles), for that works only within a given system. Lonergan had already rejected deduction as a means of transition[130] and returns to it again[131] to declare it helpless when questions arise that the system cannot account for – precisely the situation when there is a leap from one system to another.

127 Ibid. 11–12. There is an extremely interesting account of the way the same truth may be understood in greater or less degree, in *Divinarum personarum conceptio analogica* (Rome: Gregorian University Press, 1957) 17–19, where Lonergan takes us through four stages of understanding scripture. I have to omit that account here, but it cannot be stated too emphatically that his whole search for foundations was conducted in a continual engagement with actual theology, in this case, the theology of the Trinity.

128 *De intellectu et methodo* 12–14.

129 Ibid. 14–16.

130 Ibid. 12.

131 Ibid. 17–18.

Lonergan's own solution does not surprise us. It is to go behind the words, behind the concepts and judgments, in his habitual appeal to intelligence itself and its threefold formation through understanding, science, and wisdom. Wisdom is the key term, as it has been since the *Verbum* articles, being given a critical role in the selection of the first terms and principles, and in judgment on them and all their consequents. How, for example, can one judge between the various concepts of being? Not by means of some prior formula, for we are talking of the *first* term, but only by wisdom. And there are many ways of ordering the virtual totality of theology: shall we retain the old, or do we need a new? Wisdom will decide.[132]

What is different, however, in this work of 1959 – and significantly different, as we may judge with our excellent hindsight – is the searching dialectic to which Lonergan submits the notion of wisdom.[133] This critical examination can be read now as a kind of last effort to make do with the old before moving to the new. I sketch as briefly as I can the series of objections raised here against wisdom as foundation. (1) We are not born wise, or made wise necessarily by nature; so how can we even move toward wisdom? Such a step would itself require us to be wise already. (2) Wisdom is not in fact a first: it presupposes understanding and science. (3) It is useless to appeal to the wisdom of authority, for the unwise will interpret authority unwisely. (4) It is likewise useless to postulate a gradual progress through love of wisdom to wisdom itself; for, being unwise, how can we know we are really seeking true wisdom? (5) In any case, the danger of invoking wisdom is to endow with the virtue of wisdom the opinion of everyone, and thus promote relativism.

The objections, I would say, are predominantly of the 'vicious circle' type, and would therefore be valid only within the confines of a logical system. Since for Lonergan the mind has resources that easily free one from the logical ghetto, his answer will not surprise us any more than his general position did. He calls then on already established ideas. There is the intrinsic principle of the mind's dynamism (as contrasted with extrinsic terms). There is the notion of being, which already contains all knowledge in anticipation – the natural notion, of course, to be

132 Ibid. 17. Lonergan's students will recall his affection for the Thomist phrase *sapientis est ordinare*.

133 Ibid. 18–20.

distinguished from the reflected one. There is the possibility of some progress through applying the principle of contradiction to the Porphyrean tree. An analogy here, I suggest, is the game of '20 questions' – how rapidly one can zero in on a given 'x' by means of a well ordered set of questions. The reader will think: of course, but where do the questions – and the answers – come from? That is where Lonergan's next point applies: there is also the possibility of adding mastery over particular regions of being, as one grows to adult status and continues to develop. Or, briefly, to invoke an old Scholastic phrase, *sapientia non stat in indivisibili.*[134] Lonergan then goes on to answer the objections one by one, in a manner that would hardly suggest, except to the hindsight I mentioned, that wisdom will eventually give way to a modern adaptation.

Solutions to the other two problems are much shorter. Lonergan adduces his own work on the twofold way of analysis and synthesis,[135] and on the duality of human consciousness, as showing how two quite different thought-patterns can develop, with their consequent estrangement.[136] As for the problem of historicity, it is insoluble on the basis of a conceptualism that knows only how to manage concepts and judgments. But if one goes behind the concepts to their fertile source in insight, one can discover the possibility also of development of understanding, of different historical conceptions of the same reality; and thus the problem of historicity can be brought to heel.[137]

The foregoing sketch will serve, I hope, to give us an idea of the way Lonergan saw the problem of foundations and its solution in 1959. But, to keep all this in perspective, we have to remember that the overriding concern in this work, as it is in all his work at that time, is for method. The remainder of *De intellectu et methodo*, then, studies our ways of knowing, to develop and apply to theology five precepts of method.[138] To be noted is a strong insistence still on systematics.[139] Historical theology, in fact, is seen simply as systematic theology *in*

134 Ibid. 20.

135 On which see 'Theology and Understanding,' in *Collection* (1967) 127–30 [(1988) 119–22], and *Divinarum personarum conceptio analogica* 20–28.

136 *De intellectu et methodo* 22–24.

137 Ibid. 24–25.

138 Ibid. 26–72.

139 See ibid. 40–43, 50–52, on the precept *Intelligere systematice*.

fieri.[140] It is not that history is disregarded: there is reference to the lack of historical consciousness in St Thomas,[141] followed by a long study of the historical factor today;[142] but it remains rather extrinsic to what Lonergan would consider – I think we may fairly say it in this way – 'real' theology, namely, systematic understanding of revealed truth.

With this Gregorian University course of 1959 we have, I think, reached a definite plateau in Lonergan's search for foundations. In one way or another the question has been on his mind through two decades. Early reflection, however, simply carried the search back to the stable operation of the human mind, and did not explore that mind in any depth. Study of Thomist cognitional theory brought the critical problem to the fore; it was then conceived as the problem of knowing that we know, and a solution was found in terms of intellectual light and its known proportion to knowledge of the universe. Independent thinking in *Insight* changed the terms of the problem. It now was seen as a problem of discrimination, of distinguishing and relating two quite different types of knowing. The traditional form of the problem is dealt with firmly but briefly: negatively, in noting that negation of knowledge is self-destructive; and positively, in appropriating the real ground of knowing in the dynamism of human consciousness. When foundations become a theme in the Boston College lectures of 1957 Lonergan can easily apply the results of the previous ten years, and we may say that the search for cognitional foundations is concluded. Meanwhile, however, the existential subject has been coming more and more to the center of attention. Furthermore, direct engagement in the actual problems of church theology, especially of Trinitarian doctrine, has brought historical differentiations of thinking into sharper focus. This latter aspect is predominant in the 1959 search for the foundations of theology. The starting point, however, remains given: that is not the problem. Rather, it is the development of doctrine, and development in patterns of thought quite alien to those of the starting point, that must be justified. Here too the foundations that *Insight*, building on the *Verbum* articles, is able to provide are found to be adequate.

140 Ibid. 63.
141 Ibid. 54.
142 Ibid. 55 ff.

A long further climb remains before we reach *Method in Theology*[143] and the further work of the 1970s. I cannot undertake that journey here, but I do wish to look ahead and offer some comparative reflections. In 1959, I have said, two streams were meeting – one deriving from St Thomas, and one from the seven centuries following St. Thomas (a rough characterization). It seems fair to say that Lonergan was slower than most contemporaries to move beyond the Thomist context. It seems equally fair to say that, by the same token, he assimilated St Thomas more thoroughly and built on him more solidly than many of his contemporaries. At any rate there is a definite shift, from this point of view, between 1959 and 1972. There is a simple index of that: the Thomist wisdom, which was such a dominant category for many years, has all but disappeared in *Method in Theology*. Not perhaps in the functions wisdom served, but in the terminology and in the perspective from which problems are approached.[144] Even in *Insight* its functions were being taken over by the 'universal viewpoint,' and that too has yielded in *Method in Theology* to a transcendental method reaching its full human potential in dialectic, transformed then by conversions that are mainly the work of God, in order to take possession of new foundations for another formulation of the truths we live by. Moreover, this whole is complemented now by an explicit principle of feedback to help us keep in perspective the old and simpler problem of

---

143 On the question of foundations, a distinct stage is marked by the lecture of 1967, 'Theology in Its New Context.' It was first published in *Theology of Renewal*, vol. 1, ed. L.K. Shook (New York: Herder and Herder; Montreal: Palm, 1968) 34–46. It is included in *A Second Collection* 55–67.

144 There is no reference to wisdom in the Index to *Second Collection*. There is one in *Philosophy of God and Theology*, and it is to wisdom as Heraclitus saw it. There is one in *Method in Theology*, and it is to the wisdom literature of the Bible. The traditional use of the word returns however, in 'Christology Today: Methodological Reflections,' *Le Christ Hier, Aujourd'hui et Demain*, ed. Raymond Laflamme and Marcel Gervais (Quebec: Les Presses de l'Université Laval, 1976) 45–65; see 49: 'Sound judgment ... has to move us to the comprehensive reasonableness named wisdom.' [Subsequently republished in *A Third Collection* 74–99; see 78.] But to trace this history would really be to write the second part of this article, the later stages of Lonergan's search for foundations. If I cannot do that now, perhaps I may mention two ideas to investigate on the way. Dialectic is obviously one, and the other is involved in dialectic: it is the role of community; for, as Lonergan keeps saying, science is no longer a 'habit' in someone's mind, it is in the keeping of the community – and so in its own way is wisdom.

bringing the past forward into our present and preaching to Torontonians and Bostonians in 1982 rather than to Corinthians in 52.

But, if we agree on the novelty of *Method in Theology*, we may find it profitable to return to earlier work for traces of continuity. First of all, it is the human subject that is the locus of study from the beginning, and very early the subject in his or her reality. Next, it is the appropriation of that reality, sketchily in 1940, more extensively in the Thomist context of 1946–47, more directly in the self-appropriation of *Insight*, that is the positive way to foundations. Thirdly, from the early years it is the subjective conditions of ignorance, bias, underdevelopment, lack of self-appropriation, and so forth, that impede reasonable judgment and responsible decision and leave us without secure foundations. This continuity is almost labelled in the statement of *Method in Theology*: 'the basic idea of the method we are trying to develop takes its stand on discovering what human authenticity is and showing how to appeal to it.'[145] Here is a position strikingly similar to that of 1947: we know we know by knowing what we are; and to that of *Insight*: 'Prior to all writing of history, prior to all interpretation of other minds, there is the self-scrutiny of the historian, the self-knowledge of the interpreter.'[146] The form is the same, the locus of study is the same, but the material content broadens and deepens.[147]

Even in such a question as the relation of theology to its sources, I would ask whether there is not an overlooked continuity between earlier and later work. I am thinking of what seems an almost exclusive concern in earlier writings with bringing the past forward into the present, and the difficulty we have in relating that to *Method in Theology*'s concern with interior foundations, and indeed in relating inner and outer word within *Method in Theology* itself. But has not the outer word of received doctrine the same foundations in principle as the inner word of God's gift of his love? If we look to interiority for the added foundation we need in order to formulate our doctrine today, shall we not look to interiority also to account for the transitions from

145 *Method in Theology* 254.

146 *Insight* (1957) xxix [(1992) 23].

147 The similarity here of *Insight* and *Method in Theology* suggests the possibility of a fruitful analogy of the idea of the 'self-justifying.' There is self-justifying knowledge (*Insight*), self-justifying love (*Method in Theology*), and one may add the 'self-justifying joy' of the artistic experience (*Insight* [1957] 184–85, [1992] 207–209): this last needs its own investigation, which I have not been able to undertake.

one formulation to another in the past, and even to account for the original formulations of the sources themselves? I mean that, whether it be a question of evangelist, or prophet, or apostle, or Jesus himself in his human thinking, the foundations we would assign from the viewpoint of *Method in Theology* would be found in interiority – that of evangelist, or prophet, or apostle, or Jesus. The need, obviously, becomes a need for an analogy of interiority.

But, to return to the other side of the ledger, that of development, what Lonergan had to overcome along the way was the influence of those to whom he owed the greatest debt, Aristotle and Aquinas; and I suppose the very magnitude of his debt in the more fundamental questions made the task of overcoming their influence in lesser matters all the more difficult. That is the price of tradition and discipleship. Further, what he had to add were the new dimensions of the subject and his objective history that modern philosophy, science, scholarship had brought to light. He did this piecemeal at first. Some examples: history became a theme in its own right in the Thomas More Institute lecture of 1960; meaning in its many forms began to be thematized in lectures of 1962 (at Regis College and Thomas More Institute); mediation in the Gonzaga University institute of 1963; and foundations as a fourth-level function in the Georgetown University institute of 1964 (so our scanty sources indicate). From this point of view *Method in Theology* appears as a final organization of elements Lonergan had been collecting for many years.

That last sentence brings me to my concluding remark, which is a reflection on the whole business of a thinker's development, and an attempt to provide a model for seeing it as a unity over time and not just the unity of some final organization. The problem is real enough. Anyone with a bent for comprehensive thinking has presumably begun in early life and continues in later years 'to see life steadily and see it whole.' But in our world of growth and development, where results are often tentative, where there are blind alleys, sidetracks, slowdowns and pauses, there is likewise bound to be, early and late, continuing change: with Newman we have to say that to live is to change, and to have lived long is to have changed often. So how conceive the life of a comprehensive thinker, who presumably thinks more integrally and changes more profoundly than the rest of us? The model I suggest is provided by *Insight* under the general notion of emergent probability: 'If the non-systematic exists on the level of physics, then on that level there are coincidental manifolds that can be systematized by a higher chemical level without violating any physical law. If the non-systematic exists on the level of chemistry, then on that level there are coincidental manifolds that can be systematized by a higher biological level ...,' and so on through the psychic to the level of insight, reflection, and deliberation.[148] I am suggesting, then, that the data collected from the years prior to thematization stand to the thematization somewhat as a coincidental manifold does to the higher integration. I do not, however, sufficiently understand the intricacies of emergent probability to determine whether we have in such a case a real instance of emergence, or a true conceptual analogy, or merely a useful image.

I would further suggest that, if the image/analogy/instance has any value where thematization has occurred, as in foundations, it also has value where thematization has not occurred, as in the question of feedback. One can collect data on this from many of Lonergan's writings. For example, there is the wheel of progress in *Insight*: '... one thinks of the course of social change as a succession of insights, courses of action, changed situations, and fresh insights.'[149] There is the statement of *Method in Theology*: '... research tabulates the data from the past ... communications produces data in the present';[150] this is spelled out a bit on a later page: 'Execution generates feedback ... policy making and planning become ongoing processes ... continuously revised.'[151] Most of all, there is the ever present input of the Spirit. And, to add practice to statements, there is the imperious example of Lonergan's own massive engagement with modern science, modern philosophy, and modern scholarship, generating an equally massive feedback into his method (and, eventually, one hopes, into theology and its related disciplines). But this has not been thematized, either by Lonergan himself or, as far as I know, by anyone else; it remains at the moment a coincidental manifold. One consequence of this is that the statements and still more the practice go unnoticed; and it becomes possible for reviewers to say, no doubt quite honestly, that Lonergan's orientation is to the past, with little concern for input from present experience. Such a view would hardly be possible if the data I have indicated were to be thematized.

---

148 *Insight* (1957) 205 [(1992) 229–30]; and see, in the Index, 'Coincidental manifolds.'

149 *Insight* (1957) 223 [(1992) 249].

150 *Method in Theology* 135.

151 Ibid. 366.

Part Two

ESSAYS

Chapter 9

School without Graduates: The Ignatian Spiritual Exercises[1]

Education can be conceived in a stricter sense as formal education – the instruction given to the young, most often in an institutional setting. Or it can be conceived in a wider sense to include the instruction one receives from life itself throughout one's years. The two modes should not be too sharply differentiated, and in fact we are now learning (indeed, are being educated) to see them more as parts or aspects of a single process. Even the sharp distinction that once was operative between the teaching and the learning church has lost much of its relevance. We now are aware that for better or worse the whole church is a learning church. So it is no longer a matter of education versus real life. Real life is education, and becoming educated is real living.

Then, of course, the question occurs, What is real life? And we cannot but recall the 'definition' Jesus gave in his great prayer at the Last Supper: 'This is eternal life: to know you, the only true God, and Jesus Christ whom you have sent.'[2] If life and education belong to one process, there should be an educative program not just for secular life and religious doctrine, but for eternal life as well. I tried to make this clear in Chapter 6 of *Old Things and New: A Strategy for Education.*[3] In support of that chapter there is also the old tradition of calling a monastery a *schola Christi,* school of Christ. In any case a book that purported to give a transcendental and therefore universal strategy of education could

1 Original version published in Frederick E. Crowe, *Old Things and New: A Strategy for Education* (Atlanta: Scholars Press, 1985), as Appendix, 157–73.

2 John 17:3.

3 See above, note 1. Chapter 6 (133–55) is entitled 'The Christian Dimension.'

hardly omit a study of this 'higher learning' given in a school which offers no degrees, and graduates no one till it delivers its pupils into the life where knowledge is no longer partial, but 'whole, like God's knowledge of me.'[4] Consequently, I originally prepared the present essay as an appendix to that book.

My practice here and there in the book was to take a paradigm case and use it in illustration of the principles which were my main concern: the paradigm itself was then of quite secondary importance. Such was the case, for example, in my copious references to the public schools of sixty years ago in Ontario and New Brunswick. I propose to use a paradigm again and, if it were to be only a paradigm, one possible instance among many, it would again be of minor importance. But I may be forgiven for regarding this case as a bit special, for it is the *Spiritual Exercises* of St Ignatius Loyola.[5]

The saints have given us many roads to follow in knowledge of God and discipleship of Christ: the rule of St Benedict, the way of St Francis of Assisi, and dozens of others down to our times. Then too there are the renewed, or perhaps wholly new, efforts to trace a spirituality of priesthood, of secular institutes, of the laity, and so on. All of them are needed, none of them claims to exhaust the potential of what God offers us in the Son and their Spirit. But what gives the *Spiritual Exercises* a more universal application in the school of Christ and a study of education, is that they do not aim at making exercitants Ignatian in the particular sense of making them Jesuits. The aim rather is to help them find God's will. What is God's will in each case? It is not to be determined in advance. Maybe it is to be a doctor, lawyer, space traveler; maybe to enter politics, or to be a missionary nurse in the Third World; maybe, among other possibilities, to follow Ignatius in the order he founded. One does not tell the Holy Spirit the directions one wishes to

4 1 Corinthians 13:12.

5 The Latin title is *Exercitia Spiritualia*. There have been countless editions and translations. A recent and authoritative edition is found in *Monumenta Historica Societatis Iesu*, vol. 100, (Rome: Institutum Historicum Societatis Iesu, 1969). This gives four of the most ancient texts (including the autograph) in parallel columns, and adds the paragraph numbers that have become standard. For the English quotations in this essay, I use Louis J. Puhl, SJ, *The Spiritual Exercises of St Ignatius: A New Translation* (Westminster, MD: Newman Press, 1962), and will give the numbering of the 1969 Roman edition (which Puhl also was able to use in advance, p. viii).

receive: one listens and learns. From this viewpoint the *Spiritual Exercises* may serve as an especially useful paradigm.[6]

What are these famous *Exercises*? The term, 'spiritual exercise,' refers to all such activities as examination of one's conscience, praying, preparing one's soul to find the divine will, and the like.[7] So Ignatius tells us. But his own list comes nowhere near revealing the secret of his little book. That secret surely lies in the psychological and ascetical arrangement of the exercises – in the order both of the four weeks and of the exercises within each week – and is most brilliantly revealed in the key strategic exercises that give the whole set its efficacy. The four weeks deal successively with sin and its consequences, with the public life of Christ, with his passion, with his resurrection and ascension. They are enclosed by a kind of prologue (Principle and Foundation) and a kind of epilogue (Contemplation to Gain Love), though I do not mean 'prologue' and 'epilogue' to suggest that they are dispensable. Certain key exercises are regarded as Ignatian specialties: those on the Kingdom of Christ (introducing the Second Week), on Two Standards (bringing the options of life to a focus), and so on. The book also contains a great deal of ascetical advice, rules for conduct in particular circumstances, and the like; but my concern here is with the integral structure of the exercises and their total dynamics.

This schematic presentation will hardly convey to the reader the power of the *Exercises* or show sufficient reason for choosing them as paradigm. Here perhaps a little personal history will be more helpful. During forty-seven years I have made the *Exercises* every year, regularly for a period of eight days, twice for the full thirty days. One cannot go over and over the same ground, reading the same directions, using the same formulas, without pondering and pondering again the sense and drift, the meaning and purpose, of the whole maneuver, and the secret of its efficacy. I recall a remark of Newman's, simple and profound in Newman's way, about the baptismal formula and its influence on Trinitarian theology: 'it was impossible to go on using

6 While I speak of the *Exercises* as a paradigm for the educational processes of the Holy Spirit, I would point out that in themselves they are rather an *organon*, and one to which Lonergan's *organon* bears some resemblance. Just as the *Exercises* do not tell the exercitant what to find as God's will but only how to find it, so Lonergan's *Method in Theology* does not tell theologians what to find but only how they might find it. Not accidentally, both works are referred to as methods.

7 Ignatius Loyola, *Spiritual Exercises*, no. 1.

words without an insight into their meaning.'[8] That describes exactly my own experience with the *Exercises*, so much so that I can best set forth my point as the most recent in three formal attempts to analyze them, to gain 'an insight into their meaning.'

I first attempted a comprehensive analysis in my student days, when I was revelling in the *Prima secunda* of St. Thomas. Aquinas himself constructed his psychology very much along the lines of the end/means structure of Aristotelian thinking, greatly enriching Aristotle as he did so and adding a wealth of psychology that we are far from having exhausted. Naturally my first analysis followed this pattern, centering on the 'election' that is the heart of the *Exercises* and can be unpacked and set forth according to the Thomist psychology Ignatius learned at the University of Paris. Thus the purpose of human life is stated at the very beginning in the Principle and Foundation (and repeated at the Election) in these terms: 'Man is created to praise, reverence, and serve God our Lord, and by this means to save his soul.'[9] The same opening paragraphs reduce everything else on earth to the level of means to be chosen so far as they lead to the desired end. With this orientation restored and made operative by divine grace, the First Week enters into the end/means structure through a study of sin as a turning away from the end, and of repentance as a turning back to it. The Second Week functions more positively as a pursuit of the end – more specifically, as a pursuit of the end through the means given us by God in the only Son. This corresponds closely to the structure of the Thomist *Summa theologiae*: 'first we will treat of God; secondly, of the progress of rational creatures toward God; thirdly, of Christ who, insofar as he is man, is our way of tending toward God.'[10] The great strategic exercises can be fitted well enough into this pattern. The options presented by Christ in the two main life-styles, one in which he is obedient to his parents at home, and one in which he leaves them at the age of twelve to be about his Father's work, can be seen as a deliberation about means, the Thomist *consilium*.[11] The Two Standards illumi-

8 John Henry Newman, *Tracts Theological and Ecclesiastical* (London: Longmans, Green and Co., 1924) 152.

9 *Spiritual Exercises*, no. 23, and see no. 169.

10 *Summa theologiae* 1, q. 2, Prologus: 'primo tractabimus de Deo; secundo, de motu rationalis creaturae in Deum; tertio, de Christo, qui, secundum quod homo, via est nobis tendendi in Deum.'

11 *Spiritual Exercises*, no. 134; the Thomist *consilium*: *Summa theologiae* 1–2, q. 14.

nate the hidden processes at work in seemingly innocent means.[12] The Three Pairs of Men are a persuasive exercise leading to decision.[13]

There is much to ponder in a Thomist approach to the *Exercises,* nor do I think any of the positive Thomist input need be abandoned. But it serves less effectively in explanation of the Third and Fourth Weeks, which have to be seen in this analysis as mainly confirmatory of the Election and an extension of that way which is the imitation of Christ. Indeed, it does not fully exploit the virtualities of even the First and Second Weeks. This latter point occupied me again quite a few years later, in 1978, when Lonergan's *Method in Theology* had come out and I was reeling from the new ideas of Dialectic, his fourth functional specialty.[14] My new analysis moved therefore from Thomist tools to those provided by Lonergan, from a process structured by ends and means to one structured by dialectic, from the exercise of what is called horizontal liberty to that of vertical: 'Horizontal liberty is the exercise of liberty within a determinate horizon and from the basis of a corresponding existential stance. Vertical liberty is the exercise of liberty that selects that stance and the corresponding horizon.'[15] Thomist psychology does provide for such a shift in horizon, describing it as the substitution of one end for another, but this is not a major concern of the *Prima secundae.* It is a major concern of *Method in Theology,* where the shift from one horizon to another is an about-turn in the life of theologians and determinative of their mediated theology. It is not just genetic, a matter of successive stages of development, but dialectical, the dismantling of the old and the establishment of the new, in the radical transformation we call conversion.[16]

Now to effect such a radical change requires a great deal of self-searching and even more a soul-struggle of epic proportions, which is perhaps why Ignatius sets thirty days as the time to devote to his *Exercises.* But the new analysis adds to the forces at work in the change. It

---

12 *Spiritual Exercises,* no. 136.

13 Ibid., no. 149.

14 I published this effort under the title 'Dialectic and the Ignatian Spiritual Exercises,'*Science et esprit* 30 (1978) 111–27; also in *Lonergan Workshop* 1 (1978) 1–26. It was originally a paper at the 1976 Workshop.

15 *Method in Theology* 40, with acknowledgment there of the work of Joseph de Finance as his source.

16 Ibid. 106, 237, and passim; see the Index, under 'Conversion,' 'Dialectic,' 'Horizon,' etc.

does not add them as new agents – the latter are provided by God and were, presumably, as much at work in Abraham as in Ignatius – but it makes us aware of them and so enables us to respond to them more effectively. The same dynamism that was exploited in Thomist analysis is, of course, still operative: the dynamism of spirit open to the intelligible, to the true, to the good – a dynamism, let us always remember, that is graced by God as well. But dialectic adds to our understanding by invoking not only openness and response to the good but also the element of personal encounter, a challenge not so clearly provided in a more intellectualist context. This is a matter of 'meeting persons, appreciating the values they represent, criticizing their defects, and allowing one's living to be challenged at its very roots by their words and by their deeds.'[17] That list, with the exception of the third item, is verified *par excellence* in the encounter with Christ that we experience in the Ignatian *Exercises*.

Further, there is a remarkable parallel between dialectic as a theological task and the structured process of the exercise on the Two Standards. We bring to this exercise an assembly of materials from the life of Christ, and complete the operations of experience, understanding, and judgment by adding that of evaluation (though these are not four distinct tasks, as they are in theology). Again, there is a structured path in methodical theology from dialectic through foundations to doctrines: 'There are theological doctrines reached by the application of a method that distinguishes functional specialties and uses the functional specialty, foundations, to select doctrines from among the multiple choices presented by the functional specialty, dialectic.'[18] This is closely paralleled in the Two Standards, if we take doctrines in the broad sense of judgments of fact and value, of human ways, of Christ's example, of God's guidance. For that exercise leads directly to the strange and unexpected and wholly unwelcome doctrine that Christ's way is exactly the opposite of our 'natural' way that begins with love of wealth, leads on to desire for honor, and often ends in pride with its whole train of sin. The way of Christ begins with love of poverty, leads to desire for humble status, and so to humility and the whole range of virtues.[19]

---

17 Ibid. 247.
18 Ibid. 298.
19 *Spiritual Exercises*, no. 146.

There, put as briefly as possible, are my first two attempts to analyze the *Exercises*. As with Thomist ends and means, I still think Lonergan's dialectic is a valid and effective analytic tool and have seen no reason to abandon it. But I offered it in 1978 as a help toward understanding only the first half of the *Exercises*, leaving the Third and Fourth Weeks and the final Contemplation still outside the schema. At that time Lonergan had just begun to speak thematically of the two ways of human development, though they were implicit and all but thematic in *Method in Theology*'s two phases of theology. Now, alerted by his reference – in at least seven papers written from 1974 to 1977[20] – to this pair of movements in our development, I believe we can take a further step in the analysis of the *Exercises*. Here then is my third attempt.

The gist of my present view is that the analysis based on dialectic and effective for the First and Second Weeks, is notably complemented by considering the first half of the *Exercises* as basically an instance of the upward movement, and that what we need to add, for effective analysis of the second half, is the downward movement. I ask my readers to note the word 'basically.' I do not wish to be understood in a reductive and exclusive sense, as if the way of achievement, of acquisition by personal effort, were alone operative at first, and the other way, of receiving in love and trust, were alone operative later. Rather it is a matter of the emphasis falling now on one and now on the other, in such a way as to make one movement characteristic of the first two weeks and the other characteristic of the last two. Perhaps the word 'focus' and an analogy with the levels of consciousness, will be helpful. As research, though using all four levels, focuses on experience and the assembly of data, so the first two weeks of the *Exercises*, though consciously receiving and consciously relying on what is received, nevertheless focus on the acquisition of spiritual goods, in a way that is not so evident in the last two weeks.

We can invoke another pair of Thomist terms here, and say that the two phases of the *Exercises* (let us call them that, for simplicity's sake) stand to one another as a *bonum acquirendum* does to a *bonum communi-*

20 'Healing and Creating in History,' *A Third Collection* 100–109, see 106–108; 'Mission and the Spirit,' ibid. 23–34, see 30–31; 'Christology Today,' ibid. 74–99, see 76–77; 'Theology and Praxis,' ibid. 184–201, see 196–97; 'Natural Right and Historical Mindedness,' ibid. 169–83, see 180–81; 'Religious Experience,' ibid. 115–28, see 126; and 'The Human Good,' *Humanitas* 15 (1979) 113–26, see 120.

candum, as a good to be acquired does to a good to be shared. In the first we are concerned with what we may do, or achieve, or acquire, and so the dynamism of ends and means remains fully operative. Nor should this be interpreted as a selfish way: what we wish to acquire is, or may be, extremely precious and noble – self-mastery and the conquest of sin, the Christian virtues and even a place in the front lines of Christ's army, ultimately salvation. Still, it is something we strive to acquire. It is an *eros*, but an *eros* in the sense in which Nygren uses the term,[21] the sense in which the idea occurs over and over in the scriptures themselves: 'Store up treasure in heaven';[22] 'I press towards the goal to win the prize.'[23]

The *bonum communicandum* is another story, offering possibilities of another order altogether. This is not a good we reach out to grasp, however laudably and meritoriously we might do so. It is rather a spontaneous overflow, a necessity that love has for sharing whatever we possess with those we love and for entering into their state to share with them what they experience or endure. Let me use again my favorite example (with St Thomas I prefer repeating the apt example to searching my imagination for elegant variation). It is that of a mother who sits with closed eyes by the cradle of her child. She does not open them when she hears footsteps, to satisfy her curiosity of who is passing by. She does not look up in alarm when she hears brakes squealing down the street. She remains as if sightless. Why? Because she is sharing the state of her child who was born blind. What good is she doing by this renunciation? What is she achieving or acquiring? What purpose does she serve? The questions are all out of place: they belong in another context. The context now is the need love has to share with the one who is loved, not the attraction of the 'treasure,' the 'prize,' the good one may acquire.

Now this is very much our attitude in the second phase of the *Exercises*. In the Third Week we share the sorrows and sufferings of resurrection. And from love's viewpoint (if viewpoint be not a misnomer

21 Anders Nygren, *Agape and Eros*, trans P.S. Watson (London: SPCK, 1953). Notice that in unselfish acts the higher goals of *eros* overlap those of *agape*, and acquiring for ourselves overlaps acquiring for others, as when we become apostles for Christ. But the focus is still on achieving, and it is that focus which most radically distinguishes the first phase of the *Exercises*.

22 Matthew 6:20.

23 Philippians 3:14.

from the start) it does not matter, or at least is not a primary consideration, whether what we do results in some growth or gain, or whether it is pleasant or unpleasant. What matters primarily is our overarching and overwhelming need to share with the one we love. In this case, it is to be with Christ, wherever he may be: in suffering and sorrow, if he happens to be in suffering and sorrow; in peace and happiness, if that is where he is. The end/means structure has given way to a friendship/sharing one.[24]

Let me document more carefully my position on the two phases. In the first phase of the *Exercises* the emphasis falls on what, with God's grace, I may achieve or acquire. This is true of the Principle and Foundation, which tells us to make ourselves indifferent to all created things, for the sake of the supernal end. It is equally true of the First Week's struggle to turn from sin, and even of its 'for Christ' motif: what have I done, what am I doing, what ought I to do for Christ.[25] And it is true of the Second Week, with its petition, recurring in all the exercises in which we contemplate the life of Christ, for 'an intimate knowledge of our Lord, who has become man for me, that I may love Him more and follow Him more closely.'[26]

That quotation points even more directly to what is characteristic of the first phase, namely, the order of knowledge and love. Aquinas regularly gives knowledge the priority in the sense that love follows from knowledge, and the object of will is defined in terms of the good that is understood and known.[27] The Thomist influence on Lonergan was

---

24 For the *bonum communicandum* and sharing in friendship as St Thomas conceived them, one may consult such texts as these: *Summa theologiae* 1-2, q. 1, a. 4 ad 1m; q. 28, a. 4 ad 2m; q. 65, a. 5; 2-2, q. 25, a. 3; q. 26, a. 2; 3, q. 1, a. 1. Note also that the Thomist judgment 'by connaturality' corresponds to our movement from values to truth in development from above: see *Summa theologiae* 2-2, q. 45, a. 2, and passim in Thomas.

25 *Spiritual Exercises*, no. 53. The same motif is found, of course, in the Third Week (no. 197), but subordinate now to that of being with Christ. I repeat here the admonition given in note 21, to the effect that acquiring for ourselves turns into acquiring for others as we leave unselfishness behind. But we need more radical terms to distinguish and relate the two main phases of the *Exercises*, and I find them in the pair of ideas that structured my *Old Things and New* and have become applicable in this essay as the complementary pair of achieving-for and being-with.

26 *Spiritual Exercises*, no. 104.

27 The Thomist indices give numerous references for the statement: 'Bonum intellectum est obiectum voluntatis,' v.g., *Summa theologiae* 1, q. 21, a. 1 ad 2m; q. 82, a. 3 c. and ad 2m; a. 4; 1-2, q. 13, a. 5 ad 2m; etc.

tenacious, so that even in *Method in Theology*, when all the elements needed to establish the reverse order were at hand, he still tends to think of the love which precedes judgment as an exception to what is normal. This language continues in an early statement of the two ways of development,[28] but in the two great lectures of 1977 has yielded to what seems to me a more even presentation.[29] I think it would accord better with his final position to say that both ways are perfectly normal, one normal to achievement, the other to reception; and, since we are all our lives both receiving and achieving, the full normality is the complementarity of the two.

With that in mind we may notice now how characteristic it is of the first phase of the *Exercises* to put knowledge first and love second. Thus the very Ignatian Triple Colloquy of the First Week asks for 'knowledge of my sins and a feeling of abhorrence,' for an understanding of the disorder of my actions, with consequent horror, and for knowledge of the world, again with consequent horror.[30] Horror is the negative counterpart of love here,[31] but the positive side is explicit in the already quoted petition 'for an intimate knowledge of our Lord ... that I may love Him more.' This becomes the pattern for the petitions of the Second Week,[32] and returns in the changed Additions for that week: directing myself on rising so as 'to know better the eternal Word Incarnate in order to serve and follow Him more closely.'[33] Thus, too, the great pair of exercises on the Two Standards and the Three Pairs of Men are related to one another as knowing the options in all their subtlety, and choosing the right one in spite of my biases.[34] Finally, there is the most characteristic feature of all, that the first phase leads up to and culminates in the Election,[35] which is an act of will and therefore of love in the broad sense.

---

28 'Christology Today,' in *A Third Collection* 76–77.

29 'Natural Right and Historical Mindedness,' ibid. 181; and 'Theology and Praxis,' ibid. 196–97.

30 *Spiritual Exercises*, no. 63.

31 Useful here: St Thomas Aquinas, *Summa theologiae* 1-2, q. 26, *De amore*, and q. 29, *De odio.*

32 *Spiritual Exercises*, nos. 104, 113, etc.

33 Ibid., no. 130.

34 The first asks for knowledge of the ways of Satan and of Christ (no. 139), and the other for grace to choose what is more to God's glory (no. 152).

35 The Second Week ends with instructions on the Election, nos. 169–88, or (where the Ignatian election is not possible) on the reform of life (no. 189).

It remains now to document more carefully my position on the second phase of the *Exercises*. As it is characteristic, then, of the first phase to seek the good, and indeed the highest good which is the imitation of Christ as our way to God, so it is characteristic of the second to be with Christ, to share with him in the communion of love, to share in the same way with God in the final contemplation. Negatively, the emphasis is no longer on a virtue to be gained, an amendment of conduct to propose, a state of life to choose, a work to accomplish, an achievement of any kind to be effected or any good to be acquired. These remain as goals, but they are not the focus: the very notion itself of goal becomes marginal. Positively, the stress is on the communion, the sharing, the *Mitsein*, of love: sharing the suffering of Christ in the Third Week and his joy in the Fourth, then sharing with God our Creator in all that we have and are and do.[36]

Thus, in the petition of the first exercise of the Third Week, we ask for sorrow, affliction, and confusion, because on account of my sins the Lord is going to his Passion.[37] There is effort to be expended, there is great effort (*magno nisu*), but it is not directed to the reform of life or the gaining of virtue: it is directed toward feeling what Christ feels. The petition of the next exercise follows suit: we ask for sorrow with Christ full of sorrows, we ask to be broken with Christ broken, for tears and interior pain for the great pain which Christ endured for us.[38] The Fourth Week has the same generic purpose, union with Christ in his experience, only it is union with him now in his joy. So the petition is for grace to rejoice and be glad, to rejoice and be glad exceedingly, for the great glory and joy of Christ our Lord.[39] The general lines of the contrast between first and second phase emerge more clearly when we recall that throughout the Second Week the petition was for knowledge in order that love might follow, and when we notice that this sequence simply disappears from the Third and Fourth Weeks: we are to act now as if we were in a state of love.

Those familiar with the Ignatian work will have been wondering at my omission so far of any reference to the exercise called in some translations, Three Degrees, in others, Three Modes, of Humility.[40] They

---

36 *Spiritual Exercises*, nos. 203, 221, 231.

37 Ibid., no. 193; the theme, *with* Christ, is clearer in no. 203.

38 Ibid., no. 203. For the *magno nisu* phrase, see n. 195.

39 Ibid., no. 221.

40 Ibid., no. 164.

may suspect that I am in the position of a certain retreat-master who told his audience, 'I'm leaving this exercise out because I don't understand it, and don't know what to do with it.' I am not, of course, omitting it. Any analysis of the *Exercises* which failed to 'explain' this famous exercise would be self-condemned. I submit, however, that it readily yields to analysis in our terms: it will, in fact, provide illumination for the whole thrust of this essay. I will introduce my study by affirming that chronologically, in the sequence of the various exercises, it is located in the Second Week, but in idea and spirit it belongs to the Third. To understand this, and why Ignatius located it where he did, will furnish a key to the *Exercises* as a whole, and especially to the transition from first phase to second.

First, then, the idea and spirit of the Three Modes or Degrees is that of the Third Week. For the first two degrees are presented as avoidance of all sin and all imperfection of any kind, so that for no consideration whatever would the exercitant entertain for a moment the slightest thought of the slightest sin: in effect, the aim is a life of perfect virtue. Now the third degree purports to go further, but what on earth could there be that goes beyond a life of perfect virtue? Logic would say, Nothing whatever. Ignatius, however, discovers a positive answer. It is this. Given the option of poverty or riches, of opprobrium or honor, of a name for being useless and stupid or for being wise and prudent in this world, one chooses the first member in each case rather than the second. Why make such a choice? There is no evil to overcome, no good to accomplish, no purpose to serve, nor virtue to acquire, no service rendered to God. By hypothesis all these 'ends' and 'goals' are achieved in the first two degrees, where all choices 'would promote equally the service of God our Lord and the salvation of my soul.'[41] The one reason – and it is not a reason except in the sense in which Pascal said that the heart has reasons which reason does not know – is the force that is operative in the Third and Fourth Weeks: this is the way Christ went, and we follow, not in imitation of a virtue but in the communion of love. We are not, then, choosing poverty as good; we are choosing poverty with Christ poor, opprobrium with Christ dishonored, ridicule with Christ ridiculed. One might say, from this viewpoint, that the third degree does not really go beyond the first two, any more than the downward movement of tradition goes beyond the

41 Ibid., no. 166.

upward movement of achievement. It is simply a different mode, belonging in another context – one might speak, rather, of two degrees in one mode, and of a second mode which differs radically from both degrees of the first.

Three questions occur, however, on this analysis. First, why is this exercise located within the Second Week? It is because Ignatius wants it to precede the Election of a state of life,[42] and the Election should not be deferred to the Third Week. It is to precede the Election in order to promote such an election as would be made after the Third Week by one who is in love, or acts as if in love, with the crucified Christ. Thus, though love is self-justifying, and does not build on formulated grounds but only on reasons that reason does not know, still the reason (of the head) can accept such unreasoned love as ground and reason for the choices it must make in its own performances. But, secondly, why love of the crucified instead of the risen Christ? Ignatius does not say, but it is easy to supply an answer. It is surely that this choice is more suited to our short life on earth, whereas there will be eternity to share with Christ in glory, to choose joy with Christ rather than sorrow, and so on. And thirdly, why therefore does Ignatius not postpone the Election till the Third Week? The answer would seem to be simply that the Election is a task to perform, a work to do, and one of high import. To focus on such a decision would distract the exercitant from the proper attitude of the second phase: feeling and experiencing with Christ the Lord, and sharing with God his Father. As a task, therefore, it belongs rather to the Second Week, though it is not to be achieved without anticipation of the mood proper to the Third.

We come, finally, to the last exercise in the Ignatian volume: the Contemplation to Gain Love. It is essentially one in idea and spirit with the generic attitude of the Third and Fourth Weeks, only now the loved one is God our Creator in the divinity that belongs to God as God. The spirit of the exercise appears in a preliminary remark of Ignatius: 'love consists in a mutual sharing of goods.'[43] But the scope is widened to a contemplation of all that God has given me, in Christ and the benefits of creation, in the divine presence to me, in the divine work and labor on earth, and so forth. And the corresponding response is not now the following of Christ, not as such, but our side of

42 Ibid., no. 164.
43 Ibid., no. 231.

the 'mutual sharing': hence a total oblation, which I make 'as one would do who is moved by great feeling,' an oblation of liberty, memory, understanding, will, 'all that I have and possess.'[44] We noticed earlier that the order of the Second Week, where love followed on knowledge, disappeared from the Third and Fourth. It returns now, but with a difference: the emphasis is not on knowledge of a way to follow, but on knowledge of blessings received, 'that filled with gratitude for all, I may in all things love and serve the Divine Majesty.'[45] It may be that Ignatius, in this final exercise, is interweaving more closely the two threads that had been given prominence one by one in earlier exercises.

That last sentence recalls a qualification I made in the beginning. To use the analytic tools of an upward and downward movement of development in order to interpret the two phases of the *Exercises* is not to say that either phase is explained reductively and exclusively by just one of the movements. To exaggerate the case here would be to ruin it. I wish, then, to conclude my documentary work by calling attention to the presence of both strands throughout the Ignatian set of exercises. Thus, the first phase is not simply the upward way from experience through understanding and judgment to consequent decision. On the contrary the way of love is made operative very early: in the contemplation of Christ on the cross and of what he has done for me,[46] in the wondering exclamation that God has not annihilated me,[47] in thanksgiving and affection toward God who has kept me from eternal punishment.[48] Similarly, the second phase is not simply the downward way of loving reception of God's gift: there is stern effort, the *magno nisu* of the Third Week.[49] There is fruitful application to be made – the *fructum capere* of both Third and Fourth Weeks.[50] There is the very title of the last exercise, which is a contemplation to gain love. And there are the general procedures of prayer throughout the book – determining a topic, forming a picture, proposing a need to be the object of my

44 Ibid., no. 234.
45 Ibid., no. 233.
46 Ibid., no. 53.
47 Ibid., no. 60.
48 Ibid., no. 71.
49 Ibid., no. 195.
50 Ibid., nos. 194 (where the phrase occurs three times) and 222 (which refers back to no. 194).

petition, all of them more characteristic of effort toward a hoped for achievement.[51] This is brightly illuminated by the community-in-contrast of a pair of oblations made in the *Exercises*. There is the oblation made in the Kingdom exercise, which introduces the Second Week and consists of offering myself for the work: I will follow Christ and labor with him for the great purpose.[52] And there is the oblation of the last exercise in the volume, which is an offering of what I have and am.[53] There is a similar community-in-contrast when we turn to the two ways of imitating Christ. Such imitation is thematic in the Second Week, but it is that of the disciple learning true virtue from a master; now the idea occurs also in the Three Modes of Humility,[54] but here the imitation is more that of a lover sharing the state of the beloved. A brief but not inaccurate summary would seem to be that the first phase has achievement as a focus, with love as supplement, while the second phase has love as a focus, with achievement as supplementary.

One can hardly enter into the Ignatian *Exercises*, or ponder their dynamism, without a sharper realization of the need and power of images in human consciousness. Let our concluding reflections, then, return to our early effort to find an appropriate image for the two ways of human development. The original image of upward and downward movements served the useful purpose of distinguishing the two, and allowed us to relate the four conscious operations of each within a single dynamism; but it did not provide equally well for the unity of the two movements: they seem merely to cancel one another out. The image of two vectors (which I employed in chapter 1 of *Old Things and New*)[55] is still useful for ordinary education, but it introduces a measure of tension; for the two forces tend only partially in the same direction, and thus this image does not seem wholly appropriate for education in the *schola Christi*. One could think of two streams uniting to flow together to a common goal, but the characteristic differences

51 The Ignatian pattern is to state the topic and, after a preparatory prayer, to make the First Prelude, which is 'a mental representation of the place' (no. 47), and the Second Prelude, in which I 'ask God our Lord for what I want and desire' (no. 48). He adds: 'The Preparatory Prayer ... and the two Preludes ... must always be made before all contemplations and meditations' (no. 49).

52 *Spiritual Exercises*, nos. 95, 97.

53 Ibid., no. 234: 'all I possess and myself with it.'

54 Ibid., no. 167.

55 Chapter 1 (1–29) is entitled 'The Two Vector Forces of Education.'

then are not brought out. The best image that occurs to me is the unlikely one of an airplane carried forward by a combination of propeller and jet, the propeller pulling on the air in front (like one's arms pulling on the rung of a ladder) and the jet pushing on the wall of the air behind (like one's feet pushing on the rung below). Readers may easily find flaws in the comparison, or even argue which airplane engine corresponds to which way of human development; but it may help us conceive in some imperfect fashion the two ways we are carried forward, driven by a built-in dynamism that heads for the true and the good, but also

> by the love impelled
> That moves the sun in heaven and all the stars.[56]

The love that moves not only the sun in heaven and all the stars but also the minds and hearts of men and women and children is divine grace and so mystery. When we have done all that analysis can do, let us remember that our thinking, even at the very best of an Aquinas, is only straw, to be devoured finally in the flame of mystery understood.

56 The concluding words of Dante's *Divina Commedia*, trans. H.F. Cary.

Chapter 10

The Relevance of Newman to Contemporary Theology[1]

The contemporary scene in theology is vast, fluid, and diversified. If we are to say anything coherent about it and still be brief, we must be highly selective. In Part I, I have selected three features that seem to me significant. More exactly, I have chosen two features and a third – two that are familiar and admit of briefer exposition, and a third that is less familiar but of absorbing interest to me. I hope of course that it will interest you as well; in any case, here too I will aim at brevity. Then, in light of the features of contemporary theology discussed in the first part, I turn briefly in Part II to consider Newman's relevance for contemporary theology.

PART I

1 Historicity

The first of the three is historicity. Not historicity in the sense the word had fifty years ago, when the historicity of the gospels referred to the factual character of the events narrated there, but historicity in the sense the word has for most of us today, when it refers to the changing and developing nature of all things human, including the human forms of religious worship and religious doctrine.

Historicity in this sense is built into human nature. It's a permanent character of the human condition, it's a premise for anything we say

1 Originally presented at a Newman conference, St Thomas University, Miami, 5–7 January 1986. Not previously published.

about the human. Here is the way Bernard Lonergan puts it: the word means

> (1) that human concepts, theories, affirmations, courses of action are expressions of human understanding, (2) that human understanding develops over time and, as it develops, human concepts, theories, affirmations, courses of action change, (3) that such change is cumulative, and (4) that the cumulative changes in one place or time are not to be expected to coincide with those in another.[2]

I have said that historicity characterizes all things human. I mean that quite sweepingly, but I understand 'things human' as those things we bring to be in ourselves or in our works. Not human nature then as it comes forth from the creative hand of God. But the human as our creative product, the human as seen in our languages and customs, in our technology and commerce, in our arts and sciences, in our politics and culture, and in our religious doctrine and worship. In that understanding, historicity characterizes all things human without exception.

The way to see that in stark clarity is to assert this historicity of the Son of God himself as he was incarnate in Jesus of Nazareth. We are not yet used to thinking in this way. The creed says that the Son was made man, and Catholic thinking for ages tended to understand this in the most generic way: he 'became man' means he 'assumed human nature,' the human nature common to us all.

So far, so good. No one who wants to be saved by the Lord Jesus Christ is going to quarrel with that. He assumed our common human nature in order to be the Savior of us all. But contemporary theology recognizes, or has begun to recognize, that this is only half the picture. The Son of God did indeed become man, but the man he became was concrete and individual, not just abstract, generic and metaphysical.

The Word did indeed become flesh, but the flesh was Jewish. The Son did not become a Persian, Chinese, or Amerindian; he became a Jew, born in Palestine, under a Roman emperor. He grew up speaking an Aramaic language that was only one of thousands of languages on the face of the earth. He was taught, in the Psalms of his people, images of God that bore little relation to the images Amerindians formed of the Great Spirit. And he learned, in synagogue and temple, a

2 *Method in Theology* 325.

ritual and a way of worshipping God that was alien, not only to the Roman conquerors of his people, but also in some of its details to those of us who follow him today as our way, our truth, and our life.

This theology is both very old and somewhat new. It is very old, for it is part of the *kenosis*, the emptying, we read about in Paul's letter to the Philippians. But it is a new aspect of that *kenosis*. The Scholastics understood it ontologically: being divine, he assumed the being of human nature. We must understand it not only ontologically but also psychologically and culturally. In other words, this *kenosis*, this emptying, this limitation, is a limitation not only in his being, so that his new being was human with human limitations, but also a limitation in his psyche and his culture, so that his psyche was male not female, and his culture was Jewish not Chinese.

All this we express by saying that he was subject to the general human condition of historicity, limited by certain cultural particularities in his imagination, his thinking, his language, his action. He did not have our table manners; he would be baffled by our football madness; he would not even understand our theology.

If this is true, we have made our point for the whole range of our religious belief and practice in their human expression – and all of them have a human expression. The Son of God is paradigm for the entire list. If Jesus himself was subject to human historicity, then much more is the church, her dogmatic expressions, her institutional forms, her ritual and ceremony, the very experiences of her mystics, and the ways of discipleship worked out by her Basils, her Benedicts, her Loyolas. All are subject to the general law of human historicity.

One clarification before I leave this heading: it regards the difference between historicity and historical consciousness. Historicity is built into human nature: like the poor it is always with us. Historical consciousness is a development, and indeed a development of the last two centuries: it is our realization and acceptance of the historicity of our nature.

The time-conditioned character of our religion was present and operative in Jesus of Nazareth, in his forms of thought and speech, in his way of acting. It was equally operative in Paul of Tarsus, in Augustine of Hippo, in Thomas of Aquin, in Cardinal Newman and in all of us. But what was present all through the centuries could not be thematized before our times and the development of historical consciousness during the last two centuries.

That time lag is important for understanding the contemporary scene and relating it to Newman. Bossuet held it to be the mark of Catholicism to be ever the same, and the mark of Protestantism to be ever changing. If Bossuet was right, we must openly admit our Protestantism. But I think Bossuet was wrong. Newman at any rate had a different view from Bossuet's, and Newman's view has prevailed.

Of course, this creates problems: notably the problem of what is constant in all this flux, the problem of how a once-for-all event like the sending of the Son of God remains, under all the diverse forms of Christianity and through all the vicissitudes of history, a divinely operative reality, always and everywhere the focus of our religion. But problems are not meant to be swept under the carpet. The divinity of Jesus is also a problem, but we do not solve it by denying our faith in the God-man; and neither will the problem of historicity go away just because we refuse to acknowledge it.

2 Inculturation

My second heading is inculturation and, because we live in a multicultural world, this question turns into that of pluralism. The transition from our first heading seems simplicity itself: it is a transition from what has happened in the past to what we must achieve in our present and our future. That is, if the Christian message in its very origin is marked by historicity, if all the forms it has assumed over the centuries also show that character, then historicity will be a feature of our time and of every time, equally of our culture and of every culture – hence, inculturation and pluralism.

Still, what seems to be merely the same problem under another name turns out to have its own special difficulties. For one, there is a great difference between being spectators of what happened in the past and being responsible for what happens today. Once we become conscious of our historicity we also become partners and co-workers with God, responsible for the human world we help God create.

And that is not the main thing either. The real problem under this heading is the fact that we are no longer one world, and we recognize ourselves to be no longer one world. It's paradoxical, but that global village that symbolizes our unity brings out in that very unity, that togetherness, the complexity and extent of our diversity. Our global village is a league of nations that cannot talk to one another, not anyway without infinite attention and care. So, if we would preach the Christian message in this global village, we must do so in many forms and with an infinite variety of adaptations.

Now that was not the case in the past, not to the same extent. I suppose there were many subcultures in the great empires where early Christianity found its home. I do not doubt that apostles like Paul had some sense of the diversity of those to whom he preached. But the subcultures were under the domination of a superculture, and Paul's sense of our diversity was subordinated to his sense of our unity in Christ.

In any case that sense of diversity did not jell as an idea, and it certainly did not govern the church's evangelization. On the contrary, the Greco-Roman world had an overarching unity that made it one field for one Christian message preached under one form. The patristic church too was one in culture and mentality. The medieval world was even more a matter of a single Christendom in which one message could be preached in one way to one cultural group. Even the post-Reformation world for all its tragic divisions was one European world, inheritor of one European culture. Today all that has changed, and the difference, over and above our historical consciousness, is world consciousness catching up with world exploration. Catching up: because world exploration is five centuries old, but the world consciousness I speak of was delayed during most of the five. The European explorers and conquerors had a hard lesson to learn, the lesson that they could not simply transplant European culture to their colonies and carry on with business as usual.

That lesson seems at last to have been learned, largely in our own century, almost within our own generation. So we have a new recognition of the empirical nature of culture. It is not a Platonic form embodied in Greco-Roman civilization and its European successor. It is a hodge-podge, but a rich and fertile and eminently estimable hodge-podge.

This adds a new problem to theology. The problem under our first heading was how to find the unitary core in the diversity of historical forms. The problem now is how to adapt and diversify that unitary message in a way that allows it entry into all cultures without loss of identity. It's the problem John XXIII set before the Second Vatican Council, the same problem seen in its full extent. Namely, how to give an ancient faith new expression.

Twenty years of post-Vatican conflict might teach us that this is no easy task. But once more problems are given us like talents, not to be wrapped in tin foil or plastic and put in the fridge, but to exercise our minds and hearts and bring us to new heights of love and understanding.

3 A Way into the Future

I began my section on theology today with the remark that I had two headings and a third. The point of grouping the first two was that they were more familiar. I did not claim there was a consensus on either, only that they were better known. In fact there is not a consensus, but rather the contrary: violent conflict on these very topics of historicity and pluralism.

But surely beneath the violence of present conflicts there is a consensus on basic values, else why would we even bother to argue with one another? Is there no way to bring that underlying consensus to the surface, not only bring it to the surface but make it operative in our discussions? Can we not deal with theological disputes in a manner somewhat better than those congresses that are called a dialogue of the deaf? In any case in a better way than that of hurling epithets at one another?

I have asked whether there is a 'way' out of conflict. I mean useless and harmful conflict. And that simple word, 'way,' will introduce my third heading. For in Greek it is 'hodos,' from which we get 'methodos,' anglicized as 'method.' So I come to a very personal interest of mine, the theological method of Bernard Lonergan. It is especially appropriate in the context of conflict and dispute to turn to his ideas. For it was exactly the situation of bitter theological conflict, and the accompanying *odium theologicum* in the then prevailing Scholastic theology, that led him years ago to take up the question of method and deal with it perseveringly throughout most of a long life, till he had something worked out with which he could be satisfied.

I have not forgotten that my ultimate aim today, in keeping with the purpose of this conference, is to talk about Newman. This is not therefore the time or place for a lecture on Lonergan's *Method in Theology*, but only for such a sketch of its strategy as will allow us to discuss the relevance of Newman to this heading. My sketch falls into two parts corresponding to our first two headings: one part to deal with our past, another to orient ourselves in our own present toward our own future.

The past is a mighty stream, ever widening with the tributaries that pour into it from every century. More literally, it is a vast accumulation of data that must be assembled and classified with meticulous care. The past is distant in time and generally in space – and, more importantly, distant in manner of life and style of thinking. So the data have to be studied, understood in their context, and reinterpreted for our times. The past shows a steady succession of such interpretations, from the Palestinian Christianity of the early community through the Hellenic form it took in the first missionary expansion, and through the patristic, medieval, and reformation forms to our present times. So there is need of history to determine what was going forward in the past, what really happened in those distant times. The past finally is our past, the past of our community, bearing witness to us from the first Easter to this present day. So it comes to us not as mere information, but as a call, a challenge, an imperious demand for a response.

Thus, very simply, we have Lonergan's first phase of theology, the four specialties that deal with the past: research, interpretation, history, and dialectic. They are specialties latent in the performance of theologians, specialties emerging from their latent state in the scholarship of the last two centuries. But specialties given a precise identity and mutual relationship in the integral functional structure of Lonergan's first phase of theology.

But we are not mere parrots, repeating without comprehension words from the past that others drill into our heads in catechism class. From the time of Gabriel's visit to Nazareth, and the shepherds' to Bethlehem, when Mary kept the words she heard and pondered them in her heart, it has been our ideal to assimilate the word we hear, to make it our own, to give it our own meaningful expression. Further, 'what comes out of the mouth has its origins in the heart,'[3] and just as evil is evil through the evil heart in which it originates, so the good is good through its origins in a good heart.

Hence the second phase of theology, the phase in which we no longer simply repeat the past but assimilate and express it for ourselves, begins in interiority, has its new foundations in interiority. It begins there, but it does not stop there. Interiority must come to expression, in doctrine as well as in practice, which doctrine and practice are a transposition of the ancient faith, on the basis of interiority, into expressions for our time, according to the formula of John XXIII.

Still the transposition may take many shapes, be illustrated in many metaphors, be limited by the particularities of many situations. So we need some kind of coherent picture, some comprehensive overview, some intelligible unity in the many formulations – in other words, we need a system. Then finally – because the message arose in a particular

---

3 Matthew 15:18 (*NEB*).

situation, was first spoken in the idiom of that situation, even though it came from the heart of one in whom dwelt all the treasures of wisdom, and because it must return to a thousand thousand other particular situations if it is to be preached effectively, not only in Antioch in the first century, but in Miami in the twenty-first – we need adaptation, inculturations, pluralism. We need to come down from the ivory tower of system and mingle in the marketplace with the people of God.

Thus, very simply again, we have the second phase of theology, Lonergan's next four specialties: foundations, doctrines, systematics, and communications.

I have described with great simplicity the eight functions in Lonergan's way of doing theology, and with emphasis on their traditional character. So you may well wonder where their power lies. The power lies in the analysis of human consciousness with its four built-in levels and the two-way traffic from level to level. It is this that gives the functions of theology not only their distinct identity, but also their spontaneous relation to one another, and so their functional unity.

But all that is matter for another congress altogether.

PART II
The Relevance of Newman to the Contemporary Scene

It's time to talk of Newman. Few topics are more congenial to a Roman Catholic. We memorize his poetry in grade school. We read his sermons in high school. We study his apologetics in college. But for all that we do not become Newman scholars, any more than we become Shakespearean scholars through attending play after play by Shakespeare. It's Newman scholarship we need at this stage. Not having that scholarship, all I can do is advert to points in Newman that I consider relevant to my three headings and ask the scholars the questions that might help you study the matter in greater depth.

My first heading was the historicity of the human race and of all its products. Now that historicity, understood in a general way, is the very theme of *An Essay on the Development of Christian Doctrine*. 'When an idea, whether real or not, is of a nature to arrest and possess the mind, it may be said to have life.'[4] Now the evidence of life is growth.

---

4 John Henry Newman, *An Essay on the Development of Christian Doctrine*, Foreword by Gustav Weigel, SJ (Garden City, NY: Doubleday, 1960) 59–60.

'In the physical world, whatever has life is characterized by growth, so that in no respect to grow is to cease to live ... This analogy may be taken to illustrate ... development in ideas ... Thus, a power of development is a proof of life.'[5] Then, thirdly, 'an idea not only modifies but is modified, or at least influenced, by the state of things in which it is carried out.'[6] And so we come to the purest statement of the great principle of change which foreshadows modern historical consciousness: 'In a higher world it is otherwise, but here below to live is to change, and to be perfect is to have changed often.'[7]

Need we say more, or study the matter further? Can we just leave it at that? Newman's own great principle forbids us to take that easy path. So I am led to ask, as my contribution to this Newman conference, what development there may have been over the last century and a half in the very idea of development.

And first a pair of relatively simple questions. Did Newman give his idea a sufficient breadth of application to the past? To make the question concrete, did he apply it to the mind of Christ? I would incline to say, subject to instant refutation by a line you may quote from Newman, that he did not: the mind of the Savior was exempt from the historicity that is the normal lot of humanity. I would ask also whether Newman applied his idea as much to the future as to the past – or saw it as so applicable, for who can foretell the future? Or foresee in 1845 the spate of theologies of 1985? Again, I incline to think he did not. 'My stronghold is antiquity,' he says of his former Anglican days,[8] and his own need was to find in 1845 a church that was the same church as that of his beloved Greek and Latin Fathers. But what happens as a necessity of human nature, and has happened all through the past, must necessarily happen again, and this time with a greater exercise of responsibility on our part. I wonder if that responsibility occupied Newman the way it should occupy us.

But now we must go beyond this pair of simple questions and ask whether the idea itself and in itself, not just in its application and propagation, does not admit of growth and development. The answer must

5 Ibid. 189–90.
6 Ibid. 62.
7 Ibid. 63.
8 See Vincent Ferrer Blehl, *The Essential Newman* (New York: New American Library, 1953) 57.

be that of course it does. Newman himself recognized this with a quite sufficient clarity. When an idea like this enters our minds, he says 'it becomes an active principle within them, leading them to an ever new contemplation of itself, to an application of it in various directions, and a propagation of it on every side.'[9] That is, behind the application and propagation there is the 'ever new contemplation,' the developing understanding of the idea. In other words we must expect of Newman's own idea of development that it will itself develop, and undergo (I quote him once more) a 'germination and maturation ... on a larger mental field.'[10]

Can we, going beyond generalities, suggest any particular concrete development in the idea of development? I would propose for discussion this question: have we accomplished, since Newman's time, a shift from a focus on the objective to a focus on the subjective? Newman's own focus, it seems to me, not denying his great contribution to the subjective, was very clearly on the idea as objective. It is the idea that has life, the idea that modifies and is modified, the idea that germinates and matures, the idea that 'is elicited and expanded by trial,'[11] the idea whose 'beginnings are no measure of its capabilities,' the idea that changes with its surroundings.[12] Now all this takes place within a human mind; no one, I suspect, knew that better than Newman did. But I wonder if, with that turn to the subject that is so prominent in contemporary thinking, we have not shifted the focus from the idea to the subjects themselves, who, with all their biases and scotoses, their prejudices and their partisanships, their authenticity and their inauthenticity, are the ones who entertain the ideas.

My second heading was inculturation and consequent pluralism. For my first heading I had only to refer to a single work of Newman to make my point. This time, however, though reference to a single work may be possible, I can make my point out of the general knowledge we all have of his life and work. He was so obviously a man of his times, so demonstrably concerned with the needs of his contemporary church, so fully engaged in the life and movements and controversies of mid-nineteenth-century England and Europe. One might say that

9 Newman, *An Essay on the Development of Christian Doctrine* 60.
10 Ibid. 61.
11 Ibid. 62.
12 Ibid.

his very life was itself relevant to the question of inculturation; or, again, that he was the living model of theology as Lonergan defined its function: to mediate between a religion and a culture.[13]

Let me run quickly over some headlines from his history. His studies when he was an Anglican had, I venture to say, the one purpose of renewing in his time a church he loved and making it the church it should be. His great essay on development may have responded to a very personal need, but it also took up a question that occupied the national scene and perturbed many in his nation: how to find and recognize the true church of the Apostles. His penetrating reflections on the idea of a university were the direct result of being appointed Rector of the National University of Ireland, and of the need to locate the role of a university in the culture and faith of a people. His essay on consulting the faithful in matters of doctrine grew out of the study of elementary education the bishops of England were making at that time.

His whole life, then, illustrates my point: his involvement in his world. But you might prefer a sharper focus for discussion. Could we find that in his essay 'The Tamworth Reading Room'? Surely that little reading room was a minor factor in the life of a great nation, but discussion of its purposes involved great issues and questions. It aroused in a high degree Newman's sense of responsibility for his times and for his people, and he did not spare the riches of his mind to mediate in this area between his religion and his world. That essay, then, symbolizes my present point: it is so typical of Newman. And maybe better than any type or symbol is his own reflective comment on *The Idea of a University*, that 'it does but supply another instance of [the author's] lot all through life, to have been led to its publication not on any matured plan or by any view of his own, but by the duties or circumstances of the moment.'[14]

I have proposed Newman's life-work as a model of the inculturation we recognize today as so important. I have suggested a couple of particular loci for discussion. Further points of relevance I must leave to the Newman scholars. My one remaining word under this heading is again a question: was Newman still under the influence of what we

13 *Method in Theology* xi.

14 I am quoting Newman as quoted by John Coulson in his edition of Newman's *On Consulting the Faithful in Matters of Doctrine* (New York: Sheed and Ward, 1961) 8.

now call classicist culture, the Greco-Roman-European type of which he was himself so eminent a product? Was his concern for a theology to mediate between religion and culture concentrated rather much on European culture? If to live is to grow and change, and we have lived one hundred and forty years since Newman said so, I suggest for exploration the notion that for us, in a way that was not possible for Newman, the Greco-Roman-European culture is but one of a thousand, each with its own right to a place in the sun, and our theology, if it would mediate between our religion and culture, must take account, in a way Newman could not, of the other nine hundred and ninety-nine.

My third heading had to do with the creation of a method – for a very specific purpose I am going to call it an *organon* – with the creation of an *organon* for handling the acrid and interminable disputes that afflict the Body of Christ. Did Newman have anything to say on this question? He did indeed, but I need a survey of the previous twenty-two hundred years to introduce it. But, audience, be not alarmed: I will take only five minutes to cover those centuries.

You know, then, that Aristotle wrote several works of logic that his followers, many centuries later, collected into what they called an *organon*, an instrument of mind for doing philosophy. You know also that centuries afterward Francis Bacon wrote of the need for a new *organon* – *Novum Organum*, in Bacon's Latin – to do for the new inductive sciences what Aristotle's *organon* had done for philosophy and the deductive sciences. Now in 1870, when Newman's *Grammar of Assent* had just been announced, a friend of Newman wrote to say that he hoped this book would prove to be a 'Theological *Novum Organum*' that would do for theology what Bacon had done for the physical sciences. Newman replied:

> You have truly said that we need a *Novum Organum* for theology – and I shall be truly glad if I shall be found to have made any suggestions which will aid the formation of such a calculus – but it must be the strong conception and the one work of a great genius, not the obiter attempt of a person like myself, who has already attempted many things, and is at the end of his days.[15]

---

15 John Henry Newman, *The Letters and Diaries of John Henry Newman*, vol. 25 (Oxford: Clarendon Press, 1973) 76–77.

Well, this is certainly relevant to our topic, but in a rather negative way. Newman seems to forestall any attempt we might make to find in his work the needed *organon* of theological method.

Let us not, however, surrender too soon to Newman's disclaimer. First of all, we need not and should not take him at his word, or adopt his estimate of his own work. We just happen to know better, as this conference and a whole world, awake to the importance of Newman, can testify. In any case he does not rule out altogether the possibility of his relevance: he may, he admits, have made some 'suggestions' toward the creation of an *organon*. I am going to conclude my paper by pointing to what I think are some very pertinent suggestions in the work of Newman. If they turn out to anticipate what Bernard Lonergan has implemented, well, that will not surprise you.

First of all, then, there is in the *Grammar of Assent* a relevant passage that I have quoted more than once in my own writings, one that I would greatly desire to see studied and adopted by educators. The passage deals with what Newman calls 'the true way of learning.' He is speaking of credulity and skepticism, and goes on to declare his option between them.

> Of the two, I would rather have to maintain that we ought to begin with believing everything that is offered to our acceptance, than that it is our duty to doubt of everything. The former, indeed, seems the true way of learning. In that case, we soon discover and discard what is contradictory to itself; and error having always some portion of truth in it, and the truth having a reality which error has not, we may expect, that when there is an honest purpose and fair talents, we shall somehow make our way forward, the error falling off from the mind, and the truth developing and occupying it.[16]

Now I suggest that in this seemingly simple and common-sense statement we have the first step in a remarkable relationship, complex but worth the study, between Newman's work on education and Lonergan's on method.

Lonergan's work on theological method is dominated by the two phases. But the two phases themselves are preceded by the faith of the

16 John Henry Newman, *An Essay in Aid of a Grammar of Assent* (London: Longmans, Green and Co., 1930) 377.

believer, loyal to his or her tradition and church. And that is just where Newman's true way of learning begins: with a belief in what is offered to our acceptance. But then there intervenes the critical task: what Newman means by 'error falling off from the mind' and Lonergan by his four specialties of research, interpretation, history, and dialectic. Furthermore, we are not to suppose that Newman's seemingly simple approach is somewhat naive compared to the sophistication of Lonergan's. Newman's practice gives the lie to that. His research, interpretation, history – and dialectic too in the right sense – Newman's work in these areas can stand the test to which modern scholarship might subject it, and pass that test with honors. If the notion of error falling off from the mind seems too simple, we might turn to Newman's description of a university. 'What is a university?' he asks, and answers as follows.

> It is the place ... in which the intellect may safely range and speculate, sure to find its equal in some antagonist activity, and its judge in the tribunal of truth. It is a place where inquiry is pushed forward, and discoveries verified and perfected, and rashness rendered innocuous, and error exposed, by the collision of mind with mind, and knowledge with knowledge.[17]

I have no doubt, then, that Newman, both implicitly in his practice and explicitly in his thematizing, will be found directly relevant to the first phase of Lonergan's theology. What of the second phase? I'm going to press my case one step further here, relying still on the *Grammar of Assent*. I believe we have, in Newman's presentation of real as contrasted with notional apprehension and assent, the genuine precursor of Lonergan's personally grounded second phase of theology. Real assent is intensely personal, as compared with the quite impersonal attitude of notional assent. 'Human beings are mortal,' is assented to notionally. 'Grandma died this morning' – that is another matter, involving real apprehension and real assent.

It is true that Newman's first try at defining this pair of terms sets them in correlation with proper names and common nouns. We can utter notional propositions about emperors, but real propositions about Alexander the Great. Then we seem to deal merely with a question of grammar. It is true also that for Newman '[r]eal assent ...

17 John Henry Newman, *Historical Sketches*, vol. 3 (London: Longmans, Green and Co., 1924) 16.

viewed in itself ... does not lead to action.' It 'is not intrinsically operative' but only 'accidentally and indirectly.'[18] But, whatever his definitions and remarks, the whole thrust of his exposition, as well as of this whole book and his own entire life, is to relate real apprehension to what Lonergan will call fourth-level and personal involvement. Thus, we are captured, he says, through the imagination rather than through the discourse of argument.[19] Real apprehension has a vividness, a force, that kindles our hearts.[20] To sum it up, there is Newman's motto, *Cor ad cor loquitur*: Heart speaks to heart. That is Newman's real apprehension; that is Newman's life. And that too is Lonergan's second phase of theology.

18 Newman, *Grammar of Assent* 89.
19 Ibid. 92.
20 Ibid. 11–12.

Chapter 11

Lonergan and How to Live Our Lives[1]

Those of us who have trouble giving a title to what we write are considerably relieved when we find the title already provided, especially when we are allowed a comfortable margin of interpretation in determining what the suggested title means. That is the case for the present paper and, using the liberty granted me, I propose first to draw on Lonergan for an uncomplicated view on what human living is, then to add two complicating factors that suggest the untapped riches of the field, and finally to conclude with some reflections on theory and practice in living our lives.

1 A Simple Paradigm

My preliminary view takes a general approach through a remark of Aquinas, and becomes more specific through a paradigm I find in Lonergan.

Thomas Aquinas keeps repeating in his *Summa contra Gentiles*[2] that the human race has a common boundary on one side with the animal world and a common boundary on the other with the angelic. Which suggests that, if we wish to know what we are, we might look at our borders. We have little converse with the angels, however; so my preliminary view narrows down at once to half the picture, and looks only at our other border.

---

1 An earlier version of this paper was presented at the 16th annual Lonergan Workshop, Boston College, 19–23 June 1989, where the general theme was 'The Drama of Living and the Aesthetization of Truth and Value.' Not previously published.

2 Thomas Aquinas, *Summa contra Gentiles* 2, c. 69; see also 3, c. 135 and 4, c. 55.

Within the limited area thus staked out we can locate the paradigm I take from Lonergan. It concerns what we share with animals and the way we differ from them.

> It is true enough that eating and drinking are biological performances. But in man they are dignified by their spatial and psychological separation from the farm, the abattoir, the kitchen; they are ornamented by the elaborate equipment of the dining-room, by the table manners imposed upon children, by the deportment of adult convention.[3]

Nothing, it seems, could be simpler. We are one with the animals in the necessity of eating and drinking; we refuse to be one with them in the manner of our eating and drinking. For the meat-eating animal has no dining-room: capture, kill, and consumption are one undivided act, carried out in one continuous performance. For us that is impossible. We read in the same paragraph that 'man is an animal for whom mere animality is indecent,' and in a later chapter that we are 'revolted by mere animality.'[4] So we dignify our animal functions when we can, and screen them from view when they cannot be so dignified. Our meat-eating race grows a lamb on the farm, has it butchered in an abattoir, cooks it in the kitchen, and eats it in the dining-room – with tablecloth and utensils, with a code of manners whose interpretation gives ample employment to Emily Post and her successors.

Lonergan has other examples – notably, clothing and sex.[5] They are pertinent in a high degree to human living, but they fail the test of neutrality that should characterize a good paradigm. By that I mean that the paradigm should not raise problems of its own that are irrelevant to its use as a paradigm. When I learned Latin, the second-declension paradigm was *servus* and it presented no problems, but in a society in which slavery was a burning issue, it would have needlessly complicated the study of Latin accidents to use it as a paradigm. I do not say that our example of eating at table is totally neutral for everyone, and I think some of you may have winced a little when I mentioned the process from a lamb in the pasture to a lamb on the dinner-table, but it is relatively neutral for most of us, and dispassionate discussion of it remains generally possible. I will therefore continue to use it as a paradigm.

3 *Insight* (1957) 187 [(1992) 210].
4 Ibid. (1957) 385 [(1992) 410].
5 Ibid. (1957) 187 [(1992) 210].

So what can we learn from our paradigm case? What is this humanization of the animal? Lonergan speaks of the sphere of animality as dignified, ornamented, disguised, romanticized, even sanctified. But the more general and illuminating terms are those of fifteen years later: meaning and value. Meaning here is a little richer than meaning in the rather intellectualist *Verbum* articles,[6] richer even than it was in the still very intellectualist *Insight*. It is meaning rather in the sense that marriage, the institution of laws, a nation, everything truly human, and so human living itself, is constituted by meaning.

Meaning in this sense is hardly separable from value in the concrete, or in the objectives of art. About art, Lonergan comments: 'Pre-scientific and pre-philosophic, it may strain for truth and value without defining them.'[7] Thus a meal is an animal function, but an animal function that through human artistry is suffused with meaning and value. Social and cultural meaning and value: conversation and manners. Even religious meaning and value: the great Christian sacrament began at a meal, and the family meal itself, at least on special occasions, is given a religious value by grace at table.

2 Life as Summation

So far, so good. But also, so far, rather simple. Our simple paradigm with its simple analysis has to be complicated now by various factors, of which I will take only two.

The first complication is that we have been speaking of an act, exemplified in the act of eating and drinking. Living is not an act, it is an ongoing series of acts; and the meaning and value of a life is the meaning and value of the whole of life. So we have to think of the summation of acts that constitutes a life.

Lonergan deals with the notion of summation in his lectures of 1963 on mediation, first at Gonzaga University in Spokane, and then at Thomas More Institute in Montreal.[8] I do not remember any other locus in his work where it is mentioned (apart of course from mathematical contexts), or any secondary literature in which it is discussed. What

---

6 'Verbum' (1946–49); *Verbum* (1967) [(1997)].

7 *Insight* (1957) 185 [(1992) 208].

8 'The Mediation of Christ in Prayer,' *METHOD: Journal of Lonergan Studies* 2/1 (1984) 9 [*Papers 1958–1964* (1996) 170].

does the term mean? First of all, summation does not mean a summary: it means almost the opposite. I suspect Lonergan's source is the integral calculus, where I believe all the infinitesimal elements in a continuum, none whatever omitted, are summated into a whole; or perhaps it is the summing of discrete elements, as in reckoning the day's total sales from the individual items on the cash register.[9] In any case, mathematics offers only an analogy, and we might prefer to think of the 'every idle word' of scripture:[10] the point is that the summation of life omits nothing.

But the 1963 lectures consider summation more positively in the context of the intentional. There is the recurring intentional element, which is familiar enough in its three aspects: 'the act of intending; the intended object; the intending subject.'[11] But then there are the intentional summations.

> Intentional acts are summated into living, the accumulation of experience, the acquisition of skills, habits, ways of doing things. Objects are summated into situations; and the summation of situations is the environment, the world, the horizon. Subjects are summated into the intersubjectivity of community, into 'we,' into the family, the swarm, the flock, the herd, the group.[12]

This seems to me an extraordinarily rich notion; and I wonder whether, like the immanently operative dynamism of consciousness, summation in some sense is not immanently operative in our daily living. That is, on the structural side of consciousness questions are operative in a built-in pattern which we may take years to discover. Is there, on the historical side, a life-view that forms so early as to be

---

9 I owe an insight on summation to a reader for the University of Toronto Press (the same reader mentioned in my Preface), who points out that between *For a New Political Economy* (sometime in 1942-43) and *An Essay in Circulation Analysis* (1944) Lonergan introduced the summation form $\Sigma\Sigma$, a step that signalled a significant advance in his economic theory. The reader goes on to suggest that Lonergan also had this meaning for summation in mind when he used the term in 'The Mediation of Christ in Prayer.'

10 Matthew 12:36.

11 'The Mediation of Christ in Prayer,' *METHOD: Journal of Lonergan Studies* 2/1 (1984) 8 [*Papers 1958–1964* (1996) 169].

12 Ibid. (1984) 9 [(1996) 170].

almost built-in, a view of life as a whole that, without being explicitly attended to, is operative in every present moment?

Of course, there is the familiar experience of savoring yesterday's triumph and enduring all over again yesterday's humiliation, with a similar reaching out to the future in hope and fear. But I mean more than that. Is there, deeper than these transient experiences, present always but seldom reflected on, a way in which we envisage the whole of life, whether in the two less rational modes – the dreams of youth, the memories of old age – or in the more rational mode that it might pertain to this workshop to reflect on and elaborate?

This is only an idea, to be verified or falsified by experience, a procedure open to all of us for at least our youthful stage. We sometimes think of this stage as dominated by the present moment. But in fact is it not our youthful experience that the present moment is only a beachhead on the whole vast continent of the future, only marginal to that coming world that is ours, the world we have already conquered in our dreams and inhabit as our domain? Of course, the conquest is unreal. That whole future world itself is unreal, unreal in its disregard of any limits, unreal especially in its lack of limits in time. For that is the fatal flaw in the dreams of youth: for them the boundaries of life are parallel lines that never meet; but the boundaries of life are not parallel, they converge, and life as we know it here comes to an end.

There is, or can be, a similar lack of attention to the real, though with a quite different attitude, in the summation of life as we grow old. Most of you have to wait for that experience, and so must take my word for it that old age too looks on the totality of a lifetime. But the elderly can easily reduce the totality to the fruitless, empty reliving of old, sad memories. A relative of mine mothered and raised a large family, saw them grow up and scatter to the four winds, not alienated from their parents – they were devoted children – but simply carving out their own careers. Then her husband died; and, when I wrote her, she said in her reply, 'I am alone with my memories.' I do not think that, in fact, this woman merely relived her memories in the fruitless fashion of a life now empty. But her life would have been empty had it consisted simply of memories. In any case the many acts of the many years do not acquire integral meaning simply from being gathered in memory at the end of life, but only from the meaning of the whole.

So what is that meaning, and how does one achieve it? Here is a remarkable statement I recently came upon.

> To the extent that autobiography is a story of the author's inward life, its natural concluding point is not his death but the point at which the author comes to terms with himself, realizes his nature, assumes his vocation.[13]

That is a line that Lonergan could have written, had there been occasion for it; for it is the application to autobiography of what he says so often of the existential moment in life, the moment in which we decide what we are to make of our lives, of our selves.

Roy Pascal's remark looks before and after. The existential appropriation of life as a whole does not regard simply the future: we have also to incorporate our past, and what a task that is. How many thousands of flights from insight there have been in our lives. How many agonized moments when memory nevertheless breaks into consciousness. How many hours of struggle we spend in prayer, trying over and over again to accept our past, not only to admit the facts cognitionally but also to accept the burden willingly, make it part of the summation of our lives, incorporate it into the integral story.

This kind of summation gives us an analogy for the divine simultaneous presence to the whole universe of being, no matter how much single elements are separated at different moments of history. God does not summate, but has the totality present to the divine consciousness. The year 989 is present in God's eternal now just as much as the year 1989. 1989 is special to us, and this twenty-first day of June, this hour of 8 p.m. But what special significance has it for God, any more than 8 p.m. a thousand years ago, on the twenty-first of June in 989? The year 989 *is* in the sense that it belongs to the universe of being, in the sense that it is present to God, which gives it its most really real reality. In that sense we can say, not that it is contemporary with us in history, but that it is coeval with us in being: it *was* to us, it *is* to God in eternity, as we *are* to God in eternity. Our effort at summation of the whole of life can be taken as an analogy for God's eternal now.

That suggests a still deeper aspect to the matter, and it brings us to the religious summation of one's life, with implications for what we call the religious state. What does that state mean? What were they doing, Anthony of Egypt and Benedict of Nursia, Bernard, Dominic,

13 Roy Pascal, *Design and Truth in Autobiography* (Cambridge, MA: Harvard University Press, 1960) 215, quoted by William Mathews, 'Interpreting Lives: Some Hermeneutical Problems in Autobiography and Biography,' *Irish Philosophical Journal* 3 (1986) 34.

Francis of Assisi? What were they up to? There are those who would simply write them off as misguided fanatics, or at best as dreamers. That seems to me an attitude of high hubris, but in the present universal rethinking of our doctrine, practice, and institutions, the religious state also is in the crucible; and we must render an account of its meaning. I suggest an idea from the present viewpoint that might give more positive meaning to this strange way of living a human life: namely, that Anthony and his successors were integrating their lives in a new totality. They were achieving a new summation, a summation that included not only the existential but the sacred too in its totality. They were joining the good life with eternal life. They were in pursuit of the eternal now of God.

3 Mutual Self-Mediation

We seem to have come a long way from our simple paradigm of eating at table, with table-cloths and napkins, with grace before meals and conversation during them. In fact, we have approached our other boundary, the one we have in common with the angelic world; and it is time to revert to our starting point, to remember the limits we staked out as our area of investigation.

I said I would add two complicating factors to our initial paradigm, and I come now to the other. Besides the individual there is the community, and besides the summation of an individual life, there is the summation of all those individual summations in the larger community.

> Destiny is perhaps the working out of individual autonomy within community, and so the summation of destinies in a community is the history of the community.[14]

What a variety of avenues that opens for exploration, and how many of them we must leave unexplored. I will not talk, then, of autonomy, or destiny, or summation of destinies, or history. But just of community, and just of one aspect of community: mutual self-mediation.

The original paradigm that gave us a general elementary view of the human way of living has a more specific application here, for 'commu-

14 'The Mediation of Christ in Prayer,' *METHOD: Journal of Lonergan Studies* 2/1 (1984) 12 [*Papers 1958–1964* (1996) 173 plus note 16].

nity' in a general sense is found on the common boundary we have with the animal world; and it would be possible to speak of what we share under this heading, and then to study the differences that artistry and intelligence have created in the human world. There are data for this in Lonergan. First, for what we share with the animals:

> As the members of the hive or herd belong together and function together, so too men are social animals and the primordial basis of their community is not the discovery of an idea but a spontaneous intersubjectivity.[15]

Then, for our differences from them:

> Still, the network of man's social relationships has not the fixity of organization of the hive or the ant-hill; nor, again, is it primarily the product of pure intelligence devising blue-prints for human behavior. Its ground is aesthetic liberation and artistic creativity, where the artistry is limited by biological exigence, inspired by example and emulation, confirmed by admiration and approval, sustained by respect and affection.[16]

This artistry, Lonergan has just said, 'is dramatic. It is in the presence of others.' His point is confirmed by the novelist Nadine Gordimer, who has Rosa say, in a kind of soliloquy that is not a soliloquy:

> One is never talking to oneself, always one is addressed to someone. Suddenly, without knowing the reason, at different stages in one's life, one is addressing this person or that all the time, even dreams are performed before an audience. I see that. It's well known that people who commit suicide, the most solitary of all acts, are addressing someone.[17]

Clearly, there is much to explore as we leave our common boundary line with the animal world and enter the drama of human living. But in the limited time I have, I prefer to jump at once to Lonergan's notion of self-mediation, which seems quite foreign to animal ways, and then to the notion of mutual self-mediation, which is so important in his ideas on community. In our brief presentation we can take only a quick run

---

15 *Insight* (1957) 212 [(1992) 237].

16 Ibid. (1957) 188 [(1992) 211].

17 Nadine Gordimer, *Burger's Daughter* (London: Jonathan Cape, 1979) 16.

through the nest of ideas that come under these notions; but we are helped by the fact that Lonergan's interpreters have already been studying them, one of them in a previous workshop at Boston College[18]

First, self-mediation. In the old-style watch, the mainspring mediates the movement of the hands. Next, there is mutual mediation in the relation of mainspring and balance wheel, for the mainspring mediates the movement of the balance wheel as well as of the hands, and the balance wheel mediates the flow of power from the mainspring. Turning to organisms, we find a third type of mediation: 'machines are made while organisms grow. The growth of an organism is a self-mediation. The organism originates itself by giving rise to physical parts within itself,'[19] and on the larger scene lower species mediate the emergence and sustenance of higher.[20] There is a still further development when we move to the level of consciousness: 'The animal mediates itself not only organically but also intentionally.'[21] Then, for a final preliminary notion, there is self-consciousness where we take the existential step in self-mediation, when we find out for ourselves what we can make of ourselves, when we decide for ourselves what we are to be, and live out our lives in fidelity to that self-discovery and decision.[22] That is Lonergan's notion of self-mediation, and the background – terribly compressed – for understanding his notion of mutual self-mediation.

So how does he conceive of this mutual self-mediation? He does not so much define it as describe its effects, and indicate its meaning through instances: 'we are not Leibnizian monads with neither doors nor windows; we are open to the influence of others and others are open to influence by us.' The occasion of mutual self-mediation is therefore 'the encounter in all its forms.' Thus, 'There is a mutual self-mediation between equals, between brothers and sisters, between husband and wife, and between superiors and inferiors, parents and children, teachers and pupils ... There are matrices of personal relations

18 Frank Fletcher, 'Mutual Self-Mediation with Christ: Some Implications of Lonergan's and Doran's Work for Spirituality,' *Lonergan and You, Second Australian Lonergan Workshop* (Riverside, NSW, 1985) 96–99; and Peter Drilling, 'Preaching: A Mutual Self-Mediation of the Word of God, a Preacher, and a Congregation,' *Lonergan Workshop* 7 (1988) 88–101.

19 'The Mediation of Christ in Prayer,' *METHOD: Journal of Lonergan Studies* 2/1 (1984) 6 [*Papers 1958–1964* (1996) 167].

20 Ibid. (1984) 7 [(1996) 168].

21 Ibid. (1984) 8 [(1996) 169].

22 Ibid. (1984) 10 [(1996) 171].

in the neighborhood, in industry and commerce, in the professions, in ... politics.'[23]

If then we are to turn to instances, the simplest way by far to get at the idea is suggested through an almost casual remark Lonergan made at this point: 'The exploration of the field of mutual self-mediation is perhaps the work of the novelist,' and a moment later, 'the inexhaustible theme of dramatists and novelists.'[24] I found that remark extraordinarily illuminating for what novelists, ninety percent of the time, are trying to do – in the better novels, not the 'cowboys and Indians' type of story that thrilled me in my boyhood, but the ever so quiet and ever so authentic studies of mutual self-mediation in the work, say, of Barbara Pym.

But then, in the reverse direction, I find the novel illuminating for a grasp of Lonergan's notion. The novel has a natural link with our topic, since it is, I suppose, the art-form that comes closest to encompassing human living in its totality. We see that with peculiar intensity when a novel follows one person from birth to death. Further, the novel adds the power of feeling to the clarity of ideas: 'feelings ... are the mass and momentum and power of ... conscious living.'[25] 'Without feelings this experience, understanding, judgment is paper-thin.'[26]

So I want to explore novels a little, from the viewpoint of mutual self-mediation; and I believe I can make my point as clearly through the absence of such mediation as through its presence. My first choice is a novel in which there is almost complete failure of mutual self-mediation between the characters: Robert Penn Warren's *World Enough and Time*. Here we have the most strenuous efforts by both Jeremiah and Rachel to come to terms with life. There is encounter – intense and desperate. We even have moments of great tenderness. We have acts of heroic self-sacrifice. We do not have mutual self-mediation. The two do not grow through and in relation to one another; and their story ends in tragedy, useless tragedy. The chief character fault, I would say, lies in Jeremiah. He has a strong sense of the drama of life. He has a strong desire to give the totality of life a meaning, to achieve a destiny. At the end he asks, '... was I worth nothing, and my agony? Was all for naught?' But the trouble with Jeremiah is that the cast of characters in

23 Ibid. (1984) 13 [(1996) 174–75].
24 Ibid. (1984) 13, 14 [(1996) 175, 176].
25 *Method in Theology* 65.
26 'An Interview with Fr. Bernard Lonergan, S.J.,' in *A Second Collection* 221.

his drama does not really include Rachel. It consists of himself and some impersonal force that he thinks of maybe as fate, or maybe more simply, as world and time. There is no mutuality between fate and the human person.

In another illuminating novel, there is also prolonged lack of mutual self-mediation; and then at a very precise point, and in relation to a new character, the mutual mediation begins: Doris Lessing, *The Summer Before the Dark*. Kate Brown is a London woman in middle age. This particular summer her husband is away lecturing in the United States, her grown-up children have flown the nest to go hither and yon, she takes a job, encounters all kinds of people, is occupied with self-mediation (she doesn't call it that, but it describes her search very exactly) in all the situations that come up; but for two-thirds of the book there is complete lack of the mutual factor. She thinks continually, in all her adventures, of her husband, children, neighbors; but they are not there for her to interact with, and there is no mutual self-mediation with those who are there, those she does encounter. Then, in the last third of the book, she has to move to new quarters, and finds herself in 'Maureen's Flat.' Maureen is a young girl, fleeing her wealthy home, herself striving for self-mediation (still without using that term). Through the rest of the book each develops in relation to the other: mutual self-mediation. A marvellously illuminating book, if we see the contrast of first part and last part in terms of this idea.

I would very much like to go back now (were there world enough and time) and read again, with mutual self-mediation as a new heuristic, stories I read before this became a category for understanding. What light it might shed on Anna Karenina and her relationship, first with her husband, then with Count Vronsky, especially in contrast with the relationship that Levin and Kitty achieved. On father and son in Alan Paton's *Too Late the Phalarope*. On Ted and Caro in Shirley Hazzard's *The Transit of Venus*. Even on the relationship between hunter and hunted in many of Elmore Leonard's crime novels. I am not saying, of course, that this is the light in which we should read novels, but only that it is the way to read them if we would explore the fertility for human living of Lonergan's idea. (And who knows whether it might not prove a useful category for literary critics too?)

4 How to Live Our Lives

Method in Theology has greatly clarified the difference between the neutral scholarship of research or interpretation or history on the one hand

and the committed position of the believing theologian on the other. 'If one assimilates tradition, one learns that one should pass it on. If one encounters the past, one also has to take one's stand toward the future.' There is a theology 'that tells what Paul and John ... and anyone else had to say about God and the economy of salvation. But there is also a theology ... in which the theologian, enlightened by the past, confronts the problems of his own day.'[27]

The same contrast appears in regard to studies of Augustine, Aquinas, Newman, Congar, and of course Lonergan. My concern so far as been to get hold of Lonergan's ideas on human living. Despite my open endorsement of those ideas, the focus was on positive reporting: what did Lonergan hold and say? It is another question whether we wish to make his position our own, and so advance from positive reporting to a committed position. In regard to God and the economy of salvation the latter supposes faith. In regard to Augustine, Aquinas, Newman, Congar, or Lonergan, it supposes only endorsement of their ideas.

Thirdly, the contrast may apply to values in themselves – not then to study, say, of Aquinas, as when I set forth his theology with explicit or implicit personal commitment to his ideas, but to study of values in one's tradition and in their own right. This is a wide-ranging field. As Lonergan said of his eight functional specialties, 'they would be relevant to any human studies that investigated a cultural past to guide its future.'[28]

Commonly, when we study the ideas of great thinkers, our endorsement of their ideas is implicit, perhaps in our manner of presenting them, perhaps in the very choice of those ideas for study. But there is an angle in the implicit endorsement that should be brought into the open: the very clarity of such a thinker's presentation and its tacit harmony with our unexpressed experience is itself an argument for its acceptance.

All this I regard as pertinent to the present study. Everyone educated in the classic tradition knows that 'homo est animal rationale.' Not so many of them, however, get much beyond those four words in defining the human and setting it in contrast with the animal. I believe Lonergan's thought does get beyond the words and give them a recog-

27 *Method in Theology* 133.

28 'Bernard Lonergan Responds,' in Philip McShane, ed., *Foundations of Theology* (Dublin: Gill and Macmillan, 1971) 233.

nizable meaning, and I likewise believe that the clarity of his thought is itself persuasive of its validity.

Consequently, there is no urgent need for a special section in this essay to argue the value of his position and to effect the move from reporting to commitment. It is persuasion enough, I think, if I bring his ideas into focus and apply them to common experience. That move is implicit in my exposition of our paradigm case. It teaches us as a first step to give spatial and psychological separation to merely animal functions, as the abattoir is separated from the dining-room. Next, it has a word on well-mannered conversation. There is or used to be a caste system in India. Our tradition repudiates such classes among people, but the analogy is useful for present purposes: there is or should be a caste system in language for animal functions, such that some terms are and have to be outcasts from daily conversation. They are relegated to the margins of conversation and consciousness – not ignored or repudiated, for we must keep our humility, but allowed into the social situation only in self-deprecating jokes. Helpful here is the role *Insight* gives to humor: 'humor keeps the positions in contact with human limitations and human infirmity ... if satire becomes red with indignation, humor blushes with humility.'[29]

But the third level is the most important. Beyond that of language is the level of incorporation of animal functions, or in general of the material universe, into the human experience. The general theme of the workshop at which I presented the first version of this paper was 'The Drama of Human Living and the Aesthetization of Truth and Value.' My contribution to that general theme is the aesthetization of the animal in the human.

Here the analogy of caste comes into play again. I'm not dogmatic about the general question of what functions are susceptible or not susceptible of elevation into the drama of life. Our physical weight might seem the most intractable of our bodily attributes, yet the art-form of ballet succeeds in giving it an apparent weightlessness. In any case, our paradigm case of eating at table serves to define a basic need and how to implement it. The basic need is to give meaning and value, as far as possible, to what would otherwise be just an animal function. It is achieved, in Lonergan's words, when it has been enhanced by human artistry to become something of a ceremony in the humdrum of

29 *Insight* (1957) 626 [(1992) 649].

daily life: 'ornamented by the elaborate equipment of the dining-room, by the table manners imposed upon children, by the deportment of adult convention.' From this paradigm case one may easily move to other areas in which animal and human spheres intersect.

This is said in the context of our first part and its basic thesis on the relation of the human and the animal. But a similar ease of application may be discerned in my second and third parts: life as summation, and the mutuality of self-mediation. Here again there is overlapping of the two spheres, and the need for the human to go beyond the animal.

Thus, both animal and human in different ways and with more or less conscious 'planning' live beyond the present moment, and in their own way achieve an integration of their lives. Squirrels store up nuts for future need. Birds in some obscure way recognize the signs and head south for the winter. But the human being does not act only for the occasion, as do squirrels and birds. He or she is engaged in existential self-making: the determination of choices and actions 'in each case is the work of the free and responsible subject producing the first and only edition of himself.'[30] There is human use of the animal, but only to go far beyond it.

There is likewise similarity and difference in the 'community life' of animal and human beings. Ants have a community of sorts; so do bees. But the intersubjective factor in the human race goes much farther. 'A sense of belonging together provides the dynamic premise for common enterprise, for mutual aid and succor, for the sympathy that augments joys and divides sorrows.'[31]

But perhaps there is no need to spell out the application of the pattern. My essay is mainly a study of Lonergan, not of the animal–human relationship, and I believe the basic thesis is enough to bring to light a little known aspect of his thought. He is not limited to the world-historical categories of hermeneutics, historicity, horizons and biases, progress and decline, self-appropriation, method, sublation, differentiations of consciousness, and the like. He has something important to say as well on the very ordinary level on which we live our daily human-animal existence.

30 'The Subject,' in *A Second Collection* 83.

31 *Insight* (1957) 212 [(1992) 237].

Chapter 12

The Ignatian Spiritual Exercises and Jesuit Spirituality[1]

There is a tendency, seen more in passing remarks than in thematic studies, to equate Jesuit spirituality with the Spiritual Exercises of St Ignatius of Loyola. I do not know whether anyone has ever made the equation in so many words, but one hears it said that the Exercises are the wellspring of Jesuit life, that Jesuit spirituality is to be found above all in the Exercises, that the Exercises are the basis of Jesuit spirituality, that Jesuits have a vision given them by the Exercises, and so on.

There is a profound truth in all these statements, but just because the truth in them is so very profound and so very true, it seems to me all the more necessary to state explicitly that it is not the whole truth, and to think out clearly the relationship of the Exercises to Jesuit, and any other, spirituality. Otherwise part of the truth is easily made the whole truth, and thus we are led imperceptibly to identify two distinct elements in Jesuit spirituality: the Exercises, and the complex history that culminated in the Constitutions. Then, since ideas inevitably have consequences, we arrive with the same inevitability at two practical errors: the first is to point the Exercises toward a spirituality they do not intend; and the second is to deprive Jesuit spirituality of its specific individuality, as found most notably in the Constitutions.

Two simple lines of reasoning should, it seems to me, establish the point I am making.

The first is a thought-experiment that makes the case in a more graphic way than my abstract assertion. Let us imagine two men with the proper dispositions who together enter upon the Exercises. One of

---

1 Previously published in *Review for Religious* 53 (1994) 524–33.

them emerges from the thirty days with a decision to seek admission to the Jesuits. The other emerges with a decision to join the Carthusians. Is this an impossible scenario? Will anyone tell the Holy Spirit, 'You can't do that: the Exercises are identified with Jesuit spirituality, and you really cannot use them to direct someone to the Carthusians'? Or would anyone say that the Carthusian vocation here was due to a failure of the exercitant to be guided by the Spirit, that the Spirit was directing him elsewhere, that he was in fact a Jesuit *manqué*?

I mean this, of course, as a *reductio ad absurdum*, for no one would dream of taking such a position on what the Holy Spirit should or should not do, or of attributing a failure to respond if the exercitant does not decide to be a Jesuit. And a parallel statement could be made in the case of two women who emerge from their Ignatian retreat, one to become a Poor Clare, the other to become a social worker, or of a man and woman who emerge with a decision to enter matrimony.

My other line of reasoning takes us to concrete history, where we might ask: what were the first companions of Ignatius doing in the years that followed their experience of making the Exercises, say between 1534 and 1540, a period in which they were steadily seeking the divine will? Why, if the Exercises had already determined what the Jesuit spirituality and way of proceeding was to be, did they run through so many different options before they settled on that way? What, indeed, was Ignatius doing for nearly two decades after Manresa, wandering around Europe and the Holy Land before he found his destined way of life? And a still more pointed question: what was he doing in the dozen years of 'blood, toil, tears, and sweat' during which he laboriously worked out the Jesuit Constitutions? The answer seems obvious in all these questions: Ignatius and his first companions were seeking something the Exercises had not given them.

I believe that we need to face these questions, and work out with all possible accuracy what role the Exercises may play in Jesuit or any other spirituality,[2] and how that role may be complemented by the dis-

2 Eventually such a study should come to the details of particular spiritualities, but that is a further step. Here I intend the word in a broad sense, without entering into the refinements that are to be found in recent theological writing. 'Spirituality' includes therefore elements of doctrine and practice, of vocation and way of proceeding, of tradition and orientation, of rules and constitutions, and so on, without specifying what these may be for Jesuit, Carthusian, and other vocations.

tinct and specifying roles that different spiritual traditions may contribute – for Jesuits, in the way their Constitutions above all determine for them; and for Carthusians, Poor Clares, and other vocations, in ways that they also have worked out for themselves and that I need not try to determine for them here.

Is there then a spirituality in the Exercises? Yes, indeed, the very highest. If we leave aside the case of those who are not disposed to go beyond the First Week,[3] the aim of the Exercises is to bring exercitants, whatever their state in life is to be and wherever God will direct them, to choose to live under the standard of Christ. 'We shall also think about how we ought to dispose ourselves in order to come to perfection in whatsoever state or way of life God our Lord may grant us to elect.'[4] This means embracing the way of Christ: in the highest poverty, spiritual poverty certainly and if God wills it in actual poverty as well; in willingness also to bear opprobrium and injuries, in order to imitate him the better.[5] Or, again, when God is served equally by either of the two alternatives, it means to choose poverty with Christ poor rather than riches, opprobrium with Christ covered with opprobrium rather than honors, to be counted vain and stupid with Christ so counted rather than wise and prudent in this world;[6] and so forth.

The real issue is how this spirituality relates to the various specific spiritualities to which various individual exercitants may be called. I will suggest a few ways of conceiving the relation, ways that follow more traditional lines of thought and shed some light on the matter – none of them quite satisfactory, but each adding an element of understanding. And then I will propose another approach to the whole question.

The obvious pair of terms to define the relationship in question is 'generic' and 'specific.' The Exercises have a generic spirituality, the following of Christ. Then, giving more determinate content to this, we have the specific spiritualities of Jesuit, Carthusian, and so on. I have

3 *The Spiritual Exercises of Saint Ignatius: A Translation and Commentary by George E. Ganss, SJ* (St Louis: Institute of Jesuit Sources, 1992), no. 18 in the numbering that is standard for all editions. All English quotations will be from this edition.

4 Ibid., no. 135. In the Latin 'ut veniamus ad perfectionem in quocumque statu seu vita, quam Deus Dominus noster eligendum nobis dederit' (no. 135). The 'quocumque' is the 'whatever' I will presently discuss.

5 Ibid., no. 147.

6 Ibid., no. 167.

drawn on these concepts already to start discussion. They are clarifying up to a point, but they use the language of logic, which seems simply inadequate for so spiritual a question.

Another way would be to use 'infrastructure' and 'suprastructure.' To follow Christ is infrastructure for whatever way of life we choose to follow; and on this basis one builds a suprastructure of, say, the Jesuit way of proceeding. This too adds an element of understanding; and it is not limited by reference to bridge or building construction, for this pair of terms has gone beyond its engineering origins and entered largely into the human sciences. From that vantage point they could be applied with profit to our question. Still, they leave the following of Christ the invisible element, or at any rate not the focus of attention – a situation that does not correspond to any vocation emerging from the Exercises.

A third pair of terms might be 'compact' and 'differentiated,' terms that have now come into general use – mainly, I believe, through the influence of Eric Voegelin. Bernard Lonergan also has some helpful pages on the process from the compactness of the symbol, where very profound truths may be contained and grasped, to the enucleated and analyzed differentiations of scientists, philosophers, and theologians. He illustrates the process by Christology and the 'transition from a more compact symbolic consciousness expressed in the New Testament to a more enucleated theological consciousness expressed in the great Greek Councils.'[7] Once again, we have a pair of terms that provide some understanding. Certainly the various spiritualities are differentiated from one another: one has only to adduce again the example of Carthusian and Jesuit. But do those terms not also contain the unwelcome hint that the various differentiations divide up something that the compact contained in its wholeness?

A fourth pair, made familiar in social studies, is 'communal' or 'collective,' and 'particular' or 'individual.' Our communal spirituality is the way of Christ, and our individual spirituality is the particular way of life in which we follow Christ. This seems a promising approach; but

7 See *Topics in Education* 55–58; the quotation is from 57–58. On Eric Voegelin see Kenneth Keulman, *The Balance of Consciousness: Eric Voegelin's Political Theory* (University Park: Pennsylvania State University Press, 1990) 92–93: 'What the pattern of symbolizations indicates is the development from compact to differentiated forms ... The terms "compact" and "differentiated" refer not only to the symbolizations, but also to the characteristic forms of consciousness that generate them.'

we would need to work out the relation between the communal and the individual, see how the communal is explicit in the particular, and how the particular contains without loss the whole of the communal.

No doubt we could add to this list and pursue the same general line of thought with considerable profit, but I wonder whether in the end it would bring us to the heart of the matter. I wonder in fact whether our aim here is not a bit off center, whether we should not approach the problem from another perspective altogether. For in the various pairs we have considered, the first member seems to remain incomplete until the second is added, and the second must always be concerned that it incorporates the whole of the first. Further, the second term in each pair is thought of as an end-product with its meaning determined. What a Jesuit is, what a Carthusian is: these are already more or less clearly defined, belong to an established order, are in some measure static. Does such thinking deal adequately with the dynamism of the Exercises?

I would like to explore a somewhat different approach. In this line of thought it is the heuristic character, and therefore the dynamism, of the Exercises that will be the focus. But all dynamic movement, all searching, all heuristic activity, supposes and takes place within a horizon that determines the activity and defines the source of energy for the search. Therefore I first need to study the idea of horizon. For both terms, 'horizon' and 'heuristic,' I draw directly on the work of Bernard Lonergan.

For the meaning of 'horizon,' it will be best simply to quote Lonergan's account of the matter.

> In its literal sense the word, horizon, denotes the bounding circle, the line at which earth and sky appear to meet. This line is the limit of one's field of vision. As one moves about, it recedes in front and closes in behind so that, for different standpoints, there are different horizons. Moreover, for each different standpoint and horizon, there are different divisions of the totality of visible objects. Beyond the horizon lie the objects that, at least for the moment, cannot be seen. Within the horizon lie the objects that can now be seen.
>
> As our field of vision, so too the scope of our knowledge, and the range of our interests are bounded. As fields of vision vary with one's standpoint, so too the scope of one's knowledge and the range of one's interests vary with the period in which one lives, one's social background and milieu, one's education and personal development. So there has arisen a metaphorical or perhaps analogous meaning of the word, horizon. In this

> sense what lies beyond one's horizon is simply outside the range of one's knowledge and interests: one neither knows nor cares. But what lies within one's horizon is in some measure, great or small, an object of interest and of knowledge.[8]

It is easy to apply this idea to the world of the Spiritual Exercises. One enters upon them with a given horizon, vaguely or clearly conceived: 'the range of one's knowledge and interests.' For example, maybe one is led by a spirit of repentance, or by anxiety about one's salvation. One makes the First Week, remaining for the most part within such a horizon – with glimpses of something beyond, to be sure, in such passages as the Colloquy at the end of the first exercise.[9] But if one responds to the call of Christ in the Kingdom exercise,[10] one throws back the previous horizon to work within a new one, far wider, with far greater potential – a horizon that is all-encompassing, a boundary that is in fact no boundary for it encloses a territory that is boundless.

Now it is this ultimate horizon, and not any relative and confining horizon, that I would equate with the spirituality of the Exercises. The horizon of those who should not be led beyond the First Week is narrow and confining. What happens when one enters the Second Week with the mind and heart of those who would 'show greater devotion and ... distinguish themselves in total service to their eternal King and universal Lord'?[11] What happens is the discovery of a new horizon, the horizon defined by Christ the Lord. Basically, the horizon is established in the exercises on Two Standards[12] and Three Ways of Being Humble.[13] Details are added in The Mysteries of the Life of Christ Our Lord.[14] And in the Third and Fourth Weeks communion with Christ (what the Germans call *Mitsein*) fortifies the attraction of the good with the power of love and the interpersonal.

This does not happen without the grace of God and a conversion. For besides the ultimate horizon, there are relative horizons. There are shifts in our relative horizon as we move, say, from schooldays to the

8 *Method in Theology* 235–36.
9 *Spiritual Exercises*, no. 53.
10 Ibid., no. 91.
11 Ibid., no. 95.
12 Ibid., nos. 136–48.
13 Ibid., nos. 165–68.
14 Ibid., no. 261.

workforce; and this shift may occur as a normal development of potentialities. 'But it is also possible that the movement into a new horizon involves an about-face; it comes out of the old by repudiating characteristic features; it begins a new sequence that can keep revealing ever greater depth and breadth and wealth. Such an about-face and new beginning is what is meant by a conversion.'[15]

Against that background, we turn to the idea of the heuristic, taking as our context the fact that the Exercises are very basically a search. Thus the first annotation tells us that our purpose, after removing obstacles, is to seek and to find the divine will;[16] and the fifteenth annotation has advice for those who during the Exercises are seeking God's will.[17] Or, as is repeated over and over, recurring like a refrain, we are to seek what gives glory to God.[18] In the key stage of the Election, 'While continuing our contemplations of his [Christ's] life, we now begin simultaneously to explore and inquire: In which state or way of life does the Divine Majesty wish us to serve him?'[19] And still at the heart of the Exercises, in the meditation on the Three Classes of Men, we are seeking to 'desire and know what will be more pleasing to the Divine Goodness.'[20]

We are, then, in an area in which the idea of the heuristic plays a central role. My Webster's dictionary defines heuristic as 'serving to guide, discover, or reveal.' A helpful point: the famous 'eureka' of Archimedes

---

15 *Method in Theology* 237–38. I add a few helpful quotations: 'Horizontal liberty is the exercise of liberty within a determinate horizon and from the basis of a corresponding existential stance. Vertical liberty is the exercise of liberty that selects that stance and the corresponding horizon' (ibid. 40, with a reference to Joseph de Finance). 'For falling in love is a new beginning, an exercise of vertical liberty in which one's world undergoes a new organization' (ibid. 122). 'A horizontal exercise [of freedom] is a decision or choice that occurs within an established horizon. A vertical exercise is the set of judgments and decisions by which we move from one horizon to another' (ibid. 237). 'Further, deliberate decision about one's horizon is high achievement. For the most part people merely drift into some contemporary horizon. They do not advert to the multiplicity of horizons. They do not exercise their vertical liberty by migrating from the one they have inherited to another they have discovered to be better' (ibid. 269).

16 *Spiritual Exercises*, no. 1; 'Introductory Explanations ... The First Explanation.'

17 Ibid., no. 15.

18 Ibid., no. 16.

19 Ibid., no. 135.

20 Ibid., no. 151.

is from the same Greek root. It means 'I've found [it], I've discovered the secret.' Now this line of thought is thoroughly developed by Lonergan, and I find his treatment of the idea helpful for understanding the process and dynamic of the spiritual search that the Exercises are. In his usage, a heuristic notion tries to give some advance notice of what we hope to find. It is an anticipation of the answer we seek to a question. It is not a determinate concept, like various concepts in physics or chemistry or biology; rather, it is an indeterminate anticipation.

The nearly perfect word for this way of conceiving in anticipation what we have not yet determined in particular is 'whatever,' and the nearly perfect use of 'whatever' we can find right in scripture. Paul, writing to the Philippians (4:8) exhorts them to focus on 'whatever is true, whatever is honorable, whatever is just, whatever is pure, whatever is pleasing, whatever is commendable.'[21] Well, what is true? What is honorable, just, and so on? That will emerge with each new day, and meanwhile we are guided by its anticipation in that 'whatever.'

To come, then, to the present point, Ignatius and Paul are at one in conceiving by anticipation what they do not yet determine in particular. Apropos of the Election, Ignatius writes that we are to 'think about how we ought to dispose ourselves in order to come to perfection in whatsoever state or way of life God our Lord may grant us to elect.'[22]

It is possible now to bring these two ideas together in a new understanding of the relationship of the Exercises and Jesuit or other spirituality. My brief statement of the case would be that the horizon of the Exercises and the spirituality they directly intend is established in the exercise on the Two Standards[23] and the exercises that directly relate to it; further, that the heuristic of the Exercises is epitomized in the Election,[24] where we search for and discover and embrace the state of life God intends for us. And the relationship between the two is indicated in the Introduction to the Consideration of the States of Life: 'We shall also think about how we ought to dispose ourselves in order to come to perfection in whatsoever state or way of life God our Lord may grant us to elect.'[25] Perfection as defined in the Two Standards and

21 NRSV; in the Douai translation, 'whatsoever.'

22 *Spiritual Exercises*, no. 135.

23 Ibid., nos. 136–48.

24 Ibid., nos. 169–88.

25 Ibid., no. 135.

their retinue of exercises is the horizon, but 'whatsoever state' God may direct us to is another matter: it represents the heuristic element.

The Exercises do not, therefore, 'intend' any one spirituality. Their objective ordination, what the Scholastics would call their 'finis operis,' is neither Jesuit nor Carthusian spirituality, nor any other. They 'intend' what God will choose: their *finis operis* is a 'whatever.' What we therefore first conceived as generic, as infrastructure, as compact, as communal, we now conceive as a horizon; and what we first conceived as specific, as suprastructure, as differentiated, as individual, we now conceive as the area within that horizon that we discover to be God's will for us.

But in moving from one to the other we do not add something specific that was not contained in the genus; for everything is contained in the horizon, and for those who respond fully the whole spirituality of the horizon enters every vocation and every state of life. The situation is more like that of the incarnation: as the fulness of the Godhead dwells in Christ,[26] so the fulness of the horizon of Christ is the world in which we dwell, Jesuit and Carthusian and all others who respond fully to the call of the Kingdom exercise.

Similarly, the 'superstructure' we conceived as our way turns out to be what we may, if we wish, call an 'addition,' but an addition to what is already complete (like the humanity of Christ added to the eternal and infinite Word). The 'differentiation' we spoke of is not a dividing off of a part but the incorporation of the whole, and the 'individual' contains the fulness of the communal.

Thus one is everywhere safe within the all-encompassing arms of the Christian horizon. One is never in exile, never outside the shores of home, never a wanderer like the prodigal son in distant lands. One does not therefore go beyond this horizon to be a Jesuit or to be a Carthusian, or to find one's particular vocation. There is nothing there beyond it. It is the all-encompassing. Just as, within any relative horizon of geography one can go north or south, east or west, without going beyond the horizon, so within the ultimate horizon established by Christ, one can become a Jesuit or Carthusian, but one cannot go beyond the horizon set by Christ: one can only contract that horizon by living an inauthentic Jesuit life or living an inauthentic Carthusian life.

Further use of the ideas of heuristic and horizon is readily made. In

26 Colossians 1:19.

Lonergan's thought one can speak of heuristic notions and heuristic devices. There is the notion of being, the notion of the good, and so on; but there are also the heuristic structures which promote the discoveries we seek (his rather famous scissors action of heuristic method). One could say God's will is the supreme heuristic notion guiding the exercitant, and the Exercises are a heuristic device, an instrument par excellence for finding God's will, maybe with a kind of scissors action too. (I do not, however, call the Exercises the supreme heuristic device, for we do not limit God's creativity to what was divinely done in Ignatius, and we do not know what successor God may be preparing for Ignatius.) Again, still in Lonergan's thought, one can speak of interrelationships in the set of horizons, of their complementary, genetic, and dialectical differences. But that would add length to a paper that is already long enough, and introduce further specialized categories where they are already rather extensive.

Chapter 13

Linking the Splintered Disciplines: Ideas from Lonergan[1]

When I was preparing this talk, a famous line from Kipling came to mind: 'Oh East is East and West is West, and never the twain shall meet.' The association of ideas is obvious enough, for our question is about the meeting of disciplines, about dialogue between them; and when disciplines try to meet, chemistry with cultural history, say, or music with demography, they seem to have little or nothing to say to one another: they form a twain that will never meet. And a university which has ten faculties, a score of colleges, schools, and institutes, and half a hundred departments, not to mention artists in residence, can seem to be a mere congeries, a miscellany, a conglomeration, with no other bond of unity than their finance office that collects all the tuition fees and pays all the salaries.

I regularly read the *University of Toronto Bulletin*, where doctoral theses are listed every two weeks; and I see the most heterogeneous topics side by side: Leibniz's Doctrine of Evil, in the Department of Philosophy, and Modelling of Extrusion Cooking of Wheat Starch, in the Department of Chemical Engineering and Applied Chemistry. What has Jerusalem to do with Athens? – a rhetorical question of Tertullian eighteen centuries ago. And what, we may ask today, what has the history of Iceland to do with pharmaceutics? Or the Institute of Policy Analysis with the Department of Botany?

And nevertheless, to stay with Kipling for a moment, I don't have to

---

1 Originally presented as 'Insight and Interdisciplinarity' on 15 October 1992 at Lonergan College, Concordia University, Montreal, in celebration of the College's first fifteen years. Previously published in *Lonergan Review: A Multidisciplinary Journal* 3 (1994) 31–43.

tell you that the lines I quoted are not his message, not at all what he is saying to us – that to quote them in isolation from the whole poem, as we all do so often, is to distort their meaning, is in fact to make it the exact opposite of what Kipling intended. For his poem is of a genuine meeting of cultures, at the most fundamental level of humanity, in the deepest resources of human conduct. And the real message is in the last stanza, which ends: 'But there is neither East nor West, Border, nor Breed, nor Birth, When two strong men stand face to face, tho' they come from the ends of the earth' ('The Ballad of East and West').

We have to hope that in our global village a common humanity will bring open minds and generous hearts to the kind of meeting achieved by Kamal and the Colonel's son in Kipling's poem. Similarly, the existence of Lonergan University College, whose anniversary we are celebrating, and the effort at dialogue of the many diverse disciplines represented by the College Fellows, is testimony to a parallel hope in academe.

We give that hope the name 'interdisciplinary.' A mouthful, surely, even for the Teutonic peoples who delight in this kind of language, and much more for our poor English tongues: seven syllables to stumble over. Further, you have invited me to talk on the question from the perspective of Bernard Lonergan's thought; and this, in the view of some, would simply add a few more mouthfuls to stumble over. But that is not, I presume, the view of those who invited me. In any case, it is certainly not mine. And so I will speak to you of Lonergan and interdisciplinarity.

To put a semblance of order into this lecture, I propose first to mention and then set aside (or at least put on the back burner) an analogous question: namely, the question of everyday crosscultural differences; then to talk of the splintering of the disciplines and the main lines of their division; thirdly, to bring Lonergan's thought to bear on a few particular areas of interdisciplinary dialogue; finally, to take up his special contribution, the role of transcendental method in this regard. It is under the latter topic, if anywhere, that we will find our community of thought, unity at the most fundamental level, the academic parallel to the common humanity that Kipling found in the meeting of East and West.

1 Crosscultural Problems of Everyday Life

It will be useful to begin outside the university, away from the arts and sciences and academic disciplines, in the field of everyday life, with its parallel version of the problem. No doubt the disciplines deal with every aspect of life: nothing escapes the nets of sociology, anthropology, biology, immunology, and the other -ologies. But what specialists in these disciplines study, they themselves along with all of us live in everyday life; and the living is prior to the study. That living is chock full of problems analogous to those of the disciplines.

Lonergan's context for this aspect is common sense and the diverse brands of common sense.[2] Common sense is common in its procedures, its attitude toward theory, its orientation to the practical, its focus on the useful. It is not common in its ideas and judgments, its customs and values, in what it finds interesting. Exactly the contrary. The common sense of those who invaded this continent four or five centuries ago was not the common sense of the peoples native to it. English humor can be totally lost on Americans, and *vice versa*. What Romans call *Romanità* is a mystery over here. Everywhere, then, differences: differences of customs, values, ways of thinking.

For the simplest possible example, familiar to everyone, we might think of the in-law problem. A wedding can bring together two clans who don't know one another, have little to say to one another, don't want to talk to one another anyway, and can hardly wait till the celebrations are over and they can return to the safe cocoon of their own family interests. It is testimony to the power of love that it can overcome the differences in clan loyalties of bride and groom, and enable them to live in unity, till children come along to establish a new clan. (I know I exaggerate. A wedding can also be, and often is, a happy enlargement of the circle of friends; but the opposite experience is familiar enough to illustrate the point I wish to make.)

I do not intend to pursue in detail this question of everyday dialogue. The varieties of the problem are myriad, the particular cases of each are just uncountable. But it keeps touching on the parallel problem of the disciplines, especially in theology. Anyway, I can introduce our own question, and define our specific interest, if I mark off the crosscultural questions of everyday life, and distinguish them from what is directly relevant: interdisciplinary questions of a more academic nature. There are varieties here too, but they are countable; and

---

2 'There are as many brands of common sense as there are languages, social or cultural differences, almost differences of place and time.' *Method in Theology* 276.

it may be possible to put some order in the variety through the standard divisions in the disciplines.

2 Classifying the Splintered Disciplines

A preliminary point: I will be talking off and on about universities, as if the interdisciplinary problem were peculiar to them. But that is a shorthand way of speaking. Newman held that the university was a place to teach, it was not the place to do research. Research should be left to academies, or to scientific societies; at any rate it belongs outside the university.[3] The point is still debated, a hundred and forty years later. I do not enter the debate, I mention it only to leave it entirely aside. I deal with disciplines, wherever they find a home.

So we are to classify and relate the splintered disciplines, and for that purpose it will be useful to note the history of the splintering. I will do so, however, with all possible brevity, for it is not my field.

The splintering is almost synonymous with specialization, which is a modern development. I am told that it was possible in the Italian Renaissance to be *uomo universale*, a 'universal man': that is, to be a complete person, not just 'many-sided' but 'all-sided,' a type represented by Leonardo da Vinci (1452–1519). I am told also that he was one of the last representatives of a class that was vanishing, that already in him there were signs of a breakup: the separation of humanism from the artistic-technical, with their respective methodologies steadily clarifying. Again, the same source informs me that Michelangelo (1475–1564), the most universal artist of them all, represented a further separation, that of art from scientific preoccupations, the final dissolution of the Renaissance view: 'Art, science and literary humanism henceforth pursued their own independent careers.'[4]

---

3 'The view taken of a University in these Discourses is the following: – That it is a place of teaching universal knowledge. This implies that its object ... is the diffusion and extension of knowledge rather than the advancement ... [T]here are other institutions far more suited to act as instruments of stimulating philosophical inquiry, and extending the boundaries of our knowledge, than a University. Such, for instance, are the literary and scientific "Academies," which are so celebrated in Italy and France.' John Henry Newman, *The Idea of a University Defined and Illustrated* (London: Longmans, Green and Co., 1929) ix–xii.

4 Joan Kelly Gadol, 'Universal Man,' in *Dictionary of the History of Ideas*, vol. 4 (New York: Charles Scribner's Sons, 1973) 437–43 (quoted at 443).

So we are in the modern era of specialization. From Michelangelo on there was evolution and splintering in every area of life and academe: the useful arts into the various technologies, the liberal arts into branches of the humanities, the fine arts into forms many of us would not recognize as art if no one told us, the sciences dividing and subdividing endlessly. I find this glimpse of history utterly fascinating, and even a glimpse, I think, helps us see the problem; but I must leave further history to others.

When we come then to Lonergan's views on these matters, we find that the focus is on the sciences and scholarship. He deals with art, but not as artists do: in terms rather of artistic consciousness, as a methodologist does. So it is rather the sciences and their main divisions, and the division of human sciences from human studies, that are more directly in his line of vision; and it will be useful to see their general pattern and the broad lines of the way they relate to each other, before we talk of particular interdisciplinary problems.

In the natural sciences, to begin with them, for there is more clarity there, there are relations that we might call 'vertical' and others that we might call 'horizontal,' with the vertical relations being genetic, and the horizontal relations being complementary. Thus, Lonergan sees the order we are calling 'vertical' in the relations of physics, chemistry, biology: 'The laws of physics hold for subatomic elements; the laws of physics and chemistry hold for chemical elements and compounds; the laws of physics, chemistry, and biology hold for plants.'[5] There is increasing differentiation, with ever higher systems emerging, in an evolutionary and vertical relationship.

The case is different, however, in the relationship of physics and chemistry to, say, astronomy, the order we are calling 'horizontal.' 'When one turns from physics and chemistry to astronomy, one employs the same basic terms and correlations; but when one turns from physics and chemistry to biology, one is confronted with an entirely new set of basic concepts and laws.'[6]

The human sciences and human studies are more complex. There are or can be sciences here in the strict sense: in the sense, namely, of dealing with laws and principles subject to systematic ordering. But they achieve the status of science only by leaving out much that is

5 *Insight* (1957) 255 [(1992) 280].
6 Ibid. (1957) 255 [(1992) 281].

human, and dealing with human data in the same way you would deal with data on the guinea pig.[7] Human studies would fill that gap, they would go beyond the guinea pig to the truly human. And Lonergan proposed the following convention for clarity of terms in respect to the division.

> Let the term, science, be reserved for knowledge that is contained in principles and laws and either is verified universally or else is revised. Let the term, scholarship, be employed to denote the learning that consists in a commonsense grasp of the commonsense thought, speech, action of distant places and/or times. Men of letters, linguists, exegetes, historians generally would be named, not scientists, but scholars. It would be understood, however, that a man might be both a scientist and scholar.[8]

We need a general term for all the branches of learning we have been considering, and that general term seems to be 'disciplines.' There is a certain tendency to snobbishness here, to reserve honorary terms to one's own field. But Lonergan would make 'discipline' a kind of carry all. Thus, he writes, 'today the English word, science, means natural science. One descends a rung or more in the ladder when one speaks of behavioral or human sciences. Theologians finally often have to be content if their subject is included in a list not of sciences but of academic disciplines.'[9]

3 Particular Areas of Interdisciplinary Dialogue

It is time to come directly to the question: dialogue between the disciplines, and what Lonergan might contribute to such dialogue.

Is dialogue possible? Well, we have to believe and hope that it is. After all, we all belong to the same human race. Besides, we have seen the breakdown of unity following the *uomo universale* of the Renaissance, and analysis of the breakdown may suggest a reunion.

---

7 'Reductionists extend the methods of natural science to the study of man. Their results, accordingly, are valid only in so far as a man resembles a robot or a rat and, while such resemblance does exist, exclusive attention to it gives a grossly mutilated and distorted view.' *Method in Theology* 248.

8 Ibid. 233–34.

9 Ibid. 3.

We will not expect the same kind of unity. The Renaissance unity was a unity of content. Leonardo, perhaps, actually did know everything then knowable; but Lonergan's way does not require that, for it regards procedures far more than content. We will come to that in due course, in the fourth part of this presentation. Meanwhile let me say a word on community of content, for that is still possible on some sliding scale and in certain particular cases.

My first particular case is that of neighboring disciplines. Not all distances are the same distance. There are near neighbors and remote neighbors, even in the academic disciplines. There are disciplines that share a common boundary, and even disciplines that overlap, as well as disciplines that are as far apart as Leibniz's doctrine of evil and the modelling of extrusion cooking of wheat starch.

Is there not a possibility of dialogue with regard to the content of neighboring disciplines? For example, in regard to the life of the unborn, biology, neurology, and embryology should have something to say to one another. We might argue on religious or even philosophical grounds that they ought to have something to say to one another, if we are going to solve one of the most difficult, one of the most pressing problems of our time. But I would argue that simply on scientific grounds, because they are near neighbors, they do have something to say to one another. They have something in common.

What they have in common is border questions. The case is simpler, perhaps, for sciences in a horizontal relationship to one another, so let us take those that are in a vertical relationship. What kind of questions would the disciplines then discuss? Well, by and large there is agreement on the laws of physics, at least on what laws are relevant to that field. But what do you do with the events that are indeed observed in your study of physics but escape the physical laws you have agreed upon?

Of course, if you insist on mechanism, determinism, reductionism, there is no interdisciplinary problem at all. Everything reduces to one discipline, to one set of laws: the set becomes more and more complex, but all you need is a bigger and bigger brain. We are back at the Renaissance *uomo universale*, with the difference that our *uomo* is now a computer.

But if you rid yourself of such reductionism, you may ask whether those events that for physics are a non-systematic manifold, a coincidental aggregate (Lonergan's terms), whether they are systematized in chemistry. This is a new question, and indeed a new type of question:

can what is merely coincidental for the laws of physics be correlated through a quite different set of laws in chemistry? The question is common to physics and chemistry, and it may provide a common ground for conversation between the two departments. Notice that I do not ask you to accept Lonergan's affirmative answer to the question.[10] It is enough for my present purpose that the question can be asked in both departments.

That question is somewhat a priori for those of us who know neither physics nor chemistry, but we could take our example from two areas that are more familiar: the animal and the human. There are laws that pertain to the animal realm, that systematize events that pertain to that realm. But now put two animals side by side: a puppy and a child. An event occurs in one of them that does not occur in the other, the event that we call wonder and find in the look of the child's eyes long before it becomes expressed in the child's perpetual 'why?' 'Children's faces looking up/ Holding wonder like a cup.' The one recurring event creates a question for both zoology and psychology. Can that event which zoology has to regard as falling outside its system of laws be systematized in the higher science of psychology?

I have been speaking of neighboring disciplines. But now what of the widely separated disciplines – a discipline, say, where they deal with the problem of evil, and another that studies extrusion cooking of wheat starch. Is there any common scientific question, any common ground for scientific dialogue between them? Perhaps not, but that too is illuminating, as showing the limits of interdisciplinary dialogue. We should not expect to find common questions everywhere. The limits closing off an area of study are as necessary as its open possibilities.

Yet even here the case is not entirely closed. Besides scientific questions there are questions of a practical and ethical nature. For we cannot set aside our common ethical concerns, or even our common practical concerns of a lower order, though our sciences are far apart. The disciplines can meet, and often must meet, in the practical and/or ethical order, in a value judgment, in a project, in common action.

10 *Insight* (1957) 451 [(1992) 477]: '... chemical elements and compounds are higher integrations of otherwise coincidental manifolds of subatomic events; organisms are higher integrations of otherwise coincidental manifolds of chemical processes; sensitive consciousness is a higher integration of otherwise coincidental manifolds of changes in neural tissues; and accumulating insights are higher integrations of otherwise coincidental manifolds of images or of data.'

If I am building a house I must secure cooperation – from carpenters, plumbers, electricians, and so on. If three tradespeople are working on a house for me, they may have only a limited interest in cooperating. But if they are building a triplex for themselves, with carpenter, plumber, and electrician each taking a flat, the case is entirely different. The strategy, therefore, is clear: get the people in the disciplines working on a common project, where they are not only working but involved personally. This should not be too difficult, and I am not thinking of building common living quarters. For example, you have here in close relationship to Lonergan College the Loyola Jesuit Peace Institute, which could – which, I think, ought to – command the interest of every discipline on campus.

I have talked of two particular possibilities for interdisciplinary dialogue: boundary questions for neighboring disciplines, and common practical and ethical concerns for us all. I will just mention two others that are rather complex but deserve a mention because they entered so deeply into Lonergan's own work.

One is the merging of horizons that we find in the scholar, say, in students of ancient literatures, or historians.[11] They, as it were, live in one world and work in another. There is in them a merging of horizons that in itself does not differ much from the westerner who encounters the easterner, but raises an interdisciplinary problem in academe, because the scholar must return from that other world to tell the rest of us about it. The problem is acute in theology, where our sources are found in a culture very different from ours, and have to be mediated by exegetes and historians to other branches of theology.

Nor does it end there, for then systematic and pastoral theologians have to mediate to still others what they have received from exegetes and historians. They have to hand it on to the thousands of cultures around the world, as well as to the hundreds of subcultures in a city like Montreal. The problem now is a little different. In exegetes and historians there is a merging of brands of common sense; but in the systematic and pastoral field there is a merging of different patterns of consciousness. In any case we have here two cases where the interdisciplinary problem arises and is met through a merging of the disciplines in the practitioners themselves.

I cannot go into these two complex areas, but neither can I leave them

11 See Lonergan's article 'Merging Horizons: System, Common Sense, Scholarship,' *Cultural Hermeneutics* [later renamed *Philosophy and Social Criticism*] 1 (1973) 87–99.

without mentioning the area where they require further study: what has to be added here is the role of interiority. It is in the interior of mind and heart that meaning is created, formed, and expressed; and if we can appropriate our own interiority, discover meaning in its very origin, then we have a key to other cultures and their meaning, be they cultures of the ancient world or the various subcultures of a modern city.

4 The Transcendental Approach

That brief and all too cryptic mention of interiority brings me to my last point. I began by distinguishing the academic from everyday life. I then set out the academic disciplines in the relations that follow on their splintering. Thirdly, I spoke of four particular interdisciplinary possibilities, ending with remarks on the interiority that is needed for the more difficult problems. Now the area of interiority par excellence is that of the transcendental, where we find Lonergan's special contribution to our question.

What is this transcendental approach? It is overarching, if you wish, or underpinning, if you prefer. Anyway it is beyond all particular cases, it transcends them. Scholastic thinkers produced the transcendental concepts: they did so by going beyond all categories. You go beyond horses and cows to the genus, animal; but animal is still a category beside, say, plants. So you go beyond animals and plants to living things; but living things too is still a category. You get beyond all categories when you come to being. Everything that is, is an instance of being: being is one of the transcendental concepts.

Lonergan finds a way to get beyond even the transcendental concepts. He goes back to the transcendental operations of the mind that produce the transcendental concepts. Being is a transcendental concept, but how do we attain being? We attain being through the operations of experiencing, understanding, and judging. With these operations we have gone one step deeper than the Scholastics. They worked with categories. Lonergan works with what produces the categories: the operating mind and its operations. So we come to the transcendental operations, to transcendental method and the bearing it has on the interdisciplinary.[12]

12 *Method in Theology* 11–12: 'if we objectify the content of intelligent intending, we form the transcendental concept of the intelligible. If we objectify the content of reasonable intending, we form the transcendental concepts of the true and the real. If we objec-

Back in 1975 Philip McShane organized, at Mount Saint Vincent University in Halifax, 'A Workshop on Lonergan's Interdisciplinary Philosophy.' Lonergan's own lecture was 'Healing and Creating in History.' It was one he had already given at the Thomas More Institute here in Montreal, so it was not written in direct response to the interdisciplinary question, though it ends by asking 'for creativity, for an interdisciplinary theory that at first will be denounced as absurd, then will be admitted to be true but obvious and insignificant, and perhaps finally be regarded as so important that its adversaries will claim that they themselves discovered it.'[13]

So Lonergan's part in the workshop did not include a formal lecture on the interdisciplinary, but he did once take up the question directly, if only briefly. Curiously, this happened almost by accident. Someone happened to ask him in a question period, 'Can you spell out in what precise way your thinking is interdisciplinary?' And his answer is all we have from him at that conference that is directly on the question. It is interdisciplinary in this way, he said, that it studies 'what learning is in the general case, experience, understanding, judging, and all that is involved in those terms ...'

You get behind the 'learning of common sense, the learning of science, the learning of human studies, the learning of theology, the learning of history, and so on.' They are all specific cases of learning, and how are you going to bring them together? 'The Aristotelian [way] was

---

tify the content of responsible intending, we get the transcendental concept of value, of the truly good. But quite distinct from such transcendental concepts, which can be misconceived and often are, there are the prior transcendental notions that constitute the very dynamism of our conscious intending, promoting us from mere experiencing towards understanding, from mere understanding towards truth and reality, from factual knowledge to responsible action.'

Note that Lonergan distinguishes 'three meanings of the term, transcendental: the most general and all-pervasive concepts, namely, *ens*, *unum*, *verum*, *bonum*, of the Scholastics; the Kantian conditions of the possibility of knowing an object a priori; Husserl's intentionality analysis in which noêsis and noêma, act and object, are correlative' ('Religious Knowledge,' in *A Third Collection* 145 n. 8). He had said in *Method in Theology* (14 n. 4) that his use of the word is analogous to Scholastic usage, 'for it is opposed to the categorial,' but also that his actual procedure 'is transcendental in the Kantian sense, inasmuch as it brings to light the conditions of the possibility of knowing an object in so far as that knowledge is a priori.' The 'transcendental deduction' of Chapter 11 of *Insight* ([1957] 336–39, [1992] 360–62) likely shows what he means here, but his preferred usage seems close to Husserl.

13 'Healing and Creating in History,' in *A Third Collection* 108.

in terms of the object "being" ... all sciences are about being or some department of being ...' But for the modern sciences 'you have to set up a different point of unity, the point of unity of the learning subject ... The key idea becomes not the idea of some ideal science that we haven't got and won't have for a long, long ... time. But what we already have is the process of learning ... There is an element of experience involved, an element of ongoing understanding ... an element of judging ... If those three are the roots of all the disciplines, then you have a key to the interdisciplinary, you have a common basis to start out, and if they all have a common basis then they'll all have a relationship of some kind between them. And if they have a relationship of some kind between them then you are in the interdisciplinary field.'[14]

So there we have Lonergan's famous transcendental method and, in particular, its relevance and point of application to interdisciplinary dialogue. It is a matter of discovering our own interiority, the basic operations of human intentionality, their levels and the interrelations of the levels: experience, understanding, judgment, existential decision. The discovery of the four levels gives us a rule of life and work: be attentive, be intelligent, be reasonable, be responsible. Further, the four levels give a structure to cultural studies, where research collects data on the level of experience, hermeneutics interprets the data on the level of understanding, history describes what is going forward as interpretation follows interpretation, and dialectic brings us face to face with decision, the need to choose, to take a stand in regard to the world we have brought to light.

We should neither belittle nor exaggerate the role of the transcendental. It has a strong dynamic and a deep power of clarification, but it has its limits too.

I can see its power when I talk to students who are working on a doctoral dissertation, even when they work in areas of which I know very little, for I can help them determine the function of their writing. Are they doing research, collecting and ordering the data in the way Merk's *Novum Testamentum*[15] or Denzinger's *Enchiridion*

14 Q. 9, pp. 22–23, unpublished transcript of the two question sessions (on 21 and 22 October 1975) with Lonergan at the workshop. (The transcript, prepared by Nicholas Graham, is in the Lonergan Archives.)

15 Augustinus Merk, *Novum Testamentum graece et latine apparatu critico instructum*. Editio quarta retractata (Rome: Pontifical Biblical Institute, 1942). This manual was familiar to Lonergan's theological students.

symbolorum[16] is a work of research? Are they interpreting a text or texts in the way Lonergan's *Verbum* articles[17] were a work of interpretation? Are they writing history in Gilson's sense of the word, seen, for example, in *The Unity of Philosophical Experience*?[18] Are they challenging an accepted position, doing dialectic in the way much of Newman and Kierkegaard is dialectic?

Often, you find they are not doing any of these, but have some grand world-historical idea, one they think will get the whole world by the tail. If you can get them to leave the world and its tail aside till they have their doctorate, and meanwhile guide them into a dissertation that focuses on research, or interpretation, or history, or maybe even dialectic, or some combination of these, you will have done them a notable service. And you will have accomplished that in a priori fashion, simply through the application of transcendental method.

Here I think back forty years to my own dissertation. It was on Thomas Aquinas – in particular, on the conflicts in human interiority and their resolution. I did an enormous amount of work, collected passages from everywhere in Thomas, and put them in some order. But I did not have a thesis in the sense of a position. I was not attacking Scotus, or Plato, or anyone. I was not tracing a history either, say, from Augustine to Thomas. I was collecting and ordering data, and I knew it; so my subtitle was 'The Data in the Writings of Thomas Aquinas.' I am prouder of that subtitle than of the whole thesis; for I knew what I was doing in terms of transcendental activity, even though it wasn't called that yet. And I knew this because I had four years of Lonergan behind me when I started the thesis. The thesis would maybe not be accepted in some universities today, but then neither would they accept Merk's *Novum Testamentum* or Denzinger's *Enchiridion symbolorum*.

---

16 *Enchiridion symbolorum definitionum et declarationum de rebus fidei et morum*. This is another manual familiar to theological students. It was first published by Henricus Denzinger in 1854, and went through numerous editions; the 32nd was edited by Adolfus Schönmetzer in 1963 (Barcelona, Freiburg, etc.: Herder; further editions continue to appear).

17 'Verbum' (1946–49); *Verbum* (1967) [(1997)]. This five-part study was regarded by Lonergan as a work of interpretation of St. Thomas Aquinas.

18 Étienne Gilson, *The Unity of Philosophical Experience* (New York: Charles Scribner's Sons, 1941). See Gilson's 'Foreword' (vii–ix) introducing the work as 'a philosophical history of philosophy.'

I have been stressing the power of transcendental method, but we must remember that it has its limits too. It cannot dispense with the sciences and disciplines that mediate between itself and the concrete situation. I have not had time to speak of Lonergan's deep concern to interrelate moral theology and the human sciences – in particular, to relate moral theology and economics. But that is directly pertinent to interdisciplinarity, so let me in concluding return to 'Healing and Creating in History.'

> From economic theorists we have to demand, along with as many other types of analysis as they please, a new and specific type that reveals how moral precepts have both a basis in economic process and so an effective application to it. From moral theorists we have to demand, along with their other ... forms of wisdom and prudence, specifically economic precepts that arise out of economic process itself and promote its proper functioning.[19]

We have here, I think, a hint of the urgency of the question and an indication of the hope of interdisciplinary dialogue. There is an urgent need of dialogue among the disciplines. John the Baptist could tell the tax-collectors, 'Exact no more than the assessment,'[20] and he could tell the soldiers who asked for counsel, 'No bullying; no blackmail; make do with your pay.'[21] In our complex world of industry and finance, answers are not so ready to hand: they are found only through the dialogue of the disciplines.

But there is hope too in that the need is being seen and met, in the extent to which dialogue of the disciplines exists here at Lonergan University College and elsewhere. Further hope, I have been suggesting, lies in the ideas we find in the study of Bernard Lonergan – hope that

---

19 'Healing and Creating in History,' in *A Third Collection* 108. Lonergan's concern to mediate his transcendental thought to the practical order through the human sciences runs like a thread through his later writings. See, for example, 'The Example of Gibson Winter,' in *A Second Collection* 189–92; 'Moral Theology and the Human Sciences,' a paper of 1974, later published in *METHOD: Journal of Lonergan Studies* 15/1 (1997) 5–20 and in *Papers 1965–1980* (2004) 301–12), and especially his work on economics, published as vol. 15 (1999) and vol. 21 (1998) of *Collected Works of Bernard Lonergan*.

20 Luke 3:13 (*NEB*).

21 Luke 3:14.

on some fundamental level, in the deepest resources of our common nature, we will discover that there is neither East nor West, nor border, nor breed, nor birth, but a common humanity, with a common concern to be attentive, to be intelligent, to be reasonable, to be responsible, and thus have a basis for dialogue.

Chapter 14

Law and Insight[1]

Law and insight are two areas of study that for many years have been the interest of the scholar we are honoring in this issue of *The Jurist*. His interest in law, of course, needs no proof or documentation. His interest in insight, and in the cognitional theory of Bernard Lonergan in general, is probably not so well known; but it is one that I share with him, and so I venture a little way into the unknown to try to relate these two interests of Ladislas Orsy and to carry forward a line of thought that has engaged his attention through most of his career.[2] Whatever be the success or failure of my own venture, I am confident that the topic itself is close to the center of his concerns, and will not be alien to the purpose of this issue.

---

1 Previously published in *The Jurist* 56 (1996) 25–40. (Issue dedicated to Ladislas Orsy, on his seventy-fifth birthday.)

2 See, for example, the following references in Orsy's writings: 'The Canons on Ecclesiastical Laws Revisited: Glossae on Canons 8–24,' *The Jurist* 37 (1977) 112–59; 'How to Relate Theology and Canon Law,' *Origins* 22 (1992–93) 549–52; 'Legal Judgment and Legal Education: Philosophical Reflections and Practical Suggestions,' *The Jurist* 38 (1978) 1–47; 'Lonergan's Cognitional Theory and Foundational Issues in Canon Law: Method, Philosophy and Law, Theology and Canon Law,' *Studia Canonica* 13 (1979) 177–243; 'The Meaning of Novus Habitus Mentis: the Search for New Horizons,' *The Jurist* 48 (1988) 529–47. There are other articles showing Lonergan's influence. There are several reviews of Lonergan literature. There are bibliographical comments on this literature in his own book *The Evolving Church and the Sacrament of Penance* (Denville, NJ: Dimension Books, 1978) 199, 202, 206–207, 209. There is his book, *Blessed Are Those Who Have Questions* (Denville, NJ: Dimension Books, 1976). And most of all, there is his most recent book *Theology and Canon Law: New Horizons for Legislation and Interpretation* (Collegeville, MN: Liturgical Press, 1992).

The study I propose to make will unfold in the following steps: (1) the general role of insight in human living; (2) the role of insight in the sphere of human action; and (3) the role of insight in the realm of law. Each part subdivides, somewhat awkwardly, into insight as achieved and insight as applied.[3]

1 General Role of Insight in Human Living

There is a general division of insight into achievement and application – a division which, though inadequate, provides a principle of organization for what I wish to say. It is illustrated as follows in the simplest possible fashion. I learn early in the game of bridge how to finesse my opponent's king: that is an insight achieved. The insight remains with me as a habit of mind, which I need not learn all over again every time I play a hand. I may have to figure out whether or not to try the finesse (for that I need another set of insights: probabilities on the location of the king, danger of putting the wrong opponent on lead, etc.), but I need not learn again how the finesse itself works. I simply apply what I already understand.

1.1 Insight as Achieved

A good starting point for this heading is the place where insight itself starts, with a question. 'When an animal has nothing to do it goes to sleep. When a man has nothing to do he may ask questions.'[4] It is questions that first of all divide us off from the rest of the animal world, and the first question asks for an insight.[5] In the child it is simply wordless wonder: 'Children's faces looking up / Holding wonder like a cup.' Wonder is soon expressed in words (this use of language being itself

---

3 The division is inadequate and somewhat awkward, because (as I shall insist strongly) application too supposes an achievement of new insight, but is justified as indicating what is 'typical' of one or the other: it is typical of achievement to gain new insights, and typical of application to bring old insights to bear on a new situation.

4 *Insight* (1957) 10 [(1992) 34].

5 *Verbum* (1967) 4 [(1997) 17]: '... of the two Aristotelian operations of the mind "prima operatio respicit quidditatem rei; secunda respicit esse ipsius."' We may call these operations the 'what' question ('quid sit?'), asking for an understanding of form and essence, and the 'whether' question ('an sit?'), asking for a judgment on existence. Our concern in this article is mainly with 'what' questions.

an achievement of insight): what? why? how? Like the Thomist 'quid?' all these words ask for understanding, that is, for an insight. The reference, therefore, to Thomas Aquinas does not mean we are talking of an experience special to philosophers or theologians. The 'why' that is so common in a child, and sometimes so exasperating to the parent, fits quite neatly into the Thomist 'what.'[6] The 'how' of any artisan, inventor, mechanic, worker, as he or she sets about a task, be it building a boat, playing a hand of bridge, approaching the manager for a raise, getting an accused person convicted (or acquitted), or cooking the dinner – the 'how' in all of these also fits neatly into the Thomist 'what.'[7]

Neither should we think that giving insight the role described is to turn human living into a dull cerebral functioning. Who does not know the delight of making a skillful play at bridge, of finding that our approach to the manager was indeed the intelligent way, of seeing the point in a joke, of solving a stiff problem on the mathematics exam, and so on. Insight is not just a mechanical step in the assembly line, a dull category serving to mark us off from the merely animal world. It is the exuberance and joy for the individual of living a full life and, I believe, a key factor in the life of law and order in the state.

To be as brief as possible on a topic that needs a volume or two, I would say that insight, or more basically the search for insight, is the primary act distinguishing members of the human race, pervading every class and stratum of the human world. To be without insight, or worse, to be without any question seeking insight, is not just to fail to make our contribution to society. It is also to deprive ourselves of one of the chief joys of living.

1.2 *Insight as Applied*

I have indicated a few of the simplest and most general features of the act of insight. They take account, however, of only one direction in which the phenomena of insight run. They are concerned with insight

---

6 Ibid. (1967) 12–16 [(1997) 26–29].

7 See Ibid. (1967) 5, 24 [(1997) 18, 37–38], on the 'reflective pause' of the artisan, craftsman, inventor, mechanic, technician, as they ponder how to go about their task. *Insight* (1957) 82–83 [(1992) 106–107] places 'frequency' or 'how often' questions (the statistician determining probabilities of an event or an occurrence) in the same general class as 'what' and 'why' and 'how' questions.

as first achieved, but that is only half the picture. For a more adequate view we must also consider insight as applied, as turned back and operating in the reverse direction. It will be here, in fact, that some of the most interesting questions arise in regard to the role of insight in law.

I have said that, because any understanding we gain remains as a habitual possession, the insight achieved with great labor yesterday can be applied with ease today. But there are complexities in such application, chief among which for present purposes is the question of the particular and the universal. An act of understanding is, in the consecrated phrase, an insight into phantasm. It occurs with respect to a particular image or to a particular set of data presented or represented in the imagination. It is 'this' insight into 'this' phantasm, into 'these' data or presentations. But it is potentially universal and has to become universal if there is to be any further use or application of the insight. Now it becomes universal in the activity of conceiving, of expressing the insight in an inner word, of formulating the idea. In this conceptualizing activity, insight drops the particular conditions of its origins, and is set forth as a universal.[8] It thus becomes applicable again and again in the same psychological procedures with the same cognitional relationships that obtained in the genesis of the insight, but running in a direction opposite to that of the genesis.[9]

But applicable to what? That is a crucial question. Obviously, applicable to the image or presentations in which it arose. But those presentations were particular, they had what philosophers call their individuating conditions. Can they be reproduced later under exactly the same individuating conditions? Maybe so, but certainly that is not always the case. It is only the very simplest of situations that allow endless repetition of exactly the same data. Life is generally far more complex than that. The data of last week that were seen to result in rain on the weekend are not exactly the same as the data of today, and any forecast today that is based on last weekend's weather remains qualified by an 'if.' Even when they are the 'same,' they are the same only in kind, not in their individuality. Furthermore, no matter how much the data approximate to those of last week, we ourselves are not the same. In the meantime we

8 Ibid., Index under 'Universal,' esp. (1967) 39–42 [(1997) 52–56].

9 Ibid. (1967) 27–29 [(1997) 40–42].

have learned a bit more about forecasting the weather, so we come to the data with new questions.

Thus we arrive at an important contribution made by Lonergan, one that is still not widely studied, but a key element in the application of any universal concept, and an element of special interest when applications of the general are made to the particular in the realm of law. His position can be stated as follows: application of our habitual insight to any particular concrete case always involves a further insight, at least the insight that this situation is the same as the original, and more often another insight to allow for the difference from the original. This apparently simple statement has wide and multiple ramifications. It points to the enormous difference between life and logic. It is worth closer attention.

Some quotation is in order here, and I begin with a fundamental statement made in the context of Lonergan's argument that philosophers must be generalists. True enough, they must learn to deal with the particular, for that is where all knowledge must in the last analysis find its referent. But philosophers cannot take the easy path of simply adding a conclusion to premises. Mediating the transition from general to particular is a far more difficult matter than that.

> [I]t cannot be stressed too strongly that the mediation of the generalists is intelligent rather than logical: by logical mediation I understand the process from universal concepts to particular instances as just instances; by intelligent mediation I understand the process from understanding the universal to understanding the particular. The difference between the two is a difference in understanding: in logical mediation one understands no more in the instance than one did in the universal; in intelligent mediation one adds to the understanding of the universal a fuller and more determinate understanding of the particular case. The generalist that is just a logical mediator turns out to be an obtuse intruder; the generalist that is an intelligent mediator speaks not only his own mind but also the language of his interlocutor.[10]

The ramifications of this key statement are legion. Without taking space to develop them, I simply indicate three areas in which one might illustrate the point: applied science, our everyday use of prover-

10 'Questionnaire on Philosophy,' *METHOD: Journal of Lonergan Studies* 2/2 (1984) 32–33 (*Papers 1965–1980* [2004] 383).

bial wisdom, and the role of the social sciences in mediating theology to concrete practice.[11]

The scientist knows that falling bodies accelerate at the rate of 32 feet per second per second. The parachutist knows, or certainly hopes, that that is not his acceleration: the abstract law of falling bodies meets with modifying factors in the concrete. Again, proverbial wisdom tells us to look before we leap; it also tells us that the one who hesitates is lost. Which proverb is more relevant in a particular concrete situation? The proverbs themselves do not tell me: for that I need a further insight. For our third illustration, we note that ethically minded captains of industry know they must be just, but what is the just thing to do in today's complex economic situation? For judgment on that there is a crying need for a fully developed science of economics that would mediate general ethical understanding to the particular case.[12]

Notice that the need of further insight touches the lives of all of us. Medical science has to have a certain universality if what doctors learn in medical school is to have any practical use, but it touches me very directly when they decide that my case is not exactly the one they find on a certain page of the medical book. As for the application of everyday wisdom, the matter is obvious: my parents took it in good part yesterday when I rallied them a little on their old-fashioned ways, but will they do so today? Better pause first and notice their mood. Even the dismal science of economics impinges on many of us: how is the union member to vote when the union leaders call for a strike? Someone must mediate to him or her the economic repercussions of a strike, if the vote is to be cast rationally.

2 Insight in Conduct

Several of the examples I gave in the preceding section pertained to the

11 For a little more detail, I refer to my article 'The Genus "Lonergan and ..." and Feminism,' in Cynthia Crysdale, ed., *Lonergan and Feminism* (Toronto: University of Toronto Press, 1994) 13–32 [chap. 6 of the present volume]. Section 1.2, '"Application": Data Samples,' examines five cases of applying general to particular, with references especially to Lonergan's *Understanding and Being* (1980) 83–84, 106–108, [(1990) 70, 88–89, and his answer to a question on 353]; to *Insight* (1957) 46–53 [(1992) 70–76]; and to 'The Example of Gibson Winter,' in *A Second Collection* 189–92.

12 The need a moral theology has for a viable economics occupied Lonergan throughout his life. He devoted his last years to this question, and the results will appear in *Macroeconomic Dynamics: An Essay in Circulation Analysis*, vol. 15 of his *Collected Works* [subsequently published in 1999 (ed.)].

sphere of human conduct. This, of course, has special relevance to the area of law, so it needs specific study in this section. It is a sphere that claims the lion's share of attention for most of us. We do enjoy solving puzzles, and so in our modest way join hands with Newton and Einstein and Salk and even Thomas Aquinas. But we are far more like the general run of people in the New Testament, who on hearing the word of God do not ask for the definition of sanctifying grace but ask what they must do. As the rich young man asked Jesus,[13] as the Baptist's audience asked him,[14] as the first converts on Pentecost asked Peter and the apostles,[15] as their jailer asked Paul and Silas,[16] as Paul asked the Lord,[17] regularly we too ask, 'What must I do?'[18] It is in this area of praxis that we live far the greater part of our lives.

2.1 *Genesis of Insight for Conduct*

We can, if we wish, make a big thing of the difference between speculative and practical intellect.[19] For present purposes I am much more interested in what is common to the two, and the first and basic common area is defined by our first and basic question, 'What ...?' Archimedes, for all that he had an ulterior purpose in his famous problem, did not, when he found the answer, rush naked through the streets shouting for the emperor. He rushed through the streets shouting 'Eureka!' It was the joy of discovery that moved him. He had found

13 Matthew 19:16.
14 Luke 3:10.
15 Acts 2:37.
16 Acts 16:30.
17 Acts 22:10.
18 It is worth noting how important questions are in bridging the gap that historical consciousness opens up between New Testament times and ours. The people who appear in the scriptures ask their 'what' and 'whether' questions just as we do, and thereby reveal the humanity they have in common with us. I enlarged on this some years ago in 'Neither Jew nor Greek, but One Human Nature and Operation in All,' *Philippine Studies* 13 (1965) 546–71. The article was republished in the collection Michael Vertin made of scattered writings of mine, *Appropriating the Lonergan Idea* (Washington: Catholic University of America Press, 1989), as well as in the volume edited by Thomas J. Farrell and Paul A. Soukup, *Communication and Lonergan: Common Ground for Forging the New Age* (Kansas City, MO: Sheed & Ward, 1993).
19 Aquinas does not make them distinct potencies. For him they are but one potency operating now with one end, now with another. See *Summa theologiae* 1, q. 79, a. 11 (and parallels): 'Utrum intellectus speculativus et practicus sint diversae potentiae.'

a 'how' that involved a 'what' that still governs researchers and technicians in mechanics and physics. But essentially the same experience is had and felt, perhaps felt even more deeply though not expressed with such abandon, by those who after long pondering on what to do with their lives finally find an answer. True, the rich young man of the Gospels went away sad, but that was a flight from a call which we may suspect ended in a flight from insight.

In any case, 'what to do' is never in the first instance something laid out for us in black and white. Somewhere there was first the genesis of an insight. Sure, Jesus had an answer for the rich young man, as Peter did for the crowds on Pentecost, and John the Baptist did for the soldiers and tax collectors. But Peter and the Baptist, and indeed the Lord Jesus too, had to find those answers; and if they found them in a book or some other authority, then the question goes back to the book or authority: where did they get the answers? Always we are forced back to the achievement of insight. That is why ethics has so large a place in the works of Aristotle, and why Thomas Aquinas had so much to say on this sphere that he had to divide his treatise on human conduct into two books.[20]

2.2 *Application in the Sphere of Conduct*

Essentially the same procedures that we saw in the general application of insight are followed in the application of habitual understanding to the sphere of conduct. Conduct could be conceived very generally to include techniques, manners, and morals. How does one go about smoothing a piece of wood for the table one is building? Well, there are general principles of technique: for example, you don't plane against the grain; and you apply that very simply by noticing the way the grain runs. But conduct, in the usual sense of the term, relates more specifically to personal behavior as worthy of praise or blame. How does one conduct oneself at dinner? Well, I believe Emily Post has a book on that, but you still need an insight for the local situation. In Rome do as the Romans do, so how do Romans eat their spaghetti? And how does one deal with the picket lines set up by strikers at the

20 The *Prima secundae*, which treats human acts in general, and the *Secunda secundae*, which treats them in particular.

entrance to your office? Well, the answer to that can be complicated. You may have a set of guidelines from head office, but you may still need a staff meeting to apply the guidelines here.

In all such cases there is a core of knowledge, of know how, of savoir faire, of guidelines, of principles – a core that is possessed habitually but needs application to the here and now, to the present situation. I would say that in the sphere of conduct the general principles are even more remote from the concrete case than they are in the sphere of being. An 'is' question is generally simpler to handle than an 'ought' question. For example, is this an area of one acre? To answer that, one needs only the definition of an acre and the set of measuring tools used in surveying. But what is the right thing for this man and this woman to do when their marriage is threatened with breakup after thirty years? Here we are dealing with the infinitely complex field of human conduct and the infinite variety of relationships that an infinite multiplication of historical acts has set up between two people. It is a long way from the abstract principle we can find in a book to the advice a counselor may be called to give to this couple on what they ought to do.

Here belong all the refinements that the thinkers of the ages, from Aristotle to Aquinas and beyond, have brought to the study of prudence.[21] It is a history without end, and without hope of an end, and that for two reasons, as Thomas Aquinas explained when dealing with changes in human law. The first is the development of human understanding: 'it seems to be natural to human reason to come gradually from the imperfect to the perfect.'[22] The other is the changing set of human conditions under which we live, requiring a change in the law 'according to the various cases that emerge.'[23]

Here I would draw attention again to the role Lonergan assigns the human sciences and human studies as mediating between, on the one hand, a philosophy and theology and, on the other, the particular pre-

21 Defined by the Scholastics as 'recta ratio agibilium,' and treated by Thomas Aquinas, first, as part of the set of virtues, in *Summa theologiae* 1-2, q. 57, and then in itself, 2-2, qq. 47–56 (followed there, significantly, by q. 57, *De iure*, and the treatise on justice).

22 *Summa theologiae* 1-2, q. 97, a. 1 c.: 'humanae rationi naturale esse videtur ut gradatim ab imperfecto ad perfectum perveniat.'

23 Ibid., ad 1m.: 'secundum diversos casus qui emergunt.'

cepts we need to govern our practice.[24] Of course, this mediating role is found also in questions of doctrine; but far more significant and certainly more relevant to the purpose of this article is the mediating role of human sciences and human studies in the sphere of human conduct.

3 Insight in the Realm of Law

Our discussion of human conduct has already brought us into the realm of law. It remains to fulfil the promise of the title I gave this article and so to deal more specifically with the role of insight there.

3.1 Genesis of Insight for Law

An illuminating parallel is drawn by Aquinas between the self-guidance of the individual and the intervention of one who has authority to make or apply the law: 'reason has a role in a human being, with regard to what pertains to that person, like the role a ruler or judge has in the state.'[25] And as human understanding advances in every area, so also it must advance in the area of law. It is not enough to collect old laws and select the best of them: that was the method of the sophists. One must 'also work out new ones as happens in the way this is done in the other practical arts.'[26]

The similarity extends beyond the operational to a close parallel between speculative and practical reason: 'synderesis governs prudence, the way understanding of principles governs science.'[27] The entire process from first principles to particular judgments is parallel

24 See his short article 'The Example of Gibson Winter,' in *A Second Collection* 189–92, his somewhat longer paper 'Moral Theology and the Human Sciences' (written in 1974 for the International Theological Commission, later published in *METHOD: Journal of Lonergan Studies* 15/1 [1997] 5–20 and in (*Papers 1965–1980* [2004] 301–12), and especially his contribution to actual mediation with his work on economics (note 12 above).

25 *Summa theologiae* 1-2, q. 104, a. 1 ad 3m: 'ratio ... se habet in homine respectu eorum quae ad ipsum pertinent, sicut princeps vel iudex in civitate.'

26 *In decem libros Ethicorum Aristotelis ad Nicomachum Expositio*, ed. Angelus M. Pirotta (Turin: Marietti, 1934), X, lect. 16, no. 2175: 'etiam novas adinvenire ad similitudinem aliarum artium operativarum.' This is Thomas's own point, not made here by Aristotle.

27 *Summa theologiae* 2–2, q. 47, a. 6 ad 3m: 'synderesis movet prudentiam, sicut intellectus principiorum scientiam.'

for science and prudence. 'A similar process is found in the working of practical reason and speculative reason: for each of them proceeds from some kind of principles to some kind of conclusions.'[28] 'But just as it happens in speculative reason ... that some things are known naturally – of these we have understanding – and some things are known as conclusions – of these we have science – so also in practical reason some things are known naturally – ends are of this kind – and some are known as conclusions – and they are the objects of prudence.'[29]

This means that all we have said on the role of insight in general holds also for its role in law-making. Law-making, in virtue of its having the same function in the state that prudence has in the individual, assumes its true dignity as an activity of human intelligence studying the data of a situation, puzzling over the problems it presents, and arriving at a solution through insight. In fact, there is a peculiarity in the understanding of human conduct that gives an even greater role to insight here, whether it be in the making of law or in its application; but it will be more convenient to take this up in my next section.

3.2 *Application of Insight in Law*

The parallel between speculative and practical reason has served as context for bringing to the fore the role of insight in human conduct and human law. But besides the parallel there is also, as there was in the time of Thomas, a significant difference; and this, I would maintain, underlines even more heavily the role of insight here.

> Speculative reason works one way and practical reason another. For, since speculative reason deals mainly with what is necessary, with what cannot possibly be otherwise, here the truth is found in specific conclusions without any defect, just as it is found in the common principles. But practical reason deals with contingent things, which are the object of human operations; and therefore, although there is a kind of necessity in

---

28 Ibid. 1-2, q. 91, a. 3 c.: 'Similis autem processus esse invenitur rationis practicae et speculativae: utraque enim ex quibusdam principiis ad quasdam conclusiones procedit.'

29 Ibid. 2-2, q. 47, a. 6 c.: 'Sicut autem in ratione speculativa ... quaedam ut naturaliter nota, quorum est intellectus; et quaedam ... [ut] conclusiones, quorum est scientia: ita in ratione practica ... quaedam ut principia naturaliter nota, et huiusmodi sunt fines ... et quaedam ... ut conclusiones ... Et horum est prudentia.'

> the common principles, still the further you descend toward particulars, the more you recede from the necessary.[30]

And Thomas goes on to say that speculative truth is the same for all, though it may not be known by all; but practical truth is just not the same for all.

Does this mean that insight has lost its guiding role in particular law? Not at all, not even for Thomas, especially when we overcome an Aristotelian bias for the necessary as opposed to the contingent. Thomas would have no difficulty with what his master, Albert, wrote, that it was natural reason which dictated communal ownership of the earth in primitive times, and the same natural reason which dictates private property in the present state of humanity.[31] He would agree, then, with Aristotle's remark in regard to the mean of virtue, that a shoe that fits is the mean for me, but there is no use requiring everyone to wear that size.[32] And so the head of the house gives different commandments to children and adults, just as God gives different sets of laws in the Old Testament and the New,[33] kings are allowed to heap up wealth when subjects are not,[34] and we need different laws in winter

30 *Summa theologiae* 1-2, q. 94, a. 4: 'Aliter ... se habet ratio speculativa, et aliter ratio practica. Quia enim ratio speculativa praecipue negotiatur circa necessaria, quae impossibile est aliter se habere, absque aliquo defectu invenitur veritas in conclusionibus propriis, sicut et in principiis communibus. Sed ratio practica negotiatur circa contingentia, in quibus sunt operationes humanae: et ideo, etsi in communibus sit aliqua necessitas, quanto magis ad propria descenditur, tanto magis invenitur defectus.'

I studied this area at greater length in a pair of articles, 'Universal Norms and the Concrete "Operabile" in St Thomas Aquinas,' *Sciences ecclésiastiques* 7 (1955) 115–49, 257–91 [subsequently published in Frederick E. Crowe, *Three Thomist Studies*, ed. M. Vertin (Boston: Lonergan Institute of Boston College, 2000) 3–69]. A similar approach may be found in Robert Henle, 'Prudence and Insight in Moral and Legal Decisions,' *American Catholic Philosophical Association Proceedings* 56 (1982) 26–30.

31 Odon Lottin, *Psychologie et morale aux XIIe et XIIIe siècles*, vol. 2 (Louvain: Abbaye du Mont César, 1948) 98, quoting a Brussels MS.

32 *In libros Ethicorum* II, lect. 6, nos. 310–14. See Lonergan on Aristotle and equity: '... over two millennia ago Aristotle pronounced equity to be virtue and defined it as a correction of the law where the law is defective owing to its universality' ('Prolegomena to the Study of the Emerging Religious Consciousness of Our Time,' in *A Third Collection* 61, with reference to the *Nicomachean Ethics* V, 10, 1137b 27).

33 *Summa theologiae* 1-2, q. 91, a. 5 c. and ad 1m, 2m, 3m; q. 98, a. 2 ad 1m; q. 107, a. 1 c.

34 *Super Evangelium S. Matthaei Lectura*, ed. P. Raphaelis Cai (Turin, Rome: Marietti, 1951) 6, no. 611.

and summer.[35] There is nothing in Thomas to indicate that for his time such decisions are irrational or purely arbitrary or lack insight. Certainly, from Lonergan's viewpoint these examples bring out in starkest clarity his position that application of the general to the particular always requires a further insight.

Still, it must be admitted that for Aristotle and Aquinas the status of these very particular precepts was rather low in the pecking order of cognitional activities. But what Aristotle, and Aquinas insofar as he followed Aristotle, saw as a deficiency, is not regarded in that way any longer. What particular precepts lacked was the union card admitting them to the honorable status of science, and that lack stemmed from an Aristotelian notion of science that had an excessive regard for the necessary, the essential, the universal, the certain. A modern view that takes in the realms of hermeneutics, of history, of the differentiation of cultures, and so on, has revalued our cognitional activities.

Thus, modern science, as Lonergan has argued over and over, is not Aristotelian.

> [N]ecessity was a key notion for Aristotle but today it is marginal; in its place is verifiable possibility. Causality was a key notion for Aristotle but today in effect, if not in name, it is replaced by correlation. The universal and abstract were normative in Aristotelian science, but modern science uses universals as tools in its unrelenting efforts to approximate to concrete process. Where the Aristotelian claimed certitude, the modern scientist disclaims anything more than probability. Where the Aristotelian wished to know things in their essences and properties, the modern scientist is satisfied with control and results.[36]

Parallel to a new notion of science, there is a new role for philosophy.

> [P]hilosophy has invaded the field of the concrete, the particular, and the contingent, of the existential subject's decisions and of the history of peo-

35 *Super Epistolas S. Pauli Lectura: ... Ad Hebraeos*, ed. P. Raphaelis Cai (Turin, Rome: Marietti, 1953) 7, lect. 3, no. 352.

36 'The Absence of God in Modern Culture,' in *A Second Collection* 103–104 (with the correction of a misprint). An interesting reversal: where Aquinas speaks of a law being defective owing to its particularity (note 30 above), Lonergan speaks of a law being defective owing to its universality (note 32 above).

> ples, societies, and cultures; and this entry of philosophy into the realm of the existential and the historical not merely extends the role of philosophic wisdom into concrete living but also, by that very extension, curtails the functions formerly attributed to prudence.[37]

The relevance of all this to our topic is that it extends and heightens the role of insight in law. Now, more than ever, in this age of study of the particular, there is needed the exercise of intelligence. If it has been understood for centuries that only the most general laws apply everywhere and always, today it is also understood (a recovery of the wiser Aristotle) that differentiations of the general laws for different people in different situations are as much a matter of insight as are the most abstract profundities of the universal. Now more than ever we realize that the merely 'logical mediator turns out to be an obtuse intruder.' Now more than ever the need is for intelligent mediation, that is, for adding the further insight that the situation requires. As a consequence of this development we must rely much more on the intelligence of the person on the spot, and hold in much greater distrust a bureaucracy that would govern all particular situations from above.[38]

Conclusion

I leave the topic of law and insight just when it is becoming most interesting, namely, when we come to the details of law-making and law-application. Such details are beyond my competence, but let me just suggest some of the questions that occur to one approaching the question from the side of cognitional theory and insight. They will be very simple questions, as they ought to be. For the cognitional process described by Lonergan is after all a simple matter, one we use over and over spontaneously, one easy then to understand, if only (but what a big 'if') we take time to notice how our minds work.

If, then, I were transported into some hypothetical realm with my

37 'Dimensions of Meaning,' in *Collection* (1967) 261 [(1988) 240; see also 310, editorial note *g*].

38 Lonergan on bureaucracies: *Insight* (1957) 234–35 [(1992) 259–60]; *Understanding and Being* (1980) 240 [(1990) 195; see also 417–18, editorial note *c*]; *Topics in Education* 60–61; 'Prolegomena to the Study of the Emerging Religious Consciousness of Our Time,' in *A Third Collection* 60–63.

copy of *Insight* and asked to collaborate with those whose profession is the law, I would first bring up the question of the question. What questions emerge from the present situation (for we must start where we are, not where Adam and Eve were long ago)? If none emerges, how does one stimulate questions? If there are questions, how get them into some kind of order?[39]

While questions are forming and grouping one would come to realize more clearly that questions suppose a cognitional level prior to intelligence, that of data. So from the viewpoint of cognitional theory, one would ask what one does with data, what their relation is to the questions, and what their relation is to possible answers. What, then, does one do with data? One first collects and classifies them with an intelligent eye on their possible relevance to the questions before us. More directly, one sees them as holding the key to an insight. How does one turn this key? Can one operate intelligently to bring about the occurrence of an insight?

In geometry, to take an example it is easy to talk about, one 'shuffles' the data like a pack of cards: bisect an angle, extend the base, draw a parallel, try a variety of ploys, until by hook or by crook, 'The act of understanding leaps forth when the sensible data are in a suitable constellation.'[40] Then one asks for the counterpart of this in the sciences. In the natural sciences, experimentation would take the place of shuffling the data. In the human sciences, there are limits to experimentation (limits, but not an embargo, and it would be part of our task to assign the limits and understand why some people would impose an embargo); but when experiment is ruled out there remains the collection of data from parallel but widely scattered sources. My own country is struggling with the question of unity: what data are available from Belgium, Switzerland, from the history of Norway and Sweden, from recent events in what was Yugoslavia, from the newly unified Europe?

We have only sampled the questions that arise from cognitional theory, but I must hasten on. Remembering, then, the oft-quoted remark of Lonergan that insights are a dime a dozen, and his less well-known remark that for one good judgment we need to amass the multiple pos-

39 See Lonergan's remarks on the process of questioning in the search for historical understanding, *Method in Theology* 187.

40 *Verbum* (1967) 14 [(1997) 28].

sibilities provided by a variety of insights,[41] we would go on to consider judgment, where again a series of questions could be raised simply from the viewpoint of cognitional theory and on the simple basis of what judgment is, how it functions, what its relation is to the whole cognitional process.

I have been speaking of the way a collaborator, armed with a copy of *Insight* but ignorant of jurisprudence, might assist in the process of lawmaking. A parallel set of questions, raised once again from the simple viewpoint of cognitional theory, might be worked out for the application of law. Mindful of Lonergan's remark that mere logical application is obtuse intrusion, that further insights are always needed, we would regularly ask, 'What, if anything, differentiates this case from the case the law envisions? What further insight do I need to deal with it intelligently?' It is most obviously a question that judges and prosecuting attorneys must ask, but it arises much earlier in the police officer who – by contrast with the bureaucracy – is the person on the spot. What is the competence of the police in understanding the particular situation? They are the first to confront it, and the only ones to confront it in its particularity. What sort of training would increase their competence and give them the good judgment their role requires?

I have mentioned a mere fraction of the questions that arise in the realm of law from an understanding of cognitional process, and arise simply from that understanding. But I hope I have drawn attention to the role of insight in that realm, and done something to promote a greater awareness of the importance of insight in particular and of cognitional theory in general for the processes of law. If so, I would regard this article as simply a minor footnote to the contribution that Ladislas Orsy has been making throughout his long and distinguished career to the interweaving of law and insight.[42]

---

41 Implicit in his whole cognitional theory, this became explicit in a lecture of 25 February 1969, in a course 'The Alerted Mind' at Thomas More Institute, Montreal: 'Insights are a dime a dozen; only when you have a lot of them can you get somewhere' (quotation based on the tape-recording).

42 I thank my colleague Edward F. Sheridan for a critical reading of this article in typescript – a task that he performed also for the pair of articles that were its predecessor forty years ago (see note 30 above)!

Chapter 15

The Magisterium as Pupil: The Learning Teacher[1]

Magisterium means teaching function, especially that of the church. There is a great deal to be said about that teaching function: its conditions, its authority, its procedures, its limits, its agents. In all this multitude of aspects I will deal with only one in particular, which I will call the learning function of the church.

It might seem that this has nothing to do with the magisterium, which is the topic assigned me for this conference – that when I was asked to talk on one subject, I decided quite arbitrarily to talk on another of my own choosing. Teaching, I may be told, is one thing, and learning is altogether another. I would not agree, or at the very least I would claim that learning is indirectly pertinent to teaching. However, I prefer to say it is an essential condition of teaching, and for that reason pertains directly to the topic of the magisterium.

This is, I think, a neglected question in the church, and a neglected area of study. There are books and articles and talks by the hundreds on the magisterium. Hardly any term of religious doctrine occurs more often in the journals of theology or in the diocesan newspapers. But how often have you read a book or article, or heard a lecture, on the learning role of the church, on the need the magisterium has to learn before it can teach?

It is different in the secular world. There, in every aspect of human living it is presupposed that the teacher has learned the matter that is to be taught. We do not, when we are sick, choose a doctor who has

1 Originally presented on 12 February 1990 at the Paulinian Conference, St Paul's College, Winnipeg. Not previously published.

failed his or her medical examinations; similarly, we do not send our children to a school where the teachers have no training in their subject matter. This is so obvious that we don't even need to make it explicit: it is part of our spontaneous wisdom, implicit, almost instinctive.

But many feel that what we spontaneously do in human affairs is out of place in religious matters. They tend to look on the magisterium as automatically there, as something given, as needing no training or diploma in order to teach. After all, we are dealing with divinely given truth. Prophets and apostles and evangelists do not need any training or diploma to hear God's word, and God has established a teaching authority to hand on what the prophets and apostles and evangelists heard from God. Learning does not seem to enter the picture.

Of course, we hold that children should learn their catechism, that the laity should learn the church's teaching, that seminarians should be well trained in scripture and tradition. But this is learning from the magisterium, not learning by the magisterium in order to exercise its teaching role. It is learning for a part of the church, not learning for the whole church. That is, this approach thinks of the church as divided into two parts: a teaching part, and a learning part. It does not think of the whole church, including those who teach, as needing first of all to learn.

Well, my argument will be that the whole church is a learning church, that it is first of all a learning church, that there is learning all along the line, from prophet to pope, from apostle to bishop, that there always has been learning in the church, but that we have insisted so much on the teaching role that we have quite neglected the learning role and have got ourselves into a one-sided view of the matter. I am not denying, of course, when it comes to teaching, that there is a division in the church, and that one division is of those who are authorized teachers. But I think that that is a second question, and that the prior question has to do with the whole church as learning. Further, since this is a conference on the laity in the modern church, I am going to add that the laity have a major input to make in the church's learning. On that question, however, I have no special advice to offer, so I will simply introduce it and then allow discussion to take over.

I will not then deal with any of the dozens of questions that you expect to hear discussed in a talk on the magisterium. My one contribution concerns the learning function of the church, and it will consist largely in simply looking at this aspect of our history, to discover from that history that in fact we have always been learning, beginning with the original scripture and tradition and continuing through all the councils right to our own time.

Let us start with what we find in scripture on those who were the first teachers in the church. There is a clarifying episode in the Acts of the Apostles, where God is teaching Peter that Christians are not bound by the dietary laws of the Jews. Peter did not know this yet. Despite all the privileges bestowed on him by the Lord, despite all the guidance he had from the Holy Spirit after Pentecost, he did not know the freedom of Christians in this matter. He had to learn it. And learning did not mean simply taking dictation from heaven. There was help from heaven, to be sure. Peter had a vision of various animals and a voice telling him to eat. But some of the animals were unclean by Jewish law, and Peter did not want to eat them. Then, while he 'was still puzzling over the meaning of the vision,' scripture says[2] – notice that he was still puzzling, so he did not yet know – word came that messengers had arrived from the Gentile Cornelius. Then Peter came to understand, from the combination of the vision from heaven and the historical event on earth, that the Jewish dietary laws did not apply to Christians.

That example is illuminating for the principle involved, that those who teach have first to learn; but maybe it is not so helpful in our practice today, for we don't expect visions from heaven when we have a question or a problem. So let us take another example from a different situation, one that adds something to the example of Peter, one that is closer to our present situation; for this time it is a matter of the whole church learning, and learning without a vision, as is generally the case in our age.

This example has to do with the second coming of the Lord. There is no doubt that in the early church large sections of the Christian people took it for granted that Jesus would return very soon, even in the lifetime of those then living – so much so that they worried when some persons died before the return of the Lord: what would become of them on that great day?[3] I say they 'took it for granted': I do not say they made it an article of faith. Luckily – or better, providentially – the church learned that the end was not coming so soon, learned this soon enough not to make a dogma out of a mere opinion. And how did the church learn? The major factor was simply the passing of time, and the

2 Acts 10:17.
3 See 1 Thessalonians 4–5; 2 Thessalonians 2; 1 Corinthians 15:29.

non-event, as we might call it, of the Lord's coming, the failure of the Lord to return in the clouds of heaven. So they put on their thinking caps, studied the scriptures a little more carefully, and noticed that with the Lord a thousand years are as one day, so that what they thought would happen in a short time might in fact take thousands and thousands of years. That's the point of the passage in 2 Peter: 'It is not that the Lord is slow in fulfilling his promise, as some suppose' – no, because 'with the Lord one day is like a thousand years and a thousand years like one day.'[4] That second letter of Peter is putting into words what the church had learned with the passing of time and the unfulfilled expectations.

I've been talking of those who were teachers in the early church, whose history is recorded in the scriptures. What of scripture itself? For scripture too is our teacher. And my question will be, 'How did scripture come to be our teacher?' We have a doctrine that scripture is inspired, that it has God for its author, that we are to reverence it as the word of God. That is a doctrine common to all the churches. It is my doctrine too, as I am sure it is yours. But along with that article of faith there has been a view that the writer of a book of scripture is simply a passive instrument in the hand of God. A harp is a passive instrument in the hand of the harpist, and the writer of scripture is like the harp, passive under the divine Musician; and similarly the prophet or apostle speaking to the people is wholly passive. This was the view of Athenagoras, writing in the year 177.[5] It was never an article of faith, but it was a kind of unexamined supposition, and it greatly influenced our thinking right down to 1943 when Pius XII wrote his encyclical *Divino afflante Spiritu*, and set forth the human side and the human input of the sacred writer.[6]

A better way to think of it, one more in accord, I think, with the encyclical of Pius XII, is this: what God is doing is not so much using a human person as a passive instrument. He is not even dictating to a human secretary. What God is doing is teaching; and what the prophet or sacred writer is doing, first and foremost, is learning in order to teach. The clearest example of this is the Gospel of St Luke, where Luke tells us, in his introduction, of all the trouble he took to ascertain the facts before he started writing. That is, the very evangelist whom we accept as teacher was himself a learner before he turned to teaching.

4 2 Peter 3:9, 8.
5 RJ 162–63, *Legatio pro Christianis*.
6 DS 3830.

What I am saying is that we rightly learn from prophets, apostles, and evangelists: they are our teachers. But also I am saying that prophets, apostles, and evangelists themselves had to learn before they became our teachers.

This kind of learning did not cease with the last apostle or the last book of scripture. We see the same thing throughout our history, and at the highest level in the very councils of the church. In our church the first and, in my view, most important of all the councils, the Council of Nicea in 325, is our teacher on who and what Christ our Lord is. Every Sunday, every solemn feast day, we repeat a creed that, though it was written later, has its basic article from Nicea: light from light, true God from true God, begotten not made, one in being with the Father.[7]

The council taught us this, and the church continues to teach it. The church got it from the council, but where did the council get it? My answer is that the council got it through a learning process that had gone on for one hundred and fifty years in the church. It was about the year 180 that churchmen began to puzzle seriously over the status of Son and Spirit in relation to the one God. They all were baptized in the name of the holy three, they all worshipped the holy three, but they didn't think of them as three: they thought of them as the one God who had a Son and Spirit and sent the Son and Spirit into the world for our salvation. But around the year 180 different people began to talk of them as three, and then the question arose at once regarding the exact status of this Son and Spirit who are grouped with the one God.

The church had to come up with an answer, beginning with the Lord Jesus Christ. Who is he? What is he? We have twenty-seven books in the New Testament that speak of him, give him various names, and assign him various functions; but what exactly is his status in the Godhead? Is he God in the same sense as the Father is God? The church of the year 180 was not able to answer that question, because the church of the year 180 did not know the answer in an explicit fashion. It was implicit in the worship of the church, implicit in the scriptural data; but there is a long road from implicit to explicit in such questions. In fact the church of the year 180 could not even formulate the question with the clarity that was possible after Nicea. So for the next hundred and fifty years this question was slowly clarified, formulated, pondered, debated, prayed over, fought over, until finally the church was satis-

7 DS 125 (I Nicea), 150 (I Constantinople).

fied, took a position on the question, and defined the doctrine in the great council: Yes, the Son is God in exactly the same sense as the Father is. If you follow the history of Catholic thought through those years, you will have an excellent example of what I mean when I say that the church is a learning church, and must learn before she can teach.

I said that the learning process did not stop in New Testament times, but continued into the period of the great council. It did not stop with the great council either, but continued through all the councils, as I believe it will continue to the end of time; for it belongs to the nature of the people God created and to the nature of the church God established. It is not something that pertains merely to our origins in the New Testament, or merely to the fundamental article of our creed enunciated at Nicea. It is an ongoing thing: we keep on learning throughout our history, and we will continue to learn through future generations. That, I think, was the point Pope John XXIII was making when he opened the Second Vatican Council. We are not here, he said, to proclaim old dogmas. The old dogmas don't need our proclamation. We are here to take a forward leap, 'un balzo innanzi,' as he put it in his own Italian later that year. Or, to use a phrase that seemed generally accepted, 'to read the signs of the times,' and to learn from them.

Well, if the church has always been a learning church, there is no need to convert it, to change it from a non-learning to a learning church. So what am I calling for? What I am calling for is explicit recognition of our learning function, willing acceptance of the learning role, and so a methodical, intelligent, effective control of the learning process. I do not think there is explicit recognition of this role on a wide scale. And insofar as there is implicit recognition, I do not think there is a willing acceptance, so we go forward reluctantly, always dragging our feet – as Bernard Lonergan wrote, always arriving on the scene 'a little breathlessly and a little late.'[8] I do not think we have taken control of the learning process in a methodical and intelligent way. Perhaps as a result of Pope John XXIII's initiative, we had in Vatican II a council in which the learning process was more explicit perhaps than it had ever been before, but we do not seem to have kept up the momentum. And so we continue to lay enormous stress on the teaching function, and very little on the learning function. In a perhaps exaggerated image that I have sometimes used, we are like a bird that

8 *Insight* (1957) 733 [(1992) 755].

has exercised one wing and allowed the other to atrophy. How can you take flight on wings of eagles in that condition?

Let me just notice some implications of the learning process. If you are a learning church, you start by not knowing, as Peter started by not knowing about Christian freedom from the Jewish dietary laws, as the early Christians started by not knowing that there would be a long wait before the second coming of the Lord. When you are ignorant of something you do not even know at first that you are ignorant; so the first step is for someone to raise a question – as the question was raised for Peter by the entry of Gentiles into the church, as the question was raised for the early Christians by the long delay in the Lord's coming. The next step will be ideas; and ideas being a dime a dozen, there will be different ideas, some of them the exact opposite of others – as there was violent conflict in the church of Peter's time over the Jewish law. Not only that: some of the ideas will be wrong, maybe for a long time all of them will be wrong; so there will be mistakes.

This, of course, touches the exposed nerve of all those who insist one-sidedly on the teaching role of the church to the neglect of its learning role. All of us hold that there is a teaching authority in the church; all of us hold, in principle if not in practice, that there are limits to that authority; but what some have great difficulty in admitting is that there are questions to which we have as yet no answers, that when we lack the answers we have to work to learn them, and that while we are learning mistakes are possible. I think it is generally agreed now that the church made a mistake in its treatment of Galileo. Pope John Paul II went so far as to say that the church acted imprudently. Why not come right out and say the church made a mistake? It's because of our reluctance to accept the fact that we are a learning church, and to accept the implications of that fact. Again, the various decrees from the Biblical Commission early in this century, on the Johannine comma, on Moses as the author of the Pentateuch, and so on – no one, except maybe the most fundamentalist of Christians, would hold them now; but I don't know whether anyone in the Vatican has even said that we acted imprudently, much less admitted that we made a mistake.

My own view is that it would not hurt our credibility. It would on the contrary enormously enhance it, to state openly in regard to some of these declarations that we made a mistake. If that is just too difficult, and given our history it is exceedingly difficult, perhaps we could leave the past alone, but at least with regard to present and future questions make the modest statement, when it applies: 'We don't know.' Do we know, really know, whether or not women should be admitted to ordained ministry in the church?[9] Do we really know whether the Eucharist should be shared with members of other churches? Is 'I don't know' an impossible answer in our church? It might create chaos in the pastoral area, and would have to be used selectively and with prudence; but it would be something to have the principle asserted.

Now, however, I must turn to what I think might be some of the measures we could take to develop our atrophied learning wing, and what I would suggest under that heading for the role of the laity in the church.

Let us be clear first on what we are doing and what we are not doing. We are not proclaiming a new God, a new Christ, a new Holy Spirit. All these are divinely given in revelation; and just as we had nothing to do with the giving of the revelation, so we can do nothing to change it, nor should we wish to change it. We are asking, however, what God's revelation, given through Hebrew images and in Hebrew language in scriptural times and scriptural places, means for us today. We are asking how it can be expressed in terms that the people of Winnipeg can understand in 1990, in a message that will nourish their faith and hope and love.

There are *three* obvious reasons for saying we must think out the message anew in every age. The first is that the language is not always our language. Some of the gospel, of course, is limpidly clear: 'Always treat others as you would like them to treat you.'[10] But when Paul gets arguing about grace and the law, about faith and works, about authority in the home and in the state, and between master and slave, then it is not quite so simple. A second reason for rethinking the message is that new doctrinal questions arise that were not treated in scripture at all: for example, the self-consciousness of Jesus. This is a topic that came in with the psychology of last century. We all have a human con-

9 In 1994, Pope John Paul II issued *Ordinatio sacerdotalis*, an apostolic letter in which he asserted the inadmissability of women to priestly ordination (see *Origins* 24 [1994–95] 49, 51–52). Whatever the degree of authority that should be attributed to this letter or to the subsequent clarifications offered by the Congregation for the Doctine of the Faith ('Reply to the *Dubium* concerning the Teaching Contained in the Apostolic Letter *Ordinatio sacerdotalis*' [see *Origins* 25 (1995–96) 401, 403]), it should be noted that the present essay was originally presented some four years prior to *Ordinatio sacerdotalis* (ed.).

10 Matthew 7:12.

sciousness of a human self; but the Self in Jesus is divine, so what kind of self-consciousness did he have? A third reason is that new questions of conduct arise. The first question of the people who were converted by John the Baptist was 'What are we to do?' John had a ready answer for them, and for particular cases among them, for the tax-collectors in their situation, and for the soldiers in theirs; but that doesn't help a doctor today with a difficult problem in medical ethics, or a member of Parliament today with a difficult tax bill before him.

In other words, the human race and the human mind and the church of God won't stand still. In the wars of a century ago, all a rifleman needed was a good eye and a steady aim: the target stood still, or, if he were running, his speed was nothing compared to the speed of a bullet. But during World War II they developed the science of cybernetics, because the targets were moving so fast that a good eye and a steady aim were useless. You needed computers that could calculate the speed and direction of the target, the speed and direction of the missile, and put them together fast enough to aim and fire before the target disappeared. Well, God's word has been involved in an eternal cybernetics with the human race, continually adapting the aim to reach the target.

That image is not the happiest one, because it makes the human race an independent agent and something of an enemy to God, whereas it is God's creation, it belongs to God, who loves it, and wants to communicate with it, and wants to give it all the responsibility it is able to carry. But it does illustrate the fact that church expression cannot stand still.

Take the example of Jesus, angry at the commercial traffic being carried on in the temple: 'the dealers in cattle, sheep, and pigeons, and the money-changers seated at their tables.'[11] He 'made a whip of cords and drove them out of the temple, sheep, cattle, and all. He upset the tables of the money-changers, scattering their coins.'[12] Now Jesus is our way, our truth, our life. So does that mean that we should make a whip of cords and deal with evil in the way he did? Or, to put it more abstractly, is violence the way for us to deal with evil today in our world? Jesus himself did not offer violence to those who seized him on Holy Thursday night. So what is the right way for us? The way of those who would bomb abortion clinics? The way of Mahatma Gandhi? That of Mother

11 John 2:14.
12 John 2:15.

Theresa? Are all of them right? If so, since we cannot follow them all, which one is right for me?

You see it is not simply a matter of knowing your scripture, or knowing the councils of the church. It is a matter also of knowing the modern situation – the divine cybernetics of changing the aim from Palestine in the year 30 to Winnipeg in the year 1990, and transposing the message of the year 30 so that it reaches its target in the year 1990.

This is where the input of the laity is essential. In 1985 there was what was called an extraordinary synod of bishops in Rome. One of the Canadian bishops in attendance, Bernard Hubert of Saint-Jean-Longueuil, head of the Canadian Conference of Catholic Bishops, thought the synod was trying to move too fast. His proposal, as reported in *L'Osservatore Romano* was this:

> that we identify the problems that the Synod wishes to deal with and bring ourselves up-to-date next year or even later. This would allow the Synod Fathers to go back and discuss the themes considered with the members of their episcopal conferences and with all the members of the people of God responsible for the mission of the church.[13]

This brief, seemingly simple proposal gives a whole program that I find very helpful. First, raise the questions: that is, identify the problems. What exactly is the problem in regard to ordained ministry for women? Is it doctrinal? If so, is it scriptural? Is it tradition? Or, is the problem practical? Is it church discipline? Secondly, bring ourselves up-to-date. Of course, bring ourselves up-to-date on scripture, tradition, history; but Bishop Hubert means more than that. He wants 'to go back and discuss the themes' at home, 'with the members of the episcopal conferences and with all the members of the people of God responsible for the mission of the church.' That, in my view, does not leave out any adult member of the church. And what it calls for is more than scholarly acquaintance with scripture, tradition, and history. What it calls for is feedback from the people of God, based on their experience of the world we live in.

It was really feedback that led the early Christians to revise their views on the second coming of the Lord. Not feedback provided in any formal way: there were no questionnaires, there was no consultation. It was just

13 *L'Osservatore Romano*, Weekly edition, English (16 Dec. 1985) 12.

the common experience of the whole church. 'It's been a long time, and the Lord has not yet appeared; what can we make of that?' Still, in its own unorganized, informal, and quite inarticulate way, it was a primitive kind of feedback. What Bishop Hubert is calling for is feedback in a more organized, a more formal, a more articulate way; and I think he would hope that the laity will make its input in that process.

Chapter 16

'The Spirit and I' at Prayer[1]

It is almost fifty years since Pius XII spoke of 'a new and mysterious outpouring of the Holy Spirit.'[2] He was followed a few years later by John XXIII, announcing 'a new Pentecost, so to speak.'[3] Those two statements are startling, and one who took them seriously back in the 1950s might reasonably have expected history to repeat itself in a new and modern Acts of the Apostles. But that same person might also now be quite disappointed by the general lack of interest in the matter, or even disturbed by what is a barely concealed hostility. The first Pentecost came fifty days after the resurrection, and the response was immediate and enthusiastic. Our new Pentecost has met a slow and dullish reception – one is tempted to say that many of the people of God are dragging their feet.

There has been advance, of course, but it has been uneven. The charismatics seem to have created a salient; but they are a mixed bag, and I would say (somewhat hesitantly) that they have failed to attend to the institutional counterpart that must accompany enthusiasm. I have less hesitation in stating quite bluntly that the majority of theologians lag far behind. One may check the most topical question of the moment, Christianity and world religions, and see how few are the theologians of world religions who make any reference whatever to the Spirit, though the same Spirit who long ago made no distinction between Jews and Gentiles[4] might be expected to be independent of our divi-

1 Not previously published.
2 *AAS* 46 (1954) 772.
3 Ibid. 51 (1959) 832.
4 Acts 10:44–48.

sion of Christians and non-Christians. As for ecclesiastics, they range from the threatened, for a new Pentecost is bound to be disruptive of their established regime, to the sincerely willing but genuinely puzzled: 'I don't know how to respond to the charismatics; my seminary training did not equip me to deal with the Spirit.'

Well, we all do what we can, when and where we can, in the way we can. My aim in the present essay is to add another voice to those who wish to relate the Spirit more intimately to our prayer life, to bring together the Spirit and the person praying, to see the Spirit as a praying subject as well as an object of our prayer, to pray in communion with the Spirit as well as praying to the Spirit.

I am afraid that that will appear vague, but let me see if I can sharpen the idea a little. We have a strong tradition of praying *to* the Spirit, if only on rather special occasions – for example, at ordination ceremonies, or as we begin a religious conference, and especially of course at the Pentecost of the liturgical season (what a pity that in our new liturgy this season is over at midnight on Pentecost Sunday). Likewise the Spirit enters our prayer *as pertaining to the object of contemplation.* For most of us the daily food of our prayer life is the life and work and message and death of the Lord Jesus, and we contemplate the Spirit in that context. We meditate on the baptism of Jesus and so on the Spirit who descended upon him at that time.[5] We meditate on his being led into the desert, and so on the Spirit who led him there;[6] on his return in power to Galilee, and on the Spirit who gave him the power.[7] Similarly, in a number of other passages of scripture: Jesus rejoicing in the Spirit,[8] and so on.

It is in contrast to these two ways of praying, praying to the Spirit and having the Spirit as the object of contemplation, that the suggestion of this essay can be most simply understood and its scope be more fully realized. For even if prayer *to* the Spirit is not as common as perhaps it should be, it need not and indeed should not characterize all our prayer. And as for *contemplating* the Spirit, the scriptures do not provide material for this in every line. Nor do they speak in every line about the Spirit working in Jesus: to bring in the Spirit we have often therefore to supply that aspect as understood. It remains that my suggestion would *involve* the Spirit with us in every prayerful exercise.

5 Matthew 3:16.

6 Matthew 4:1.

7 Luke 4:14.

8 Luke 10:21.

For the sake of our prayer, to exploit (in the good sense of the phrase) the Spirit's presence is my present purpose. True, the sending of the Spirit is one of the mighty acts of God, made public and visible in the roaring wind and the tongues of fire, and thus objectified for the scriptural record and for our contemplation. But the sending of the Spirit is also a very individual and private affair for each one of us, and that underlies the aspect I would examine here: 'the Spirit and I' at prayer together, the Spirit on our side in prayer, our solidarity with the Spirit as we pray, two subjects at prayer – the Spirit and I.

A few soundings in scripture will give us the general orientation. The title of the essay is meant to suggest a link with Acts 15:28, as translated in the NRSV: 'For it has seemed good to the Holy Spirit and to us to impose on you no further burden than these essentials ...' In the area of discipline, then, with implications for dogma, there is a partnership, a collaboration, teamwork, cooperation, between the Spirit and the church. Further, we have scriptural support for extending this partnership from disciplinary matters in the church to the prayer life of individual Christians. For Paul tells us, speaking of our need for help: 'Likewise the Spirit helps us in our weakness; for we do not know how to pray as we ought, but that very Spirit intercedes with sighs too deep for words.'[9] What applies, then, to 'the Spirit and us' in the government of the church can reasonably be said to apply to 'the Spirit and me' in my prayer life.

These references, so explicit on the activity of the Spirit among God's people, can serve as a guide where the matter is not quite so clear. For example, they illuminate a tradition of Israel and the church where a similar idea is implicit. The tradition is most obvious in the strong sense Israel had of nearness to her God, the classic expression of which is found in the words of Moses: 'For what other great nation has a god so near to it as the Lord our God is whenever we call to him?'[10] The same idea appears in the Psalms: 'The Lord is near to all who call on him, to all who call on him in truth';[11] and again: 'He declares his word to Jacob, his statutes and ordinances to Israel. He has not dealt thus with any other nation; they do not know his ordinances.'[12]

9 Romans 8:26.
10 Deuteronomy 4:7.
11 Psalms 145:18.
12 Psalm 147: 19–20.

Now this nearness of God and Israel becomes a solidarity and is extended to the solidarity of God and Christ, in C.H. Dodd's interpretation of John's Gospel.[13] The argument revolves around the phrase, 'I-he,' or 'I and he,' which 'signifies the solidarity of God with His people,' especially in their tribulations. This phrase was represented in the Septuagint by 'ego eimi' (I am), and Dodd thinks it highly probable that John's use of 'ego eimi'[14] alludes to the divine name and implies that God has given his own name to Christ. Dodd observes further that John's 'ego kai ho pempsas me'[15] is equivalent to the Hebrew 'I and he' as understood in the later tradition with which John may have been acquainted. 'The substitution of Christ for Israel in the expression of solidarity is in harmony with early Christian procedure in general, and in particular with that of the Fourth Gospel.'[16]

We have then a religious tradition of the solidarity of God and Israel expressed in the phrase 'I and he,' and we have a likely linking of that tradition with John's 'I and the one who sent me.' What I am suggesting is a simple development or extension of that theme. If John could transfer this expression of solidarity from God and Israel to God and Christ, may we not transfer it from God and Christ to the Spirit and ourselves?

We have surely a profound intimacy of union with the Holy Spirit resident within us. John speaks movingly of the intimacy of the beloved disciple with Jesus. At the Last Supper he leaned on Jesus' breast to ask who the betrayer was,[17] and this sense of intimacy pervades the opening lines of John's first letter: 'what we have heard, what we have seen with our eyes, what we have looked at and touched with our hands.' Well, is it not a simple step to think in the same way of the Spirit? Can we not celebrate, in the interior union we enjoy with the indwelling Spirit, that which John celebrates in the external union of Jesus and his disciples? To ask the question in that way is already to answer it.

13 See 'The Name of God,' in C.H. Dodd, *The Interpretation of the Fourth Gospel* (Cambridge: University Press, 1953) 93–96.

14 John 8:28 and passim.

15 John 8:16, 'I and the one who sent me.'

16 Dodd, *The Interpretation of the Fourth Gospel* 96.

17 John 13:25, as in NRSV; in *Good News for Modern Man: The New Testament in Today's English Version* (New York: American Bible Society, 1996): 'moved closer to Jesus' side.'

There is, then, at least a *prima facie* case for the thesis of a partnership in prayer of the Spirit and myself.[18] But instead of continuing to validate further a doctrine that will in the end depend more on the *sensus fidelium* than on proof of a thesis, I wish to turn to ideas and implications that belong more to the systematic side of theology and may be found useful once the role of the Spirit in our prayer receives the attention it deserves.

One point of insertion for a systematics might be found in the word 'interior,' for it points to a fundamental lack in our theology of the indwelling Spirit – the lack, namely, of a philosophy of interiority by means of which we might construct a theology of interiority. There is no guilt or shame attached to this lack. We are all extroverts at birth: very early on, we begin to see and hear and touch. Further, if we philosophize on this human condition, we very easily become behaviorists. Quite readily then do we imagine Jesus before us to see and hear and touch him. But when we are born again in the Spirit, we have an interior presence that is just as real and just as much a presence of the divine (more so, one could argue) as the presence of Jesus in the Holy Land; but we do not know how to handle it. We do not even know how to study our own human interiority, as a step toward study of the interior presence of the Spirit.

To remedy that state of affairs is a basic task for theology today. And the first step in the remedy is to acknowledge the need. What is not the first preoccupation of our extroverted consciousness can nevertheless become a focus of our attention. As Bernard Lonergan has stressed, we need 'studies of religious interiority: historical, phenomenological, psychological, sociological.'[19] With a philosophy of interiority we could organize our rich tradition on the discernment of spirits, on the gift of prophecy for reading the signs of the times, on joining the mystical and

18 How much has been omitted from our *prima facie* case will be obvious to readers. The first paragraphs of an article by John McDade ('Jesus and the Spirit,' *The Month* [December 1994] 498–503), alerted me to the existence of a very old tradition on 'the Spirit and me' at prayer, but I have not tried to put together a bibliography on the question. Of the many areas that might be studied, however, I would mention in particular the mystic union enjoyed by the great contemplatives, and its relevance to our own everyday union with the Spirit.

19 *Method in Theology* 290. I would add that equally we need a philosophy of interiority, and that Lonergan's own work went a long way toward meeting that need; but we have hardly begun to exploit the legacy he left us.

charismatic to the institutional and organizational, on relating the consensus of the faithful to dogma and the tradition, on consulting religious experience to moderate the application of external power – and so on through a whole range of questions that trouble us today. Then also we might attend more to the new Pentecost and enter more fully into companionship with the Spirit.

Secondly, we need a theology and consequently a philosophy of intersubjectivity. Again, I find it convenient to appeal to Lonergan, who mediates to us on this question the findings of personalist and phenomenological philosophy. Thus he describes the sequence beginning from a prior 'we' that is not made thematic but is simply lived, a sequence in which we move through encounter with others and the resultant categories of 'I' and 'you,' and so arrive at the formally thematized 'we' of the everyday adult world. The familiar example of that primary and unthematized 'we' is the mother and child, but anthropologists discover it also in primitive peoples, and students of the Old Testament find it in the origins of Hebrew religion.

It was perhaps in the great revolution that Jaspers calls the axis of history that the individual members of the tribe emerged with individual responsibilities, and the prophets discovered the individual accountability of each person: 'What do you mean by repeating this proverb concerning the land of Israel, "The parents have eaten sour grapes, and the children's teeth are set on edge"? As I live, says the Lord God, this proverb shall no more be used by you in Israel. Know that all lives are mine ... it is only the person who sins that shall die.'[20] Similarly, in a process that replays for the individual the history of the tribe, it is within the 'we' of the family that there emerge the 'I' of the child and the possibility of another 'we.' For the child grows into adulthood, as does another child in a perhaps distant land; the two meet and fall in love. That 'mutual love is the intertwining of two lives. It transforms an "I" and "thou" into a "we" so intimate, so secure, so permanent, that each attends, imagines, thinks, plans, feels, speaks, acts in concern for both.'[21]

---

20 Ezekiel 18:2–4.

21 *Method in Theology* 33. Then the cycle starts again: 'From the "we" of the parents comes the symbiosis of mother and child. From the "we" of the parents and the symbiosis of mother and child comes the "we" of the family. Within the "we" of the family emerges the "I" of the child' (*Philosophy of God, and Theology* 58 [*Papers 1965–1980* (2004) 210]).

Now Lonergan sees this as having an application to the theology of the Trinity. 'Recently, the phenomenologists have been scrutinizing the mutual communion of "I" and "thou" and thereby opening up the possibility of another dimension to Trinitarian thought.'[22] He was thinking, I believe, of an analogy for what theologians call the essential or immanent Trinity, but of course what is valid for the Three in themselves is valid for them in their presence among us, that is, for the economic Trinity, and in particular for the Holy Spirit resident in our hearts.

Thirdly, under the heading of intersubjectivity we may pay particular attention to the category of mutual self-mediation. There is a self-mediation when we use what we *are* to become what we *should be.* There is self-mediation through another when our encounter with others reveals new possibilities of what we may be, and challenges us to realize them. There is mutual self-mediation when the encounter and resulting growth are reciprocal.

Lonergan applies this to the mutual self-mediation of Christ and ourselves: we obviously grow in relation to Christ, but Christ too grew in relation to his mission to be our Saviour and Redeemer. May there not be something analogous in the reciprocal relation between the Spirit and myself? Granted that the Spirit does not 'grow' in the way Christ grew, might there not nevertheless be an adaptation of the Spirit's role in our lives, an adjustment in the variety of gifts of the Spirit, according to our response? If we can in some sense grieve the Spirit, if the Spirit can join with a church assembly to provide for our changing needs, if the Spirit's role in the world is not fixed by an eternal decree but is responsive to the situation, it does not seem wholly fantastic to speak, analogously and with modifications, of a mutual self-mediation of the Spirit and myself.

It is as important to take account of obstacles and difficulties as it is to present the more positive side of an idea, and so I would conclude with a few remarks on the 'hang-ups' we have in our thinking about the Spirit. That expression is more commonly used in regard to psychic and emotional snags, but our reluctance to open our eyes to the presence and activity of the Spirit, and to a corresponding development of our doctrine and practice, has such a resemblance to psychic hang-ups as to warrant the use of the expression here.

22 'Philosophy and Theology,' in *A Second Collection* 200.

One hang-up is fear of experimentation. To overcome this, a certain boldness is in place, a willingness to try and to be proved wrong, to try again, and so finally to discover God's will. I think of the vicissitudes in the life of Ignatius Loyola before he came to his tried and tested vocation. More generally, religious orders are experimenting with new life-styles, new mission outreach, new applications of their founding charism, new forms of collaboration with one another, and even with a certain federalism. This is a straightforward tactic in a time of change, in which old guidelines are no longer sufficient and new ones must be found.

So I would recommend a measure of experimentation in personal prayer. It is a little formal, perhaps, to say to the Spirit, 'Let us pray,' but informally we may recognize, as we begin our prayer, that the Spirit is contemplating the same gospel scene as we are, and doing it in communion with us. Of course, we will conduct our bold experiment with due caution, realizing that we contemplate to inquire and learn, whereas the Spirit 'contemplates' to teach and reveal. Nevertheless, we pray with a deep sense of our need, and we know that the Spirit comes to help us in our need.[23] To experiment in this direction might help us realize better that the Spirit prays in solidarity with us, in the same solidarity that God had with the people of Israel in their tribulations, the same solidarity that, on the other side of the ledger, causes the Spirit to grieve over our unworthy conduct.[24]

Another hang-up is the fear of moving outside the boundaries of Scholastic categories. St Thomas Aquinas had occasion half a dozen times in his two *Summae* to deal with the text from Romans on the Spirit praying,[25] and on every occasion he explained it in the same way. As divine the Spirit does not pray. What then does the text mean? It means that the Spirit inspires us with holy desires and causes us to pray: 'Spiritus ... in hoc adiuvat infirmitatem nostram quod, inspirando nobis sancta desideria, recte postulare nos facit.'[26] One cannot fault this reasoning as long as the explanation moves within the horizon of efficient causes. But we need to add modern philosophy to medieval philosophy on this point. If we think, as we must today, in terms of an inter-

23 Romans 8:26.

24 Ephesians 4:30.

25 Romans 8:26.

26 *Summa theologiae* 2-2, q. 83, a. 5, ad 1m.

subjectivity that gives to thought a dimension beyond causality, we may be able to go back to the Hebrew 'I and he' and add new considerations to the Thomist position. There is a primordial 'we' of the Holy Spirit and me, in which categories of causality may apply, as the laws of biochemistry apply to our thinking, but in which also causality is not a sufficient principle of explanation, as biochemistry does not give an adequate account of our thoughts.[27]

A third hang-up is the most fundamental, and the hardest to dislodge: our sense of what is real, of what is really real, of what is problematically real. For the commonsense and 'no nonsense' person, the tree out there is real. If I can walk up and touch it, it is really real. But the insight – brought to me by study – into what a tree is and thus what this tree is, is problematically real; and so is its metaphysical counterpart, the 'substantial form' of the tree. How can I be sure of the reality of anything? Well, it's there to be seen! My face lights up, I even walk on air, or maybe rush naked into the streets when I have a really profound insight. There is lots of reality there, and the incident is chock full of reality. But is the insight itself real? Is the 'formal cause' of the tree real?

Thus, if traditional Catholics were asked, 'Was the Spirit really sent into the world?' they would surely and without hesitation answer 'yes.' 'And is the Spirit really present in the world?' 'Well, yes' (slight hesitation there for some). But press the question a little: 'Is the Spirit as really present now as the Son of God was nineteen centuries ago?' That would definitely give them pause – so pervasive among us is the original sin of philosophy, behaviorism.

There is no remedy for these hang-ups except in a thorough rethinking of interiority and intersubjectivity, of the word 'is' and of the validity of our use of it. But lest our philosophy itself lose touch with reality, we must return to experience – in this case, to our own experience of

27 An angle of this 'hang-up' is the fact that the Spirit has no human nature, such as the Son has, to be the principle of change. But this difference in the missions of Son and Spirit has preoccupied us too much. All along the line we have to be more open to parallels and counterparts. I wonder, for example, if, corresponding to the *kenosis* of the Son, we must not speak of something parallel in the submission of the Spirit to existence in our hearts. God made the Son 'to be sin' for our sake (2 Corinthians 5:21); may we not suppose that the infinitely pure Spirit 'suffered' in an analogous way on being sent into our sinful hearts, to remain with us in spite of our continual failures to respond?

the 'new and mysterious outpouring of the Holy Spirit' that Pius XII spoke of, to John XXIII's 'new Pentecost.' Then the 'I' and 'You' of prayer to the Spirit might become the 'We' of the Spirit and myself at prayer, recovering the original and primordial and unthematized 'We' of our rebirth in the Spirit. May witness to this experience grow ever clearer and stronger, so that the Acts of the Apostles may not only record the history of first-generation Christians but also be an exemplar for repetition over and over again in the continuing history of the people of God.[28]

28 I am grateful to Michael Kolarcik, of Regis College, Toronto, for helping me understand the basis in Hebrew of Dodd's interpretation of John (note 13 above).

Chapter 17

Why We Have to Die[1]

The question why we have to die seems at first sight to be a non-question, or one for which the answer is there already, spelled out in the pages of scripture on the history of the human race. Adam and Eve failed their test, and death was the punishment: 'Therefore, just as sin came into the world through one man, and death came through sin, and so death spread to all ...'[2]

But is the sin of Adam and Eve the ultimate explanation of the entry of death into our world? St Thomas Aquinas has taught us that we must question everything, even the fundamentals of our faith, even the existence of God – not, to be sure, in a state of doubt, but to find the ultimate reason why. Further he has given us a clue on how to find the ultimate reason why, namely, the great difference between what is first for us and what is first in itself. What is first for us is the immediate explanation, the proximate 'why' or cause of what we experience, of what we see or hear. But what is first in itself is the final explanation, the ultimate reason why, the fundamental cause of that experience; and this is not immediate at all, but may be quite remote from our first understanding. Thus, the immediate cause of daylight is the rising of the sun, and that is first for us; but when we search out the underlying causes, we come to the spinning of the earth, and after that to its orbit around the sun, and then to the way the planets were long ago propelled into space, and so on, as far as science can take us, till we come to the remote and fundamental explanation of the solar system.

1 Not previously published.
2 Romans 5:12.

Now what is remote and ultimate for us is first in God's thinking, and so to ask for the ultimate reason for death is to try to think the way we imagine God to think. The stress here is on 'try' and 'imagine': we cannot think the divine way, seeing the whole reality all at once in a flash of understanding, but must proceed step by ponderous step. These steps we then attribute to God, but at least following St Thomas's clue, we will not proceed in the order natural to us, but in the order we imagine as 'natural' to God.

This order of the steps of God's 'reasoning,' as I imagine it and will set it forth here, is the following. God wishes to share the divine life, and this involves at once the creation of a hybrid: part creature, part divine. Next, the creaturely part will be a 'nature' and this means it should fulfil itself as a nature, in a stage where there is only the promise and not yet the reality of divine being. Thirdly, there must be a passage from the state of being in which we live in hope, to the state of being in which we share as fully as possible the divine being, and this involves dying, a leaving behind – a leaving, to be sure, in order to recover, but still a total divesting of oneself as human: Dust thou art, and to dust thou shalt return.

1 God's Idea of Sharing the Divine Life

In our first step we may think, then, of the divine Three deliberating among themselves as they consider what they might do with their infinite power. 'Goodness is self-extending,' they might say[3] as they begin, 'and a good thing ought to radiate beyond itself. Now we enjoy the highest possible form of the good life, and so we should consider how to spread this good thing around, how to share it with others, how to give them the divine and infinitely blessed life that is ours.'

If we take that as their starting point, then, since to share requires others and there is as yet no one besides the Three, their very first step would have to be the creation of others out of the nothing of the universe. With that very first step, however, there arises the very first difficulty: anything created will necessarily be finite, and nothing finite is fit to receive the infinite or to be the proper subject of an infinitely

---

3 See St Thomas Aquinas, quoting Dionysius: 'bonum est diffusivum sui esse,' *Summa theologiae* 1, q. 5, a. 4 ob. 2 (and passim in Thomas).

good life. The original desire to share the divine life seems to involve from the start an intrinsic contradiction.

This first hurdle that thought encounters is taken in stride in God's thinking, but it is a crucial one for us, so let us pause here, think out in human steps the divine flash of understanding, and make sure the point is clear. If the Three are to share, there must be others; if others are to be, they must be created. But then comes the sticky point: what is created must be 'something'; it will be 'this' or 'that,' with a potency to become more than it is, but it will still be a 'something.' What receives the divine life will be a certain definite 'what.' Further, this creation must somehow form a unity with the divine life it is to receive. Whatever it is, it will have to be obedient to the divine command to receive in its finite nature the gift of the infinite and form a unity with it.

This is true whether God decides to create an angelic world, a human world, or some other world that we can scarcely imagine. But our interest, of course, is in the human. In one of the possible world orders in the divine mind, there would be people and someone called Abraham. In that same universe there could also be stones, and those stones would have to obey the divine command, should God issue it, to become children of Abraham.

How that is possible we may leave to God and the theologians to work out in detail, but perhaps it would be a wise precaution to assure readers of one point. In saying that, if God decides to create, the work created must be a nature, we are not saying that in this actual world God created what theologians would call 'natura pura' (pure nature), with a world order that would be intelligible in itself as an entity and a unity. That idea is useful as a hypothesis against which theologians might set in comparison the actual world order that we know. Whether 'pure nature' was a real possibility for God is something that could be argued for and against, but the question is marginal and academic, for God's actual decision was to create a human race destined for, longing for, oriented toward the divine, and therefore in some sense already living a life touched by the divine. The unity of the universe and in particular of the human-divine was built into the creative idea from the start.

The first great step in divine thinking involved God, therefore, in certain constraints. As in our world the wealthy may wish to share their wealth, but find at once that they suffer all kinds of constraints (like those from the tax collectors), so God too must face the limitations inherent in the divine plan. To share means there must be another, and that other must be created. If that other is created, it must be finite. But something finite created to share the infinite is a hybrid, and would be a 'monster' in the order of the universe, did not infinite wisdom and divine omnipotence know how to make it an intelligible, reasonable unity.

2 The Human Race in Its 'Natural' Habitat

If we leave to God and the theologians the basic metaphysics of creating the human world and ensuring its unity, there are other questions that we may not so easily avoid. The decision to create involves a human being that would have a 'nature,' would belong by 'nature' in a world proportionate to that nature.

And what that nature would be, and what that world, and how much scope God would allow that nature to be itself in a human world, and why such relative 'independence' would be wise and good, these are questions that bear directly on the reason why we have to die. It seems then that the next question in the divine thinking out of the plan to share involves a closer look at the human race in its 'natural' habitat.

God's thinking starts with the end-product, so the decision to share the divine life with a human race centers first on the human race in its final state – what we call the state of blessedness. But God is a thorough thinker, and various options occur at this point. A basic one is this: should the human race be created from the beginning in the state of the end-product, that of the blessed, or should there be a prior and preparatory state in which the human race lives, as it were, in its 'natural' habitat? The answer was that it had to be the latter. The decision was easy. Knowing already – what St Thomas, as we shall see, would later discover – that natures should not be otiose, God decided that there should be, in the order of the universe, a role for human nature in its 'natural' world and environment.

But, again, what is easy for God, and is seen in a flash of divine understanding, is a crucial step in our thinking and must be spelled out. Why then was it quite inappropriate to create the human race to exist from the start in its final state? Why must there be a preliminary stage before we enter the state of the blessed? It is because human nature would have next to no role to play in the alternative scenario. What role could human nature have if it were immersed, without previous experience of itself, in the immensity of the divine? If a tiny drop of water were immersed in a mighty ocean, what kind of personal identity, what kind of life, what kind of history would the droplet experience? What interest would it have in developing its own 'natural' potentialities? But suppose the droplet, instead of that overwhelming immersion from the beginning, had the experience first of being formed in the cloud world, of falling to earth, of joining a stream and flowing down to the ocean, suppose it brought this history and these memories to its life in the ocean, something 'personal' and individual would remain with it always.

For reasons that are somewhat similar, there must therefore be a human world, a human life, human experience, human history, and it must have its own existence, be in some partial sense independent and self-contained. There must be the opportunity for it to grow, to realize its potential, and of course also to become aware of its deficiencies, its needs. We might adopt and adapt St Vincent of Lerins here. In a famous passage taken up by the First Vatican Council, he said in regard to the development of doctrine: 'Therefore, let there be growth ... and all possible progress in understanding, knowledge, and wisdom whether in single individuals or in the whole body, in each person as well as in the entire Church, according to the stage of their development.'[4]

Let us pursue this point, which is altogether basic to the ultimate explanation of why we have to die, and examine more deeply the question why there must first be a world in which people live as people, before they enter the world in which people will live as God does. We might start with a word from Thomas Aquinas. Speculating about the experimental knowledge the Son of God made human might have, he remarked that, despite all the divinely given knowledge Jesus had, which seemed to cover the same territory as experience would, there would still have to be this experimental knowledge, because it belongs to the idea and reality of an agent intellect that it not be just a fiction, that it have its proper function and play its proper role in the universe: 'propter convenientiam intellectus agentis, ne eius actio sit otiosa.'[5]

---

4 'Crescat igitur oportet et multum vehementerque proficiat tam singulorum quam omnium, tam unius hominis quam totius ecclesiae, aetatum ac saeculorum gradibus, intellegentia, scientia, sapientia' (*Commonitorium* 23; RJ 2174; or see DS 3020). I have quoted *The Church Teaches: Documents of the Church in English Translation* (St Louis: B. Herder Book Co., 1955) 34 – various translators – but only the positive side (making a slight change); Vincent goes on more negatively to register cautions.

5 *Summa theologiae* 3, q. 12, a. 1 c.

There is a world of wisdom in that short and cryptic phrase, 'ne eius actio sit otiosa,' and a very wide application. Think of a human being who was made a doctor of philosophy without any schooling, primary, secondary, or post-secondary: this would render useless the whole human potency to be educated. Think of a male or female person who entered the world fully grown as a mature adult without passing through the stages of childhood and adolescence: this would render useless the whole biological, neural, psychic, and intellectual system built for gradual development. Think of a football team that was declared champion without ever having played a game against opponents: this would render useless the training of athletes and the whole system of competitive sports.

It is not only agent intellect, therefore, that must be itself and not just a fiction. It is not just that the vine should be 'free' to produce grapes and the thornbush to be thorny, that the fig tree should produce figs and not thistles. The point applies to the whole universe that God created with its capacities, its resources, its potential, its nature and way of operating. This human universe must grow in its totality according to its own nature and laws, and each human being must enter into that universe in an appropriate way and similarly grow to maturity.

There is an extremely important point to add, though I can but touch on it. I have spoken of this stage as prior, as preparatory, as preliminary. And now I must correct the impression that those words are bound to form. For they suggest that this stage is over and done with once we enter the final state. Nothing could be further from the truth. It is not incidental at all in the divine plan, but intrinsic and essential, that each human life and the whole of human history has an 'eternal' existence in the sense of eternity looking forwards; from the moment of creation it is and does not cease to be. It 'is' in the present of the timeless God and every part of it 'is'; my grandparents 'are' as truly as I 'am.' The 'is' which we divide into 'was, is now, will be,' has no such division for God; once the world is, it simply is. Adam and Eve, Mary and Joseph, our great grandparents, they all simply 'are' to God, and likewise the whole of human history simply 'is' to God. And what 'is' to God 'is' also to those who share God's life.

How that human life and history, which in our present experience seems to pass inexorably into the nothingness of yesterday, how it enters the consciousness of the blessed and is joined to their experience and knowledge of God, how what is eternal to God can be eternal also to us as we share God's life and being, that is a most pressing question for theology today. It arises out of the age-old longing of the human race for retaining the past, but it has a special echo in our time in the hunger people experience for something permanent in this world and in our temporal life. Presently, we shall speak of 'leaving' this world behind in death, but we shall also see that we leave it only to find it again exactly as it 'is' in its eternal being on the other side of death. (Saddest of all sadnesses for suicides, to be confronted at once with what they had just tried so desperately to escape!) This is an essential factor in giving human 'nature' its place and role in the divine scenario, but it needs elaboration in its own right, instead of being reduced to a couple of paragraphs here.[6]

3 And Therefore We Must Die

We have set up the background of the question why we have to die, but have not yet answered the question itself. Think again of the options, or what seem to us to be options, for the creating God. Granted that, even while oriented toward the divine, the human race must live through (and permanently in) a stage that is really human, is there not an alternative way to the final state? Must we go through the dark exit of death? Might not God receive us alive and well, adding eternal life peaceably to the good life that belongs to the human idea, transferring us and all our human freight without interruption into the eternal mansions?

The answer, of course, is no. But why? It is because what we thought out in our second section was only the positive side of the picture. Human nature must be given its place in the divine plan, it must develop, become aware of itself, work out its intrinsic possibilities, be here and hereafter truly human. What we have not yet thought out is the negative side. That is the task and argument of our third section.

Recall the situation. We are destined to a life that is beyond our understanding, beyond the proportion of the human: 'What no eye has seen, nor ear heard, nor the human heart conceived, what God has prepared for those who love him.'[7] But we are living a finite human life,

6 I have spelled it out in 'Rethinking Eternal Life: Philosophical Notions from Lonergan,' *Science et esprit* 45 (1993) 25–39. It ties in with a strong groundswell in religious thinking that gives existence in this world a deeper and more permanent being and meaning.

7 1 Corinthians 2:9.

with the already mentioned modification that God built into our world, and made intrinsic to our world, an openness to, an orientation towards, a capacity for, and on the present hypothesis a need for the divine. We must make the transition in our thinking from that situation to the need to die, and I would argue the point as follows.

We are 'capax Dei'[8] and the capacity is a longing: 'Thou hast made us for Thyself and our hearts are restless till they rest in Thee.[9] Positively, God gave us our nature; positively, we must develop it to the full extent of our powers. Negatively, however, it is not enough. Negatively, we must become aware that it is not enough. Somehow we must all experience what Augustine felt as a divine restlessness, what the mystics go through in the dark night of the senses and the dark night of the spirit.

It is basic here that we recognize our need of the divine. We could in theory lead a life of relative happiness in our human world, given divine help on this or that point (in regard, for example, to our moral impotence). Likewise, we could in theory pass from life to eternal life as easily as we pass from day to day after a night's sleep. As long as there was no death in our universe, a plan might be devised for a life in which there would be no agony or tears or sorrow. But would it be right for the infinite to absorb a finite that is unconscious of its limitations and its helplessness and its need? Would it be right for the human race to be treated like stones from which children of Abraham, without any sense of what was happening, could be raised up?[10] With the history of God's own dear Son before our eyes, and the way that was appointed for him, we know it is not right; but the example of Jesus is not yet ultimate, for we have to ask why God chose that way for the Son, and the answer gives us the culminating point in our understanding of why we have to die.

To make this point in the context of examples previously used, would students who had not desired, striven for, been anxious about a doctorate, would they appreciate the doctorate finally bestowed? Would the adult person who had not struggled through childhood and adolescence be at peace in a state he or she had never understood to be an

---

8 Gilles Langevin, '*Capax Dei*': *La créature intellectuelle et l'intimité de Dieu* (Bruges and Paris: Desclée de Brouwer, 1966).

9 *The Confessions of St Augustine*, 1, 1; trans. F.J. Sheed (London and New York, 1944, 6th impression).

10 Matthew 3:9; Luke 3:8.

achievement of grace over nature? Would the winning team enjoy its triumph to the full if it had not experienced the pre-game nervousness of those who keenly desire to win but have to view that prospect as contingent on the struggle?

Let us return from our analogies to the case in point. If we led a relatively happy life on earth and, without 'leaving' it, without relinquishing any of its joys and comforts, went on without break or interruption to receive in addition the divine life, what prior sense of need would there be? Our universe, in which death was unknown, would be expanded by another universe for which we felt no really agonizing need. Of course, once the divine life became ours, we would see the relative nothingness of the human, of even the highest in the human, but we would see it somewhat abstractly, not having experienced it, not having in the prior life on earth longed for the other world the way Paul did.[11] We would not have faced extinction, or a ghostly, shadowy existence in Sheol. In short it is intrinsic to human existence, as a creature of potency, to know the need that that potency is, and to desire its actuation; and the possibility of such knowledge and such desire is confrontation with extinction in death.

On the deeper level of interpersonal communion with our Creator, would we be happy to enter into our inheritance and receive from the Father who adopted us the full legacy of a divine parent, had we not done something to 'earn' our legacy? And given that no positive work of ours is able to earn it, does any other way remain but simple faith and trust in the work of our Maker, and is there any better way of showing that faith and trust than by committing our spirit into the hands of God and going through the dark exit?

Such is perhaps the way that God thought it all through as an idea and proceeded to execute the idea, but then ... Enter Adam, Eve, and the serpent. Now what was a well-planned order is contaminated with disorder. What would have been a necessity of a divine idea turns into a bitter destiny. What would have been a reasonable course, seen as reasonable and accepted as reasonable, becomes an absurdity to the unbeliever and a dreaded punishment to the believer. What would have been an intimate union of divine and human cooperation is broken, and the Son of God endures the *kenosis*, becomes one of us, to

11 2 Corinthians 5:2, 8.

repair the damage. In this way the ultimate reason why is concealed behind the immediate reason for our dying in the way we do.

But let us not commit the hubris of thinking that our thinking got it all right, or got even part of it right. As the final point in understanding our need to die is to realize our need to put ourselves into the hand of God, to go through the dark exit in faith and trust, so our final evaluation of this 'explanation' is that it does not really explain. Just as in facing death we must throughout life gradually learn to leave everything in affection, the way Ignatius in the exercise on the Two Standards bids us leave already in affection what God may ask us to leave in actuality, so also we must leave the very explanation of our need to die. For no explanation really explains; it is a glimpse only:

> Those shaken mists a space unsettle, then
> Round the half-glimpsèd turrets slowly wash again.[12]

12 Francis Thompson, 'The Hound of Heaven.'

Chapter 18

Rhyme and Reason: On Lonergan's Foundations for Works of the Spirit[1]

Our topic is cognitional foundations. More precisely, we are concerned with the two approaches to those foundations represented by reason with its first principles and by Lonergan with his foundations in authentic subjectivity. The focus is on the second: the whole effort is to find out what Lonergan means by that much quoted statement, 'Genuine objectivity is the fruit of authentic subjectivity.'[2] What is the relationship between those two functions? What are the mechanics of their collaboration? Vegetables are the fruit of gardening: that I understand. A conclusion is the fruit of premises: that too I understand. But how is objectivity the fruit of subjectivity? What do I do to get subjectivity operating? What level of consciousness do I invoke? What intentionality buttons do I push? That is my question.

There is, of course, a context for discussion of foundations; and without that context the question of this paper would hardly have arisen, nor would Lonergan's position be of much interest outside the circle of those who study his thought.[3] Nevertheless, except for his background

---

1 Originally presented on 26 October 1996 at Regent College, Vancouver, and subsequently at a Lonergan Research Institute Seminar, Toronto. Previously published in *METHOD: Journal of Lonergan Studies* 17 (1999) 27–45.

2 *Method in Theology* 292; see also 265. Note that there is much the same difficulty in understanding how method uses foundations 'to select doctrines from among the multiple choices presented by ... dialectic' (ibid. 298; and see also 132, 142, 298, 299, 349, 355).

3 For the anti-foundationalism of philosophers see Hans Albert, *Treatise on Critical Reason*, trans. Mary Varney Rorty (Princeton, NJ: Princeton University Press, 1985) 18: '... if one demands a justification for everything ... one must choose ... between ... 1. an

in Aristotle and Aquinas, I ignore that context. There is a real question about Lonergan's own meaning, and a real need to pin down his position. That is task enough for one short paper, and the only onus I assume in my present contribution.

1 Scholastic Background

I might, indeed, find a starting point common to many theologians in 1 Peter 3:15: 'Be always ready with your defence whenever you are called to account for the hope that is in you.' But I would part company with most of them when I turn to Aristotle's *Posterior Analytics*. There is a little passage there that is a good springboard for any discussion of foundations. Taking some liberty with Aristotle, I paraphrase it as follows. An Athenian family is at dinner when there is a knock on the door. The head of the house goes to answer it, and returns shortly to be questioned by the children, the 'agent intellects' of the family. 'Who was it?' 'It was X, our next-door neighbor.' 'What did X want?' 'Some money.' 'Why money?' 'To pay a debt.' 'Why should one pay a debt?' 'Because it's the right thing to do.'[4]

It's an example, beautiful in its simplicity, of the search for foundations. For Aristotle the question regarded the foundations of knowledge. When do you really know? When you come to a fact that doesn't need another fact to explain it, that doesn't evoke a why. The knock on the door needs explanation: it has a why. The need for money needs explanation: it too has a why. The obligation to pay a debt needs explanation: why pay a debt? But right and wrong need no explanation. When you come to what in Aristotle's terms is the right thing to do, you have reached what in our terms we call foundations.

The Scholastics continued this line of thinking. They spoke of first

infinite regress ... 2. a logical circle ... 3. the breaking-off of the process at a particular point, which, admittedly, can always be done in principle, but involves an arbitrary suspension of the principle of sufficient justification,' or, in other words, abandoning the search for foundations. (I owe the Albert reference to the Ph.D. dissertation of Lance Miles Grigg, 'Bernard Lonergan's Philosophy for Education,' University of Calgary, 1995, p. 3.) For a theological objection to foundations there is the well-known position of Karl Barth, who sees the search for foundations as compromising the integrity of the word of God.

4 Aristotle, *Posterior Analytics* (I, 24, 85b 30), trans. G.R.G. Mure (Richard McKeon edition, *The Basic Works of Aristotle* [New York: Random House, 1941] 149).

principles. These, when really first, are self-justifying: in Scholastic terms '*per se nota*,' which translates quite well as 'self-evident.' On the basis of these first principles you could build (demonstrate) the further levels of knowledge (conclusions, science). Those further levels had their foundations, then, in immediate knowledge, the naturally known premises from which they were demonstrated.

But there is a difficulty with that simple view of foundations. Imagine another series than that of Aristotle. 'Why did X come?' 'To get some money.' 'Why the need of money?' 'To buy a gun.' 'Why the need of a gun?' 'To kill Y?' 'And why kill Y?' 'In revenge: for the honor of the family.' That is a possible scenario, not at all far-fetched. There are peoples, tribes, families where family honor would in certain circumstances demand revenge: it is the right thing to do, it is based on foundations. But such foundations are worthless for those who judge that the right thing to do is to forgive. Foundations for one person are not foundations for another: they tell me to take revenge or to forgive, depending on my choice. When our first principles differ, we have lost objectively valid foundations. Then everything depends on subjective positions and dispositions that vary with religion, culture, education, whatever.

Thomas Aquinas saw that problem and had his answer for it. There are first principles that are self-evident *quoad se* (or, *secundum se*), and they apply objectively to our first X doing what is right, and to our second X seeking revenge; but these first principles may not be self-evident *quoad nos*, and so you get different first principles assumed as foundations. Now, *quoad se* and *quoad nos* need translation. They seem to me to translate almost exactly into 'objectively' and 'subjectively.' Objectively, *quoad se*, the principles are clear, they are self-evident; but there are those who subjectively do not see them. And what does the subject need in order to see them? Thomas's answer is that the subject needs wisdom! The wise will see what the unwise will not see.[5]

With that answer, however, Pandora's box is wide open. The 'subject' who had been kept locked up while we explored logical objectivity, tracing conclusions back to immediate first principles, has been set

5 Thomas Aquinas, *Summa theologiae* 1-2, q. 94, a. 2 c.: 'Quaedam vero propositiones sunt per se notae solis sapientibus.' See also ibid., q. 1, a. 7, on the various ultimate ends that guide people: riches, the voluptuous life, and so on. In this set of options, who judges rightly? The one 'habens affectum bene dispositum.' More sharply q. 2, a. 1 ad 1m: 'Iudicium ... de bonis humanis non debet sumi a stultis, sed a sapientibus ...'

free to take up nonfoundationalism along with relativism and who knows how many other isms. Lonergan's thought emerged in this context, so we have to begin our study with his relation to Thomas on the question.

2 Lonergan and Thomist Scholasticism

There are three themes in terms of which Lonergan's position relates to that of Thomas Aquinas: the role of wisdom; choices predetermined by character; and knowledge by connaturality.

I begin with wisdom. In Thomas it is a multi-faceted endowment, but perhaps for present purposes we may simply adopt Lonergan's sketch of its two main forms.

In its higher form, Aquinas considered it a gift of the Holy Spirit and connected it with mystical experience. In its lower form, Aquinas identified it with Aristotle's first philosophy, defined as the knowledge of all things in their ultimate causes. Clearly enough, the problem of metaphysical method demands a third form of wisdom. For the problem is not to be solved by presupposing a religion, a theology, or mystical experience. Similarly, the problem is not to be solved by presupposing a metaphysics, for what is wanted is the wisdom that generates the principles on which the metaphysics is to rest. But it does not seem that Aquinas treated explicitly the third type of wisdom.[6]

It seems to be that third type that Lonergan tries to develop in his 1959 course at the Gregorian University, *De intellectu et methodo*. Granting that the wise will see what the unwise cannot, we have the problem: How do you become wise? It is a beautiful problem. For you start with the supposition that you are dealing with people who are not wise, or that possibly you yourself are not wise. (There is no need for an already wise person to become wise.) But you need wisdom even in order to search for wisdom: if you are not wise, you will not know you are not wise, you will not know your need to search for wisdom, and

6 *Insight* (1957) 407 [(1992) 432]. Lonergan in his *Verbum* studies (1946–49) had already tried to come to grips with Aquinas on wisdom; see the Index to *Verbum* (1967) [(1997)]. Here wisdom has a rather metaphysical cast: it is knowledge of the real as real, of the *ratio* of being and non-being, and so on. Lonergan studies this at some length, searching for a more epistemological view. But his most extensive presentation of wisdom, to my knowledge, is found in his course *De intellectu et methodo*, 1959: see the next note.

you are certainly in no condition at all to carry out the search. And it is useless to appeal to the wisdom of authority, for the unwise will interpret authority unwisely. In any case, the danger of appealing to wisdom as a foundation is to endow with the virtue of wisdom the opinion of every Tom, Dick, and Harry, and thus promote relativism.[7]

The objections, I would say, are predominantly of the 'vicious circle' type, and would therefore be valid only within the confines of a logical system. For Lonergan the mind has other resources than logic. There is the intrinsic principle of the mind's dynamism, as contrasted with the terms and concepts it objectifies. There is the notion of being which already contains all knowledge in anticipation. There is the possibility of some progress by applying the principle of contradiction to the Porphyrean tree. There is the possibility of adding mastery over particular regions of being, as one grows to adult status and continues to develop.[8]

What Lonergan said in 1959 is, I think, still valid in itself and continuous with his later work, especially the principle of growth, which enables us to break victoriously out of all logical prisons. But, as in a general way his *Insight* is sublated by his *Method in Theology*, so the 1959 position on wisdom is sublated in the role of authentic subjectivity.

A second way that Lonergan relates to Aquinas regards choices allegedly predetermined by character. It is treated by Thomas more as an objection than as a positive factor in laying foundations. We might say that he opened a way that would lead beyond his own Thomist position, but that he did so almost unwittingly. Of course, this applies to Aristotle too, for whom the context was the question of our responsibility for our vices, and likewise for our virtues. He put an objection in lapidary fashion in the statement, 'the end appears to each man in a form answering to his character.'[9] And here is the Latin for those who want to get the full force of what Thomas read in medieval translations

7 *De intellectu et methodo,* student notes of a course at the Gregorian University in the spring semester, 1959, pp. 18–19 of the MS ('Obiectiones contra fundamentum positum in sapientia').

8 Ibid., pp. 19–21 ('Gressus initialis solutionis problematis fundamenti') and 21–22 ('Solutio obiectionum').

9 Aristotle, *Nicomachean Ethics* III, 5, 1114a 30 f. Though I don't read Aristotle in his own language, here for the experts is what he said: 'hopoios poth'hekastos esti, toiouto kai to telos phainetai autoi.' The phrase is underlined in Lonergan's personal copy of the *Ethics*. The English translation I gave is that of W.D. Ross (p. 973, McKeon ed.; see note 4 above).

of Aristotle: *Qualis est unusquisque, talis et finis videtur ei.*[10] The best I can do in a literal rendering is to say, 'Such as a person is, such also will the end appear to that person.'

But if Thomas and Aristotle contribute through this principle to a doctrine on foundations, they do so, I have suggested, almost unwittingly. While not blind to the positive side of the principle they see it mainly as an objection to liberty: Thomas quotes it in the arguments *Videtur quod* ... which he must answer.[11] And if we propose to develop it in a positive way for a doctrine on foundations, we may not forget the troublesome fact that it will give someone else foundations, similarly arrived at, for a position just the opposite of ours.

Lonergan's solution to this problem is provided by his doctrine on conversion, which is as little confined within logical forms as is wisdom. Conversion makes a positive factor of what to Aristotle and Aquinas was first of all an objection. 'Foundational reality ... is conversion: religious, moral, and intellectual.'[12] The scriptural equivalent is in 1 Corinthians 2:14-15: one 'who is unspiritual refuses what belongs to the Spirit of God; it is folly to him'; but one 'gifted with the Spirit can judge the worth of everything.'

The new position is illustrated in the way fundamental theology is now conceived. Once it was a set of doctrines, and these doctrines were premises from which other doctrines were deduced. 'In contrast, foundations present, not doctrines, but the horizon within which the meaning of doctrines can be apprehended.'[13] Again, 'the threefold conversion is not foundational in the sense that it offers the premisses from which all desirable conclusions are to be drawn. The threefold conversion is, not a set of propositions that a theologian utters, but a fundamental and momentous change in the human reality that a theologian is.'[14]

10 Thomas Aquinas, III, lect. 13, in his *In decem libros Ethicorum Aristotelis ad Nicomachum expositio*, Marietti edition (cura Angeli Pirotta), 1934, no. 516; or *Summa theologiae* 1, q. 83, a. 1 obi. 5a.

11 For example, *Summa theologiae* 1-2, q. 10, a. 3 obi. 2; and see note 8 above. The answer to the objection is that the evil person made himself or herself evil and so is responsible for that later lack of liberty. But the point is that they admit the premise; there is a sense in which what we are determines our ends.

12 *Method in Theology* 267.

13 Ibid. 131.

14 Ibid. 270.

The third way Lonergan relates to Aquinas regards what the latter calls judging by connaturality. The classic Thomist text is in the *Secunda secundae*. The general topic of question 45 of that part – very interesting as context – is the gift of wisdom. In discussing the particular question whether the gift of wisdom resides in the faculty of intellect, Thomas has this to say. Wisdom means right judgment, and there are two ways of judging rightly: one is by the good use of reason, but the other is by a certain connaturality with the object on which we are passing judgment. Thus by the use of reason moral theology can give us right judgment about chastity, but chaste people without any moral theology can have right judgment in this matter by connaturality. And thus too someone with the gift of charity and wisdom has a connaturality with things divine, and so judges about them rightly.[15] This, it seems to me, is the Thomist anticipation of Lonergan's authentic subjectivity; but the latter, as something to be achieved, with the way to achieve it expressly indicated, carries us forward in a new concept of foundations.

A moment ago the word 'horizon' appeared on the scene: 'foundations present, not doctrines, but the horizon within which the meaning of doctrines can be apprehended.' That idea is closely related to Thomist connaturality. In its literal sense, it applies to the range of our vision: we see what lies within the horizon, we do not see what lies beyond it. This is transposed in philosophy and theology to mean the scope of our knowledge and interests: '... what lies within one's horizon is in some measure ... an object of interest and of knowledge,' but 'what lies beyond one's horizon is simply outside the range of one's knowledge and interests: one neither knows nor cares.'[16]

'Horizon' therefore relates to all three elements of the Thomist position. The wise person sees beyond the horizon of the unwise. The term 'horizon' replaces the Thomist 'qualis' and the Aristotelian 'hopoios'; and where Thomas says a person's end is such as the person is, Lonergan says a person's horizon determines what that person cares about, that is, what is connatural to that person.[17]

15 Thomas Aquinas, *Summa theologiae* 2-2, q. 45, a. 2. See also ibid., 1-2, q. 23, a. 4 c.; q. 27, a. 1 c. etc.; *In X Ethicorum*, lect. 10, no. 2083 (Pirotta edition); *De veritate*, q. 26, a. 3 ad 18m; *De caritate*, q. unica, a. 12 c. (where Thomas refers to 1 Corinthians 2:14, 'animalis homo non percipit ea quae sunt Spiritus Dei').

16 *Method in Theology* 236.

17 It is strange that Lonergan seems only late in life to have noted the relevance to his work of Thomist knowledge by connaturality; see the last paper he gave (1982), 'Unity and Plurality: The Coherence of Christian Truth,' in *A Third Collection* 250 n. 9.

3 Subjectivity and Objectivity: Six Tangents

We are ready to approach, though not yet confront, our focal question: How does Lonergan understand the relation of authentic subjectivity to genuine objectivity? Our approach will be to walk round the question first and make six points that touch it at tangents. The sixth point will bring us face to face with the question.

My first point is negative: subjectivity does not dictate to objectivity. In a laconic answer to a question (how often a good question is the occasion for especially helpful remarks), Lonergan stated that 'method controls operations, not conclusions.'[18] That five-word quotation really says it all, but it is the negative side that is presently relevant: method or the subjective factor does not control conclusions; there is no logical route from subjectivity to objectivity.

My second point is to reject unduly ambitious aims: we will not pursue foundations in a univocal sense when the only available and realistic goal is foundations in an analogous sense. This strategy has wide application in Lonergan studies. Knowing is a compound activity with three steps, each of which is cognitional but analogously so. Willing is a compound activity involving will of the end, deliberation on possible options, and choice of the means: each of these steps is 'voluntary' as a step in the compound but analogously so. To neglect that analogy gives naive realism cognitionally (a 'look' is the standard all cognitional activity must attain), and a parallel naivete volitionally ('freedom' is the standard all voluntary activity must attain to be named voluntary). Well, reaching foundations is similarly a compound activity, with various foundational steps that are analogously foundational. To look for the same foundations in logic and in epistemology and in morality is to lose the battle before you have begun it. Why borrow money? Why pay a debt? Why do what is right? The three why's lead to immediate, remote, and ultimate foundations, but 'foundations' has become an analogous term. To neglect that analogy adds a third naivete to our list.

18 Discussions, Toronto Congress on the Theology of Renewal of the Church, 1967, mimeograph report transcribed from tapes, Institute of Mediaeval Studies, Toronto, 1968, p. 7. The occasion of this beautifully concise statement was a question from a layman (J.T. Weir, QC): 'Is methodology an element of theology or a determinant for measuring?' Lonergan goes on at once from the quoted five words to add a consequence: 'One must be careful not to transpose from the operational level (theology) to the deductivist level (religion).'

Thirdly, the role and influence of subjectivity is indirect: it controls operations, and the operations reach conclusions. That is, subjectivity tells you how to think, not what to think. This point is complementary to my first: subjectivity does not dictate conclusions, and furthermore its influence is not direct in the manner of a premise. A good example of that is natural law in Lonergan's sense. As he conceives it, the natural law does not give you a position on, say, capital punishment; it tells you to be attentive, intelligent, reasonable, and responsible as you consider the question.[19]

My fourth and fifth points begin as questions. One question: does the concept of scissors action[20] illuminate our problem? There is some resemblance, for just as in subjectivity-objectivity, you have two disparate factors that nevertheless work in combination to give results. The other question: does the concept of sublation shed some light here? Again, there is some resemblance; two factors, the sublated and the sublating, for example, intellectual conversion and moral, work in closest harmony.[21] Is objectivity sublated in a similar way by subjectivity?

---

19 'The natural law is Be attentive, Be intelligent, Be reasonable, Be responsible' (transcript of the question sessions, Boston College Lonergan Workshop 1974, session 5, p. 17). See the 1976 workshop, question session 4, p. 1: '... cosmopolis is just a matter of the first two precepts of the natural law, Be attentive, Be intelligent ...' And 'The Response of the Jesuit as Priest and Apostle in the Modern World,' in *A Second Collection* 169: '... human authenticity is a matter of following the built-in law of the human spirit,' followed by an account of the four (transcendental) precepts. The same position is all but explicit in *Method in Theology* 231, 302, and in various papers.

It is, I think, typical that the term 'natural law' occurs in discussion with others: it is they who introduce it. The term does not regularly appear in Lonergan's independent compositions, where the focus is not on objectifications but on intentionality analysis and foundations.

A simpler example of such indirect influence is found in Lonergan's account of British colonial praxis (which he uses for illustration without condoning it). London could not dictate decisions in India in 1797: they would always be six months behind events. Still they controlled those decisions indirectly, through the education given their colonial agents; see *Topics in Education* 102–103.

20 See the Index to *Insight*, under 'Heuristic method, scissors-action of.'

21 Take the example I used of one whose intellectual conversion is sublated by moral: this 'in no way interferes with or weakens his devotion to truth. He still needs truth ... The truth he needs is still the truth attained in accord with the exigences of rational consciousness. But now his pursuit of it is all the more secure ... all the more meaningful ...' (*Method in Theology* 242). The other main use of sublation occurs in the move from level to level of consciousness (ibid. 316, 340).

I believe that in fact both comparisons are helpful and might be exploited to greater advantage. In an obscure area we accept whatever help we can get (Lonergan relished Charlie Brown on this: We need all the friends we can get). But neither one offers an exact parallel to the subjectivity-objectivity pair. As to the first, where the factors in scissors action operate, as it were, in parallel, our two elements operate more like a series in tandem. As to the second: subjectivity can hardly be said to incorporate intrinsically the arguments it indirectly influences, whereas sublation does incorporate intrinsically the sublated elements. Understanding includes experience, truth includes understanding, and decision includes truth. Nevertheless, the questions about scissors action and sublation, and especially the latter, lead us to a sixth point in our walk around the question, and this in turn will force us to confront our question head-on. As follows.

We notice about scissors action and sublation that in both cases there is a positive corollary to a negative point, the positive affirmation, namely, that the 'lower' element has its strip of autonomy. The upper blade of scissors action does not determine the data supplied by the lower; the corollary is that data have their own source and their own autonomy. Again a sublating element joins to itself a lower element without destroying in any degree that lower element; the corollary is that truth has its own criterion, its own strip of autonomy, even when sublated by moral intentionality, even in controlled experiments. Well, advertence to this fact gives us a corollary to our first point. To the negative position that subjectivity does not dictate to objectivity we have now to add the positive corollary: the status of objective argument does not change with conversion to an authentic horizon.

This corollary becomes the sixth in our series of tangents to the main question. It is an important, indeed crucial step in our argument, and it must be clearly nailed down. It is, then, not enough to say that subjectivity does not interfere with objectivity, or that it supplies for the intrinsic defects of objectivity. We have to add that objective argument must stand on its own feet. On their own level and in their own area of competence, reasons and arguments are still valid, still necessary, still the responsibility of those who wish to be attentive, intelligent, and reasonable. Authentic subjectivity does not eliminate the force or the need of objective proofs. It starts by simply giving them a chance to be heard. To take our recurring example: if we argue a position on capital punishment, either for or against, we do not achieve our goal just by converting people to be intelligent, reasonable, responsible, loving, and religious;

we still have to prove our case. We may not say, 'I am attentive, intelligent, and reasonable, and I am against capital punishment; therefore ...' If then objectivity asks, 'Where do I get my arguments against capital punishment?' subjectivity answers, 'You get them where you ought to get them, from objective arguments based on objective principles.'[22]

4 Subjectivity and Objectivity: Direct Approach

With the sixth step in our approach by tangents we have laid bare the gap between objective arguments and subjective influence, and seem no nearer a solution to the problem of foundations than were the Scholastics. In fact, we seem to be back to Aquinas's position that self-evident principles, though not grasped by all, will be evident at least to the wise.

This impasse appears as soon as we come to a concrete question on which there is controversy. Suppose then two opposed positions on capital punishment. Both sides collect the data: data on capital punishment as a deterrent against crime, on conversions of those on death row, on 'mistakes' when innocent persons are executed, on whatever seems relevant. On this basis argument proceeds. Sooner or later one comes to a principle: on one side, let us say, the sacred character of human life; on the other, say, the right and duty of the state to protect its citizens from the lawless. For each side its principle is foundational, so it is clear that foundations in the sense of first principles are not sufficient: by themselves they simply do not work. What then will work? The question leads us to confront our problem directly.

Such a direct confrontation has been our aim from the beginning and especially in our third section, but I believe our previous discussion will enable us to isolate the main question. The six points of the preceding section may have their value, but all of them approached the question at a tangent. A direct study of the relationship between sub-

22 Lonergan's position on our knowledge of God's existence belongs in this context: 'I do not think that in this life people arrive at natural knowledge of God without God's grace, but what I do not doubt is that the knowledge they so attain is natural' ('Natural Knowledge of God,' in *A Second Collection* 133). In other words, this natural knowledge is subject to the ordinary rules of reason; but we would not use our reason properly (that awful Chapter 19 of *Insight*) without God's grace. Knowledge must indeed stand on its own feet, but it won't stand at all without subjective support, in this case, the support of divine grace.

jectivity and objectivity is another matter. It introduces a new factor in our argument, and it requires a new and radically different approach.

My proposal, therefore, is that we take the line Lonergan adopted in his study of cognitional theory: examine your own introspective experience; discern what happens in your mind when you come to know; it is there and there alone that you will discover what knowing is.[23] I believe that, using a strategy that is generically the same, we should examine our own experience of the subjectivity–objectivity relationship: what actually happens to us interiorly when authentic subjectivity yields genuine objectivity?

This means, of course, that the Lonergan approach is not at the moment proving anything but only issuing an invitation, just as the book *Insight* is not a position argued but rather an invitation to self-appropriation.[24] It also means that, though the strategy may be excellent, results are first obtained only personally and in private. The field of battle is one's own interiority. Any expression we give it is only the report of a witness and not yet an objective argument: argument is temporarily replaced by witness.

I will come in a moment to a more decisive step, but even at this very personal level there are objective factors we can call to our aid. One is the provision of examples that may have a catalytic effect. *Insight* took several hundred pages to issue its invitation. What was the book doing in all that time? Tactically it was at least reporting examples of insight that might suggest to readers what to look for in their own personal exercises. Perhaps the same tactic is available here.

For example, theologians might examine the difference and the relations between their religion and their academic theology. The first is the result of personal conversion, the second is a matter for discussion in the university. In particular, it is clear that, without any religious commitment, one can do a great deal of theology on the level of Lonergan's first three functional specialties: research, interpretation, and history.[25] It is equally clear that with the move to dialectic and foundations the

23 *Insight* (1957) xviii [(1992) 13]: 'The crucial issue is an experimental issue, and the experiment will be performed not publicly but privately.'

24 Ibid. (1957) 744 [(1992) 766]: We have been 'inviting subjects to a personal appropriation of their own rational self-consciousness'; see also (1957) xix [(1992) 13].

25 *Method in Theology* 268: '... anyone can do research, interpret, write history, line up opposed positions.'

subjective factor emerges as an influence.[26] What is happening in that move from history through dialectic and conversion to commitment, and what relation has it to the objectivity of the positions we make our own in the functional specialty of doctrines?

Another possibility is biographical study of famous men and women who have described their conversion experience and the effect it had on their beliefs and values. We can try to discern in them the relationship of subjectivity to objectivity. One thinks, of course, of the great Augustine and his *Confessions*. True, we are still dealing with witness, but the witness is not to a position on our question, and so it may have a somewhat more objective value for us: what was *vécu* in the witness we can make *thématique* for our purposes. Less well known but also worth study is the deposition of Ignatius Loyola on his experience.[27] And are there data in Paul's writings to illuminate our question?

5 Subjectivity and Objectivity: The Interpersonal Factor

To stop with section 4 would be to truncate Lonergan's theology in a radical way, leaving the searcher isolated, stranded on the desert island of personal experience, lacking anyone with whom to communicate, against whom to test personal experience. But communication is vital to Lonergan's perspective and doubly so in regard to the objectivity of our judgments. For him, though 'conversion is intensely personal, utterly intimate, still it is not so private as to be solitary. It can happen to many and they can form a community ...'[28] So we are

26 Ibid. 267 on the move through foundations from neutral reporting to personal commitment. On the role of dialectic in this move, ibid. 298: method 'uses the functional specialty, foundations, to select doctrines from among the multiple choices presented by the functional specialty, dialectic.'

The event of conversion is not itself a work of theology: to the objection that conversion lies outside the eight functional specialties, Lonergan admits the fact. 'Well, it is. It's a personal event, and it occurs in all sort of contexts. Religious conversion is transferring oneself into the world of worship; theology is in the academy, the classroom, the seminar, it isn't in the Church but about the Church' ('An Interview with Fr. Bernard Lonergan, S.J.,' in *A Second Collection* 217–18).

27 *A Pilgrim's Journey: The Autobiography of Ignatius of Loyola*, introduction, translation and commentary by Joseph N. Tylenda (Wilmington, DE: Michael Glazier, 1985; reprinted 1989).

28 'Theology in Its New Context,' in *A Second Collection* 66. The theme is recurrent; see, for example, *Method in Theology* 130.

brought to the role of encounter with others, and to our final point on the relationship of subjectivity and objectivity. Besides the personal there is the interpersonal and the intersubjective, and it is operative in two contexts: that of dialogue here and now with my contemporaries, and that of the 'experiment of history.'

Dialogue with contemporaries means encounter. 'Encounter' in the present sense is a late term in Lonergan;[29] its emergence seems to parallel the rather late move from science as a virtue tucked in a single mind to science as a product of the community.[30] But it emerges as a category of central significance in the *Method in Theology* period, in the context of the two functional specialties, dialectic and foundations. That works out in the concrete in the complex interplay of intersubjectivity.

> I ... have proposed a dialectic in which investigators are urged both to expand what they consider authentic in the followers of a religion they are studying and, as well, to reverse what they consider unauthentic. The result will be a projective test in which interpreters reveal their own notions of authenticity and unauthenticity both to others and to themselves. In the short run both the more authentic will discover what they have in common, and so too will the less authentic. In the long run the authentic should be able to reveal the strength of their position by the penetration of their investigations, by the growing number in the scientific community attracted to their assumptions and procedures, and eventually, by the reduction of the opposition to the hard-line dogmatists that defend an inadequate method no matter what its deficiencies.[31]

---

29 Occurrences of 'encounter' in *Method in Theology*: 119, 136, 168, 170, 232, 247. The term in our present sense comes into prominence in the 1963 lectures at Gonzaga University, Spokane ('Knowledge and Learning,' 15–26 July 1973, unpublished), when the subtopic is mutual self-mediation.

30 'On the Aristotelian notion of science, science could be a habit in the mind of a man, and its principles could be logical premises. On the modern notion, science is the cumulative product of a scientific community' (Lonergan's 1974 article, 'Moral Theology and the Human Sciences,' published in *METHOD: Journal of Lonergan Studies* 15/1 [1997] 11 [*Papers 1965–1980* (2004) 306], with a reference to Thomas Kuhn on this point. See also the 1976 article 'Questionnaire on Philosophy,' ibid., 2/2 [1984] 4–5 [*Papers 1965–1980* (2004) 356], for the same point with the same reference to Kuhn).

31 'Philosophy and the Religious Phenomenon,' *METHOD: Journal of Lonergan Studies* 12/2 (1994) 137–38 [*Papers 1965–1980* (2004) 403].

The word 'test' is to be taken literally. Encounter is more than the first three functional specialties of research, interpretation, and history.

> It is meeting persons, appreciating the values they represent, criticizing their defects, and allowing one's living to be challenged at its very roots by their words and by their deeds. Moreover, such an encounter is not just an optional addition to interpretation and to history. Interpretation depends on one's self-understanding; the history one writes depends on one's horizon; and encounter is the one way in which self-understanding and horizon can be put to the test.[32]

The phrase 'one way' is also to be taken seriously and in an exclusive sense: its occurrence here is not an isolated case.[33] Further, it has some analogy to a standard procedure in empirical science.

> Such an objectification of subjectivity is in the style of the crucial experiment. While it will not be automatically efficacious, it will provide the open-minded, the serious, the sincere with the occasion to ask themselves some basic questions, first, about others but eventually, even about themselves. It will make conversion a topic and thereby promote it.[34]

We are at the heart of the question: we change, we grow, we develop, we become, our moral sense (to take the obvious example) is refined.[35] Most of our remote ancestors saw nothing wrong in the practice of slavery. Then someone, somewhere, at some time achieved a new understanding of human dignity and human rights; the cause of abolition of slavery became 'connatural' to that person; and from this as a center it

---

32 *Method in Theology* 247.

33 See also the Question Sessions of the Boston College Lonergan Workshop of 1976 (p. 24 of the transcript). How resolve the question of value judgments? 'Dialectic ... solves it in the only way in which it can be viz. dialogue.'

34 *Method in Theology* 253.

35 It is quite illuminating to trace Lonergan's references in *Method in Theology* to refinement of feelings and the moral sense. 32: 'feelings are enriched and refined'; 38: 'moral feelings have to be cultivated ... refined'; 39: 'growth ... knowledge ... increasing in extent ... refinement'; 40: 'Such judgments [of value] ... attain ... their clarity and refinement, only through ... development'; 240: 'As ... our responses to human values are strengthened and refined'; 289: 'the illuminative way in which one's discernment of values is refined'; 320: 'I ... suggest that ... the refinement of human feelings is the area to be explored.'

spread through the civilized world. Today abhorrence of slavery is 'connatural' to most of the human race.[36] But this is a cognitive position; it has a why; reasons can be given for it. Further, the reasons reduce to a first principle which really is first and is grasped as such by those with a refined moral sense. Finally, such refinement is not a cultic secret. It is something we can all learn, nor will anyone reach foundations without such learning. We do indeed arrive at something close to the Thomist position on the role of the wise, but the new wisdom has become a methodical human achievement and is a possession of the community.

When we turn to the role of history in our question, we examine from another angle a relationship we already noticed in discussing witnesses to interiority. Our new approach is concerned less with witness than with communication, encounter, dialectic, dialogue. Of course, those terms have a somewhat different sense when we deal with figures of the past: dialogue with Augustine is necessarily one-sided. Still, besides the dialectic of intersubjectivity among contemporaries there is what we might call the dialectic of intersubjectivity across the centuries, and it has a decisive role to play.

A passage just quoted gives us the lead: there is 'the short run' and there is 'the long run.' If the short run is more a matter of forming clear battle-lines in the present, the long run, especially when it becomes the very long run of centuries, eventually brings about the consensus of the authentic and 'the reduction of the opposition to the hard-line dogmatists that defend an inadequate method no matter what its deficiencies.' The human race does not learn overnight to abhor slavery, or child labor, or genocide, or the oppression of women, or capital punishment.

Thus the final word is given by the experiment of history,[37] and our input to this vast experiment is simply to show how Lonergan aligns himself with the development of the last two centuries.

---

36 To be noted is the fact that results are not guaranteed: the method is not 'automatically efficacious'; we are dealing with people, not robots. A while back I asked, If objective arguments will not work, what then will work? It is clear now that the question is not well put. I am reminded of an exchange in which X said to Y, 'I tried your suggestion and it didn't work.' To which Y replied, 'Among other things, your grammar is wrong. What you mean is that you tried my suggestion and you didn't work!'

37 The idea of the experiment of history had a deep appeal for Lonergan. See the *Collected Works* edition of *Insight* (1992) 779, editorial note *c*. It reveals the great chasm between the dialectical manner of proceeding and the way of a conclusions theology.

> [T]he nineteenth and twentieth centuries have witnessed a series of attempts to get beyond Kant and, in one way or another, these attempts have consisted in an insistence on the subject to offset and compensate for Kant's excessive attention to sensible objects. This was already apparent in the absolute idealisms of Fichte, Schelling, and Hegel. It took a more personal form with Kierkegaard's emphasis on the contingently existing subject and with the emphasis on will in Schopenhauer and Nietzsche. The phenomenological studies of intersubjectivity by Edmund Husserl and Max Scheler and the various forms of existentialism have set up against the objectivist world of impersonal science a not-to-be-objectified inner world of subjects striving for authenticity.[38]

The turn to the subject that the dialectic of history has brought about is the context for Lonergan's view of foundations. We began with Aristotle's series of questions that take us back and back till we come to rest in a beginning. But what kind of rest and what kind of beginning? It cannot be just another unit in the series, something in the same genre but more remote. That way there is no escape that I can see from Hans Albert's trilemma.[39] We may contend that self-evident propositions are another genre that free us from the trilemma, but a proposition has no 'self' to deal with 'evidence.' The only real 'self' is that of the subject examining the proposition, and there we run into the many selves that interpret the proposition in many different ways.

It becomes necessary then to examine that examining subject, but this requires us to shift the gears of thought in a radical way, to examine not only the proposition but the person uttering the proposition. The relevant person is in the first instance myself, but that is a lonely self indeed, and in the last analysis we are led to test our personal mindset in the arena of dialogue. We find a very modern use of Augustine's old adage, 'Securus iudicat orbis terrarum': when the whole world agrees you can trust its judgment.[40]

---

38 'Natural Knowledge of God,' in *A Second Collection* 122–23.

39 See note 3 above. What does the authentic critic of foundations do with such a block in the path of philosophy? Just give up philosophy as a department of knowledge? That is the escape of some very eminent thinkers, as I gather from John Verhaar, 'Quel sens au postmodernisme?' (*Etudes* 380 [March 1994] 367–73), and I myself see no other option. But I am departing here from my purpose, which has basically been to ascertain Lonergan's meaning, however much my sympathy with his position has led me beyond reporting to argument.

40 *Contra epistolam Parmeniani* III, 4, no. 24 (*Patrologia latina* 43, 101).

Augustine's security was that of the church's faith, but the security in question here is not so well-founded. It has only the foundation proper to any human enterprise. The results of dialogue will not be automatic; we cannot change ourselves or others in a mechanical way; there are no free rides on some logical automobile. We are content, for a start, with making conversion a topic. We grope toward a finish line, only to find that someone has moved the finish line a little farther ahead. We grow. And that word supplies the continuity between the Scholastic Lonergan dealing with the way to become wise, and the modern Lonergan dealing with people learning through dialogue.

There is another word still at a loose end. My title speaks of rhyme and reason, and I have yet to explain my choice of that word 'rhyme.' The choice of 'reason' for the objective side is clear enough, but what of 'rhyme' for the subjective? It is, true enough, a catchword with some value in announcing a coming lecture. Yet it is not wholly out of place as representing the subjective. We have seen the position of Thomas Aquinas on the judgments we make because of a certain connaturality or affinity that we have with the topic under discussion for judgment. 'Rhyme,' you could say, is the connaturality or affinity in verse of one sound with another, and so metaphorically it may perhaps stand for the connaturality and affinity of an attentive, intelligent, reasonable, responsible subject with an attentive, intelligent, reasonable, responsible objective position.

Chapter 19

For Inserting a New Question (26A) in the *Pars prima*[1]

Just over fifty years ago Bernard Lonergan finished his series of articles 'The Concept of *Verbum* in the Writings of St Thomas Aquinas';[2] and though his general thesis has made an impact on Thomist studies and been recognized in the wider academic world,[3] there are still many particular points to study and many implications of the main thesis to explore. The present article explores the meaning and implications of an intriguing statement Lonergan makes in the concluding pages of his study: 'Thus, the Augustinian psychological analogy makes trinitarian theology a prolongation of natural theology, a deeper insight into what God is ...'[4] I interpret this deeper insight as the discovery of a new divine attribute; and I will argue that discussion of this new divine attribute belongs between questions 26 and 27 of the *Pars prima*, where it functions as a new and unifying transition from the questions on God as one to the questions on God as three, so that questions 2 to 43, instead of being two treatises (God as one, God as three) can be seen as one treatise on God, with no jump to a new consideration at question 27.

To mark this proposal, I would insert a new question between the present question 26 and the present question 27, tentatively calling it

---

1 Previously published in *The Thomist* 64 (2000) 565–80.

2 'Verbum' (1946–49); *Verbum* (1967) [(1997)].

3 For example, Anthony Kenny, *Aquinas* (London: Oxford University Press, 1980) 83: 'The best book in English about Aquinas's philosophy of mind is Bernard Lonergan's *Verbum* ...'

4 *Verbum* (1967) 208 [(1997) 215]. Lonergan really meant this point to be taken seriously, for a little later on the same page he repeats it: 'the psychological analogy truly gives a deeper insight into what God is.'

question 26A. I will first show the opening Thomas leaves for an insertion here, then set forth the relevant human perfection uncovered by Lonergan, transfer it in the usual way of analogy to a divine attribute, and conclude with brief reflections on repercussions this proposal may have on our doctrine of God.

1 The Thomist Order of the *Pars prima*

The grand sweep of Thomas's master plan for his *Summa theologiae* has been a fertile field for Thomist exegesis. It is not part of my commitment to study the literature on this, but I may mention by way of example the justifiably famous analysis proposed by M.-D. Chenu. He saw the whole *Summa* under the heading of an 'émanation et ... retour ... la *Ia Pars* et la *IIa Pars* sont entre elles comme *exitus* et ... *reditus* ... deux branches de la courbe qui, partant de Dieu, ramène tout à lui,' with Part III figuring as the means God chose for that return.[5] The rationale of this division is of the highest interest to Thomists, but it has no immediate reference to our present question. If we turn now to Thomas himself, we find that within the *Pars prima* there is an introductory question on *sacra doctrina,* after which Thomas unfolds his plan, laid out according to the intention of this *sacra doctrina,* namely, 'to discuss [our] knowledge of God, and not only as he is in himself, but also as he is the cause of [created] things and their final end.'[6] The treatise on God 'as he is in himself' covers questions 2 to 43, and that on God as principle of creation, the rest of the *Pars prima.* Once more the rationale of this division has no immediate reference to our topic.

But now within the treatise on God 'as he is in himself' we come to a division and order that is highly relevant to our topic. Thomas divides this section to consider, first, 'those things that pertain to the divine essence' – questions 2 to 26, and then 'those things that pertain to the distinction of persons' – questions 27 to 43.[7]

---

5 M.-D. Chenu, *Introduction à l'étude de saint Thomas d'Aquin,* 2nd ed. (Montreal: Institut d'études mediévales; Paris: J. Vrin, 1954) 266; and see pp. 260–64, also 266–73 which are devoted to 'La construction de la Somme.'

6 Prologue to question 2: 'Dei cognitionem tradere, et non solum secundum quod in se est, sed etiam secundum quod est principium rerum et finis earum.'

7 Ibid.: 'ea quae ad essentiam divinam pertinent' and 'ea quae pertinent ad distinctionem personarum.' Note that Thomas regards the whole *Pars prima* as a treatise on God, setting it in contradistinction to the treatise 'de motu rationalis creaturae in

The twenty-five questions from 2 to 26 consider such matters as God's existence, perfection, goodness, infinity, eternity, unity, knowledge, will, power – I select some well-known ones by way of illustration only. Then, with question 27 Thomas begins to treat 'of those things which pertain to the trinity of persons in divinity'; and because the persons are distinguished according to origin, he will treat first the question of origin or procession, then that of relations, and thirdly that of persons,[8] before going on to the many questions that arise in regard to individual persons, the comparison of persons, and so on.[9] In this way Thomas came to his first trinitarian question, 'whether there is procession in God.'[10]

Now I believe Thomas has left an opening here for a new question, for he makes the transition from the divine essence (questions 2 to 26) to the Trinity (questions 27 to 43) without assigning grounds for that transition, and indeed without assigning grounds for this order of the treatises. Of course, Thomas has reasons for his procedure. That God is one and God is three is part of his faith, so he must consider both. Further, if you consider two things, there must be an order of one after the other; and he chooses to take essence first and distinction of persons second. Nothing could be simpler. The Thomist order is perfectly normal. But it is an ordering of our beliefs, not an ordering according to theological reasons. We believe God to be one and we believe God to be three, and we have reasons for each of these beliefs; but that does not give us a theological reason for the order of the *Pars prima*. Why, for example, do we not begin with the triune God and proceed in the second place to the unitary God? One might well argue that the triune God has a stronger claim than the unitary to be basic in our concepts.

In any case, since Thomas is writing according to a reasoned series,

---

Deum' (on the movement of a rational creature to God), covered in *Pars secunda* (ibid.). Also that the treatise on God is 'tripartita' (ibid.), including as its third part a treatise on 'ea quae pertinent ad processum creaturarum ab ipso' (those things which pertain to the procession of creatures from him – questions 44 to 119) – again a division that touches our question only because the procession of creatures *from* God could be seen by analogy as continuous with the processions of Son and Spirit *internal to* God.

8 Prologue to question 27: 'de his quae pertinent ad trinitatem personarum in divinis.'

9 Prologue to question 29.

10 Q. 27, a. 1, prologue: 'Utrum processio sit in divinis.'

'according to the order of teaching,'[11] there seems to be need and room here to give a theological justification of the order, whatever it be, that we happen to choose. Can we justify the Thomist order, starting with the divine essence and turning from a treatise on God as one to a treatise on God as three? It will be part of my contention that by assigning a new attribute to the divine essence we can do just that: give a rationale for the order Thomas uses, justify his transition from questions *de Deo uno* to questions *de Deo trino*, and see that transition less as a transition and more as a link to make one integral treatise out of two.

There is, however, a real oddity in the role of question 26 in the Thomist 'plan' which must be mentioned here, though what relation it may have to our topic is not clear. The oddity is that Thomas twice rounds off the questions that pertain to the unity of the divine essence, as if ready in each case to proceed to the distinction of persons, but in the first of these transitions turns, not to the distinction of persons, but to a question on divine beatitude. Thus in his prologue to question 26 he says the following: 'Finally, after considering those things that pertain to the unity of the divine essence we have to consider ...' Surely, we think, he means to turn now to the distinction of persons. Not so. His topic is beatitude: after considering what pertains to the unity of God 'we have to consider the divine beatitude.'[12] As if beatitude did not pertain to the divine essence! Then, in the prologue to question 27, he again rounds off the questions pertaining to the divine unity, and this time proceeds to trinitarian questions: 'Having considered the things that pertain to the unity of the divine essence, it remains ...' and comes now to the Trinity: it remains 'to consider the things that pertain to the trinity of persons in God.'[13]

The perplexity is compounded by the further oddity that the question on beatitude is not announced in any of the carefully drawn plans of the *Pars prima*, nor is any rationale for its inclusion given in question 26 itself.[14] It seems to be an afterthought of Thomas, but even so we would

---

11 Prologue to *Summa* and to the *Pars prima*: 'secundum ordinem disciplinae.'

12 Prologue to question 26: 'Ultimo autem, post considerationem eorum quae ad divinae essentiae unitatem pertinent, considerandum est de divina beatitudine.'

13 Prologue to question 27: 'Consideratis autem his quae ad divinae essentiae unitatem pertinent, restat considerare de his quae pertinent ad trinitatem personarum in divinis.'

14 The oddity continues in that Cajetan, in his commentary published with the Leonine edition of Thomas, does not advert to the problem.

expect his 'Finally' sentence to read, 'Finally, among those things that pertain to the unity of the divine essence we have to consider beatitude.' I remarked that this oddity has no special significance for our topic, but it does prompt the question whether Thomas felt the need of some transitional idea from God as one to God as three.[15]

2 A New Perfection of Human Spirit: Rational Consciousness

The contention of this article is that Lonergan's *Verbum* study uncovers a new human perfection, that this suggests a new attribute under which to consider the divine essence, that this new attribute affects quite radically the Thomist transition from question 26 to question 27, and that notable clarifications of general trinitarian questions result as byproducts. I proceed now to the first of these claims.

What I am calling here a new human perfection needs its own name. Lonergan, after the example of Aquinas, is more concerned with meaning than with words,[16] so the term he uses here is 'rationality,' and the new divine attribute would be the rationality of God. The connotations of this term make it less than happy as a concept for the divine, and in fact Lonergan does not seem to have used it for God. It is ambiguous even for human psychology; for what Lonergan proposes is not some generic rationality but a quite specific one and, though he later names it more specifically 'reflective rationality,'[17] the term 'reflective' is also

---

15 This is the kind of question without data that encourages guessing, a quite harmless pastime as long as we know we are guessing. Here is one guess. The *Pars prima secundae*, dealing with our 'reditus' to God, begins with our last end, which is beatitude. Did Thomas, on writing this part, realize 'But I said nothing about beatitude in God,' and so go back to insert question 26 in the *Pars prima* without tidying up the details of the prologues outlining his plan?

16 For some data on this, see *Verbum* (1967) 106 [(1997) 115]: 'so far was Aquinas from the stereotyped terminology that sometimes is attributed to him that he could write "a wise person is not fussy about words"' (Aquinas, *Super II Sententiarum*, d. 3, q. 1, a. 1 sol.: 'sapientis enim est non curare de nominibus'). See also *Verbum* (1967) 118, 122 [(1997) 127, 130]. The whole of chapter 3, 'Procession and Related Notions,' is worth reading for perspective on terminology. See also *Grace and Freedom* (2000) 146: 'as if to insist upon meaning and to contemn terminological primness'; also page 72.

17 *Verbum* (1967) 199 [(1997) 207]. We avoid giving the word 'reflective' the sense of a second act supervening on direct understanding and knowledge; it means rather that reflection in a special sense is internal to every procession of a word in us; it means the same as the 'because of' character of our inner words.

in need of explanation and further specification. Let us not cavil, however, about the term, but look to the meaning as it emerges in Lonergan's explanation, first in abbreviated form, then at greater length.

The brief explanation runs as follows: 'To introduce a term that will summarize all this, we may say that the inner word is rational, not indeed with the derived rationality of discourse, of reasoning from premises to conclusions, but with the basic and essential rationality of rational consciousness, with the rationality that can be discerned in any judgment, with the rationality that now we have to observe in all concepts.'[18] This makes the point positively and negatively, but it *is* somewhat cryptic, an abbreviation, introducing 'a term that will summarize'; so we must turn to the full explanation as given in *Verbum*.

The proximate context and occasion for the *Verbum* study was the need, as Lonergan saw it, to overcome the conceptualism that afflicted much of Thomistic exegesis: the disposition, namely, to take concepts for granted as a basic given, to compare the concepts in judgments, and to compare the judgments in syllogisms, and only secondly to search for understanding. For Lonergan this represents a blackout of the whole rich universe of insights that are the fertile source of concepts, and an oversight of the intelligible procession of concepts (and judgments and syllogisms) from an act of understanding. Instead of that rich universe bequeathed to us by Aristotle and Aquinas, and the intelligible procession of concepts which was added by Aquinas, we have what Lonergan rather caustically describes as a 'metaphysical sausage machine, at one end slicing species off phantasm, and at the other popping out concepts' – a poor substitute for what he sees as 'an operation of rational consciousness.'[19]

To this negating element there must be added the positive side. We have to pin down this 'basic and essential rationality of rational consciousness,' this 'operation of rational consciousness.' Lonergan does this by contrast with natural process, the process, say, of heating: 'The intelligibility of natural process is passive and potential ... but it is not the very stuff of intellect.' Or, if we turn to the laws by which we understand natural process, we find that they have 'the intelligibility of some specific natural law ... but never the intelligibility of the very idea of intelligible law.' Even then, 'the intelligibility of natural

18 Ibid. (1967) 34 [(1997) 47].
19 Ibid. (1967) 34 [(1997) 48].

process is imposed from without; natures act intelligibly,' but not intelligently.

On all three of these points Lonergan contrasts the intelligibility of the procession of an inner word.

> [T]he intelligibility of the procession of an inner word is not passive nor potential; it is active and actual ... [I]t is intelligible, not as the possible object of understanding is intelligible, but as understanding itself and the activity of understanding is intelligible. Again, its intelligibility defies formulation in any specific law ... [It] is the pure case of intelligible law ... Thirdly, it is native and natural for the procession of inner word to be intelligible, actively intelligible, and the genus of all intelligible process ... intelligence in act does not follow laws imposed from without, but rather it is the ground of the intelligibility in act of law, it is constitutive and, as it were, creative of law; and the laws of intelligible procession of an inner word are not any particular laws but the general constituents of any law ...
>
> ... [A]n inner word not merely has a sufficient ground in the act of understanding it expresses; it also has a knowing as sufficient ground, and that ground is operative precisely as a knowing, knowing itself to be sufficient.[20]

With this Lonergan comes to the short form of his key statement, already quoted: 'To introduce a term that will summarize all this, we may say that the inner word is rational, not indeed with the derived rationality of discourse, of reasoning from premises to conclusions, but with the basic and essential rationality of rational consciousness ...'

This amounts to saying we have discovered a new perfection of human spirit and human consciousness: a new perfection, we might add, that borrows the use of an old name. But there is a hint of where we might find a new name, for later Lonergan adds a contrast between 'caused by' and 'because of,' a way of putting it that might be converted into a better name than rationality.

> [I]nner words do not proceed with mere natural spontaneity as any effect does from any cause; they proceed with reflective rationality ... not merely from a sufficient cause but from sufficient grounds known to be sufficient

20 Ibid. (1967) 33–34 [(1997) 47].

> and because they are known to be sufficient ... The inner word of defining is not only *caused by* but also *because of* the act of understanding.[21]

Thus this 'basic and essential rationality of rational consciousness,' this 'operation of rational consciousness' has to do with internal process. It is a process within intelligence. It is an intelligible process; more, it is an intelligent process. It is a process from knowledge to knowledge, from knowledge as insight, as perfection, as insight into a particular phantasm, to knowledge as the expression of the insight, knowledge as conceived, objectified, made universal. It has a 'because of' character. It is a 'because of' intrinsically in itself and not just as seen in an object. We could call it a 'because-of-ness,' were not that phrase such a mouthful in English.

My own preferred term for this perfection is 'ipsum quia' (a little shorter in the Latin than 'because-of-ness-itself'!) coined on the pattern of 'ipsum intelligere' (understanding itself, the very essence of understanding) and 'ipsum amare' (loving itself, the very essence of loving), where 'quia' has the same essential dynamism as 'intelligere' and 'amare,' and adds the new dynamism of 'from ... to': it is the 'because of' linking 'from X' and 'to Y.' If the form 'ipsum quia' suggests a divine attribute in parity with 'ipsum intelligere' and 'ipsum amare,' that is all to the good, because I propose it as a divine essential dynamism, as pertaining to the essence of the one God, and as a better name for the new attribute than the rather infelicitous 'rationality,' even if we convert the latter to 'rationality itself.'

I have so far avoided the Latin term *emanatio intelligibilis* (intelligible emanation), though it figures so prominently in Lonergan's thought. This very Thomist phrase is the carrier for his exposition of rationality, but it is a problem to many. The great Karl Rahner is said to have been puzzled by Lonergan's use of it, and to have asked someone supposedly in the know, 'What does he mean by *emanatio intelligibilis*?' It is useful to adduce this item of news, coming to us by the academic grape-vine but apparently authentic, for it suggests that *emanatio intelligibilis* is not part of the stock-in-trade of current Thomism and that it

21 Ibid. (1967) 199 [(1997) 207]; see 213 (220): '... thought because of understanding, and love because of both, where 'because' means not the logical relation between propositions but the real *processio intelligibilis* of an intellectual substance.'

may have a meaning not yet widely recovered in our 'traditional' interpretation of Thomas.

The term, then, though not frequent in Thomas, is definitely Thomist; and the core purpose of Lonergan's *Verbum* articles was to recover the idea Thomas had of it,[22] which is simply another way of stating what we have already said, namely, that his purpose was to overcome a conceptualism that had no room for an *emanatio intelligibilis. Emanatio intelligibilis* is, in fact, the complete antithesis of that 'metaphysical sausage machine' mentioned above.

In any case the phrase is definitely a key to Thomas's trinitarian thought. In the very first article of his trinitarian questions in the *Pars prima,* he lists and sets aside various modes of procession to arrive at *emanatio intelligibilis* as the only procession that elucidates our faith in the divine Word: 'Procession [in God] is not then to be understood the way it occurs in the corporeal world, either through local motion or through the action of some cause to produce an external effect, as heat [proceeds] from the heater to the heated, but is to be understood as intelligible emanation, as of an intelligible word from the speaker.'[23]

Further, in the justly famous treatment in book 4 of the *Contra Gentiles* Thomas goes through in far greater detail a similar series of emanations that are to be set aside in order to conclude: 'It remains therefore that divine generation is to be understood as intellectual emanation.'[24] The occurrence of the phrase in these two key loci for Thomist trinitarian doctrine cannot but be significant for the meaning Thomas attached to the phrase. As for the meaning it has for Lonergan, it is simply a Latin form of 'basic and essential rationality of rational consciousness,' or of the 'operation of rational consciousness.'

---

22 Ibid. (1967) 215 [(1997) 222]: 'my purpose has been to understand what Aquinas meant by the intelligible procession of an inner word.' The focused treatment is *Verbum* (1967) 33–45 [(1997) 46–59]; pp. 198–201 (206–208) list the equivalent phrases, of which the preferred one seems to be *processio intelligibilis*. However, it looks as if Thomas himself did not use the term *emanatio intelligibilis* frequently, and this may account for our neglect of it.

23 *Summa theologiae* 1, q, 27, a. 1 c. ad fin.: 'Non ergo accipienda est processio secundum quod est in corporalibus vel per modum localem, vel per actionem alicuius causae in exteriorem effectum, ut calor a calefaciente in calefactum, sed secundum emanationem intelligibilem, utpote verbi intelligibilis a dicente.'

24 *Summa contra Gentiles* 4, c. 1 (paragraph 8 in the Leonine manual edition, ad fin.): 'Relinquitur igitur quod generatio divina secundum intellectualem emanationem sit intelligenda.'

Now we need another step before we proceed to speak of 'reflective rationality' or 'ipsum quia' as an attribute of God. This rationality has an aspect we may call generic in the sense that it applies to the procession of both concept and judgment in us (these are one in the procession of God's one Word) and to the procession of love as well. We may call it transcendental in the sense not only that it is not limited to any one of these three occurrences, but also in the sense that it is an attribute of consciousness and the condition of possibility of any of the occurrences.[25]

This, I believe, is of some importance for our transfer of the human attribute to God. I would illustrate it by a parallel in Lonergan's position on what may be called the transcendental character of 'is.' 'Is,' Lonergan says,[26] may be thought of in two ways. First, it may be viewed as contrasted with 'was' and with 'will be.' But there is a second way to think of it, a way in which 'is' is not contrasted with 'was' or 'will be,' a way rather which finds a common and fundamental reference to being in all three. There is an aspect of 'is' that underlies its use in the three temporal meanings and prescinds altogether from temporal connotations. If we get hold of the aspect which is common to all three, which underlies all three, which pervades all three, which does not include a reference to time, we will have a radical sense of 'is' – and, I have argued elsewhere, a radical new meaning for eternal life and eternal being.[27] In a similar way, I would argue now, there is a 'because of' character that pertains to the dynamism of the human mind in a way that is prior to all particular instances of rational consciousness, and so provides an analogy for the divine dynamism where we conceive 'ipsum quia' as an essential divine attribute and as in our thinking prior to and grounding the two trinitarian processions.

25 For Lonergan's use of 'transcendental': *A Second Collection* 207, 'in the Scholastic sense (it is not confined to any particular genus or category ...) and in the Kantian sense (it is the condition of possibility ... of any categorial method).' *A Third Collection* 145, n. 8: 'three meanings ... the most general ... concepts ... of the Scholastics; the Kantian conditions of the possibility of knowing an object *a priori*; Husserl's intentionality analysis in which ... act and object, are correlative'; and see pp. 82–83.

26 Bernard Lonergan, *De scientia atque voluntate Dei: Supplementum schematicum*, unpublished notes for students of the course *De praedestinatione*, College of Christ the King (now Regis College), Toronto, March 1950, caput 3.

27 Frederick E. Crowe, 'Complacency and Concern in the Risen Life,' *Lonergan Workshop* 13 (1997) 18–19. For the original presentation of this idea, see Crowe, 'Rethinking Eternal Life: Philosophical Notions from Lonergan,' *Science et Esprit* 45 (1993) 25–39.

3 A New Attribute of the Divine Essence: *Ipsum Quia*

Our human word is not only caused by an insight; it is also consciously 'because of' the insight; and while the ontological 'caused by' is irrelevant to trinitarian theology,[28] the cognitional 'because of,' as a property and perfection of the human, provides the possibility of analogous understanding of *ipsum quia* as a divine attribute. There is in God not only the procession of an inner Word and the procession of inner Love, and so three divine persons. There is also in the divine essence a radical dynamism that has the character of 'because of,' that can be named 'ipsum quia,' that in our human thinking is the ground of the processions of Word and Love, that is a divine fermentation such that those processions can be.

It is this rationality, conceived as a human perfection and therefore as pertaining in the 'via eminentiae' (the way of eminence) to the being and essence of God, that we have now to study in its divine form. An indirect and preparatory step is to open our minds to the concept and possibility of an internal infinite and eternal dynamism in God. Here I draw on a Thomist professor (from Toronto's Pontifical Institute of Mediaeval Studies, I believe, but I am dependent on my unreliable memories of fifty years ago). To overcome the appearance of the 'static' in the divine 'is,' an appearance of the static that we too readily attach to 'is' used as a copula, he proposed that when we say 'God is,' we think of God as 'is-ing.' It is a striking expression, and though it is not directly relevant to the concept of 'rationality' in God, it can play a supportive role, I believe, in our conception of rationality as a divine dynamic and eternal perfection.

To come directly now to our own point I would first conceive this new attribute in its purest form, in its most generic aspect, by simply saying that God is 'such' as to have in the divine essence an attribute that underlies our human concept of the divine processions. That, I believe, would readily be conceded, for it is little more than an analytic proposition: there are processions internal to God, therefore the being

28 With the mature Thomas we avoid saying the Word is 'caused by' the Father's 'dicere,' or that proceeding Love, the welling forth of Love, is 'caused by' the Utterance and the Word. Though Thomas did speak of the proceeding person as being produced (*Summa theologiae* 1, q. 37, a. 2 ad 3m), this is not characteristic of his language; see *Verbum* (1967) 196, 198–99 [(1997) 204, 206].

of God is such as to have internal processions. We first conceive this divine attribute, then, simply as a 'suchness': God is 'such' as to have two internal processions. At this 'abstract' stage we already have an attribute of the divine essence conceived in relationship to the divine processions, and so the possibility of an ordered transition from question 26 to question 27 of the *Pars prima*, and a quite natural transition from a treatise *De Deo uno* to a treatise *De Deo trino*.

It is desirable, however, to conceive this 'suchness' in a more concrete way; for as yet we have little positive content for our new question 26A, and could propose the question in Thomist form only as 'Whether God is such as to be able to have internal processions' (Utrum Deus sit talis ut possit habere processiones internas). For that more positive understanding I call again on the brilliant passage in Thomas already referred to, that we can use as a springboard to our conception. For his trinitarian theology in the *Contra Gentiles* he sets up a series of higher and higher emanations in which principle and term come closer and closer to identity, while the emanation remains and, we may even say, grows in perfection. A baseball proceeds (emanates) from the bat of the batter, and is totally extrinsic to the bat. A plant proceeds from a seed, and is also extrinsic to the seed; still, the process began within the principle of the emanation, inasmuch as the seed was formed there. We take a further step with an animal, in which the image proceeds from the sensation, and is extrinsic to it, since at this level of life sensitive potency does not reflect on itself; still, both principle and term are now internal to the animal: they are now more nearly one. But then we come to the life of intellect, which is able to reflect on itself, so that the principle and term approach identity – less perfectly in human intelligence, since the process starts outside in the object sensed; more perfectly in the angel, in whom the process is totally internal; and with absolute perfection in God, in whom principle and term are perfectly one in being.[29]

Here we have a series of the same type as that which Newman constructed for the approach of a polygon to a circle. Increase the number of sides in the polygon as much as you please: with each step you come closer to the circle; but you never reach the circle, you simply find a way to point to it.[30] In the same way Thomas, in this illuminating series

29 *Contra Gentiles* 4, c. 11, nos. 1–5.

30 John Henry Newman, *An Essay in Aid of a Grammar of Assent* (London: Longmans, Green and Co., 1930) 320–21.

of emanations in the *Contra Gentiles*, approaches ever more closely to the identity in being of Father and Son, while their distinction, signified and grounded by the emanation, is preserved untouched. The distinction of being is disappearing while the reality of the procession and the distinction of persons remain. The series points to its goal – reality of procession without difference in being – but cannot reach it except by analogy and the way of eminence.

We need a similar series to point to our goal of conceiving rationality, *ipsum quia*, without principle or term, a series that shows the *ipsum quia* to remain while the distinction of a term that is 'cognitional cause' and a term that is 'because of' vanishes. Could we simply take over and adapt the Thomist series? To a certain extent I believe that might be possible. For Thomas the task was to show the identity of being of principle and term of the emanation, while maintaining the reality of the emanation. Ours would be to show the identity of a divine rationality, the oneness of the 'because-of-ness' character of rational process, while maintaining the reality of the 'emanatio intelligibilis' and so the distinction of an antecedent and what is 'because of' that antecedent. Just as the Thomist sequence brings principle and term of an ontological process closer and closer together in one identical being (the context for Thomas is the divine generation of a Son, hence it has a clear ontological cast), so a focus on the rational side of the Thomist process would bring the rational 'cause' and the rational 'consequence' closer and closer to the identity of one rationality as an essential attribute, while maintaining the reality of the 'because of,' and so the distinction of the divine persons. Unfortunately, however, we would not be able to duplicate all the Thomist steps, for the material and sensitive emanations have no place in the world of 'because of.' We await another Thomas, then, to construct the series we need!

At the start of section 2 above, I proposed as a second step in our essay that this new attribute, *ipsum quia*, affects quite radically the Thomist transition from question 26 to question 27. We are ready now for that step, but it can be handled quite briefly. Our new question 26A, then, dealing with that new attribute, would at once assume a natural locus between question 26 and question 27 in the *Pars prima*. It would follow on question 26 as a new dynamic attribute follows on the more static attributes, though 'static' suggests a kind of inertia and is not a happy term for things divine. But clearly, and without unhappy connotations, the new attribute would take its place prior to question 27 and point to question 27. It really would provide the springboard to question 27 that is not explicit in the *Pars prima*. Thus questions 2 to 43 of the *Pars prima* would form one 'integral' treatise on one 'integral' God; God would be conceived by us the way that that God is, namely, as three in natural unity; and there would be nothing awkward in the transition from question 26 to question 27 of the Thomist treatise.[31]

4 Byproducts of the New Attribute

A first and obvious byproduct of inserting this new attribute into the *Pars prima* is the negative side of what I put more positively in speaking of a natural transition from question 26 to question 27. That is to say, to the charge that a treatise *De Deo uno* followed by a treatise *De Deo trino* divides our doctrine of God into two parts, I would claim that Lonergan's new and deeper insight gets the two parts back together again, so that we avoid the appearance of a somewhat arbitrary jump, or of bringing in a 'processio ex machina' in order to begin the trinitarian study. For the question of the processions has no 'ex machina' appearance now. Instead it arises quite naturally from the new concept we have of God. And thus the unitary God is linked naturally with the trinitarian God, the trinitarian God is continuous in human thought with the unitary God, and we have the Trinity emerging from within the nature of God instead of being considered in a separate set of questions.

Not that we conceive the processions as processions from the *ipsum quia*: that would be the *processio operationis* that Lonergan repudiates in favor of a *processio operati*.[32] But as a human mind has to think of the divine *ipsum intelligere* in two ways, as in the Father as *Dicens* and as in the Son as *Verbum*, so we have to think of the divine *ipsum quia* in two ways, as in the Father as in 'that because of which' and as in the Son as in the 'becaused' or the *emanans*.

In another byproduct, we avoid to some extent the impression inevitably formed by speaking of 'first, second, and third' persons. In the

31 We realize, of course, that Thomas did not number his questions; nevertheless the traditional numbering is sacrosanct and if a new question is to be introduced it has to be numbered 26A. An unwieldy alternative would be to modify question 27 somewhat to bring it back to include a question on the divine essence.

32 *Verbum* (1967) 198–99 [(1997) 205–206]. See the index of the book for several references to *processio operationis, processio operati* (procession of an operation, procession of a product of the operation).

imagination of the believer a 'first' person is somehow before and above and superior to the second and third persons: the 'first' person has *a se* something the other two 'receive' and would otherwise lack. In the new perspective all three are immediately related in our thinking to the 'because of' attribute, for it is an attribute of the divine essence. Of course, in the traditional conception, once the Trinity is conceived *in facto esse* (as already constituted), then all attributes are from the Father and are communicated to Son and Spirit. Thus, for example, the divine simplicity is communicated to Son and Spirit by the Father. So also, then, is *ipsum quia* communicated to Son and Spirit by the Father. But there is a difference. The communication of the divine simplicity from Father to Son is a notional act following on the Trinity as conceived *in facto esse.* On the other hand, the relation of *ipsum quia* to a possible procession is antecedent to the Trinity as conceived *in facto esse*: while our concept of the Trinity is still *in fieri* (as on the way to being constituted), the potential for an *emanatio intelligibilis* and so for the distinction of the Three is already intrinsic to the conception.[33] When the psychological analogy is set forth, the Father will still be seen as 'first,' and the Son and Spirit as 'second' and 'third'; but prior to the order of the psychological analogy there is the new attribute that potentially regards all three without assigning the order of first, second, and third.[34]

33 The importance of the two orders of our concepts of the Trinity, one *in fieri* and one *in facto esse,* is set forth by Lonergan, ibid. (1967) 206–209 [(1997) 213–16].

34 This is not the place to discuss the history of theological thought on the Trinity, but I may at least indicate the relevance of this essay to the controversy between those who consider Augustinian-Thomist thinking a decline from Cappadocian thought and those who consider it an advance.

Chapter 20

The Future: Charting the Unknown with Lonergan[1]

> We cannot chart the future ... Our course is in the night, our control is only rough and approximate. We have to believe and trust, to risk and dare.
>
> Bernard Lonergan, 10 October 1974[2]

In keeping with the theme of this workshop my question here began as a question about the future of Lonergan studies. That is still a major interest, but it is framed now by a general interest in the future. As the question became generalized, the attempt at an answer followed suit, and will be given only in the most general terms. That is no cause for apology, since students of Lonergan are supposed to be generalists,[3] but my audience should be warned that I have no details on tomorrow's weather, no tip on the stock market. My means are likewise general. I have no crystal ball or pack of cards to help me: I rely on a study

1 Originally presented at the 27th annual Lonergan Workshop, Boston College, 12–16 June 2000, where the general theme was 'Looking Ahead: Lonergan for the 21st Century.' (The ideas in this essay first began to emerge in a panel discussion at the June 1996 Lonergan Workshop. They were developed into a lecture for a Lonergan Weekend in Vancouver in October of that year. The essay approached its present form in a presentation to the Lonergan Research Institute Seminar, Toronto, in October 1998. Its style shows its relation to a live audience.) Previously published in *Lonergan Workshop* 17 (2002) 1–21.

2 See 'Self-Transcendence: Intellectual, Moral, Religious,' a public lecture at Hobart and William Smith Colleges, Geneva, NY, 10 October 1974, p. 4 of the first draft of a transcription by Marcela Dayao of the tape-recording. Published in *Papers 1965–1980* (2004) 313–31; see 315.

3 'Questionnaire on Philosophy,' *METHOD: Journal of Lonergan Studies* 2/2 (1984) 32 (*Papers 1965–1980* [2004] 382).

of what it is to be human. My interest moreover is sober: I am less interested in what will be overthrown in the next revolution than in what will endure. In brief, don't expect too much.

The title of the paper suggests the order of its parts. It aims at tracing a faint trail in the unknown area of the future, and it would take Lonergan as a guide on the journey. This supposes a certain view of the relevant features in his work. So, on the good Thomist principle that what is last in intention is first in execution, my first part will attempt an overall view of Lonergan's work; my second will sketch his views on past history as context for the 'history' of the future; and my third section will venture into that unknown area.

1 'Instant' Lonergan: An Overall View

To offer an overall view of Lonergan's thought sounds like a threat. Will it include all that has been said in these workshops since 1974? Be not afraid. For present purposes I offer an 'instant' Lonergan: a pair of headings that are comprehensive in intent but omit all details. I am told that one can put half of physics into seven typing spaces: $E = mc^2$. I present a formula like that for my overall view of Lonergan.

The formula, then, states that there are two components in his thinking. There is the structural principle. This focuses on the invariant, the hard and fast, the fixed and determined. But there is also what we may call the historical principle, which is not invariant at all but subject to continual change, is not hard and fast but open to development or to decline, is not fixed and determined but insecure and precarious, does not provide some instant utopia but would lead the human race forward in a steady process of learning.

Lonergan himself provides support for this formula: 'A contemporary ontology,' he says, 'would distinguish two components in concrete human reality: on the one hand, a constant, human nature; on the other hand, a variable, human historicity. Nature is given man at birth. Historicity is what man makes of man.'[4] That is a statement in ontology. Transfer it from ontology to his work and thought, and you have my instant Lonergan.

Still, even an instant view may be allowed some expansion. I will expand my first principle very briefly, and my second at greater length.

---

4 'Natural Right and Historical Mindedness,' in *A Third Collection* 170.

The obvious illustration of the structural principle is the four levels of consciousness.[5] You have heard about those levels a dozen times, and it would bore you to tears to hear me go through them again. From my viewpoint it should bore you, as it should bore future generations: that's a position I'll take when I come to its future in part 3. So it needs no further discussion at the moment.

Next, the historical principle. The framework remains steady and becomes familiar with use, but what happens within the framework can be quite new and unfamiliar, infinitely various, infinitely rich, and very exciting. When I first worked on this talk, I happened to be reading an old book, *The Tales of Tchehov*.[6] The 'Introduction,' by Edward Garnett, speaks of Chekhov's 'picture of life's teeming freshness and fulness,' of the way he conveys 'a mysterious sense ... of life's ceaseless intricacy.' He points out how Chekhov's 'flexible and transparent method reproduces the pulse and beat of life, its pressure, its fluidity, its momentum, its rhythm and change ...'[7] This may not at first sound much like Lonergan. On reflection, however, and thinking of the two principles in our instant formula, we might agree that it is the perfect partner to his thought on history. Garnett says of history in artistic terms what Lonergan says of it in his more theoretic terms. It is the addition of history, with its endless variety, to structure; it is not the steady framework, it is what happens within the framework.

And what is it that happens? What happens is Homer singing of Ulysses, Plato writing his dialogues, Archimedes taking a bath, Augustine hearing the child say 'Take up and read.' Thomas Aquinas happens, and so does Dante, so does Isaac Newton. Jean Vanier establishes his L'Arche communities, while others climb Mount Everest or land on the moon or give their lives for the poor and oppressed of the third world. Well, you get the idea: in 'the pulse and beat of life' anything and everything and everybody happens.

Such endless variety cannot be handled the way the structural principle was. It needs more study, and that brings me to part 2.

---

5 For a quick view of levels 1 to 3, see chapter 9 of *Insight*. For level 4, add chapter 1 of *Method in Theology*.

6 *The Tales of Tchehov*, vol. 1: *The Darling and Other Stories*, trans. Constance Garnett (London: Chatto & Windus, 1925; original publication, 1916).

7 Ibid., 'Introduction' (pp. v–ix), by Edward Garnett.

2 The Historical Principle

First, a few clarifications. There are two senses of history: the history that happens, and the history that is written about those happenings. Again, there is Lonergan's personal history, and there is his thinking about history. And yet again, there are his views, and there is my interpretation of his views. Much more important, there is his view of history, and there is the objective history he discusses. However, I note at once that in my approach both elements of the latter distinction come to the same thing: if his views are valid, then objective history is what he claims it is; if his views are not valid, then my whole project collapses, and we'd better take a long coffee break before the next paper. Another point: the question regards history; therefore it studies transitions in time, not concepts in their supposed timelessness. Scholasticism is a concept and as such has a permanent place among ideas, but history asks how it arose, how it related to its past, where it was heading. Finally, I will speak continually in terms of time, past and future; yet 'history,' not time, is the central term: this is not an essay on time as a predicament, but on human activities in time – that is, on history.

I hope through these early clarifications to forestall a good deal of possible confusion. There may be some oscillation from idea to idea, as well as some overlapping in discussion; but the ideas are all quite simple, and the context will determine which of them is in question.

So we turn to Lonergan's historical principle, his counterpart to Chekhov's 'picture of life's teeming freshness and fulness,' his way of dealing with 'the pulse and beat of life, its pressure, its fluidity, its momentum, its rhythm and change ...'

2.1 The 'Essential' Lonergan

What is the role of history in Lonergan's thinking? I would claim that the need to understand history, basic history, the history that happens, is the chief dynamic element in all his academic work. From start to finish history is the pervasive theme: not insight, not method, not economics, not emergent probability, but history. I suggested something like that in this workshop a few years ago. The idea didn't exactly catch fire. Nevertheless I present it again. I will even call it the 'essential' Lonergan, and I will try to make a better case for it this time.

Any number of books use the word 'essential' in their title – *The*

Essential Augustine, The Essential Confucius, The Essential Darwin, for example. I suspect that most of them offer a selection of writings, and the selection is meant to convey the main ideas of a particular thinker. That is a legitimate use of 'essential' but it is not the usage here. I am not referring to a selection of writings; I am referring rather to the key to such a selection, and the key to someone's mind and life and works.

Notice that my 'essential Lonergan' is not the 'instant Lonergan' I began with. That was a miniature 'table of contents': it gave us two pegs to hang ideas on. It was a summarizing word, the term of a process of reduction. But my 'essential' describes a principle rather than a term. It is not a later summary of works, but the prior inspiration that would make the summary; and it can be a tacit influence even when it is not declared.

Think of it in terms of intentionality. What is the total intended goal of the total intending thought of Bernard Lonergan? What lies behind all his particular intendings, and all his achieved results? Behind all his labor to construct an organon, and all his efforts to apply it? He has taught us to recognize the intention of being latent in every concept.[8] I would claim that there is a similar intention of universal history latent in all his writings, even in the great *Insight* and *Method,* which function then, not as the goal, but as an organon to move him toward the goal. This, I submit, is the essential and characteristic Lonergan.

Can such a claim be proven? In a sense it doesn't need proof, for it just puts in other terms what we would all say, that Lonergan was concerned all his life with the real world: method, he would say, is not an end but a means; withdrawal is only for a return. But the real world is the world of people and what they do; and the sum total of what they do is their history. Of course, we study physics and chemistry and biology and the natural sciences generally, but mainly because and insofar as they are part of our human world.

My position then hardly needs argument. Nevertheless I will argue. Think of prospectors in search of precious minerals: they watch for outcroppings of a hidden lode. Our outcroppings are certain little phrases that keep popping up: 'the transition from feudal to bourgeois society';[9]

8 See *Verbum* (1967) 43–45 [(1997) 57–59].

9 'Prolegomena to the Study of the Emerging Religious Consciousness of Our Time,' in *A Third Collection* 65.

'systems on the move';[10] 'ongoing discovery of mind';[11] 'the emergence of ethical value';[12] the 'long transition from primitive fruit-gatherers, hunters, and fishers to the large-scale agriculture of the temple states';[13] 'from the compactness of the symbol to the differentiation of philosophic, scientific, theological, and historical consciousness';[14] 'how is there effected the transition from one level or stage in human culture to another later level or stage';[15] and so on, and so on.

'On the move,' 'ongoing,' 'transition,' 'emergence,' 'from ... to' – they are all outcroppings of a lode, signs of a mindset, pointers to the essential Lonergan. Aristotle and Aquinas say that character is manifested in sudden reactions to the unexpected, 'ex repentinis.'[16] These phrases have the same effect. They show us one whose second nature is to think in terms of change, development, history. They suggest the need to add to '*Insight* Revisited' a more comprehensive 'History, or Lonergan Revisited.'

Let's revisit him at least at the start and finish of his career. There is that letter of 1938 when he said to his religious superior that 'philosophy of history is as yet not recognised as the essential branch of philosophy that it is,' and asked for freedom to work on that needed branch.[17] Likewise in 1982 at the end of his career, in the last paper he gave, he was still deep into history: 'It is cultural change that has made Scholas-

---

10 *Insight* (1957) 536 [(1992) 559].

11 *Method in Theology* 305.

12 *Topics in Education* 38.

13 *Philosophy of God, and Theology* 2–3 (*Papers 1965–1980* [2004] 163).

14 *Topics in Education* 55.

15 'Questionnaire on Philosophy' 24 (*Papers 1965–1980* [2004] 375).

16 *Summa theologiae* 1-2, q. 109, a. 8: '... in repentinis homo operatur ... secundum habitum praeexistentem' (with a reference to Aristotle, *Ethica III*, c. 11, 1117a 18–22. See Thomas, *In III Ethicam*, lect. 17, no. 579: '... in repentinis homo non potest deliberare. Unde videtur operari ex interiori inclinatione, quae est secundum habitum.' Also *Summa theologiae* 2-2, q. 123, a. 9: '... in repentinis periculis maxime manifestatur fortitudinis habitus.'

17 Letter to Henry Keane, Provincial Superior, 10 August 1938, asking approval of his plan to maintain interest in the philosophy of history. I would note also the significance of the motto from Thomas Aquinas that he prefixed to his student essay of 1935, 'Pantôn Anakephalaiôsis' (*METHOD: Journal of Lonergan Studies* 9/2 [1991] 139–72, at 139). It is not the famous statement on insight into phantasm; it is Thomas on the development of human thinking (*Summa theologiae* 1, q. 85, a. 3).

ticism no longer relevant and demands the development of a new theological method and style, continuous indeed with the old, yet meeting all the genuine exigences both of Christian religion and of up-to-date philosophy, science, and scholarship.'[18] How many works can you find between 1938 and 1982 that do *not* include some reference to the transitions of history? I do not mean that you can find the word in every paragraph or even every chapter but, as an ascetic finds God in a multiplication table, so in Lonergan, at a deeper level in his spirit, the intention of history is always operative.

These pointers are only my build-up: his own statements clinch the matter. In his 1958 lectures on education he stated that 'reflection on history is one of the richest, profoundest, and most significant things there is. In the past few centuries any great movement has been historical in its inspiration and its formulation.'[19] Almost twenty years later he stated that 'to understand men and their institutions we have to study their history. For it is in history that man's making of man occurs, that it progresses and regresses, that through such changes there may be discerned a certain unity in an otherwise disconcerting multiplicity.'[20] He links the two great works of his organon to a theory of history: 'I have a general theory of history implicit in *Insight* and in *Method*.'[21] He sees it as explaining doctrinal development: 'the intelligibility proper to developing doctrines is the intelligibility immanent in

---

18 *A Third Collection*, in 'Unity and Plurality: The Coherence of Christian Truth' 247. And see the analyses of history here and there in that chapter: 244 on 'the issue ... transported from the fifth century to the thirteenth ... and to the twentieth'; 245 on the five steps in the great medieval task – Abelard, Gilbert of Porreta, the books of *Sentences*, commentaries on those books, and fifthly, Thomas Aquinas.

19 *Topics in Education* 233–34.

20 *A Third Collection*, in 'Natural Right and Historical Mindedness' at 171. He speaks (ibid.) of the German Historical School and 'its massive, ongoing effort to reveal, not man in the abstract, but mankind in its concrete self-realization.' Elsewhere ('Questionnaire on Philosophy' 15 [*Papers 1965–1980* (2004) 366]), urging us to live and operate on the level of the times, he says: 'To put it bluntly, until we move onto the level of historical dynamics, we shall face our secularist and atheist opponents, as the Red Indians, armed with bows and arrows, faced European muskets.'

21 Interview with Lonergan conducted by Eric O'Connor and Cathleen Going, 'Questions with Regard to Method: History and Economics,' in Cathleen M. Going, ed., *Dialogues in Celebration* (Montreal: Thomas More Institute, 1980) 305.

historical process.'[22] And he expressly relates his 1938 position to that of twenty-five years later.[23]

So much for the question *whether* it is a fact that history has a pervasive role in his mindset. Let us return to the question *what*. What are Lonergan's views on that history of the past which I hope to extend in part 3 into the 'history' of the future? I have three headings for this: the underlying structure of history; the possibility of history; and the actual transitions of history.

2.2 *The Underlying Structure of History*

One may ask: What is 'structure' doing here? At the very start we distinguished it from history. Why then does it intrude in this historical section? I might respond that it is a boundary question, overlapping both sides, but that would not explain much. Some explanation is needed, for the 'structure' of history ranks high in Lonergan's thinking – certainly one of his top ten ideas, if we play the 'top ten' game. His first title for the final chapter of *Insight* was 'The Structure of History,'[24] and we saw that he still thought that way in '*Insight* Revisited.'

It is structure, however, in a special sense, different from that of the four levels, so I call it the 'underlying' structure. It means the three factors of progress, decline, and redemption. That triad was worked out in the papers of 1937–38,[25] and it was never abandoned.[26] In a sense it belongs to the first part of my instant Lonergan, for it is not a matter of historical transitions, but a permanent and constitutive feature of human life, always operative in human affairs, a continual dialectic at work within the human subject: we are always at one and the same

---

22 *Method in Theology* 319.

23 See '*Insight* Revisited,' *A Second Collection* 271–72, where he tells of his work in 1937–38 and declares: 'The whole idea was presented in chapter twenty of *Insight*.'

24 In a table of contents sketched while he was writing the book, Archives, Batch 4, Folder 2.

25 File 713 of the Archives. For a study of these papers of the 1930s, see Michael Shute, *The Origins of Lonergan's Notion of the Dialectic of History: A Study of Lonergan's Early Writings on History* (Lanham-New York-London: University Press of America, 1993).

26 For a late declaration (1976) see 'Questionnaire on Philosophy' (*Papers 1965–1980* [2004] 383) 33: '... any attempt to introduce a new program of studies will find itself involved in the dialectic of progress, decline, and redemption.' Also *A Second Collection* in 'The Transition from a Classicist World-View to Historical-Mindedness' (written 1966) 6–7.

time making progress, falling into decline, and being renewed. In language much in use now, the three factors are synchronic: in the very act of making progress we may be guilty of hubris, and hubris from its first movement may be challenged by divine grace.[27]

Why then does Lonergan call it a structure of *history*? Maybe it was diachronic when he first worked it out, thinking the way theologians commonly thought of paradise, the fall, and redemption: there we have the succession of states that fits a history. When he later realized it was not a matter of transitions but synchronic, he kept the name 'history.' More likely, he thought of it as a special case of 'what was going forward,' to use his later terminology for history.[28] The structure really does carry human affairs forward, not in a historical succession of events, but in the ongoing dialectic of growth, and in that sense it belongs to history. In any case, I venture the view that this threefold structure is the philosophy of history of his letter to Father Henry Keane in 1938,[29] a philosophy that would, I think, be better named a theology of history.

2.3 *The Possibility of History*

My next heading is the possibility of history. On one occasion Lonergan distinguished possibility from potency; 'I would distinguish possibility as something conceptual and potency as something real.'[30] I'm not sure that he used the distinction very much himself, but it forces us to reflect on our usage. So I speak of real possibility. The conceptual possibility of history would lie, I suppose, in the ability to get our ideas straight and formulate a concept that at one remove intends being,

---

27 The synchronic point is made in *Topics in Education* 69: the three factors 'have been described in isolation; I considered first intellectual development, then sin, and finally redemption; but in the concrete all three function together. They are intertwined. They do not exist in isolation but they have to be described separately before they can be considered together.'

28 *Method in Theology* 178.

29 See note 17 above.

30 'Bernard Lonergan Responds,' in Philip McShane, ed., *Language Truth and Meaning* (Dublin: Gill and Macmillan, 1972) 311. But this distinction does not seem to have become a fixed usage: see Lonergan's thought on possibility in 'The Natural Desire to See God,' *Collection* (1967) 93–95 [(1988) 88–91]; also in 'A Note on Geometrical Possibility,' ibid. 107–13 (102–107); also *Insight* (1957) 337–38 [(1992) 361–62] and *Topics in Education* 256–57.

intends it in the way every concept does. But real possibility is fully concrete; it intends *this* being as potentially in *this* matter. Lonergan's term for that possibility is potentiality, so we have to talk about that.

Potentiality needs far more study than it gets. It is a sleeper word: it seems of little consequence but turns out to be quite fertile. Or call it another outcropping, for it keeps popping up like history itself, another sign of a rich mineral lode. Potentiality comes out of the past but heads directly into the future and is understood through its future. It means the future, it has no meaning of itself except with regard to the future. And it is infinite: infinite on the side of the physical world, infinite on the side of experience and potency to ideas, infinite on the side of the human world to be created by meaning and values. In view of Lonergan's work on economics in the evening of his life, it is most interesting that he sees that science as a link, maybe the chief link, between the merely material world and the world of human culture, joining the potentiality of one to the actuality of the other: 'between the potentialities of nature, whether physical, chemical, vegetal, animal or human, and on the other hand the standard of living, there is a gap to be bridged. ... some effort to make. Such an effort is termed *economic activity*.'[31]

The potentiality of the material world is for the human, but the potentiality of that human world is another infinity, going far beyond the field of economics. One may compare it, first, with the animal world: 'For the animals, safely sheathed in biological routines, are not questions to themselves. But man's artistry testifies to his freedom. As he can do, so he can be what he pleases.'[32] Then, in comparison with the world of the infant: 'The world of the infant is no bigger than the nursery, but the world of the adult extends from the present back to its past and forward to its future. It includes not only the factual but also the possible, the ideal, the normative.'[33] The infant world is the potentiality of that adult world.

We need to ponder that. Since this time a year ago a hundred million babies have been born into the world – the annual crop of barbarians, to

31 See Lonergan, *For a New Political Economy* [ed. P. McShane, *Collected Works of Bernard Lonergan*, vol. 21 (Toronto: University of Toronto Press, 1998)] 205–206. See also *A Third Collection*, in 'A Post-Hegelian Philosophy of Religion' 211: 'meaning is efficient ... We imagine, we plan, we investigate possibilities ... Over the world given us by nature, there is an artificial, man-made world.'

32 *Insight* (1957) 185 [(1992) 208–209].

33 *A Third Collection*, in 'A Post-Hegelian Philosophy of Religion' 211.

adapt Lonergan's striking phrase (borrowed maybe in part from Toynbee): 'The annual crop of infants is a potential invasion of barbarians, and education may be conceived as the first line of defense.'[34] They really were born as barbarians. But they are the future of the human race: *spem gregis,* in a phrase I dimly recall from my Latin studies. They have to be brought to the level of our world, which is a world mediated by meaning and motivated by value. Think of a hundred million adult barbarians, not helpless like infants in their cribs, but some adult Neanderthal race, really invading our world, meeting us face to face, with power to annihilate us: how might we bring them to our level? That's the problem Lonergan so often refers to as the socialization, acculturation, and education of new arrivals, the process of actuating the potentialities of our infant barbarians, of saving our future.

Here is the place to mention his view on the plasticity of the human infant. He compares the infinite potentiality of human offspring with the fixed patterns of the animal. Piaget's studies of his own children 'revealed that, if the human infant acquired slowly and laboriously what came to the animal cub spontaneously or at least rapidly, still the great advantage was on the side of the infant. The infant was slow because of its enormously greater plasticity, and it took longer because it learned immeasurably more.'[35]

There is another field in which potentiality plays a basic role: religion. Here we turn from infants to Feuerbach. Feuerbach saw religion as a projection of human qualities into an object of worship. Lonergan's answer is intriguing. The human quest 'is not mere quality but potentiality and finality; and it is potentiality and finality not confined

34 *Topics in Education* 59. On the process of socialization, acculturation, and education, see 119, 122, 156, 181, 197, 217.

35 *A Third Collection,* in 'Aquinas Today: Tradition and Innovation' 38. Also ibid. in 'Religious Experience' 119: 'Where the kitten or puppy is born with built-in instincts and skills, the human infant is born with a helplessness that leaves room for an indefinite plasticity.' And ibid. in 'Religious Knowledge' 133: 'In man ... there is an all but endless plasticity that permits the whole of our bodily reality to be fine-tuned to the beck and call' of the person. 'The agility of the acrobat, the endurance of the athlete, the fingers of the concert pianist, the tongue of those that speak and the ears of those who listen and the eyes of those that read,' leading up to free images, insight, judgment, empathy. Also *Insight* (1957) 189 [(1992) 213]: the 'initial plasticity and indeterminacy' of the human child grounds 'the later variety'; and see the Index of the book under 'Flexibility.' It is remarkable how often Lonergan returned to this idea.

to some category but ... scorning any arbitrary burking of questions.'[36] In other words he is saying: Let's get to the point. It's potentiality, not quality, that is the key to our human nature and our history and our religion.

There are two other terms I must mention but can only mention: finality and emergent probability. Lonergan linked finality to potentiality in his answer to Feuerbach. Indeed they are closely linked, almost identical; and when we add the third factor of emergent probability, we have the basis of possibility. Finality, however, has its own mini-treatise in *Insight* and needs no exposition here.[37] The same is true of emergent probability, though I remind you that emergent probability is a factor in human affairs too, not just in the world of nature.[38] The three factors form a unity, for potentiality is related to finality as openness to dynamism, and finality is related to emergent probability as dynamism to its instrument. In these three factors we have the basic possibility of history.

2.4 Lonergan's Analyses of History

So we come to Lonergan's analyses of actual historical transitions. It's a huge area, and this should be the major part of my paper. However, I won't attempt the impossible: I'll just do what I can. What I perhaps can do is provide two samples, again one early in life and another late, not to study his argument, but just to indicate the character of his thinking. Then I will suggest, very tentatively, a tactic that might help us order the impossible multiplicity of his other analyses.

Sample one. Back in the 1930s when Lonergan was a student in Rome he wrote the essay 'Philosophy of History.' It finds four main stages in the actual course of history, ordered in relation to social philosophy, which was a strong interest of his at the time. First: 'The world prior to the discovery of philosophy, that is, up to Socrates, Plato and Aristotle.' Next: 'The failure of philosophy to fulfil its social mission, that is, from Plato to the Dark Age.' His third stage: 'The automatic cultural expansion following upon the Dark Age and continuing

---

36 *A Third Collection*, in 'A Post-Hegelian Philosophy of Religion' 218.

37 *Insight* (1957) 444–51 [(1992) 470–76].

38 See the Index to *Insight* under 'Emergent probability.' For its relevance to human affairs: 209–11 (234–37).

up to the present.' The fourth stage is simply: 'The future.'[39] That fourth stage is concrete in a way you might not expect. It starts with 'the antinomy of church and state' (113); it names liberalism (114) and bolshevism (116) as the enemies; and it finds the counter to them in 'scholastic social theory culminating in the encyclicals of His Holiness, Pius XI' (117, with correction of a typo).[40]

Sample two. If we jump now to his 'Philosophy and the Religious Phenomenon,' we see the change that forty years have wrought. He first distinguishes 'the terms whose meaning shifts' from 'the factors bringing about such shifts in meaning.' The former are (1) social contexts: 'accepted modes of human cooperation grouped under such headings as family and mores, community and education, state and law, economics and technology.' And (2) cultural contexts: 'such areas are art, religion, science, philosophy, history.'[41]

Obviously there is still a strong sociological interest, but it is a good deal wider. What is quite new, however, is the way he organizes the factors that cause the 'shifts in meaning' in the social and cultural fields. He now sees them in relation to language: the linguistic, the literate, the logical, the methodical.

> Each of these stages includes those that precede but adds a new factor of its own. In the linguistic stage people speak and listen. In the literate they read and write. In the logical they operate on propositions; they promote clarity, coherence, and rigor of statement; they move towards systems that are thought to be permanently valid. In the methodical stage the construction of systems remains, but the permanently valid system has

---

39 'Philosophy of History' 102 (with further references given in my text). This is one of the papers in File 713 of the Archives (see note 25 above).

40 For a far more detailed account of this document, see Michael Shute (note 25 above) 74–99. It is useful to remember two factors in the context. First, in 1937–38 (and likewise in the earlier 1930s) Lonergan was still a philosopher by vocation, expecting to specialize in that field and already working on a philosophy of history. Second, this was a period of social and political turbulence, during which he looked to the Pope for doctrinal guidance and to the Mystical Body of Christ as the social force to meet current aberrations.

41 'Philosophy and the Religious Phenomenon,' *METHOD: Journal of Lonergan Studies* 12 (1994) 138 (*Papers 1965–1980* [2004] 404). This is an undated paper in the Archives, but the evidence points to late 1977 or early 1978 as the date of composition: see the editorial preface to the published paper, 121–24 (*Papers* 391–92 n. 1.).

> become an abandoned ideal; any system is presumed to be the precursor of another and better system; and the role of method is the discernment of invariants and variables in the ongoing sequences of systems.[42]

Then he works out the series concretely, in religious history, and in Christian history.

These two sketches may give some sense of the categories Lonergan uses, of the way he organizes them, and of the broad sweep of his vision. As for the analyses I have omitted, there may be a simpler approach: not a detailed study of all his historical analyses, but not just a list of his analyses either – rather, something like a middle way. Anyway I suggest for this the concept of 'operators.' Operators are pivotal for understanding the levels of human intentionality: can we use them in some transferred sense to understand the analyses of history as well? If this tactic works, we might do an end run around an impossible task, and gain some general understanding of Lonergan's analyses by an easier route.

Thus, the operator in 'Philosophy of History' was the turbulent political situation of the times and the social thought of the Papal Encyclicals. A few years later essays on the 'analytic concept' of history[43] focused on the structure of progress, decline, and redemption. One suspects the influence of Hegel, but in the second 'analytic concept' essay he declares: 'By the dialectic we do not mean Plato's orderly conversation, nor Hegel's expansion of concepts, nor Marx's fiction of an alternative to mechanical materialism.'[44] The operator here would therefore seem to be his own creative thinking transposing Hegel. His dissertation on *gratia operans* in Aquinas studied a historical pattern emerging in the eight centuries between Augustine and Aquinas, a pattern that he called the form of speculative development.[45] He expressly meant this to be a scientific statement of a verifiable hypothesis, and the operator would be the challenge to a positivism that excludes understanding. Positivism was still an enemy in the *Verbum* articles, though now it

42 Ibid. 139.

43 The term occurs with slight variations in the title of three of the essays: see Shute 64.

44 'Analytic Concept of History' (identified by this simple title; the other two essays on the analytic concept have variants in the title) 11. Further to the question of Lonergan's sources, he speaks of the idea as his own: 'I worked out an analysis on the model of a threefold approximation' (*A Second Collection* 271).

45 Chapter II-1 in *Grace and Freedom* (2000).

takes second place to conceptualism, and the main operator is the recovery of a role for intelligence in Thomistic thought.[46] And so on. If this approach works it will have the further advantage of linking up with his *curriculum vitae* and with the 'essential' Lonergan I spoke of earlier.

3 Charting the Unknown

According to the program for this workshop I am to chart the future. According to the quotation I put at the head of my paper, 'We cannot chart the future ... Our course is in the night, our control is only rough and approximate. We have to believe and trust, to risk and dare.'[47] Was I bluffing when I proposed this topic to the workshop's director? It's time to find out.

And first I have to come to terms with my mentor. Naturally I have to agree with him that we cannot chart the future in any detail. But he does allow for a control that is 'rough and approximate,' and maybe the night is not total, not quite as 'Black as the pit from pole to pole' ('Invictus'). The future, after all, is the continuation of the present. It is also the second half of universal history: I used Lonergan himself for my study of the past, which is the first half, and the two form a unity – otherwise we could not speak of 'our' past and 'our' future.

I do not of course use 'half' quantitively as a measure of time, but only in the sense that in a table of contents of time, the headings 'past' and 'future' take up equal space on the page. There is no way of measuring their relative length in reality. At one end of time some philosophers would argue for a beginning: 'Why is there something and not nothing?'[48] Theologians do so on the grounds of the Book of Genesis. It's a further question how it started: was it with a big bang? If so, that's fine with me. As for the other pole, the end of time, science may argue that the world must run down; philosophy may be silent on the

46 See the Index to *Verbum* under 'Conceptualism': especially helpful are (1967) 183–91 [(1997) 192–99].

47 See note 2 above.

48 Leibniz's question, made famous by Heidegger. See Werner Brock in Heidegger, *Existence and Being* (London: Vision Press, 1949) 238: 'Aptly does Heidegger close his Inaugural Lecture about the problem of "nothingness" by renewing the question which the aged Leibniz once advanced ...' The question was put by Lonergan in his own terms, *Understanding and Being* (1980) 300–301 [(1990) 244].

question; theology struggles with the apocalyptic nightmares in religious literature; and we all live in fear that the crazies will push the wrong button and end everything. So we prophesy the shape of the future always with the proviso 'if there is to be a future.'

There are prophets in a religious sense, to whom God may have revealed the future: I am not in that class. There are modern prophets, whose expertise is really a keener insight into present trends, the 'signs of the times.' They are not really prophets, but they have a good set of antennae for the present (Harvey Cox is said to have the best set of theological antennae in the United States). I am not in their class either. But thirdly, there are those who study the past and discern patterns that seem to belong to our race, to be so much a part of the human condition that we can predict their extension into whatever future we may have: here all of us have a chance to say something.

3.1 *The Future of the Structural Principle*

My first step is the one I promised at the start: the future of Lonergan's four-leveled structure. I am optimistic on that. My hope is that by the end of this century the basic idea of the four levels will be part of our general culture – so much so that to explain them, and still more to prove them, will be quite boring. Pupils leaving primary school will be as familiar with this structure as they are with, say, the golden rule.

Consider that example. Who would attend a lecture that promises to prove or explain the golden rule? You would have to pay people to go. Not because they don't believe in the golden rule, but because they do, and do so by second nature: everyone holds it. Yet someone somewhere sometime long ago first formulated that rule. It was new then, and just because it was new, it had to be proved and defended. It's that way with any new idea. First, opposition. Then, opponents die off. The idea catches on. Finally, it becomes part of tradition. 'Sure, we always held that.' Well, I believe the same will happen with the four levels. They are so simple and compelling: once the opposition dies off, they will win a hearing and be here to stay.

That does not mean that the whole area of the structural is quite static. To say that is like saying all works of benevolence will cease once the golden rule is accepted: in fact, they will just be starting. It's the same with the four levels. First of all, they have infinite applications, possibilities without end, and every application is a new thrill. Further, within the structure itself there is always more to learn, all sorts of questions too erudite to be taught in primary school. Who among us is ready to explain, for example, the *emanatio intelligibilis* of concept from insight? Or the functioning of the operator on the downward path from level to level? Or the open-ended character of the structure above level four and below level one? Or the diverse relationships of the levels to the arts and sciences, to cultures and religions? And what of the 'boundary' questions, the reciprocal effect of the two principles on each other?[49] There is plenty of room for new discoveries. My point is simply that we don't expect radical changes in the basic structure, at least not every day.

On the side of the structural principle, then, I see a prosperous future, a future without many surprises, a comfortable future in which we wear the idea like an old shoe: it has been accepted, it fits. We have to get Lonergan in perspective on this question, and that is difficult when *Insight* and *Method*, the books and the ideas, fill the horizon.

3.2 *The Future of the Historical Principle*

The question is quite different for the complex historical principle. I would say, then, that the concern of what I called the 'essential Lonergan'will continue to struggle against heavy odds to become, at least in some cases, the concern of the 'essential human.' Our human world and its history will always find students, but they will always have to struggle for a place in the sun: the Philistines are always with us, and they will always want to turn our universities into technical schools.

I would say, secondly, that the tripartite structure of progress, decline, and redemption, will remain: progress, because no tyrant can forever suppress our questions; decline, because of our recurring flight from understanding and the precarious nature of our achievements; redemption, because God's love is stronger than our biases and fail-

49 In the Lonergan Research Institute Seminar, where an early version of this paper was presented, Robert Doran reminded us of some of these more recondite questions, questions that could hardly be grasped except by more advanced students: for example, the objectification of insights in concepts, and the contrast of common sense and science – things in relation to us, and things in relation to one another. Lonergan himself late in life proposed that we think of the structure as open at both ends, that is, to higher and lower 'levels,' in 'Philosophy and the Religious Phenomenon' 134 (*Papers 1965–1980* [2004] 400).

ures. It's part of our human condition under God, and the only question is whether we will recognize it as such and cooperate.

Thirdly, I would say that the possibility of intelligible history, founded on human potentiality, finality, and emergent probability, will remain. To deny potentiality to the human race is to cancel the human, for from *non posse* to *non esse valet illatio*: it's good logic to say that what cannot be will not be. Next, to deny finality is to reduce human nature to the inert condition of sticks and stones. And lastly, to deny emergent probability is to condemn ourselves to perpetual chaos or some cycle of eternal return. Against that, it's good to remember that survival of the fittest still has meaning and a degree of validity, and that it's good statistical science to say that in the long run what can be will be.

Fourthly, what of the various analyses of historical transitions that Lonergan has made? They are much more interesting: will they endure? It might help to look at the wider world of our own time. When I came to the study of theology in the 1940s kerygmatic theology was coming in strong, the result largely of wartime experience in Austria. It was followed by biblical theology, which grew rapidly in the wake of *Divino afflante Spiritu*. There were also revivals: monastic theology, Neo-Scholastic theology, theology of the cross. Meanwhile new theologies multiplied: liberation theology, postmodern theology, and the latest I've seen – radical orthodoxy. These all arose as movements, and the movements belong to history. Once they have settled into place, however, they are less interesting to the historian, though historians may continue to reinterpret them.

In the light of the last half-century, then, we may consider the movements Lonergan studied. Are they still operative, or have they reached their term? In any case is his analysis of them accurate enough to stand the criticism of the centuries? It depends. Some of them pertain to particular movements, like the transition from scriptural categories to theological. Some of them are great 'sweeps' through the long centuries of macrohistory, like the stages of meaning. His analyses therefore allow no simple prophecy. We are dealing with mountains of data: from a past that continues to be discovered, from a present that continues to create still more data. We are dealing also with a moving object: for example, the war to end all wars is a view of history that was very soon contradicted by the moving object of events. We are dealing with human historians, and every day the historians enlarge their horizons, so that they have to rewrite in 2000 the history they carefully charted in 1990. Lonergan himself was fifty years old when he came to accept the new learning in scriptural studies; what other gaps remained in his thinking at the end?

This much, I think, is true in general: that the more fundamental the factors effecting shifts in meaning, the more likely the movement is to have an ongoing future. Similarly, the more fundamental the categories in which Lonergan analyzed history, the more likely his views are to endure. In the 1930s liberalism and bolshevism loomed rather larger in the context of church and state than they do in the year 2000: as movements they may have had their day, but I think Lonergan's analysis in terms of sociology and philosophy may be more enduring. I would certainly expect his analysis of the dialectical development in theology from Tertullian through Origen to Athanasius to be a permanent acquisition. I would also expect his 1977 analysis of shifts in meaning, using the categories of linguistic, literate, logical and methodical, to survive the erosion of time.

So much for what I think is 'true in general.' I leave more particular questions to prophets or interpreters of the times with better antennae than I have. As for myself, I fall back on my mentor and say, 'We cannot chart the future ... Our course is in the night.' I leave it to the future itself, if there is to be a future, to pronounce the verdict.

3.3 *The Limits of Charting: The Unknown*

Movements may come and go or they may come and stay. The great world can accommodate them all, if there is a world. I've talked about the survival of Lonergan's ideas, but neither his ideas nor anyone else's will survive without a world to host them. So what of that world itself: will it survive? When I say 'if there is to be a future,' I raise a question that we must take seriously. The 'if' is real, and was real to Lonergan.[50] It is real with a vengeance to us today. Like the Philistines, the crazies are always with us, and today they have power without precedent to destroy us. Fifty years ago we lived on the edge of extinction, waiting till the US or USSR, each fearful that the other might act first, pushed the button to end it all. Then that situation eased a bit but

50 On the destructive element in our times, typical phrases are 'horror of mere destructiveness,' *A Second Collection* 99; 'destructive power,' ibid. 113; the need to 'banish all tendencies to hatred, reviling, destroying,' ibid. 187. But I have lost the reference to his statement on the real possibility of our destroying our world.

we began to worry about the 'rogue nations' that now are able to do as much damage as a superpower. But at least we were dealing in both cases with national leaders who knew what the buttons meant, who calculated consequences, and even had some sense of responsibility we could appeal to. Not so today. Today we are at the mercy of any irresponsible maverick ten thousand miles away, who pushes buttons at random in the internet world. Who knows what their random actions may bring up?[51] Not likely *The Lost Chord*; much more likely the lost universe.

But let us suppose a world where sanity reigns. There are two sober considerations that still raise the question of the world's future. They are intrinsic to the very notion of a free God and to the idea of a contingent creation, and I will end with a word on them.

First, divine freedom. Here my approach is entirely a priori, which means stating what I think I would do if I were God. Consider the possibilities. If this world fails this time, will God try it again? That would make God a divine Sisyphus, pushing a world up the mountain of eternity, losing grip and seeing it roll back to the bottom; then try again. I think we may rule that out.

But maybe this world, while not a failure, could be terminated as a project good enough to round off and preserve in the divine storehouse of being. Lonergan rounded off *Insight* when he was only halfway through, and that half seems a presentable work all by itself. Well, what he or any one of us can do is surely possible to God too. A world that produced Francis of Assisi, Aquinas, Shakespeare, and Mother Theresa seems worth while: God might look on this creation in the year 2000, see that it is good, and say 'It is finished; store it in the universe of being.' Then God who has worlds without number in the divine mind could proceed to create another. This, if I were God, I just might see as an intelligent, reasonable, and responsible decision.

On the same principle, however, that for a world to be worthwhile it must have an intelligible unity, I would look farther than human greatness for that unity. I would think of the divine Three as entering our world. The divine Word has joined us and is recognized, in doctrine and worship and life. The divine Spirit has joined us and is recognized in doctrine, but not fully recognized in worship and life. The divine

51 This paper was first presented fifteen months before the events of 11 September 2001 (ed.).

Mystery has not yet entered our world in the present sense of enter. I would say, then, that when the Spirit is given the role in the world that belongs to her, and when the divine Mystery is present in the mystic life of all believers, then the created universe is an intelligible unity and that God could look on it, say, 'It is good, it is very good.' But what at that point God might choose to do, whether to maintain this world in its now optimum state or to transfer it whole and entire into another state, that is still hidden in the divine counsels. In any case the world, up to that point and to some extent after it, remains contingent, and our responsibility for its future remains.

Next, contingency, where the real problem lies for philosophy and theology. What is, is, and now necessarily is. In the example beloved of St Thomas: Socrates, if he is seated, necessarily is seated; the condition expressed by the 'if' has been fulfilled. But as long as the 'if' remains, so long does the 'to be or not to be' of the contingent future remain. It would be meaningless to affirm the contingency of future events and at the same time to surround those events with a protective shield that guarantees their coming to be. What is true of events is true of the universe: if its future is contingent, then it is possible that that future may not come to be. Or, in the human universe, it is meaningless to say the human race has power to destroy itself, and yet at the same time say that such destruction can never be. A contingent world means a possible non-world. It also means a degree of human responsibility for the world that is and will be.

Now if our world is contingent, if to be or not to be is an open question on our future, it follows that there is not as yet in the divine counsels a decree one way or another. That is, there is no divine decree that there will be a future, and there is no divine decree that there will not be a future. For as soon as there is a truth in place in regard to the future, then the future is bound to correspond to that truth. Since the time of Aristotle, philosophers including Aquinas and Lonergan have discussed this in the context of the sea-battle of Salamis. The question regards the truth today of a free and so contingent event tomorrow: Will there be or will there not be a sea-battle tomorrow between the Greeks and the Persians? Logic seems to say it must be one or the other. Lonergan says no: that would be applying a two-valued logic where you need a three-valued logic, namely, (1) the truth is that it will be, (2) the truth is that it will not be, (3) the truth is still indeterminate. For as soon as the truth is determinately yes or no, the contingent future ceases to be contingent: it has to correspond to that determination. By the same token, responsibility for that no longer contingent future, insofar as it is no longer contingent, ceases to be ours.

But what about the crazies? How will God deal with them? Let us locate and specify the problem. The problem is not some frustration of the divine plan: scripture assures us that God is not frustrated. The problem is not the freedom of the crazies: God's transcendence gets its way without violating human freedom – St Thomas took care of that problem.[52] No, the problem regards the contingency of the world, and it is partly a question of what God may have decreed and partly a question of theological understanding.

If God has decreed the future of the world, then, first, the world is no longer contingent, and second, there has to be an extrinsic denominator as counterpart to that decree.[53] But the contingency of creation is a belief based not only on divine freedom but on the nothing out of which God creates. And what would the extrinsic denominator be for what is certainly a contingent statement about a divine decree?

These are real questions. In circles where the pursuit of truth is a delusive goal, they will be doubly indictable, prolonging the pursuit beyond this world, where it is already judged and found wanting, into another which is by our own admission impenetrable. But they are questions beloved of Thomas Aquinas and of his pupil Bernard Lonergan. And some of us who follow in their steps find it impossible to brush the questions aside. Let me add at once that they are questions mainly for academic theology. While theology works at their solution, the rest of the world (and we along with it) may continue to exercise what limited responsibility we have, and to do so in an atmosphere of religious hope. 'We have to believe and trust, to risk and dare.'

52 See *In I Peri hermeneias*, lect. 13–14. For Lonergan on Aquinas, see *Grace and Freedom*.

53 An extrinsic denominator is the created reality needed for the truth of a contingent statement regarding God. To say 'God created' is to make a contingent statement about God. If it is true, there has to be a corresponding reality. That reality cannot be in God, in whom nothing is contingent; rather, it is in creation, existing as an extrinsic denominator of that contingent truth about God. See 'On God and Secondary Causes,' in *Collection* (1967) 59 [(1988) 58]. Also *Insight* (see the Index, under 'Denomination'); and *De Deo trino*, vol. 2 (1964), Assertum XV, pp. 217–19, where it is called 'conveniens terminus ad extra.'

The Writings of Frederick E. Crowe

1. 'Conflict and Unification in Man: The Data in the Writings of St Thomas Aquinas.' Doctoral dissertation. Rome: Gregorian University, 1953. Excerpts published by Gregorian University Press, 1953.
2. 'Convention of the Catholic Theological Society of America.' *Sciences ecclésiastiques* [later *Science et esprit*] 6 (1954) 262–65.
3. 'Universal Norms and the Concrete *operabile* in St Thomas Aquinas.' *Sciences ecclęsiastiques* 7 (1955) 115–49, 257–91.

3a. 'Universal Norms and the Concrete *operabile* in St Thomas Aquinas.' In Frederick E. Crowe, *Three Thomist Studies*, ed. Michael Vertin. Boston: Lonergan Institute of Boston College, 2000, 1–69. (Reprint of no. 3, adding English translations of all Latin words.)

4. 'Devotion to the Holy Eucharist.' *Canadian Messenger of the Sacred Heart* 66 (1956) 685–90.
5. 'Index.' In Bernard Lonergan, *Insight: A Study of Human Understanding*, London: Longmans, Green; New York: Philosophical Library, 1957, 749–81.
6. 'The Origin and Scope of Bernard Lonergan's *Insight*.' *Sciences ecclésiastiques* 9 (1957) 203–95.

6a. 'The Origin and Scope of Bernard Lonergan's *Insight*.' In Frederick E. Crowe, *Appropriating the Lonergan Idea*, ed. Michael Vertin. Washington: Catholic University of America Press, 1989, 13–30. (Reprint of 263–79 of no. 6.)

7. 'Pastoral Care in Large Cities.' *Canadian Messenger of the Sacred Heart* 68 (1958) 277–83.
8. 'Complacency and Concern in the Thought of St Thomas.' *Theological Studies* 20 (1959) 1–39, 198–230, 343–95.

8a. 'Complacency and Concern in the Thought of St Thomas.' In *Three Thomist Studies*, 71–203. (Reprint of no. 8, adding English translations of all Latin words.)

9. 'Complacency and Concern.' *Cross and Crown* 11 (1959) 180–90.
10. 'Reign of the Sacred Heart.' *Canadian Messenger of the Sacred Heart* 69/6 (June 1959) 4–6, 43.
11. 'Review: *Experimental Knowledge of the Indwelling Trinity: An Historical Study of the Doctrine of St Thomas*, by J. Dedek.' *Theological Studies* 21 (1960) 687–88.
12. 'St Thomas and the Isomorphism of Human Knowing and Its Proper Object.' *Sciences ecclésiastiques* 13 (1961) 167–90.
12a. 'St Thomas and the Isomorphism of Human Knowing and Its Proper Object.' In *Three Thomist Studies*, 207–35. (Reprint of no. 12, adding English translations of all Latin words.)
13. 'How Infallible Is Catholic Dogma?' *Crosslight* 2/4 (Summer 1961) 14–26.
13a. 'Development of Doctrine and the Ecumenical Problem.' *Theological Studies* 23 (1962) 27–46. (Reprint, with minor changes, of no. 13.)
14. 'Review: *Les missions divines selon saint Augustin*, by J.-L. Maier.' *Theological Studies* 22 (1961) 476–78.
15. *The Most Holy Trinity*. Mimeographed notes. Toronto: Loyola Institute of Sacred Studies, 1962.
15a. *Il Dogma Trinitario*. Trans. J. Navone. Rome: Gregorian University, n.d. (Italian translation of no. 15.)
16. 'Review: *Structures et méthode dans la somme théologique de saint Thomas d'Aquin*, by G. Lafont.' *Theological Studies* 23 (1962) 314–16.
17. 'On the Method of Theology.' *Theological Studies* 23 (1962) 637–42.
18. Editor. *Spirit as Inquiry: Studies in Honor of Bernard Lonergan. Continuum* 2 (1964) 301–552.
18a. Editor, *Spirit as Inquiry: Studies in Honor of Bernard Lonergan*. Chicago: St Xavier College, 1964. (Reprint of no. 18.)
19. 'Introduction.' In *Spirit as Inquiry: Studies in Honor of Bernard Lonergan*, 306–307.
20. 'The Exigent Mind: Bernard Lonergan's Intellectualism.' In *Spirit as Inquiry: Studies in Honor of Bernard Lonergan*, 316–33.
21. 'Bibiography of the Writings of Bernard Lonergan.' In *Spirit as Inquiry: Studies in Honor of Bernard Lonergan*, 543–49.
22. 'A Birthday to Notice.' *America* 111 (July–December 1964) 804–805.
23. 'Neither Jew nor Greek, but One Human Nature and Operation in All.' *Philippine Studies* 13 (1965) 546–71.
23a. 'Neither Jew nor Greek, but One Human Nature and Operation in All.' In *Appropriating the Lonergan Idea*, 31-50. (Reprint of no. 23.)
23b. 'Neither Jew nor Greek, but One Human Nature and Operation in All.' In Thomas J. Farrell and Paul A. Soukup, eds, *Communication and Lonergan: Common Ground for Forging the New Age* (Kansas City, MO: Sheed & Ward, 1993) 89–107. (Reprint of no. 23.)

24. *The Doctrine of the Most Holy Trinity*. Mimeographed notes. Toronto: Regis College, 1965.

25. 'Development of Doctrine: Aid or Barrier to Christian Unity?' *Catholic Theological Society of America Proceedings* 21 (1966) 1–20.

25a. 'Kyoogi no Hatten: Kirisuto kyoo Itchi no Tasuke to naru ka.' Trans. M. Kooitchi. *Shigaku Digesto*, Natsu, 1968, 49–56. (Digest, in Japanese translation, of no. 25.)

26. 'Review: *The Second Vatican Council and the New Catholicism*, by G. Berkouwer.' *Canadian Journal of Theology* 12 (1966) 142–43.

27. 'Review: *Salut et rédemption chez saint Thomas d'Aquin: L'Acte sauveur du Christ*, by B. Catao.' *Theological Studies* 27 (1966) 282–84.

28. 'Full Communion with the Separated East.' *Canadian Messenger of the Sacred Heart* 76 (November 1966) 6, 8–9.

29. 'Insight.' *New Catholic Encyclopedia*, vol. 7 (1967) 545.

30. 'Intuition.' *New Catholic Encyclopedia*, vol. 7 (1967) 598–600.

31. 'Theological Terminology.' *New Catholic Encyclopedia*, vol. 14 (1967) 37–38.

32. 'Understanding.' *New Catholic Encyclopedia*, vol. 14 (1967) 389–91.

33. With David Burrell. 'Index.' In Bernard Lonergan, *Verbum: Word and Idea in Aquinas*. Notre Dame: University of Notre Dame Press, 1967, 221–300.

34. Editor. *Collection: Papers by Bernard Lonergan, S.J.* New York: Herder and Herder; London: Darton Longman & Todd, 1967.

35. 'Introduction.' In *Collection: Papers by Bernard Lonergan, S.J.*, vii–xxxv.

35a. 'The Growing Idea.' In *Appropriating the Lonergan Idea*, 3–12. (Reprint, with minor changes, of viii–xix of no. 35.)

36. 'Index.' In *Collection: Papers by Bernard Lonergan, S.J.*, 269–80.

37. '*Aggiornamento*: Eternal Truth in a Changing World.' *Canadian Messenger of the Sacred Heart* 77/2 (February 1967) 8–12.

38. '*Aggiornamento*: Changing Forms of Life and Worship.' *Canadian Messenger of the Sacred Heart* 77/3 (March 1967) 10–14.

39. '*Aggiornamento*: Do Dogmas Change?' *Canadian Messenger of the Sacred Heart* 77/4 (April 1967) 18–22.

40. '*Aggiornamento*: Is There a New Morality?' *Canadian Messenger of the Sacred Heart* 77/5 (May 1967) 18–23.

41. '*Aggiornamento*: The Church in the Modern World.' *Canadian Messenger of the Sacred Heart* 77/6 (June 1967) 18–23.

42. '*Aggiornamento*: The Wide World My Parish.' *Canadian Messenger of the Sacred Heart* 77/7–8 (July–August 1967) 8–11.

43. '*Aggiornamento*: The Church and the Churches.' *Canadian Messenger of the Sacred Heart* 77/9 (September 1967) 16–19.

44. 'Your Questions.' [Comments on questions submitted by readers of nos. 37–43.] *Canadian Messenger of the Sacred Heart* 77/10 (October 1967) 15;

77/11 (November 1967) 17; 78/1 (January 1968) 14–15; 78/4 (April 1968) 9; 78/5 (May 1968) 15; 78/7–8 (July–August 1968) 16; 78/9 (September 1968) 14; 78/10 (October 1968) 8.

45. 'A Jesuit Makes a Pilgrimage to Martin Luther's Shrine.' *Toronto Daily Star*, 28 October 1967, 16.

46. 'Bernard Lonergan.' In Thomas E. Bird, ed., *Modern Theologians, Christians and Jews*. Notre Dame: University of Notre Dame Press, 1967, 126–51.

47. 'Christology and Contemporary Philosophy.' *Commonweal* 87 (October 1967–March 1968) 242–47.

47a. 'Christology and Contemporary Philosophy.' In Daniel Callahan, ed., *God, Jesus, and Spirit*. New York: Herder and Herder, 1969, 137–52. (Reprint of no. 47.)

48. 'Review: *Newman on Tradition*, by G. Biemer.' *Theological Studies* 28 (1967) 590–92.

49. 'Fear, Hate, and Sin at the German Wall.' *United Church Observer* 29/22 (15 February 1968) 26–27.

50. 'Sorrow and Hope at Bonhoeffer's Death Camp.' *United Church Observer* 30/3 (1 April 1968) 25–26.

51. *A Time of Change: Guidelines for the Perplexed Catholic*. Milwaukee: Bruce, 1968. (Chaps. 1–7 are reprints of nos. 37–43 respectively.)

52. 'Christologies: How Up-to-Date Is Yours?' *Theological Studies* 29 (1968) 87–101.

53. 'Review: *Bible et tradition chez Newman: Aux origines de la théorie du développement*, by J. Stern.' *Theological Studies* 29 (1968) 777–79.

54. 'Development of Doctrine.' *American Ecclesiastical Review* 159 (1968) 233–47.

55. 'Review: *Revelation and Theology*, by E. Schillebeeckx.' *Theological Studies* 29 (1968) 339–40.

56. 'Salvation as Wholeness: Theological Background for an Ecumenical Programme.' *Canadian Journal of Theology* 14 (1968) 228–37.

57. 'Review: *Revelation and Theology* 2, by E. Schillebeeckx.' *Theological Studies* 29 (1968) 779–81.

58. 'Pull of the Future and Link with the Past: On the Need for Theological Method.' *Continuum* 7 (1969) 39–49.

59. 'What Can Join Us to the Love of Christ?' *Canadian Messenger of the Sacred Heart* 79/6 (June 1969) 1, 13–15.

60. 'But Is There a Fault in the Very Foundations?' *Continuum* 7 (1969) 323–31.

61. 'Dogma versus the Self-Correcting Process of Learning.' *Theological Studies* 31 (1970) 605–24.

61a. 'Dogma versus the Self-Correcting Process of Learning.' In Philip McShane, ed., *Foundations of Theology: Papers from the International Lonergan Congress 1970*. Dublin: Gill and Macmillan, 1971, 22–40. (Reprint of no. 61.)

62. 'First International Lonergan Congress: A Report.' *America* 122 (January–June 1970) 452–53.
63. 'The Conscience of the Theologian with Reference to the Encyclical.' In William C. Bier, ed., *Conscience: Its Freedom and Limitations*. New York: Fordham University Press, 1971, 312–32.
63a. 'The Responsibility of the Theologian, and the Learning Church.' In *Appropriating the Lonergan Idea*, 172–92. (Reprint, with minor changes, of no. 63.)
64. 'Introduction.' In Bernard Lonergan, *Grace and Freedom: Operative Grace in the Thought of St Thomas Aquinas*. London: Darton, Longman & Todd; New York: Herder and Herder, 1971, ix–xi.
65. 'Jerusalem at the Heart of Athens: The Christian University.' *The Maroon & White* 19/7 (June 1971) 1–3.
65a. 'Jerusalem at the Heart of Athens: The Christian University.' In *Appropriating the Lonergan Idea*, 163–71. (Reprint of no. 65.)
66. 'Early Jottings on Bernard Lonergan's Method in Theology.' *Science et esprit* 25 (1973) 121–38.
67. Editor, assisted by Conn O'Donovan and Giovanni Sala. *The Early Latin Works of Bernard J.F. Lonergan*. Typescript, Regis edition. 4 vols. Toronto: Regis College, 1973.
68. 'General Introduction.' In *The Early Latin Works of Bernard J.F. Lonergan*, each vol., ii–vii.
69. 'Editor's Introduction.' In *The Early Latin Works of Bernard J.F. Lonergan*. Vol. 1: De notione sacrificii, ix–x.
70. 'Editor's Introduction.' In *The Early Latin Works of Bernard J.F. Lonergan*. Vol. 2: De ente supernaturali, ix–xiii.
71. 'Editor's Introduction.' In *The Early Latin Works of Bernard J.F. Lonergan*. Vol. 3: De scientia atque voluntate dei, ix–xii.
72. 'Editor's Introduction.' In *The Early Latin Works of Bernard J.F. Lonergan*. Vol. 4: Analysis fidei, ix–x.
73. 'Dogmatic Theology.' *New Catholic Encyclopedia*, vol. 16 (supplement, 1974) 132–33.
74. With Philip and Fiona McShane. 'Index of Subjects.' In *A Second Collection: Papers by Bernard J.F. Lonergan, S.J.* London: Darton, Longman & Todd; Philadelphia: Westminster, 1974, 284–300.
75. 'Eschaton and Worldly Mission in the Mind and Heart of Jesus.' In Joseph Papin, ed., *The Eschaton: A Community of Love*. Villanova, PA: Villanova University Press, 1974 [c. 1971], 105–44.
75a. *Escatologia e missione terrene in Gesù di Nazareth*. Trans. G. Sala. Catania: Edizioni Paoline, 1976. (Italian translation of no. 75.)
75b. 'Eschaton and Worldly Mission in the Mind and Heart of Jesus.' In *Appropriating the Lonergan Idea*, 193–204. (Reprint of no. 75.)

76. 'The Mind of Jesus.' *Communio: International Catholic Review* 1 (1974) 365–84.
76a. 'The Mind of Jesus.' In Richard Laflamme and Marcel Gervais, eds, *Le Christ hier, aujourd'hui et demain*. Quebec: Laval University Press, 1976, 143–56. (Reprint of no. 76.)
77. 'The Power of the Scriptures: Attempt at Analysis.' In Joseph Plevnik, ed., *Word and Spirit: Essays in Honor of David Michael Stanley*. Toronto: Regis College, 1975, 323–47.
78. 'The Lonergan Center.' *The Jesuit Bulletin 1975*, 3–6, 27.
79. 'A People of Serene Joy: Memories of an African Congress.' *Annals of the Propagation of the Faith* 33/1 (February–March 1976) 4–7.
80. 'Doctrines and Historicity in the Context of Lonergan's *Method*: A Review-Article.' *Theological Studies* 38 (1977) 115–24.
81. 'An Exploration of Lonergan's New Notion of Value.' *Science et esprit* 29 (1977) 123–43.
81a. 'An Exploration of Lonergan's New Notion of Value.' *Lonergan Workshop* 3 (1982) 1–24. (Reprint of no. 81.)
81b. 'An Exploration of Lonergan's New Notion of Value.' In *Appropriating the Lonergan Idea*, 31–50. (Reprint of no. 81.)
82. *Theology of the Christian Word: A Study in History*. New York: Paulist Press, 1978.
83. 'Dialectic and the Ignatian Spiritual Exercises.' *Science et esprit* 30 (1978) 111–27.
83a. 'Dialectic and the Ignatian Spiritual Exercises.' *Lonergan Workshop* 1 (1978), 1–26. (Reprint of no. 83.)
83b. 'Dialectic and the Ignatian Spiritual Exercises.' In *Appropriating the Lonergan Idea*, 235–51. (Reprint of no. 83.)
84. With Sara Butler, Anne Carr, Margaret Farley, and Edward Kilmartin. *A Report on the Status of Women in Church and Society: Considered in Light of the Question of Women's Ordination*. New York: Catholic Theological Society of America, 1978.
85. 'Review: *Newman and His Theological Method: A Guide for the Theologian Today*, by T. Norris.' *Doctrine and Life* 29 (1978) 391–92.
86. 'Foundational Theology.' *New Catholic Encyclopedia*, vol. 17 (supplement, 1979) 235–37.
87. 'Theology and the Past: Changing Views on the Sources.' *Science et esprit* 31 (1979) 21–32.
87a. 'Theology and the Past: Changing Views on the Sources.' In *Appropriating the Lonergan Idea*, 252–64. (Reprint of no. 87.)
88. 'Theology and the Future: Responsible Innovation.' *Science et esprit* 31 (1979) 147–57.

88a. 'Theology and the Future: Responsible Innovation.' In *Appropriating the Lonergan Idea*, 265–76. (Reprint of no. 88.)

89. *Method in Theology: An Organon for Our Time.* The Pere Marquette Theology Lecture. Milwaukee: Marquette University Press, 1980.

90. *The Lonergan Enterprise.* Cambridge, MA: Cowley Press, 1980. (Chap. 1 is a reprint of no. 89.)

91. 'Report on the Regis College Lonergan Center.' *Lonergan Studies Newsletter* 1/2 (April 1980) 6–8.

92. 'Birthday Celebrations.' *News Letter: Upper Canada Province* 55/4 (May–June 1980) 5–6.

93. '"Interiority" Going Forward?' In Cathleen M. Going, ed., *Dialogues in Celebration*. Montreal: Thomas More Institute, 1980, 260–85.

94. 'Bernard Lonergan's Thought on Ultimate Reality and Meaning.' *Ultimate Reality and Meaning* 4 (1981) 58–89.

94a. 'Bernard Lonergan's Thought on Ultimate Reality and Meaning.' In *Appropriating the Lonergan Idea*, 71–105. (Reprint of no. 94.)

95. '*Creativity and Method*: Index to a Movement. A Review Article.' *Science et esprit* 34 (1982) 107–13.

96. 'The Present State of the Lonergan Movement.' *Lonergan Studies Newsletter* 3 (1982) 9–10.

97. 'Lonergan's Early Use of Analogy: A Research Note, with Reflections.' *METHOD: Journal of Lonergan Studies* 1/1 (Spring 1983) 31–46.

98. 'The Janus Problematic: Tradition versus Innovation.' In Joseph B. Gavin, ed., *Tradition and Innovation: Faith and Consent. Essays by Jesuits from a Canadian Perspective.* Regina: Campion College Press, 1983, 13–36.

98a. 'The Janus Problematic: Tradition versus Innovation.' In *Appropriating the Lonergan Idea*, 277–96. (Reprint of no. 98.)

99. 'Son and Spirit: Tension in the Divine Missions?' *Science et esprit* 35 (1983) 153–69.

99a. 'Son and Spirit: Tension in the Divine Missions?' *Lonergan Workshop* 5 (1985) 1–21. (Reprint of no. 99.)

99b. 'Son and Spirit: Tension in the Divine Missions?' In *Appropriating the Lonergan Idea*, 297–314. (Reprint of no. 99.)

100. 'Lonergan's Search for Foundations: The Early Years, 1940–1959.' In Philip McShane, ed., *Searching for Cultural Foundations*. Lanham, MD: University Press of America, 1984, 113–39.

100a. 'Lonergan's Search for Foundations: The Early Years, 1940–1959.' In Frederick E. Crowe, *Developing the Lonergan Legacy*, ed. Michael Vertin. Toronto: University of Toronto Press, 2004, 164–93. (Reprint of no. 100.)

101. 'The Human Mind and Ultimate Reality: A Lonerganian Comment on Dr. Leahy.' *Ultimate Reality and Meaning* 7 (1984) 67–74.

101a. 'The Human Mind and Ultimate Reality.' In *Appropriating the Lonergan Idea*, 106–15. (Reprint of no. 101.)

102. 'Transcendental Deduction: A Lonerganian Meaning and Use.' *METHOD: Journal of Lonergan Studies* 2/1 (March 1984) 21–40.

103. Editor. *A Third Collection: Papers by Bernard Lonergan, S.J.* New York: Paulist Press; London: Geoffrey Chapman, 1985.

104. 'Editor's Introduction.' In *A Third Collection*, 1–2.

105. 'Index.' In *A Third Collection*, 251–56.

106. 'Lonergan's Last Year.' *Lonergan Studies Newsletter*, special commemorative issue (February 1985) 5–6.

107. 'Reflections on Fr. Lonergan's Funeral and Burial.' *Lonergan Studies Newsletter*, special commemorative issue (February 1985) 7.

108. Co-editor, with Robert M. Doran. *Compass: A Jesuit Journal*, special issue honouring Bernard Lonergan, SJ, 1904–1984 (March 1985).

109. 'Collège de l'Immaculée-Conception: Where It All Began.' *Compass: A Jesuit Journal*, special issue honouring Bernard Lonergan, SJ, 1904–1984 (March 1985) 9.

109a. 'Le Collège de l'Immaculée-Conception: Où tout a commencé.' Trans. E. Richer. *Nouvelles de la Province du Canada-français* 4/4 (April 1985) no pagination. (French translation of no. 109.)

110. 'Homily, Funeral of Father Bernard Lonergan, S.J.' *Compass: A Jesuit Journal*, special issue honouring Bernard Lonergan, SJ, 1904–1984 (March 1985) 21–23.

110a. *Homily, Funeral of Father Bernard Lonergan, S.J.* Toronto: Regis College Press, 1985. (Reprint of no. 110.)

110b. 'Homily at the Funeral of Bernard Lonergan.' In *Appropriating the Lonergan Idea*, 385–90. (Reprint of no. 110.)

111. *Old Things and New: A Strategy for Education.* Supplementary issue of *Lonergan Workshop* 5. Atlanta: Scholars Press, 1985.

111a. 'School without Graduates: The Ignatian Spiritual Exercises.' In *Developing the Lonergan Legacy*, 197–212. (Reprint of Appendix of no. 111.)

112. 'A Note on the Prefaces of Insight.' *METHOD: Journal of Lonergan Studies* 3/1 (March 1985) 1–3.

113. Editor. 'The Original Preface,' by Bernard Lonergan. *METHOD: Journal of Lonergan Studies* 3/1 (March 1985) 3–7.

114. 'Bernard J.F. Lonergan, S.J., 1904–1984.' *Canadian Theological Society Newsletter* 5/1 (March 1985) 6–8.

115. *Son of God, Holy Spirit, and World Religions: The Contribution of Bernard Lonergan to the Wider Ecumenism.* Toronto: Regis College Press, 1985.

115a. 'Son of God, Holy Spirit, and World Religions.' In *Appropriating the Lonergan Idea*, 324–43. (Reprint of no. 115.)

116. 'Father Bernard J.F. Lonergan, S.J.' *News Letter: Upper Canada Province* 60/3 (May–June, 1985) 15–18.
117. 'A Note on Lonergan's Dissertation and Its Introductory Pages.' *METHOD: Journal of Lonergan Studies* 3/2 (October 1985) 1–8.
118. Editor. 'The *Gratia operans* Dissertation: Preface and Introduction,' by Bernard Lonergan. *METHOD: Journal of Lonergan Studies* 3/2 (October 1985) 9–49.
119. 'Bernard Lonergan and Liberation Theology.' In Walter Ysaac, ed., *The Third World and Bernard Lonergan: A Tribute to a Concerned Thinker*. Manila: Cardinal Bea Institute, 1986, 1–15.
119a. 'Bernard Lonergan y la teologia de la liberación.' *Humanidades Anuario* (Universidad Iberoamericana) 8 (1984–85) 11–23. (Spanish translation of no. 119.)
119b. 'Bernard Lonergan and Liberation Theology.' In *Appropriating the Lonergan Idea*, 116–26. (Reprint of no. 119.)
120. 'A Threefold Kenôsis of the Son of God.' In Joseph Armenti, ed., *The Papin Gedenkschrift, Dimensions in the Human Religious Quest. Essays in Memory of Joseph Papin*, Vol. I: Theological Dimensions. Ann Arbor: University Microfilms International, 1986, 54–64.
120a. 'A Threefold Kenôsis of the Son of God.' In *Appropriating the Lonergan Idea*. 315–23. (Reprint of no. 120.)
121. 'Bernard Lonergan as Pastoral Theologian.' *Gregorianum* 67 (1986) 451–70.
121a. 'Bernard Lonergan as Pastoral Theologian.' In *Appropriating the Lonergan Idea*, 127–44. (Reprint of no. 121.)
122. 'Graduation: End or Beginning?' *Christ the King Seminary News* 50/3 (Summer 1986) 2–4.
123. 'Lonergan, Bernard.' In Mircea Eliade, ed., *The Encyclopedia of Religion* (1987), vol. 9, 19–20.
124. 'The Task of Interpreting Lonergan: A Preliminary to the Symposium.' In Timothy Fallon and Philip Riley, eds, *Religion and Culture: Essays in Honor of Bernard Lonergan, S.J.* Albany: State University of New York Press, 1987, 3–16.
124a. 'The Task of Interpreting Lonergan.' In *Appropriating the Lonergan Idea*, 145–60. (Reprint of no. 124.)
125. '"The Role of a Catholic University in the Modern World" – An Update.' In Frederick Lawrence, ed., *Communicating a Dangerous Memory. Soundings in Political Theology*. Supplementary issue of *Lonergan Workshop* 6. Atlanta: Scholars Press, 1987, 1–16.
125a. 'The Church as Learner: Two Crises: One Kairos.' In *Appropriating the Lonergan Idea*, 370–84. (Reprint, with revisions, of no. 125.)

126. 'An Expansion of Lonergan's Notion of Value.' *Lonergan Workshop* 7 (1987) 35–57.

126a. 'An Expansion of Lonergan's Notion of Value.' In *Appropriating the Lonergan Idea*, 344–59. (Reprint of no. 126.)

127. 'The Life of the Unborn: Notions from Bernard Lonergan.' In *Appropriating the Lonergan Idea*, 360–69.

128. Co-editor, with Robert M. Doran. *Collected Works of Bernard Lonergan*. 24 vols. anticipated. Toronto: University of Toronto Press, 1988–.

129. 'Preface.' In *Appropriating the Lonergan Idea*, xi–xii.

130. *Appropriating the Lonergan Idea*. Ed. Michael Vertin. Washington: Catholic University of America Press, 1989. (Collection comprising nos. 6a, 23a, 35a, 63a, 65a, 75b, 81b, 83b, 87a, 88a, 94a, 98a, 99b, 101a, 110b, 115a, 119b, 120a, 121a, 124a, 125a, 126a, 127, and 129.)

131. 'From Kerygma to Inculturation: The Odyssey of Gospel Meaning.' In *Developing the Lonergan Legacy*, 21–31.

132. 'Insight: Genesis and Ongoing Context.' *Lonergan Workshop* 8 (1990) 61–83.

132a. 'Insight: Genesis and Ongoing Context.' In *Developing the Lonergan Legacy*, 32–52. (Reprint of no. 132.)

133. 'Rethinking the Religious State: Categories from Lonergan.' *Science et esprit* 40 (1988) 75–90.

134. 'Rethinking Moral Judgments: Categories from Lonergan.' *Science et esprit* 40 (1988) 137–52.

135. 'Rethinking God-with-us: Categories from Lonergan.' *Science et esprit* 41 (1989) 167–88.

136. 'Lonergan Research Institute.' *News Letter: Upper Canada Province*, Supplement no. 23 (June–July–August 1990: Appendix to Supplement no. 22), p. 14ff.

137. 'Newman: A Glory to Our Human Race.' *Compass: A Jesuit Journal* 8/3 (July 1990) 36.

138. 'Thomas Aquinas and the Will: A Note on Interpretations.' *METHOD: Journal of Lonergan Studies* 8/2 (October 1990) 129–34.

139. With Robert M. Doran. 'Editors' Preface.' Bernard Lonergan, 'Pantôn Anakephalaiôsis (The Restoration of All Things).' *METHOD: Journal of Lonergan Studies* 9/2 (October 1991) 134–38.

140. *Bernard Lonergan and the Community of Canadians: An Essay in Aid of Canadian Identity*. Toronto: Lonergan Research Institute, and Canadian Institute of Jesuit Studies, 1992. (Pamphlet.)

141. 'Lonergan's Nottingham Lecture on Method.' *METHOD: Journal of Lonergan Studies* 10 (Spring 1992) 1–2 (with Editorial Notes, 24–26).

142. 'Introduction' (27–28) and 'Editorial Notes' (29–30) to Lonergan's article

'Savings Certificates and Catholic Action.' *Lonergan Studies Newsletter* 13 (1992).

143. *Lonergan*. London: Geoffrey Chapman, and Collegeville, MN: Liturgical Press, 1992. (In series Outstanding Christian Thinkers, ed. Brian Davies.)

143a. *Bernard J.F. Lonergan: Progresso e tappe del suo pensiero*. Ed. Natalino Spaccapelo and Saturnino Muratore. Trans. Gabriele Bonetti, with revisions by L. Armando and N. Spaccapelo. Rome: Città Nuova, 1995. (Translation of no. 143, with presentation by the editors [7–8], and a preface for the Italian edition by the author [11–14].)

144. 'Rethinking Eternal Life: Philosophical Notions from Lonergan.' *Science et esprit* 45 (1993) 25–39.

145. 'Rethinking Eternal Life: Theological Notions from Lonergan.' *Science et esprit* 45 (1993) 145–59. (Sequel to no. 144.)

146. 'The Spectrum of "Communication" in Lonergan.' In Thomas J. Farrell and Paul A. Soukup, eds, *Communication and Lonergan: Common Ground for Forging the New Age*. Kansas City, MO: Sheed & Ward, 1993, 67–86.

146a. 'The Spectrum of "Communication" in Lonergan.' In *Developing the Lonergan Legacy*, 53–77. (Reprint of no. 146.)

147. 'Fr Vincent J. MacKenzie, S.J. 1918–1993.' *Province Newsletter Jesuits of Upper Canada* 69/2 (Spring 1994) 13–14.

148. '"All my work has been introducing history into Catholic theology" (Lonergan, March 28, 1980).' *Lonergan Workshop* 10 (1994) 49–81.

148a. '"All my work has been introducing history into Catholic theology" (Lonergan, March 28, 1980).' In *Developing the Lonergan Legacy*, 78–110. (Reprint of no. 148.)

149. 'The Ignatian Spiritual Exercises and Jesuit Spirituality.' *Review for Religious* 53 (1994) 524–33.

149a. 'The Ignatian Spiritual Exercises and Jesuit Spirituality.' In *Developing the Lonergan Legacy*, 242–51. (Reprint of no. 149.)

150. 'The Genus "Lonergan and ..." and Feminism.' In Cynthia Crysdale, ed., *Lonergan and Feminism*. (Toronto: University of Toronto Press, 1994) 13–32.

150a. 'The Genus "Lonergan and ..." and Feminism.' In *Developing the Lonergan Legacy*, 142–63. (Reprint of no. 150.)

151. 'Linking the Splintered Disciplines: Ideas from Lonergan.' *Lonergan Review: A Multidisciplinary Journal* 3 (1994) 131–43. (A public lecture at Lonergan University College, Montreal, celebrating the first fifteen years of the College [1978–93].)

151a. 'Linking the Splintered Disciplines: Ideas from Lonergan.' In *Developing the Lonergan Legacy*, 252–66. (Reprint of no. 151.)

152. 'Lonergan's Universalist View of Religion.' *METHOD: Journal of Lonergan Studies* 12 (1994) 147–79.
152a. 'Lonergan's Universalist View of Religion.' In *Developing the Lonergan Legacy*, 111–41. (Reprint of no. 152.)
153. Translator of Giovanni B. Sala, 'Kant and Lonergan on Insight into the Sensible.' *METHOD: Journal of Lonergan Studies* 13 (1995) 89–97.
154. 'Rethinking the Trinity: Taking Seriously the "Homoousios."' *Science et esprit* 47 (1995) 13–31.
155. '"A Bridge of Dialogue": Foundations for the Bridge.' *LuCe: A quarterly publication of the Lonergan Communications Center, Manila* (3, but unnumbered: Christmas 1995) 4–5. (Reflections on the metaphor used in the subtitle in the LuCe masthead.)
156. 'Law and Insight.' *The Jurist* 56 (1996) 25–40. (Issue dedicated to Ladislas Orsy, SJ, on his seventy-fifth birthday.)
156a. 'Law and Insight.' In *Developing the Lonergan Legacy*, 267–82. (Reprint of no. 156.)
157. 'Christian Thinker: Fr. Bernard Lonergan, S.J.' *Company: A Magazine of the American Jesuits* 13:3 (Spring 1996) 10–11. (Part of an issue devoted especially to the Jesuits of Mexico and Canada, neighbours to south and north of the American Jesuits.)
158. 'La Vocazione di Lonergan Quale Pensatore Cristiano.' *Rassegna di Teologia* 37 (1996) 313–31. (Translation by Saturnino Muratore of the lecture given at the Lonergan conference in Milan, 28 January 1995.)
158a. 'Lonergan's Vocation as a Christian Thinker.' In *Developing the Lonergan Legacy*, 3–20. (Original English of no. 158.)
159. 'Lonergan's "Moral Theology and the Human Sciences": Editor's Introduction.' *METHOD: Journal of Lonergan Studies* 15 (1997) 1–3.
160. 'Complacency and Concern in the Risen Life.' *Lonergan Workshop* 13 (1997) 17–32.
161. 'Now I Begin.' *Canadian Religious Conference Bulletin* 38:3 (Fall 1998) 14–15. (An issue focused on transitions for religious.)
162. 'The Date of "For a New Political Economy."' Appendix to Philip McShane, ed., *For a New Political Economy*, vol. 21 of *Collected Works of Bernard Lonergan* (Toronto: University of Toronto Press, 1998) 319–24.
163. 'Rhyme and Reason: On Lonergan's Foundations for Works of the Spirit.' *METHOD: Journal of Lonergan Studies* 17 (1999) 27–45.
163a. 'Rhyme and Reason: On Lonergan's Foundations for Works of the Spirit.' In *Developing the Lonergan Legacy*, 314–31. (Reprint of no. 163.)
164. 'The "World" from Anthony of Egypt to Vatican II.' *Review for Religious* 58 (1999) 470–80.

165. 'Interview.' With Christine Jamieson, Peter Monette, and Paul Allen. *Ottawa Lonergan Website* (www.lonergan.on.ca), 10 July 1999.
166. 'For a Phenomenology of Rational Consciousness.' *METHOD: Journal of Lonergan Studies* 18 (2000) 67–90.
167. 'Putting Old Heads on Young Shoulders.' *Canadian Messenger of the Sacred Heart* 110:9 (October 2000) 22–24.
167a. 'Putting Old Heads on Young Shoulders.' *Pioneer* (Dublin), March 2003, 10–11. (Reprint, with slight change, of no. 166.)
168. 'Objectivity versus Projection in Lonergan.' *International Philosophical Quarterly* 40 (2000) 327–38.
169. 'Author's Preface.' In *Three Thomist Studies*, xvii–xix.
170. *Three Thomist Studies*. Ed. Michael Vertin. Supplementary issue of *Lonergan Workshop*, vol. 16. Boston: Lonergan Center of Boston College, 2000. (Collection comprising nos. 3a, 8a, 12a, and 169.)
171. 'For Inserting a New Question (26A) in the *Pars prima*.' *The Thomist* 64 (2000) 565–80.
171a. 'For Inserting a New Question (26A) in the *Pars prima*.' In *Developing the Lonergan Legacy*, 332–46. (Reprint of no. 171.)
172. 'Lonergan, Bernard Joseph Francis.' *Diccionario Històrico de la Compañia de Jesùs: Biogràfico-Temàtico* (Rome: Institutum Historicum, S.I.: 2000), 2409–10.
173. 'Analogy of Proportion: Note on a Favorite Lonergan Thought-Pattern.' *Theoforum* 32 (2001) 419–25.
174. '"Stare at a triangle ...": A Note on How to Get an Insight, and How Not to.' *METHOD: Journal of Lonergan Studies* 19 (2001) 173–80.
175. 'The Dynamics of Spirit-Body Communication: Some Case Studies.' *Josephinum Journal of Theology* 9 (2002) 95–107.
176. 'The Future: Charting the Unknown with Lonergan.' *Lonergan Workshop* 17 (2002) 1–21.
176a. 'The Future: Charting the Unknown with Lonergan.' In *Developing the Lonergan Legacy*, 347–68. (Reprint of no. 176.)
177. 'Lonergan at the Edges of Understanding.' *METHOD: Journal of Lonergan Studies* 20 (2002) 175–98.
178. 'History That Is Written: A Note on Patrick Brown's "System and History."' *Journal of Macrodynamic Analysis* 2 (2002) 115–24.
179. 'The Puzzle of the Subject as Subject in Lonergan.' *International Philosophical Quarterly* 43 (2003) 187–205.
180. 'McShane's Puzzles: Apologia for Those Who Flunk Them.' *Journal of Macrodynamic Analysis* 3 (2003) 186–93.
181. 'The Relevance of Newman to Contemporary Theology.' In *Developing the Lonergan Legacy*, 213–27.

182. 'Lonergan and How to Live Our Lives.' In *Developing the Lonergan Legacy*, 228–41.

183. 'The Magisterium as Pupil: The Learning Teacher.' In *Developing the Lonergan Legacy*, 283–93.

184. '"The Spirit and I" at Prayer.' In *Developing the Lonergan Legacy*, 294–303.

185. 'Why We Have to Die.' In *Developing the Lonergan Legacy*, 304–13.

186. 'Author's Preface.' In *Developing the Lonergan Legacy*, xi–xiii.

187. *Developing the Lonergan Legacy*. Ed. Michael Vertin. Toronto: University of Toronto Press, 2004. (Collection comprising nos. 100a, 111a, 131, 132a, 146a, 148a, 149a, 150a. 151a, 152a, 156a, 158a, 163a, 171a, 176a, 181, 182, 183, 184, 185, & 186.)

188. 'Images for Sin in the Ignatian Exercises.' *Spirituality Review: An Interactive Journal* [semi-annual supplement to *Review for Religious*] (Lent/Easter 2004) 16–21.

189. 'Aquinas, Pascal, Lonergan, and the Dynamic of the Spiritual Exercises' (to appear).

190. *Christ and History: The Christology of Bernard Lonergan, 1935–1982* (to appear).

Index

www.ingramcontent.com/pod-product-compliance
Lightning Source LLC
LaVergne TN
LVHW090800070826
844660LV00022B/1041

9781487520533